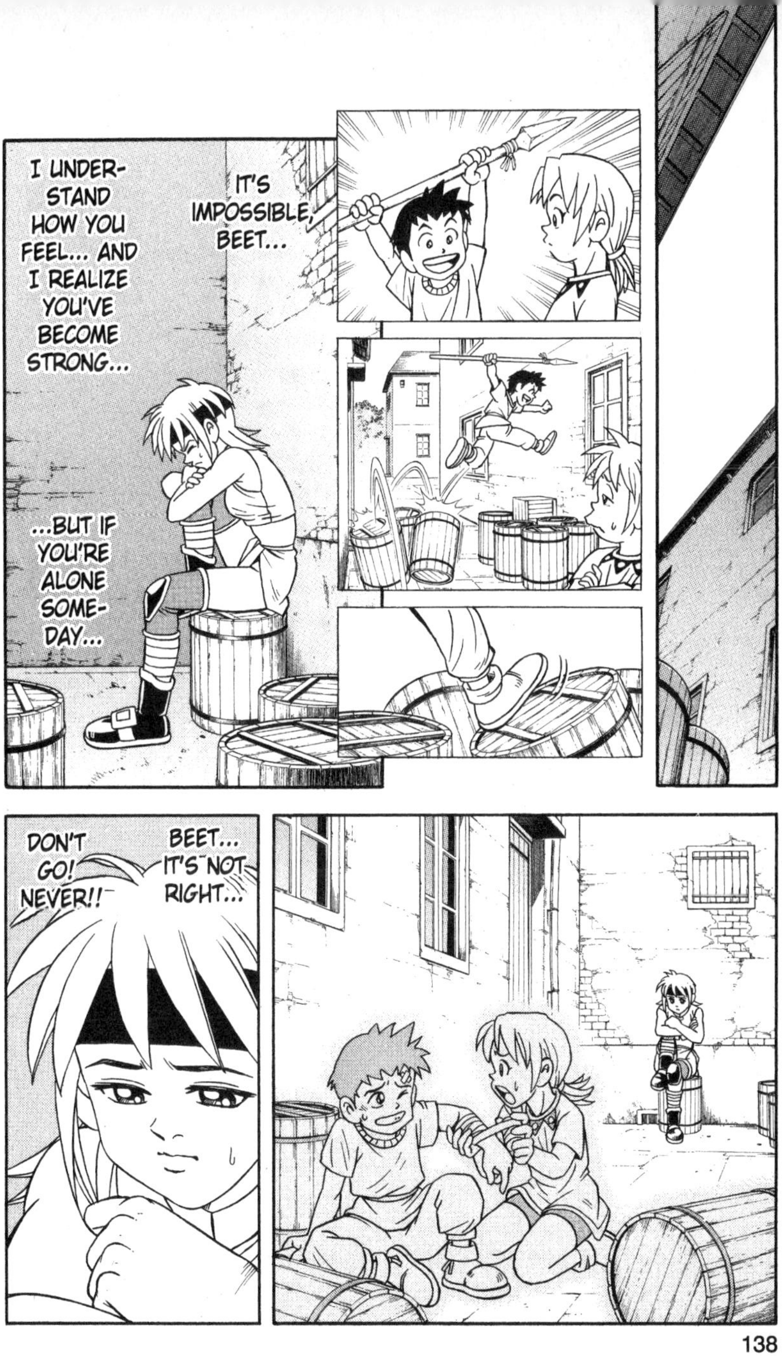
IT'S IMPOSSIBLE, BEET...
I UNDERSTAND HOW YOU FEEL... AND I REALIZE YOU'VE BECOME STRONG...
...BUT IF YOU'RE ALONE SOMEDAY...
BEET... IT'S NOT RIGHT...
DON'T GO! NEVER!!

三条　陸・稲田浩司

Thanks for waiting, everyone!
Here is the first volume of *Beet!* Unlike
Dai's Adventure, which was set in a
world not too different from our own, for
this story we've constructed a new world
from scratch, setting up new rules for
the world, the Vandels and the monsters.
It's the biggest struggle we deal with, but
it also gives us pleasure to take on the
unpredictable. We'll continue to do our
best, so please cheer us on!
— Riku Sanjo

Author Riku Sanjo and artist Koji Inada were
both born in Tokyo in 1964. Riku began his
career writing a radio-controlled car manga for
the comic Bonbon. Koji debuted with
Kussotare Daze!! in Weekly Shonen Jump.
Riku and Koji first worked together on the
highly successful Dragon Quest–Dai's Big
Adventure. Beet, their latest collaboration,
debuted in Monthly Shonen Jump in 2002
and was an immediate hit, inspiring an action-
packed video game and an animated series on
Japanese TV.

BEET THE VANDEL BUSTER
VOL. 1
The SHONEN JUMP Graphic Novel Edition

STORY BY RIKU SANJO
ART BY KOJI INADA

English Adaptation/Shaenon K. Garrity
Translation/Naomi Kokubo
Touch-Up & Lettering/Mark McMurray
Graphics & Cover Design/Sean Lee
Editor/Richard Kadrey

Managing Editor/Elizabeth Kawasaki
Director of Production/Noboru Watanabe
Editorial Director/Alvin Lu
Executive Vice President & Editor in Chief/Hyoe Narita
Sr. Director of Licensing & Acquisitions/Rika Inouye
Vice President of Sales/Joe Morici
Vice President of Marketing/Liza Coppola
Vice President of Strategic Development/Yumi Hoashi
Publisher/Seiji Horibuchi

Printed in the U.S.A.

Published by VIZ, LLC
P.O. Box 77064
San Francisco, CA 94107

SHONEN JUMP Graphic Novel Edition
10 9 8 7 6 5 4 3 2 1
First printing, September 2004

PARENTAL ADVISORY
BEET THE VANDEL BUSTER is rated A
for All Ages. It contains fantasy violence.
It is recommended for all ages.

THE WORLD'S
MOST POPULAR MANGA

SHONEN JUMP
GRAPHIC NOVEL
www.shonenjump.com

www.viz.com

SHONEN JUMP GRAPHIC NOVEL

Beet™ The Vandel Buster

Volume 1

Story by **Riku Sanjo**

Art by **Koji Inada**

Chapter 1
The Boy Rises!
5

Chapter 2
He Who Returned!
71

Chapter 3
The Time of Departure!
117

Special Feature
Beet: The World (Part 1)
169

Chapter 1 – The Boy Rises!

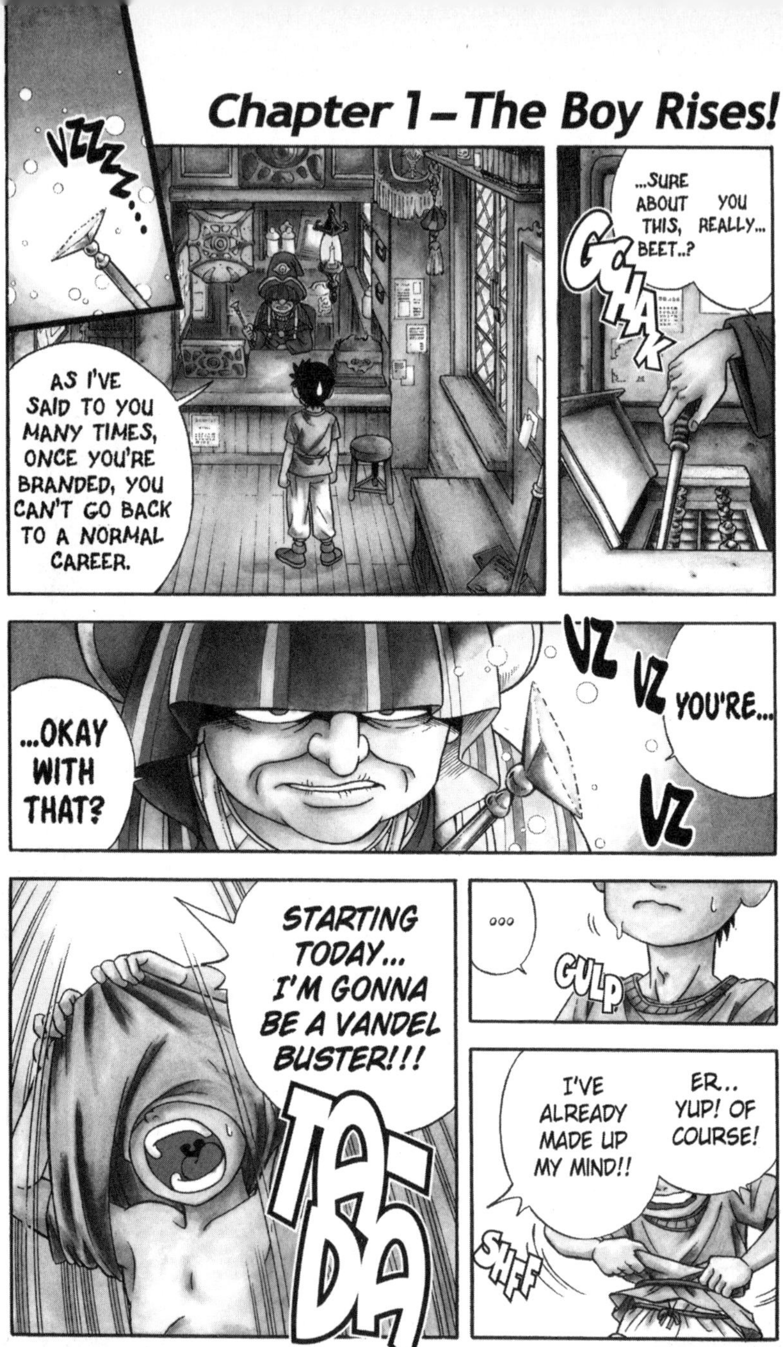

YOU REALLY...
...SURE ABOUT THIS, BEET..?
GOHAK
AS I'VE SAID TO YOU MANY TIMES, ONCE YOU'RE BRANDED, YOU CAN'T GO BACK TO A NORMAL CAREER.
VZZZZ...
VZ
VZ
YOU'RE...
VZ
...OKAY WITH THAT?
...
GULP
ER.. YUP! OF COURSE!
I'VE ALREADY MADE UP MY MIND!!
SHFF
STARTING TODAY... I'M GONNA BE A VANDEL BUSTER!!!
TA-DA

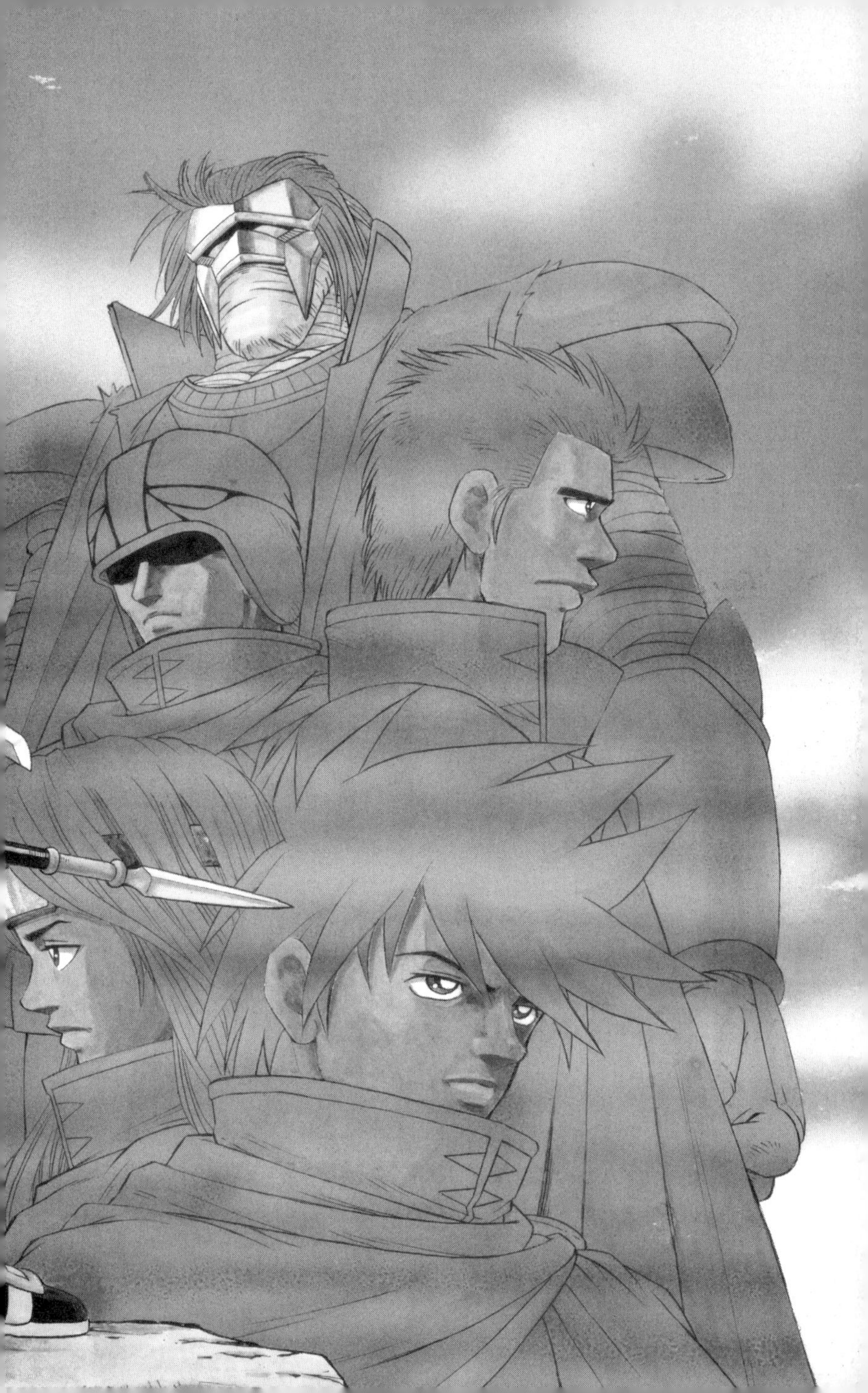

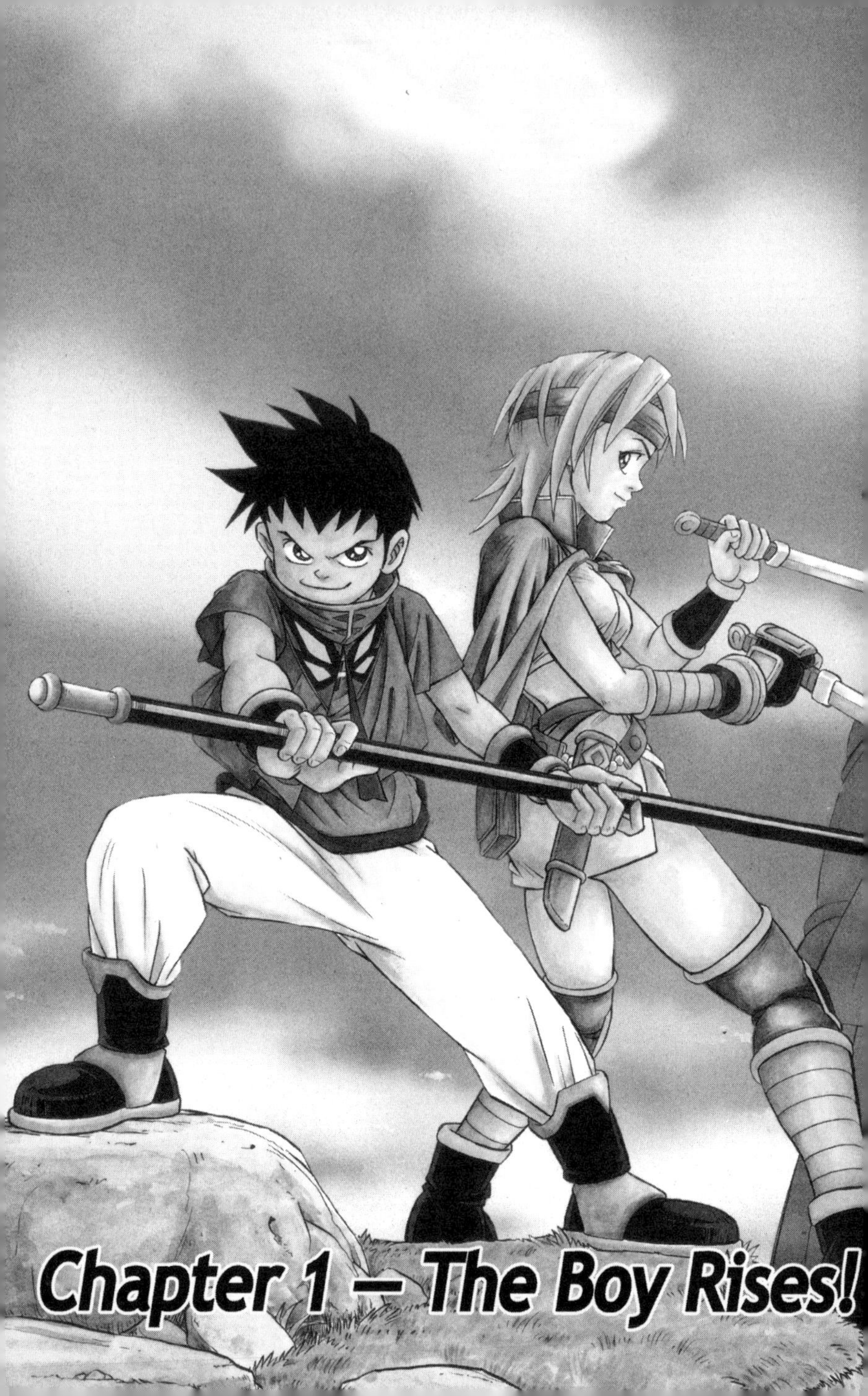
Chapter 1 — The Boy Rises!

BEET
THE VANDEL BUSTER

READ THIS WAY

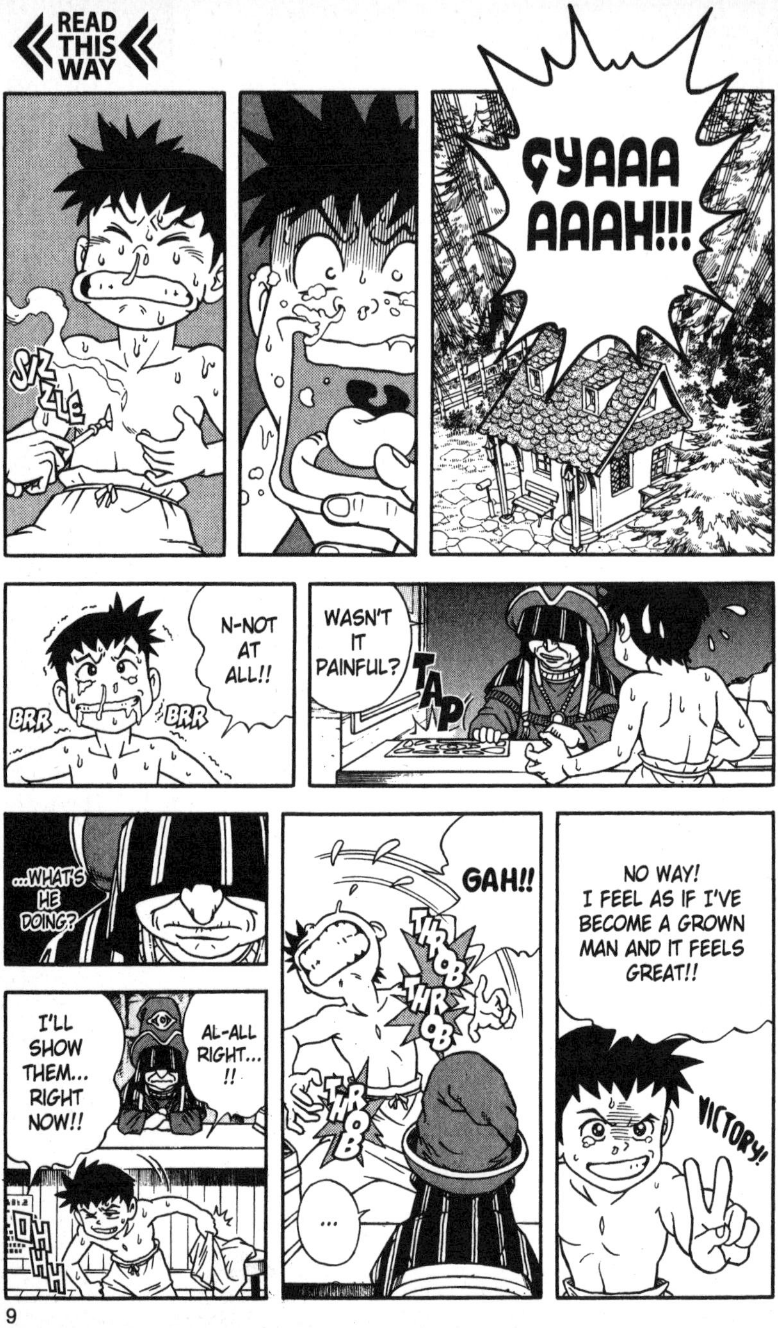
GYAAA AAAH!!!
SIZZLE
WASN'T IT PAINFUL?
TAP
N-NOT AT ALL!!
BRR
BRR
NO WAY! I FEEL AS IF I'VE BECOME A GROWN MAN AND IT FEELS GREAT!!
VICTORY!
GAH!!
THROB
THROB
THROB
...
...WHAT'S HE DOING?
AL-ALL RIGHT... !!
I'LL SHOW THEM... RIGHT NOW!!
OHHH

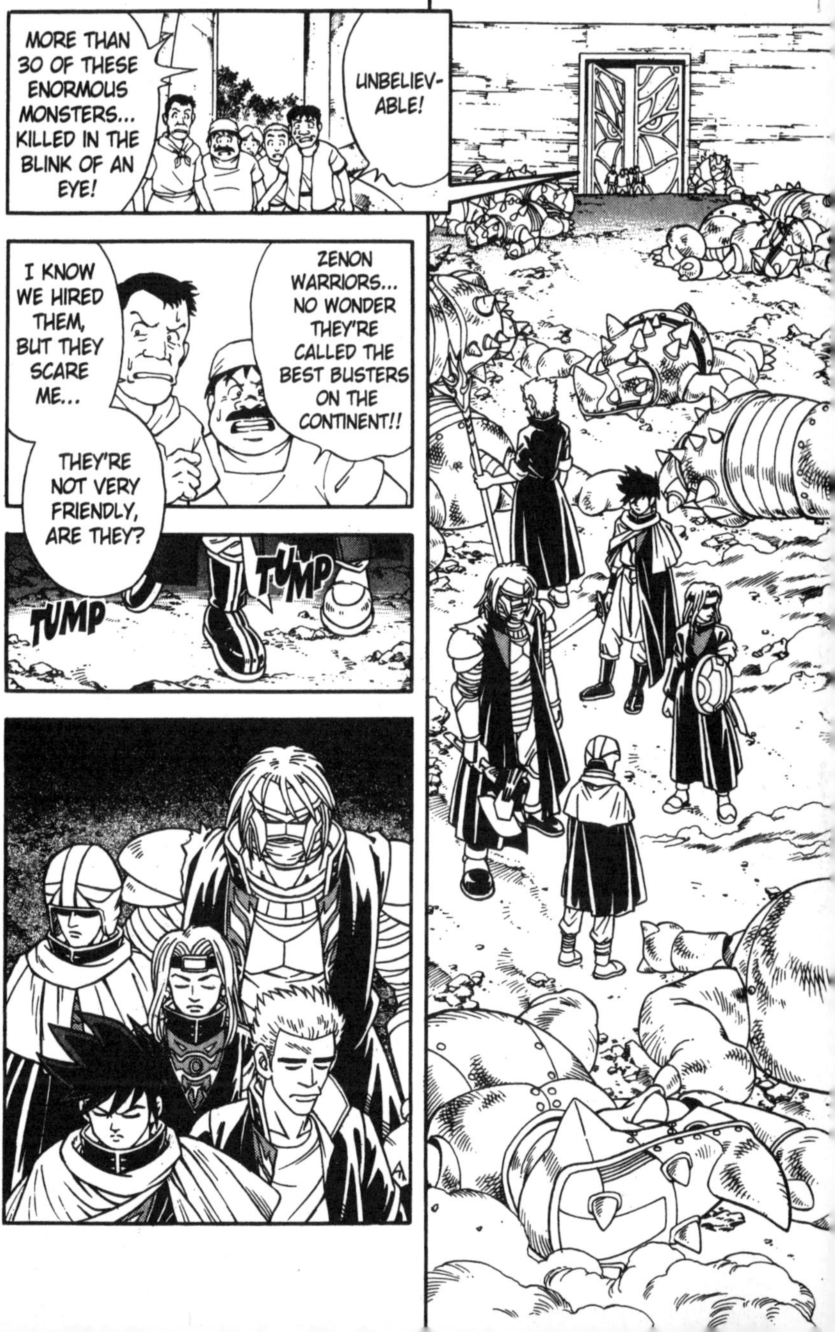
UNBELIEV-ABLE!
MORE THAN 30 OF THESE ENORMOUS MONSTERS... KILLED IN THE BLINK OF AN EYE!
ZENON WARRIORS... NO WONDER THEY'RE CALLED THE BEST BUSTERS ON THE CONTINENT!!
I KNOW WE HIRED THEM, BUT THEY SCARE ME...
THEY'RE NOT VERY FRIENDLY, ARE THEY?
TUMP
TUMP

READ THIS WAY

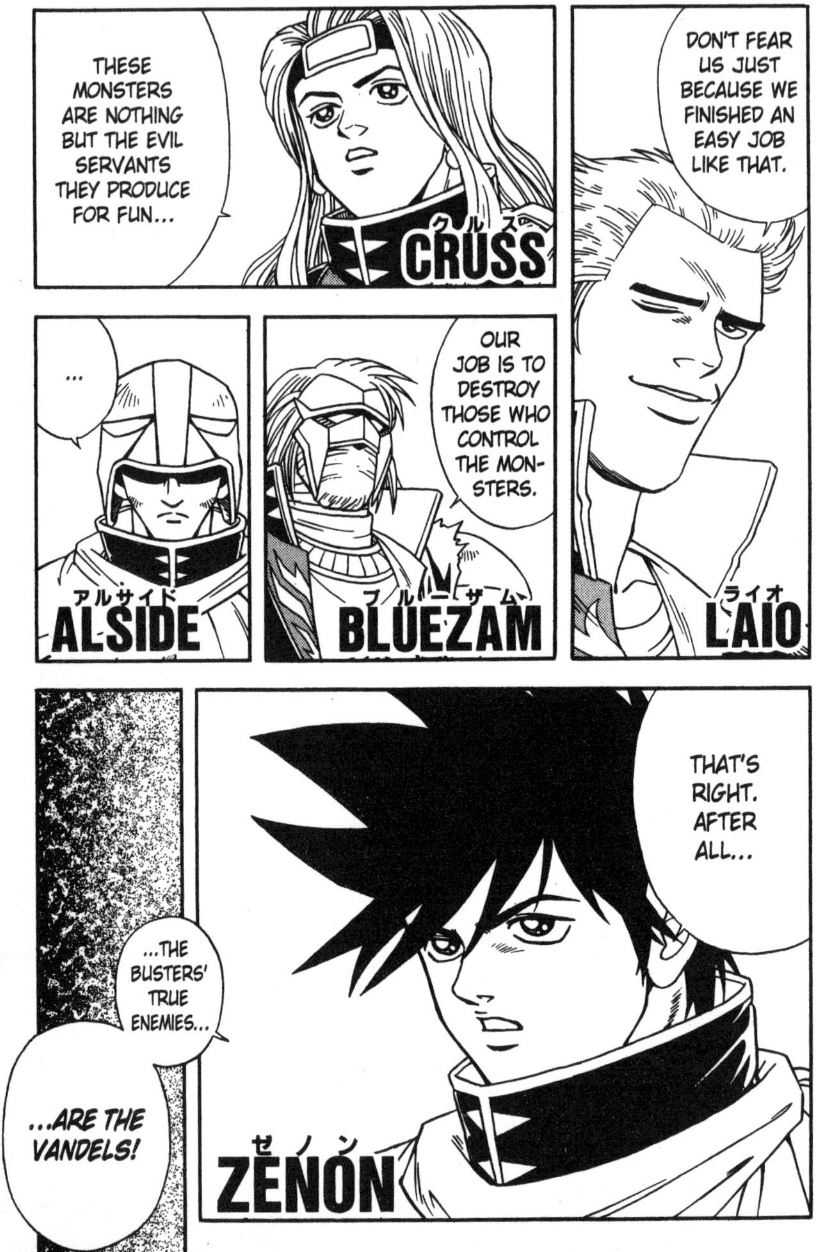

DON'T FEAR US JUST BECAUSE WE FINISHED AN EASY JOB LIKE THAT.
ライオ
LAIO
THESE MONSTERS ARE NOTHING BUT THE EVIL SERVANTS THEY PRODUCE FOR FUN...
クルス
CRUSS
OUR JOB IS TO DESTROY THOSE WHO CONTROL THE MONSTERS.
ブルーザム
BLUEZAM
...
アルサイド
ALSIDE
THAT'S RIGHT. AFTER ALL...
...THE BUSTERS' TRUE ENEMIES...
...ARE THE VANDELS!
ゼノン
ZENON

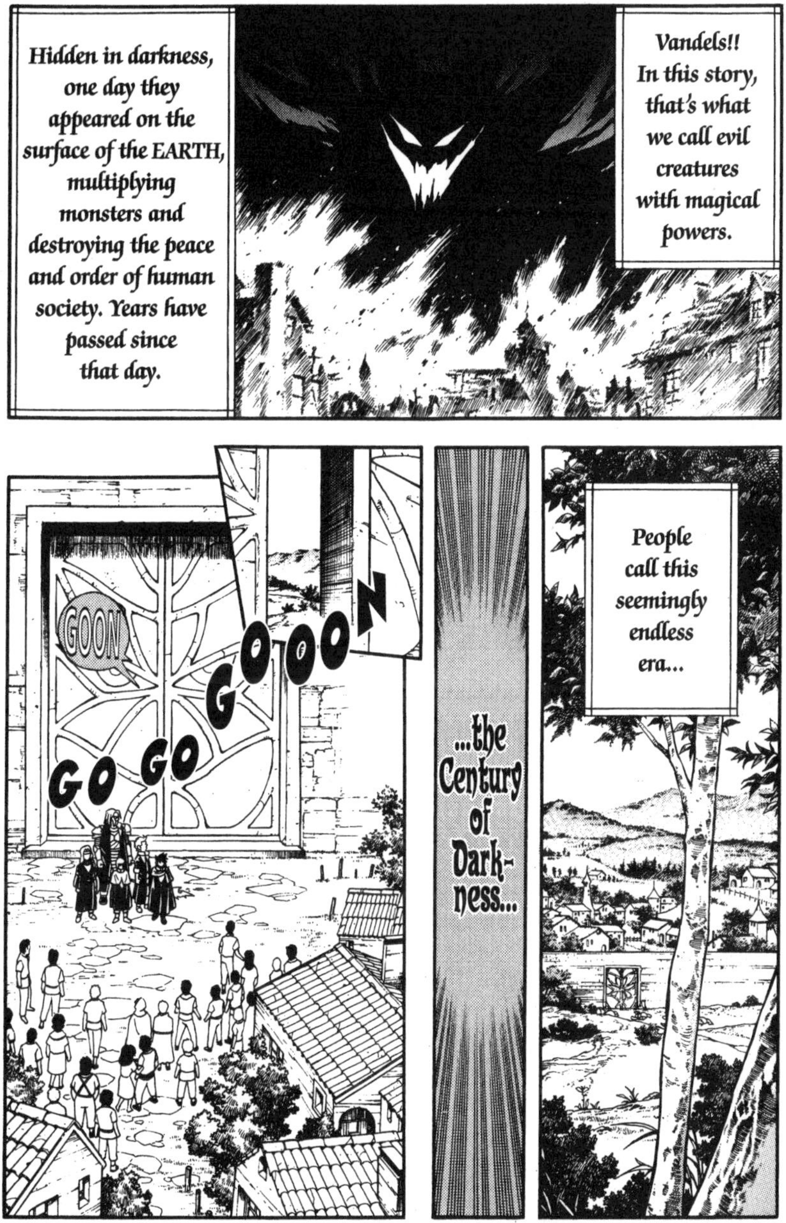
Vandels!! In this story, that's what we call evil creatures with magical powers.
Hidden in darkness, one day they appeared on the surface of the EARTH, multiplying monsters and destroying the peace and order of human society. Years have passed since that day.
People call this seemingly endless era...
...the Century of Darkness...
GOON
GO GO GOOOON

READ THIS WAY

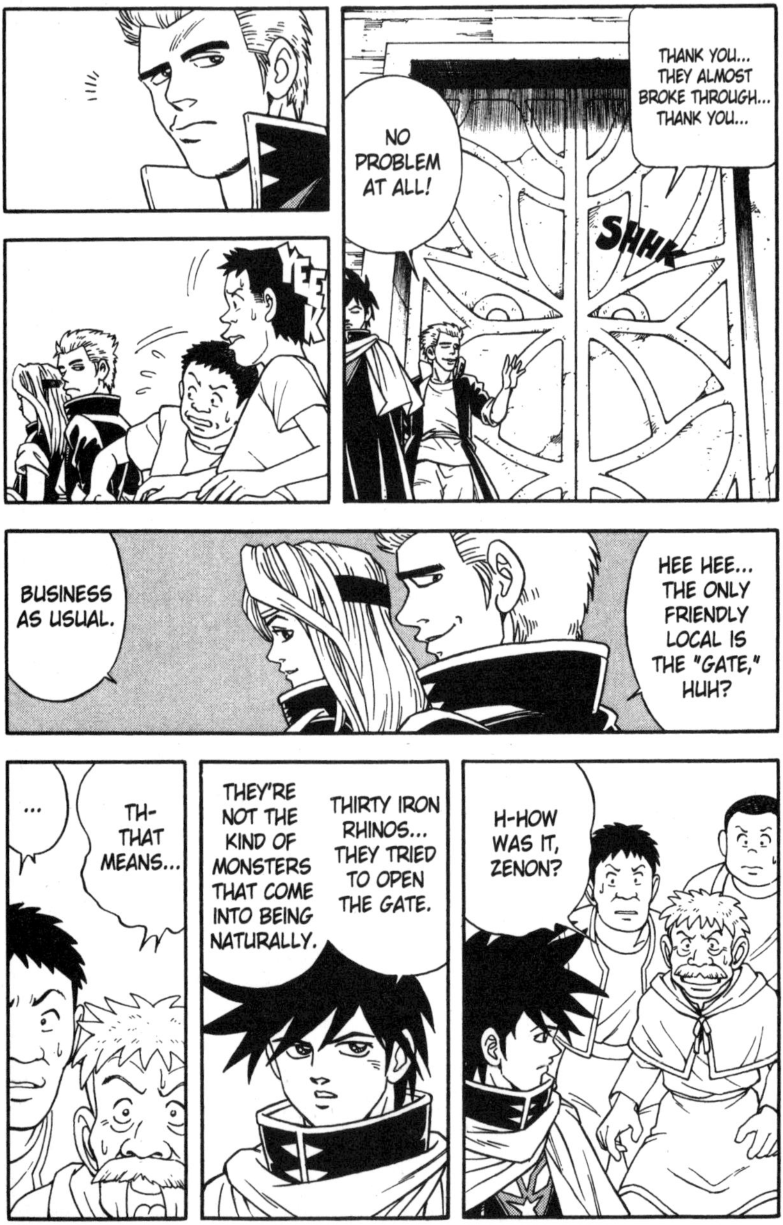
THANK YOU... THEY ALMOST BROKE THROUGH... THANK YOU...
NO PROBLEM AT ALL!
SHHK
YEEEK
HEE HEE... THE ONLY FRIENDLY LOCAL IS THE "GATE," HUH?
BUSINESS AS USUAL.
H-HOW WAS IT, ZENON?
THIRTY IRON RHINOS... THEY TRIED TO OPEN THE GATE.
THEY'RE NOT THE KIND OF MONSTERS THAT COME INTO BEING NATURALLY.
TH- THAT MEANS...
...

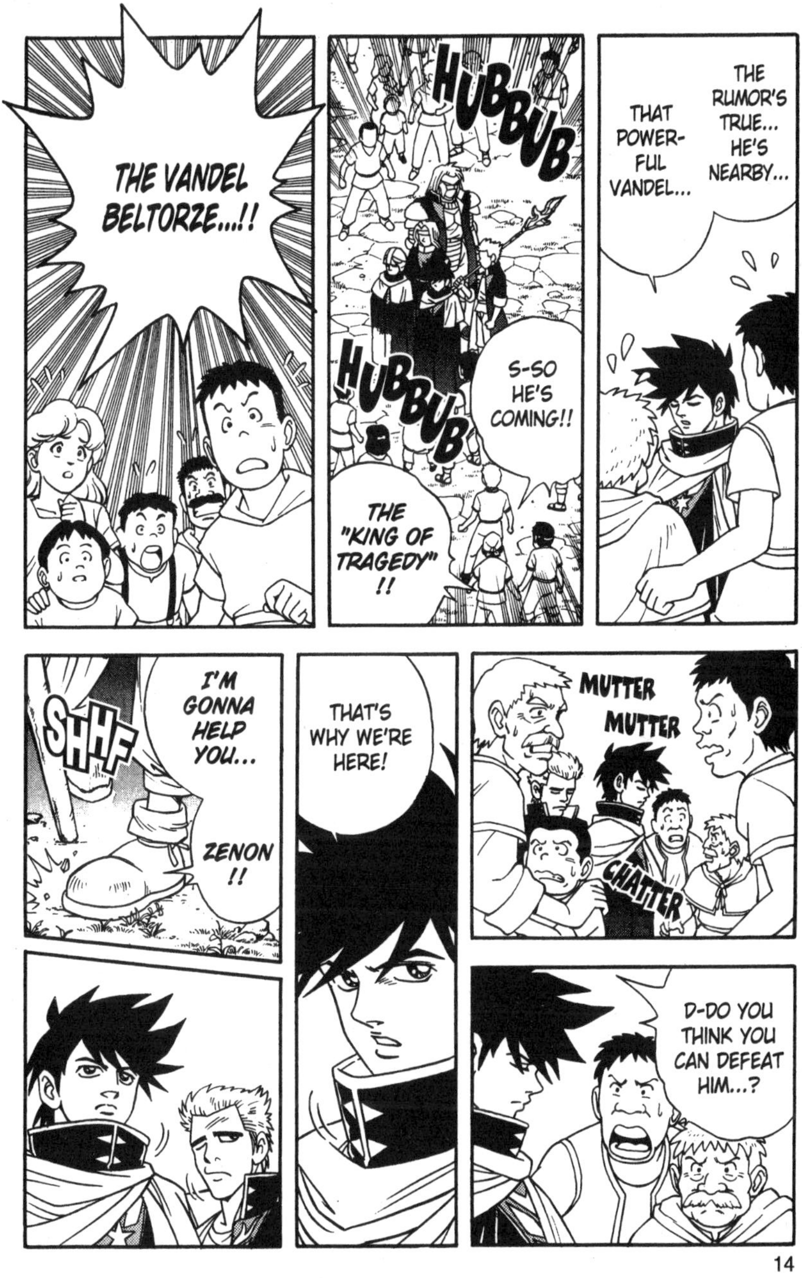
THE RUMOR'S TRUE... HE'S NEARBY...
THAT POWER-FUL VANDEL...
HUBBUB
S-SO HE'S COMING!!
HUBBUB
THE "KING OF TRAGEDY"!!
THE VANDEL BELTORZE...!!
MUTTER
MUTTER
CHATTER
D-DO YOU THINK YOU CAN DEFEAT HIM...?
THAT'S WHY WE'RE HERE!
SHHF
I'M GONNA HELP YOU...
ZENON!!

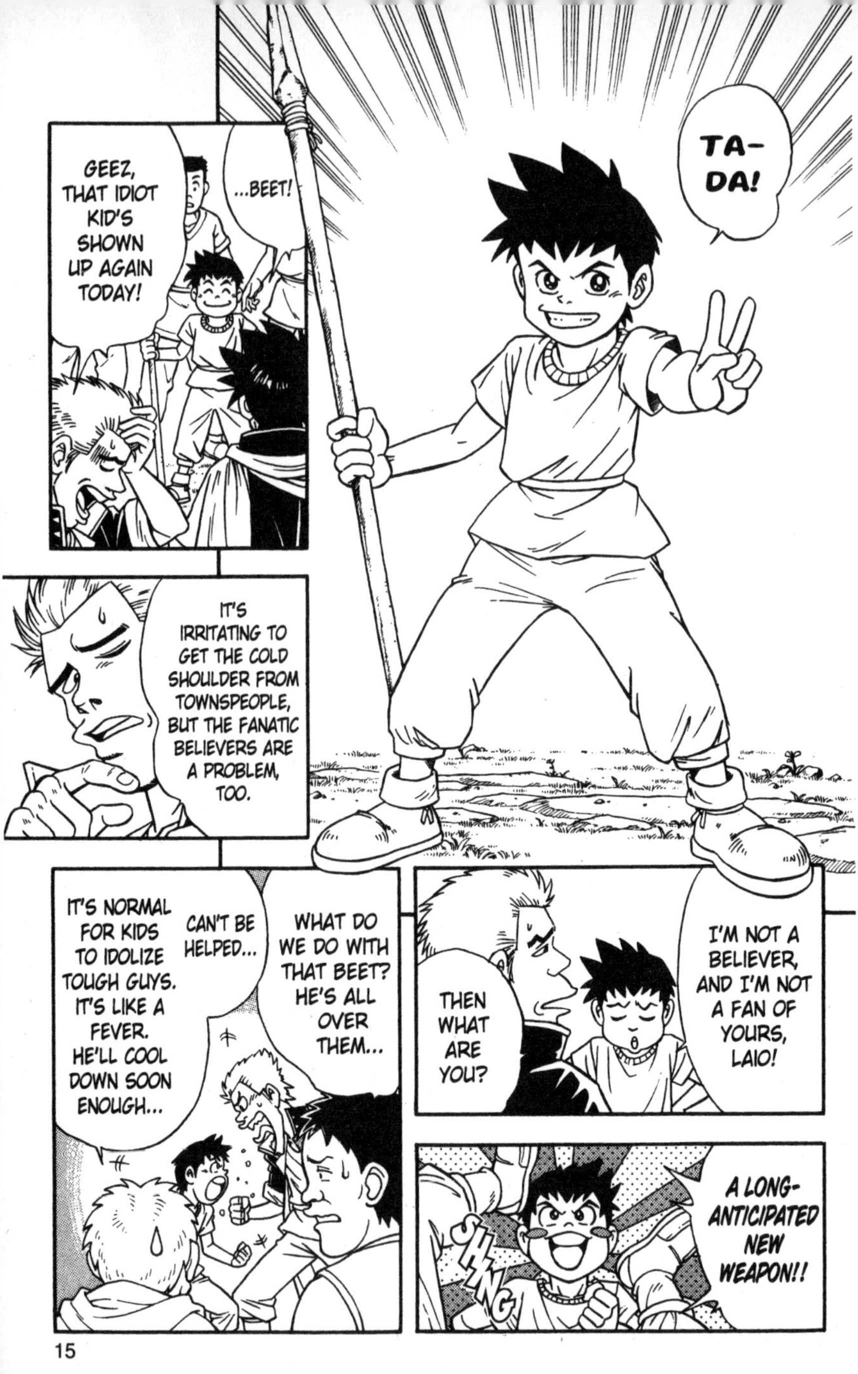
TA-DA!
...BEET!
GEEZ, THAT IDIOT KID'S SHOWN UP AGAIN TODAY!
IT'S IRRITATING TO GET THE COLD SHOULDER FROM TOWNSPEOPLE, BUT THE FANATIC BELIEVERS ARE A PROBLEM, TOO.
I'M NOT A BELIEVER, AND I'M NOT A FAN OF YOURS, LAIO!
THEN WHAT ARE YOU?
A LONG-ANTICIPATED NEW WEAPON!!
SHING
WHAT DO WE DO WITH THAT BEET? HE'S ALL OVER THEM...
CAN'T BE HELPED...
IT'S NORMAL FOR KIDS TO IDOLIZE TOUGH GUYS. IT'S LIKE A FEVER. HE'LL COOL DOWN SOON ENOUGH...

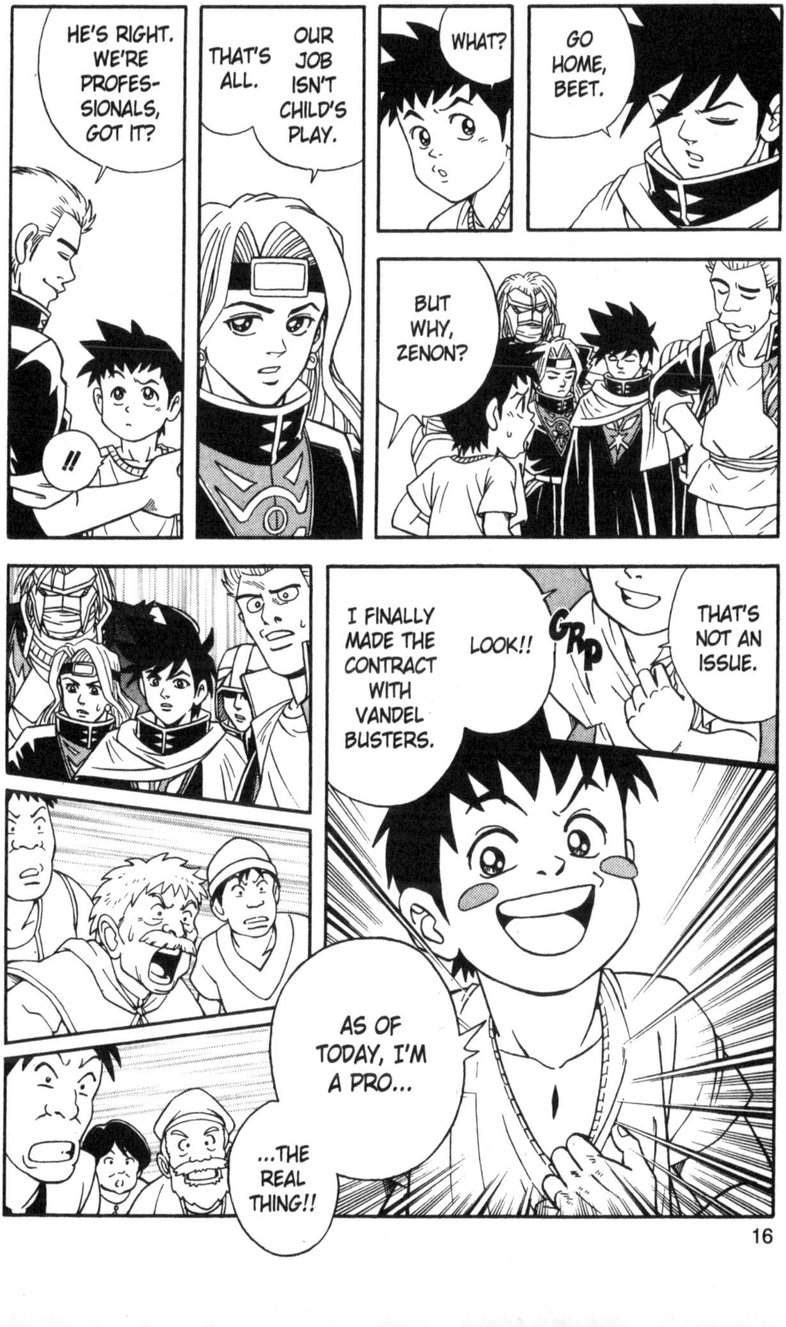
GO HOME, BEET.
WHAT?
BUT WHY, ZENON?
OUR JOB ISN'T CHILD'S PLAY.
THAT'S ALL.
HE'S RIGHT. WE'RE PROFES-SIONALS, GOT IT?
!!
THAT'S NOT AN ISSUE.
GRP
LOOK!!
I FINALLY MADE THE CONTRACT WITH VANDEL BUSTERS.
AS OF TODAY, I'M A PRO...
...THE REAL THING!!

READ THIS WAY

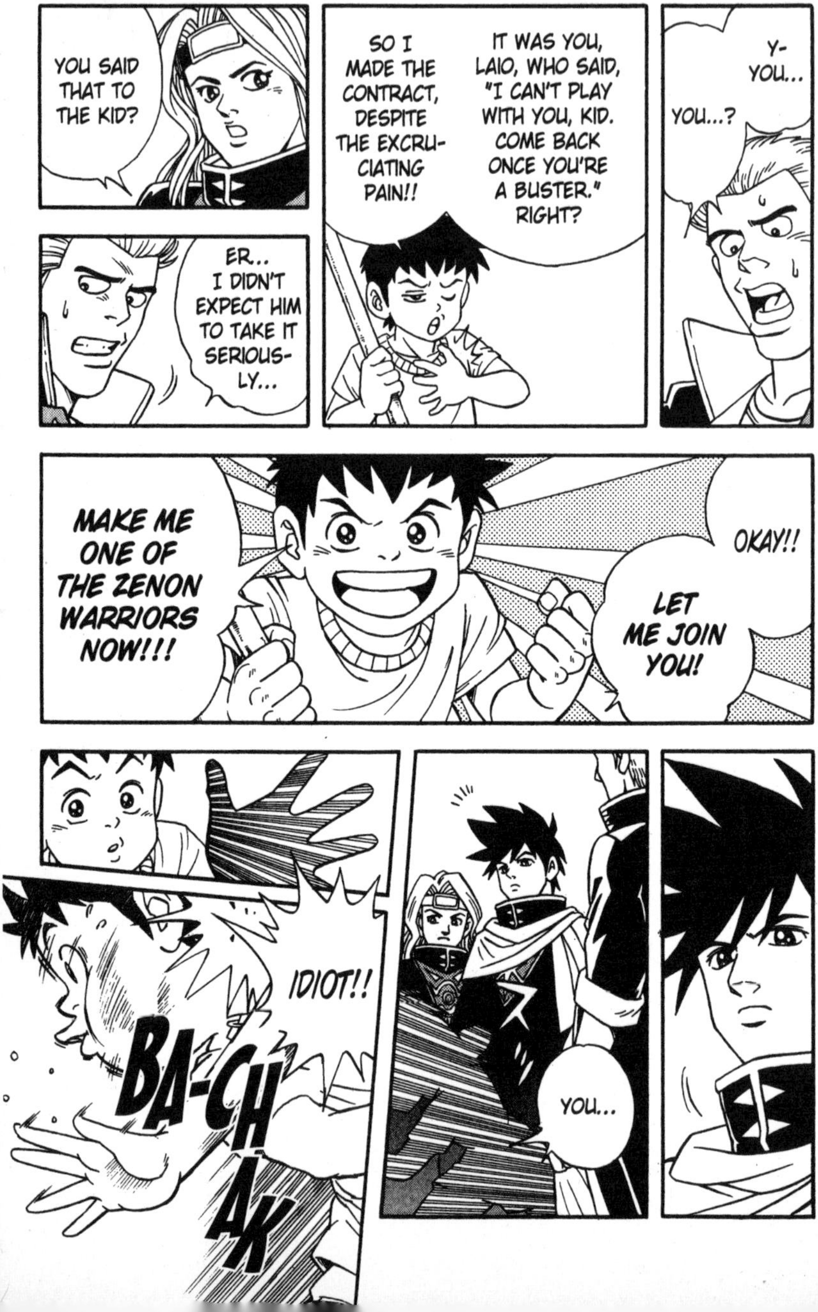
Y- YOU...
YOU...?
IT WAS YOU, LAIO, WHO SAID, "I CAN'T PLAY WITH YOU, KID. COME BACK ONCE YOU'RE A BUSTER." RIGHT?
SO I MADE THE CONTRACT, DESPITE THE EXCRUCIATING PAIN!!
YOU SAID THAT TO THE KID?
ER.. I DIDN'T EXPECT HIM TO TAKE IT SERIOUSLY...
OKAY!!
LET ME JOIN YOU!
MAKE ME ONE OF THE ZENON WARRIORS NOW!!!
YOU...
IDIOT!!
BA-CHAK

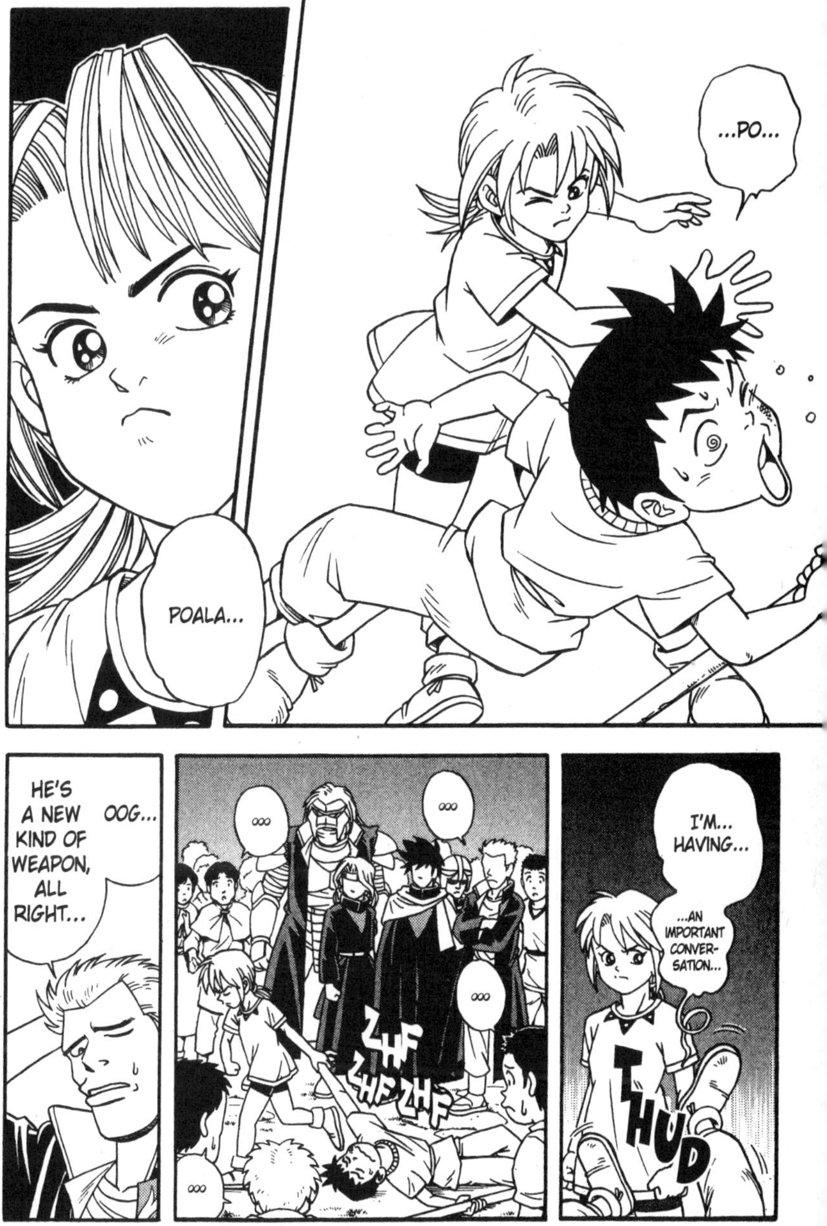
...PO...
POALA...
I'M... HAVING...
...AN IMPORTANT CONVER-SATION...
THUD
ooo
ooo
ooo
ZHF ZHF ZHF
ooo
OOG...
HE'S A NEW KIND OF WEAPON, ALL RIGHT...

READ THIS WAY

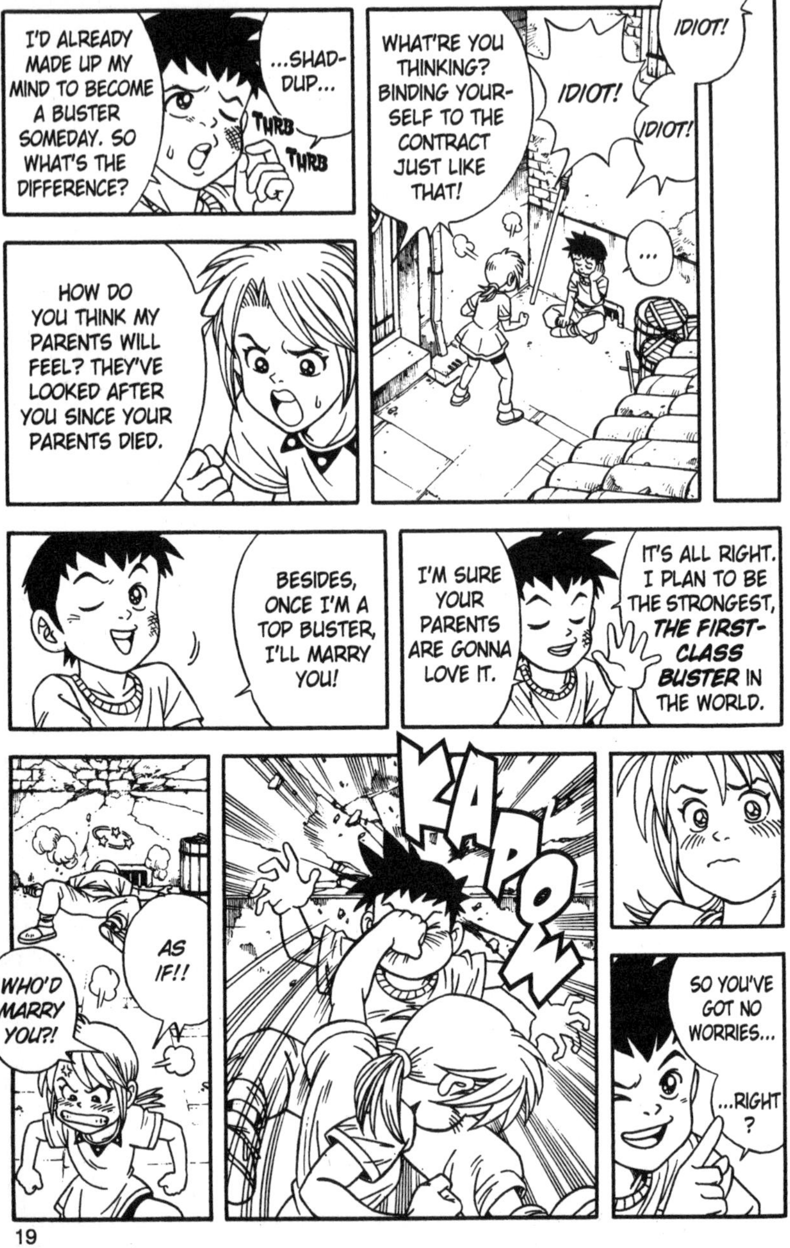
IDIOT!
IDIOT!
IDIOT!
WHAT'RE YOU THINKING? BINDING YOURSELF TO THE CONTRACT JUST LIKE THAT!
...
...SHAD-DUP...
THRB
THRB
I'D ALREADY MADE UP MY MIND TO BECOME A BUSTER SOMEDAY. SO WHAT'S THE DIFFERENCE?
HOW DO YOU THINK MY PARENTS WILL FEEL? THEY'VE LOOKED AFTER YOU SINCE YOUR PARENTS DIED.
IT'S ALL RIGHT. I PLAN TO BE THE STRONGEST, ***THE FIRST-CLASS BUSTER*** IN THE WORLD.
I'M SURE YOUR PARENTS ARE GONNA LOVE IT.
BESIDES, ONCE I'M A TOP BUSTER, I'LL MARRY YOU!
SO YOU'VE GOT NO WORRIES...
...RIGHT?
KAPOW
AS IF!!
WHO'D MARRY YOU?!

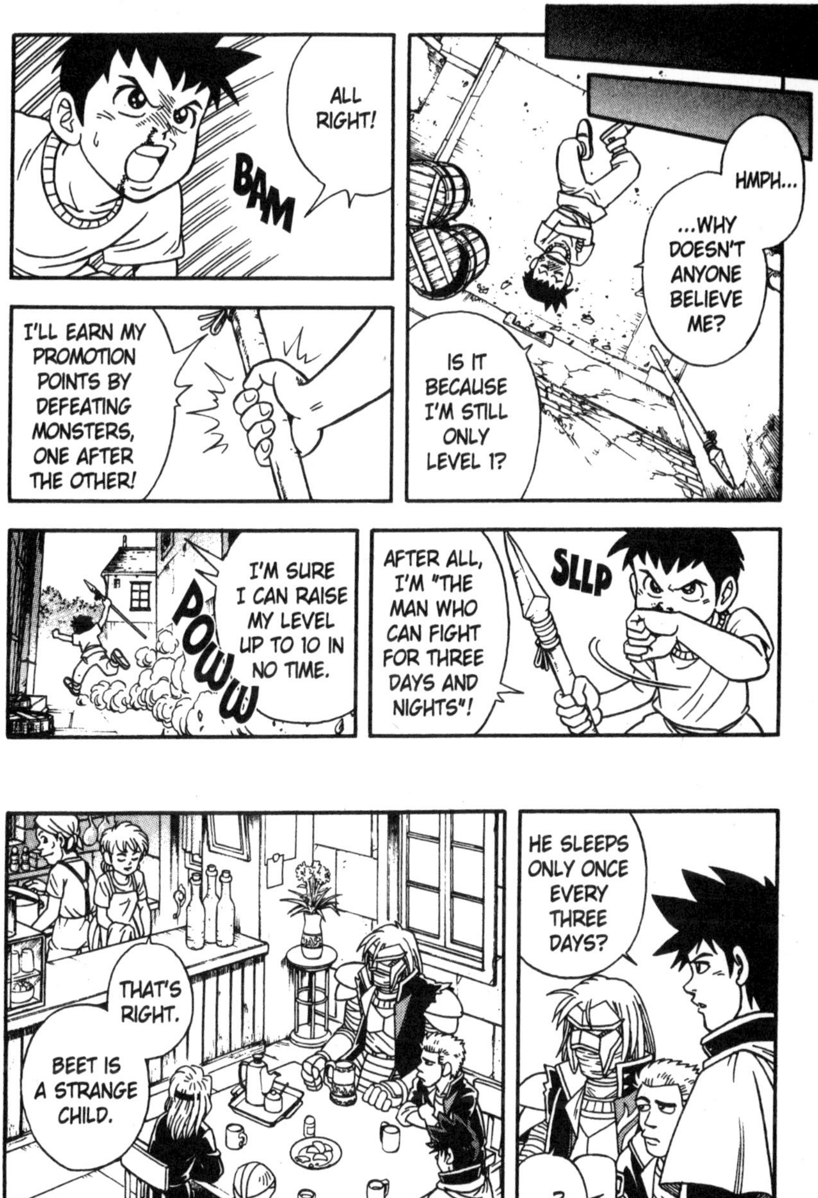
HMPH...
...WHY DOESN'T ANYONE BELIEVE ME?
IS IT BECAUSE I'M STILL ONLY LEVEL 1?
ALL RIGHT!
BAM
I'LL EARN MY PROMOTION POINTS BY DEFEATING MONSTERS, ONE AFTER THE OTHER!
SLLP
AFTER ALL, I'M "THE MAN WHO CAN FIGHT FOR THREE DAYS AND NIGHTS"!
I'M SURE I CAN RAISE MY LEVEL UP TO 10 IN NO TIME.
POWWW
HE SLEEPS ONLY ONCE EVERY THREE DAYS?
...?
THAT'S RIGHT.
BEET IS A STRANGE CHILD.

READ THIS WAY

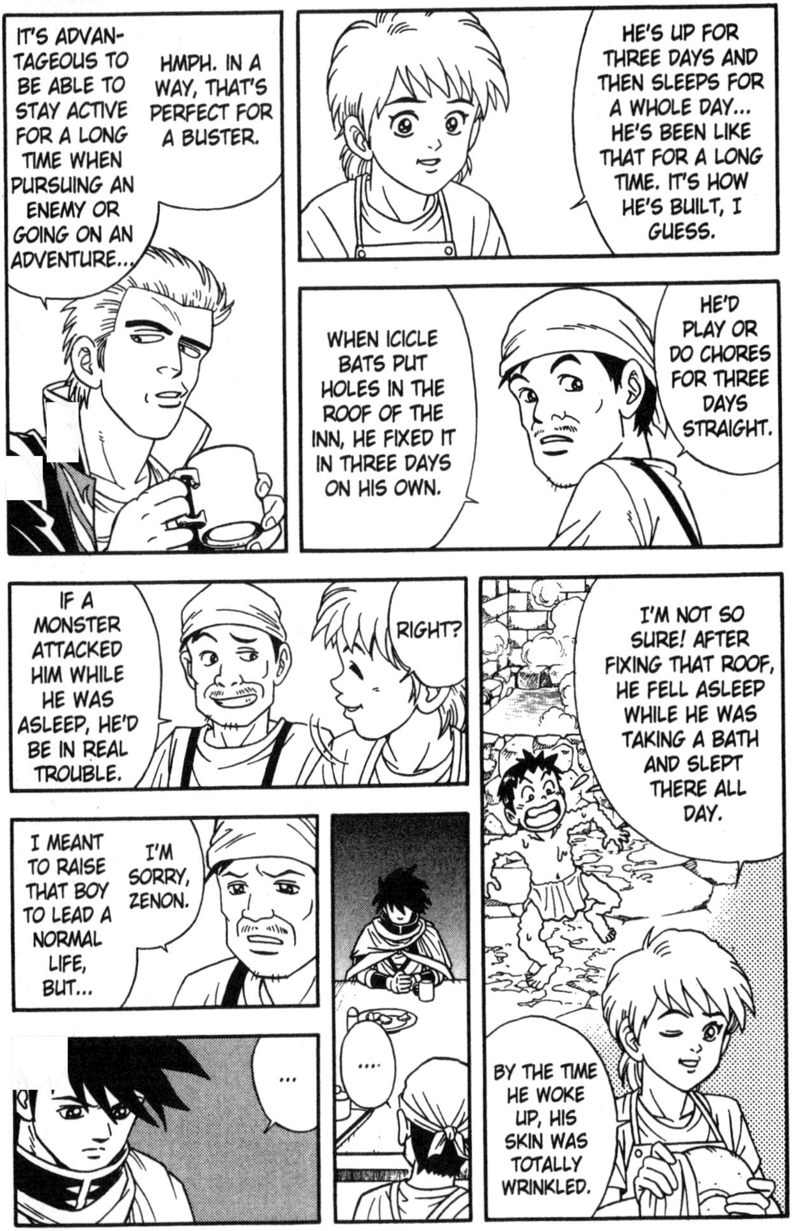
HE'S UP FOR THREE DAYS AND THEN SLEEPS FOR A WHOLE DAY... HE'S BEEN LIKE THAT FOR A LONG TIME. IT'S HOW HE'S BUILT, I GUESS.
HE'D PLAY OR DO CHORES FOR THREE DAYS STRAIGHT.
WHEN ICICLE BATS PUT HOLES IN THE ROOF OF THE INN, HE FIXED IT IN THREE DAYS ON HIS OWN.
HMPH. IN A WAY, THAT'S PERFECT FOR A BUSTER.
IT'S ADVAN-TAGEOUS TO BE ABLE TO STAY ACTIVE FOR A LONG TIME WHEN PURSUING AN ENEMY OR GOING ON AN ADVENTURE...
I'M NOT SO SURE! AFTER FIXING THAT ROOF, HE FELL ASLEEP WHILE HE WAS TAKING A BATH AND SLEPT THERE ALL DAY.
BY THE TIME HE WOKE UP, HIS SKIN WAS TOTALLY WRINKLED.
RIGHT?
IF A MONSTER ATTACKED HIM WHILE HE WAS ASLEEP, HE'D BE IN REAL TROUBLE.
....
I'M SORRY, ZENON.
I MEANT TO RAISE THAT BOY TO LEAD A NORMAL LIFE, BUT...
...

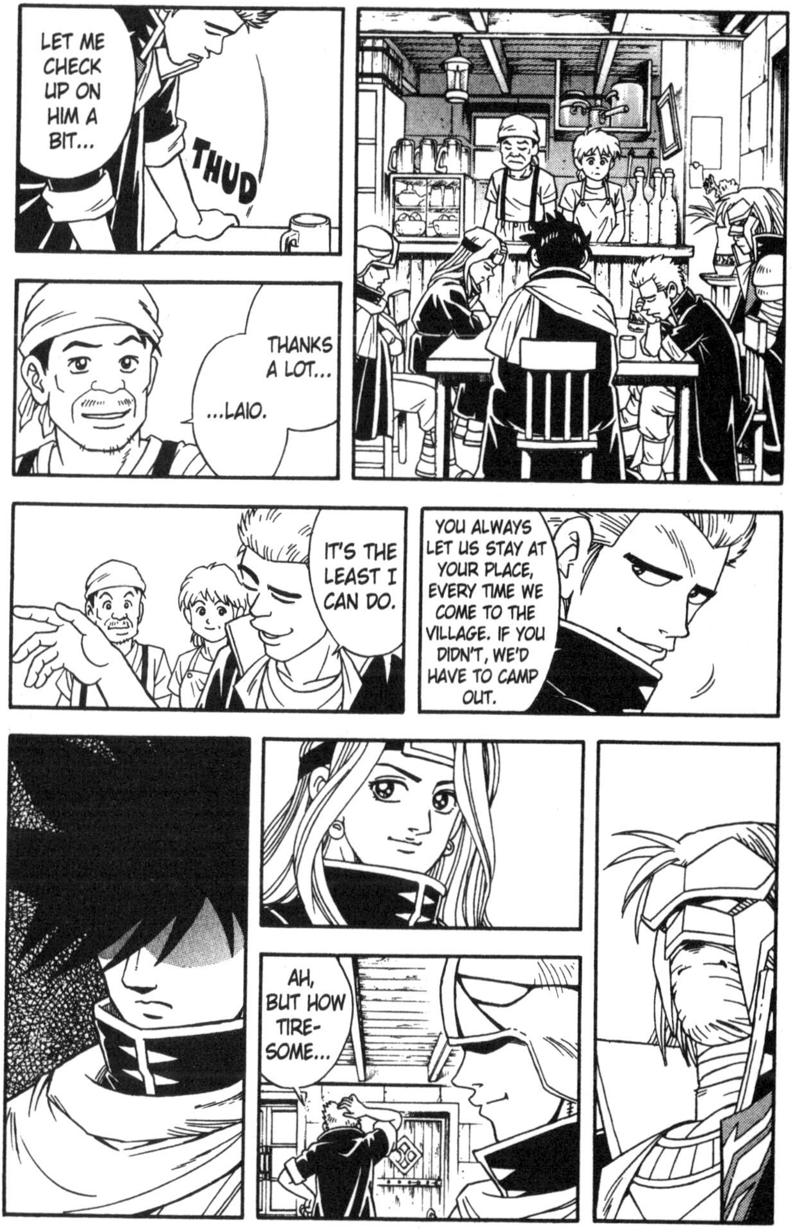
LET ME CHECK UP ON HIM A BIT...
THUD
THANKS A LOT...
...LAIO.
YOU ALWAYS LET US STAY AT YOUR PLACE, EVERY TIME WE COME TO THE VILLAGE. IF YOU DIDN'T, WE'D HAVE TO CAMP OUT.
IT'S THE LEAST I CAN DO.
AH, BUT HOW TIRE-SOME...

READ THIS WAY

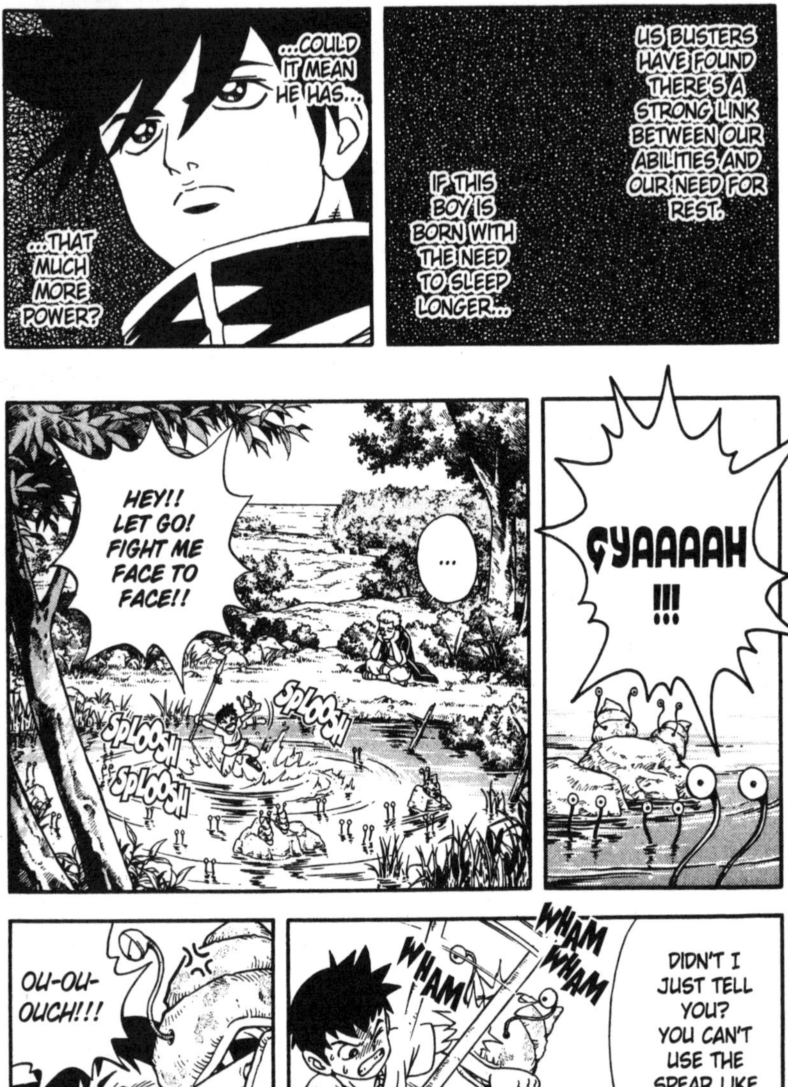
US BUSTERS HAVE FOUND THERE'S A STRONG LINK BETWEEN OUR ABILITIES AND OUR NEED FOR REST.
IF THIS BOY IS BORN WITH THE NEED TO SLEEP LONGER...
...COULD IT MEAN HE HAS...
...THAT MUCH MORE POWER?
GYAAAAH !!!
...
HEY!! LET GO! FIGHT ME FACE TO FACE!!
SPLOOSH
SPLOOSH
SPLOOSH
WHAM WHAM
WHAM
DIDN'T I JUST TELL YOU? YOU CAN'T USE THE SPEAR LIKE THAT WHEN YOU ATTACK...
OU-OU-OUCH!!!

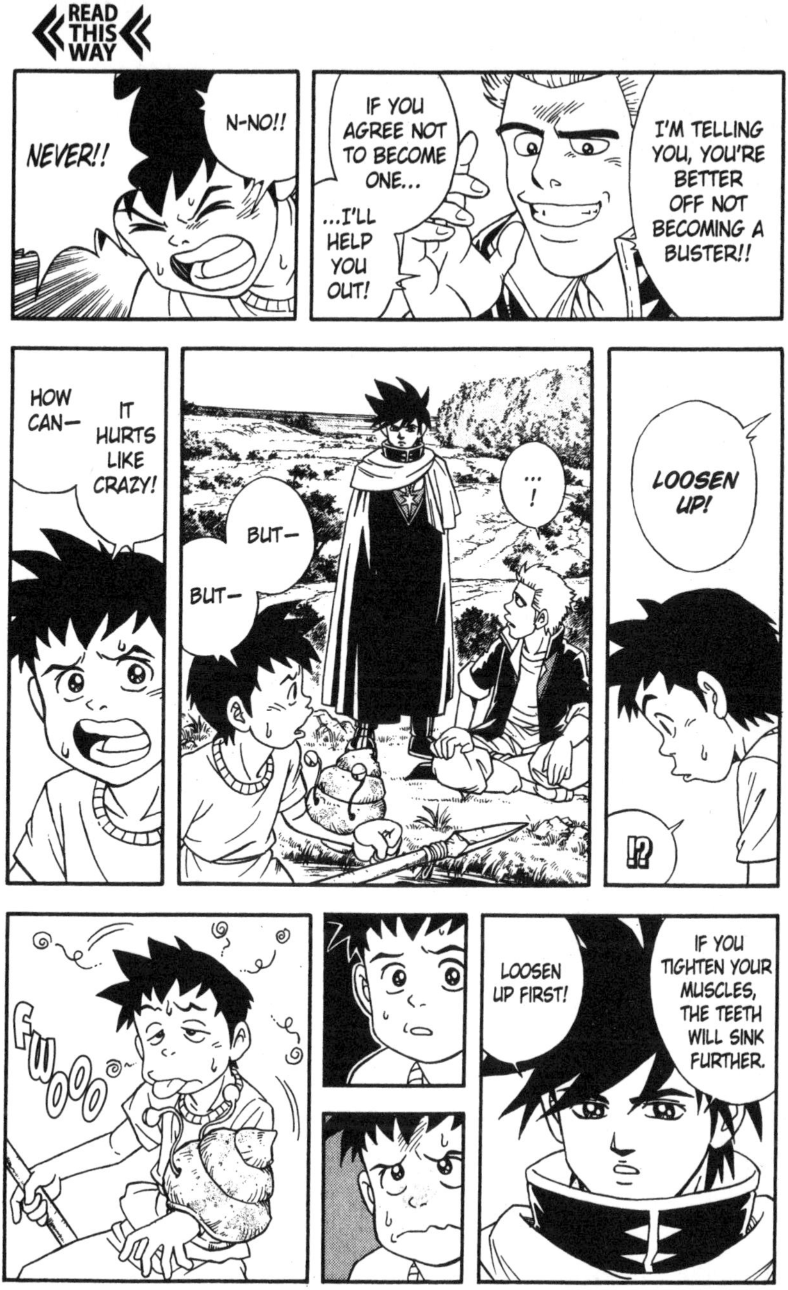
READ THIS WAY
I'M TELLING YOU, YOU'RE BETTER OFF NOT BECOMING A BUSTER!!
IF YOU AGREE NOT TO BECOME ONE...
...I'LL HELP YOU OUT!
N-NO!!
NEVER!!
LOOSEN UP!
!?
...!
BUT—
BUT—
IT HURTS LIKE CRAZY!
HOW CAN—
IF YOU TIGHTEN YOUR MUSCLES, THE TEETH WILL SINK FURTHER.
LOOSEN UP FIRST!
FWOOO

READ THIS WAY

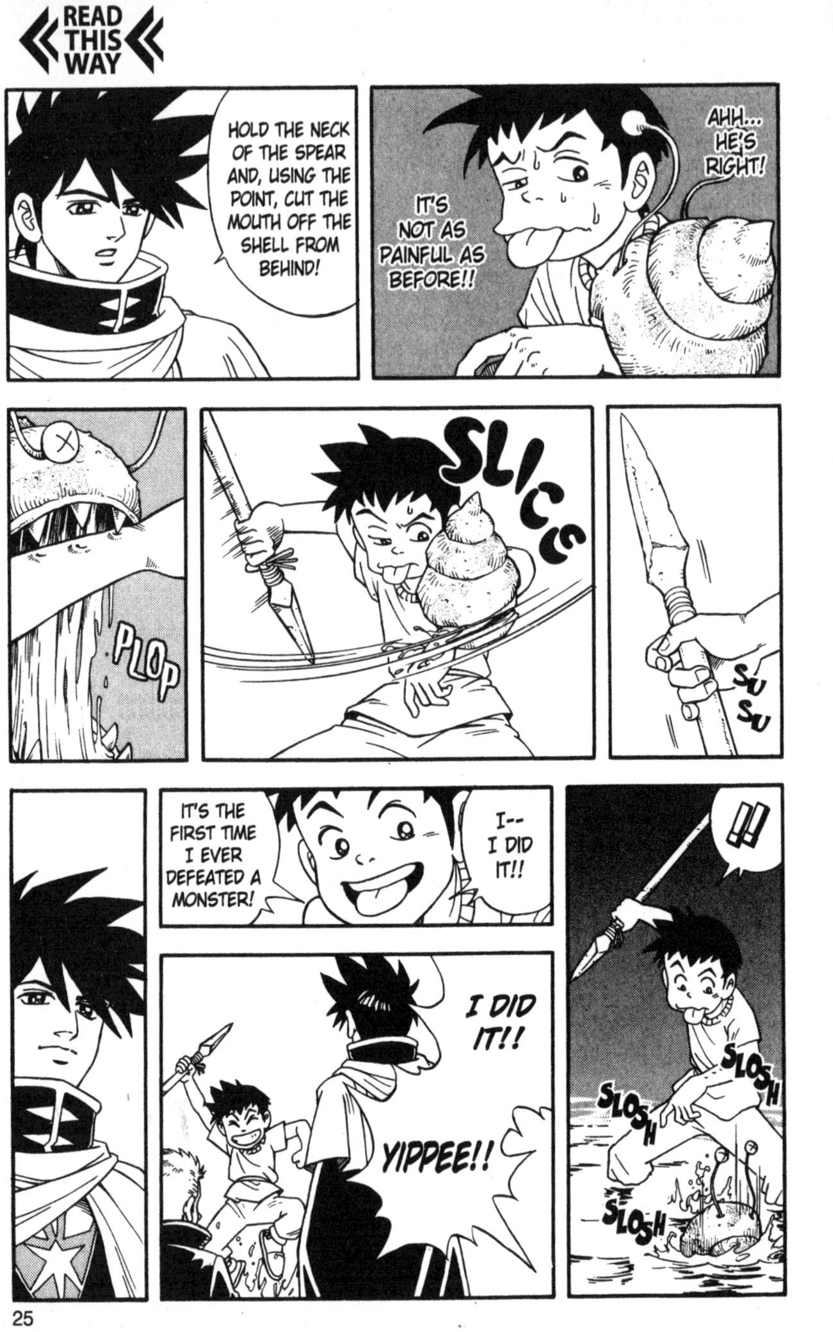

AHH... HE'S RIGHT!
IT'S NOT AS PAINFUL AS BEFORE!!
HOLD THE NECK OF THE SPEAR AND, USING THE POINT, CUT THE MOUTH OFF THE SHELL FROM BEHIND!
SU SU
SLICE
PLOP
!!
SLOSH
SLOSH
SLOSH
I-- I DID IT!!
IT'S THE FIRST TIME I EVER DEFEATED A MONSTER!
I DID IT!!
YIPPEE!!

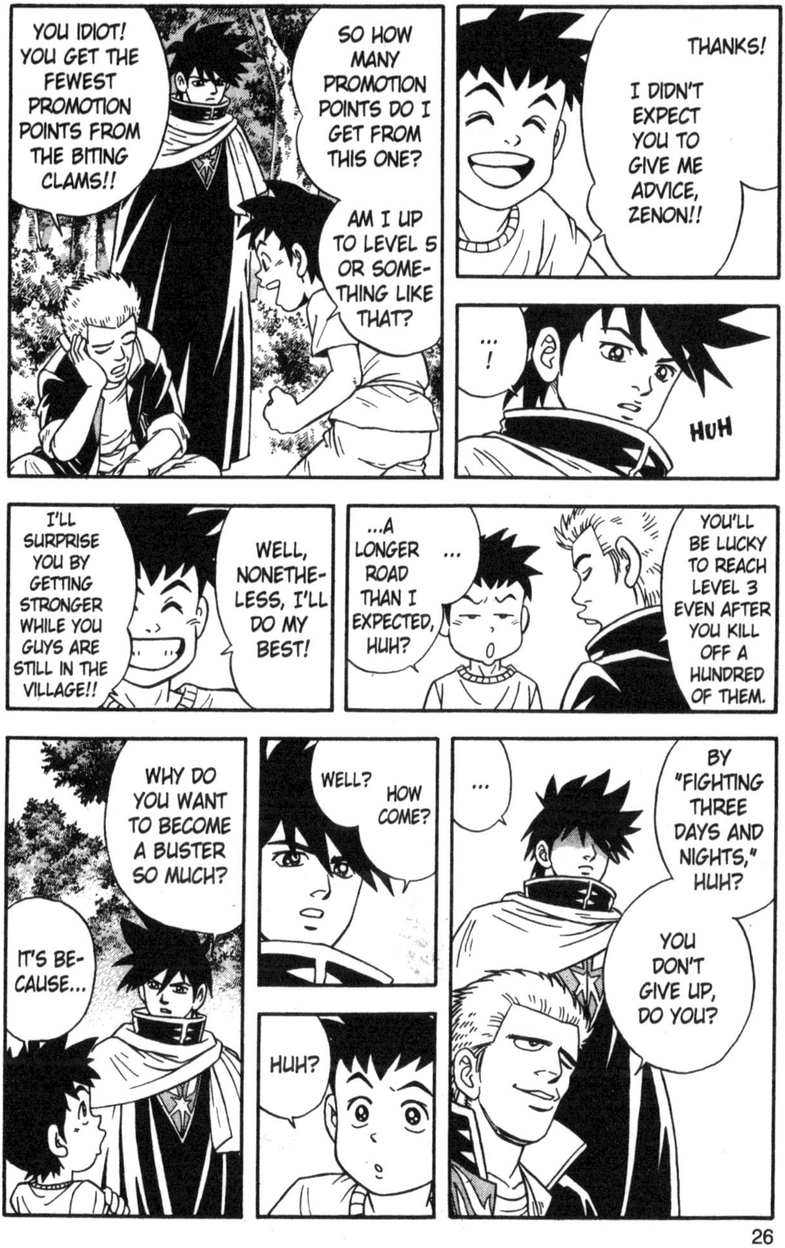
THANKS!
I DIDN'T EXPECT YOU TO GIVE ME ADVICE, ZENON!!
...!
HUH
SO HOW MANY PROMOTION POINTS DO I GET FROM THIS ONE?
AM I UP TO LEVEL 5 OR SOME-THING LIKE THAT?
YOU IDIOT! YOU GET THE FEWEST PROMOTION POINTS FROM THE BITING CLAMS!!
YOU'LL BE LUCKY TO REACH LEVEL 3 EVEN AFTER YOU KILL OFF A HUNDRED OF THEM.
...
...A LONGER ROAD THAN I EXPECTED, HUH?
WELL, NONETHE-LESS, I'LL DO MY BEST!
I'LL SURPRISE YOU BY GETTING STRONGER WHILE YOU GUYS ARE STILL IN THE VILLAGE!!
BY "FIGHTING THREE DAYS AND NIGHTS," HUH?
...
YOU DON'T GIVE UP, DO YOU?
WELL?
HOW COME?
HUH?
WHY DO YOU WANT TO BECOME A BUSTER SO MUCH?
IT'S BE-CAUSE...

READ THIS WAY

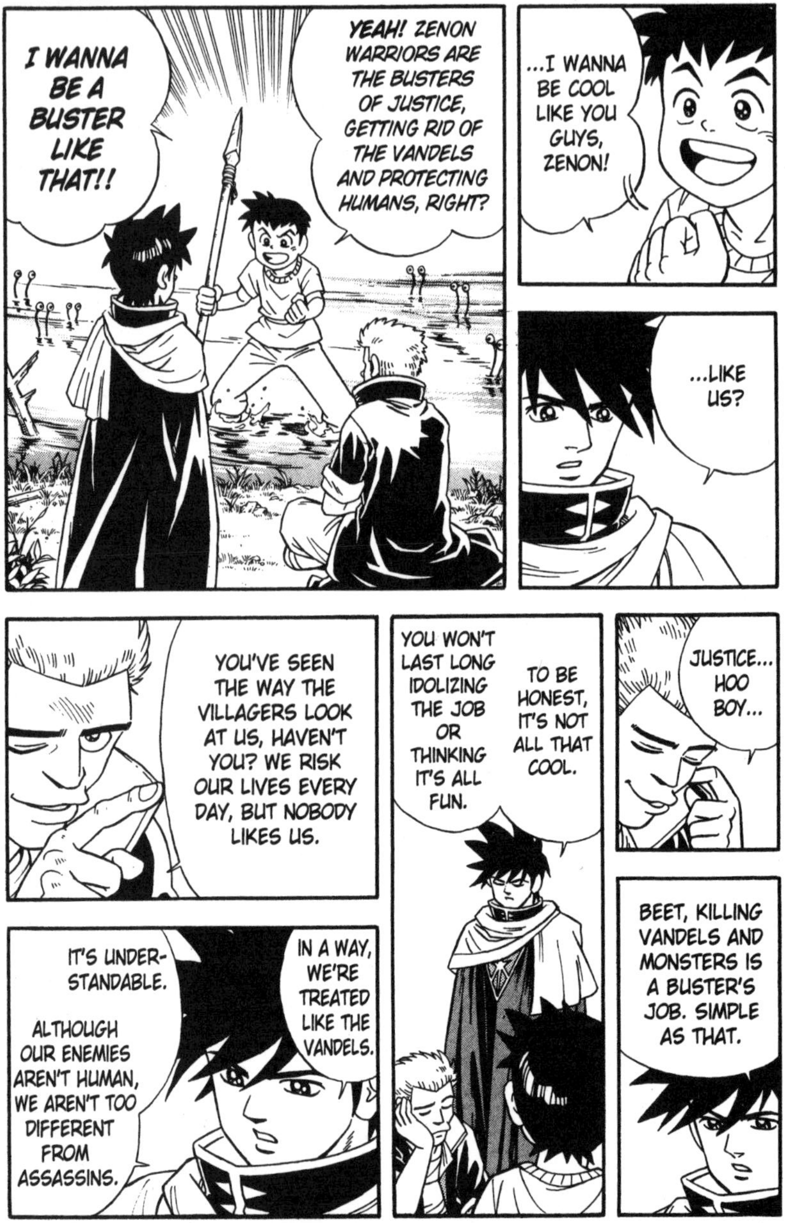

...I WANNA BE COOL LIKE YOU GUYS, ZENON!
...LIKE US?
YEAH! ZENON WARRIORS ARE THE BUSTERS OF JUSTICE, GETTING RID OF THE VANDELS AND PROTECTING HUMANS, RIGHT?
I WANNA BE A BUSTER LIKE THAT!!
JUSTICE... HOO BOY...
BEET, KILLING VANDELS AND MONSTERS IS A BUSTER'S JOB. SIMPLE AS THAT.
TO BE HONEST, IT'S NOT ALL THAT COOL.
YOU WON'T LAST LONG IDOLIZING THE JOB OR THINKING IT'S ALL FUN.
YOU'VE SEEN THE WAY THE VILLAGERS LOOK AT US, HAVEN'T YOU? WE RISK OUR LIVES EVERY DAY, BUT NOBODY LIKES US.
IN A WAY, WE'RE TREATED LIKE THE VANDELS.
IT'S UNDER-STANDABLE.
ALTHOUGH OUR ENEMIES AREN'T HUMAN, WE AREN'T TOO DIFFERENT FROM ASSASSINS.

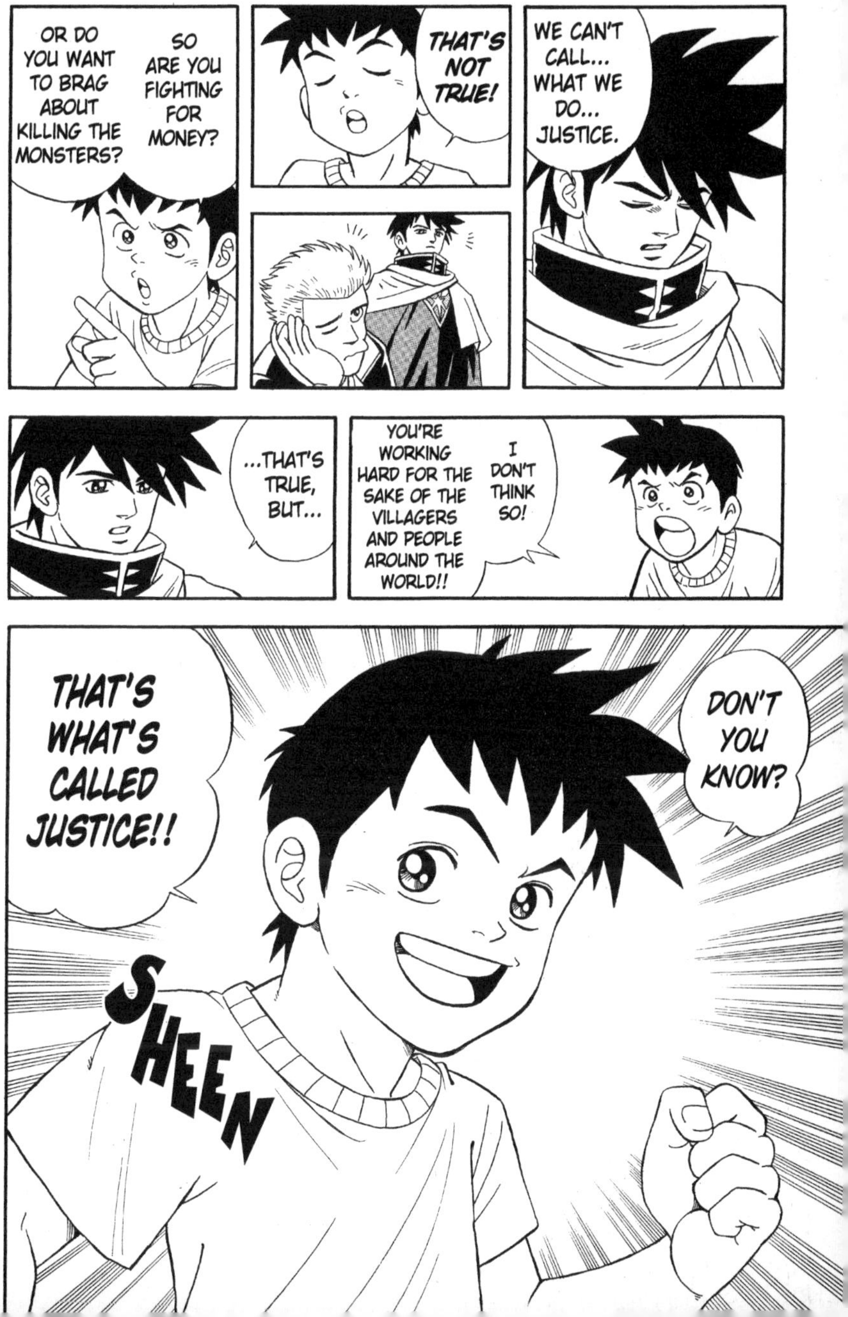
WE CAN'T CALL... WHAT WE DO... JUSTICE.
THAT'S NOT TRUE!
SO ARE YOU FIGHTING FOR MONEY?
OR DO YOU WANT TO BRAG ABOUT KILLING THE MONSTERS?
I DON'T THINK SO!
YOU'RE WORKING HARD FOR THE SAKE OF THE VILLAGERS AND PEOPLE AROUND THE WORLD!!
...THAT'S TRUE, BUT...
DON'T YOU KNOW?
THAT'S WHAT'S CALLED JUSTICE!!
SHEEN

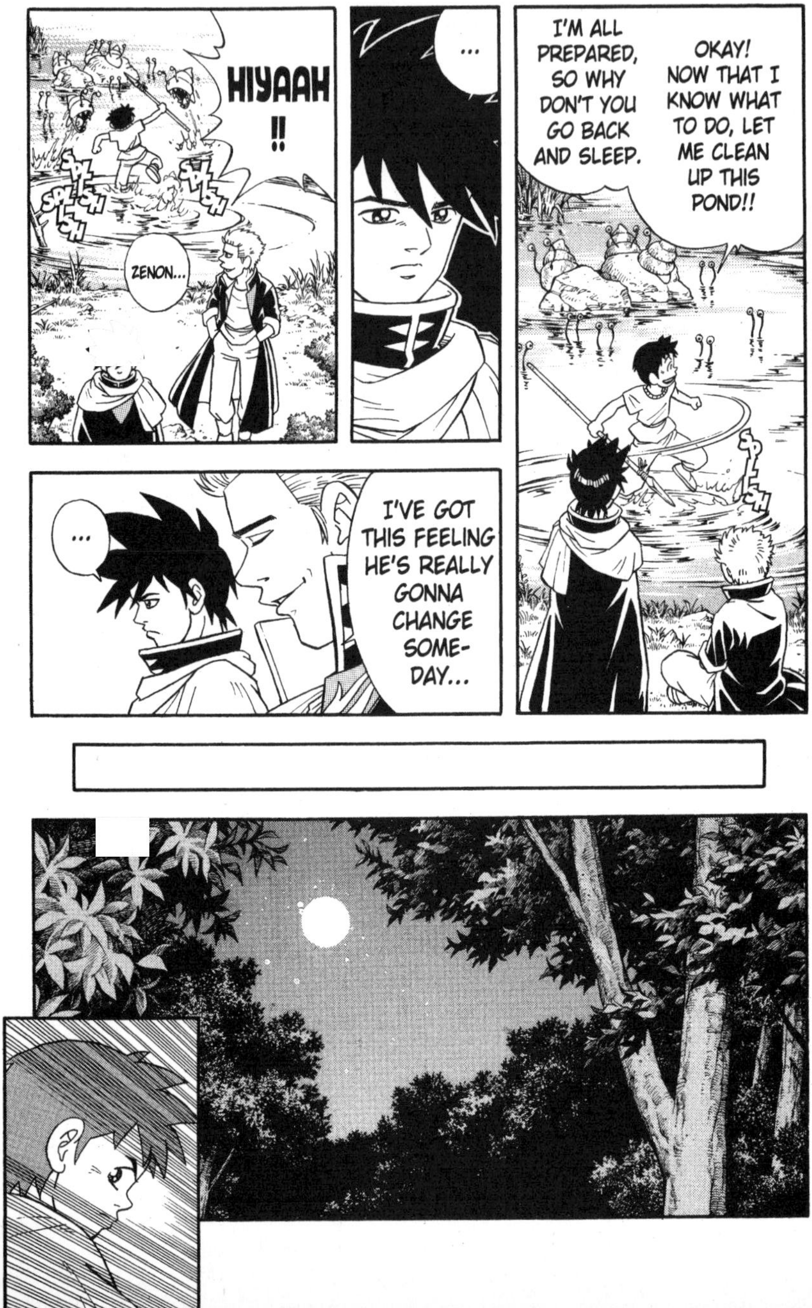
I'M ALL PREPARED, SO WHY DON'T YOU GO BACK AND SLEEP.
OKAY! NOW THAT I KNOW WHAT TO DO, LET ME CLEAN UP THIS POND!!
SPLISH
...
HIYAAH!!
SPLISH
SPLISH
SPLISH
ZENON...
I'VE GOT THIS FEELING HE'S REALLY GONNA CHANGE SOME-DAY...
...

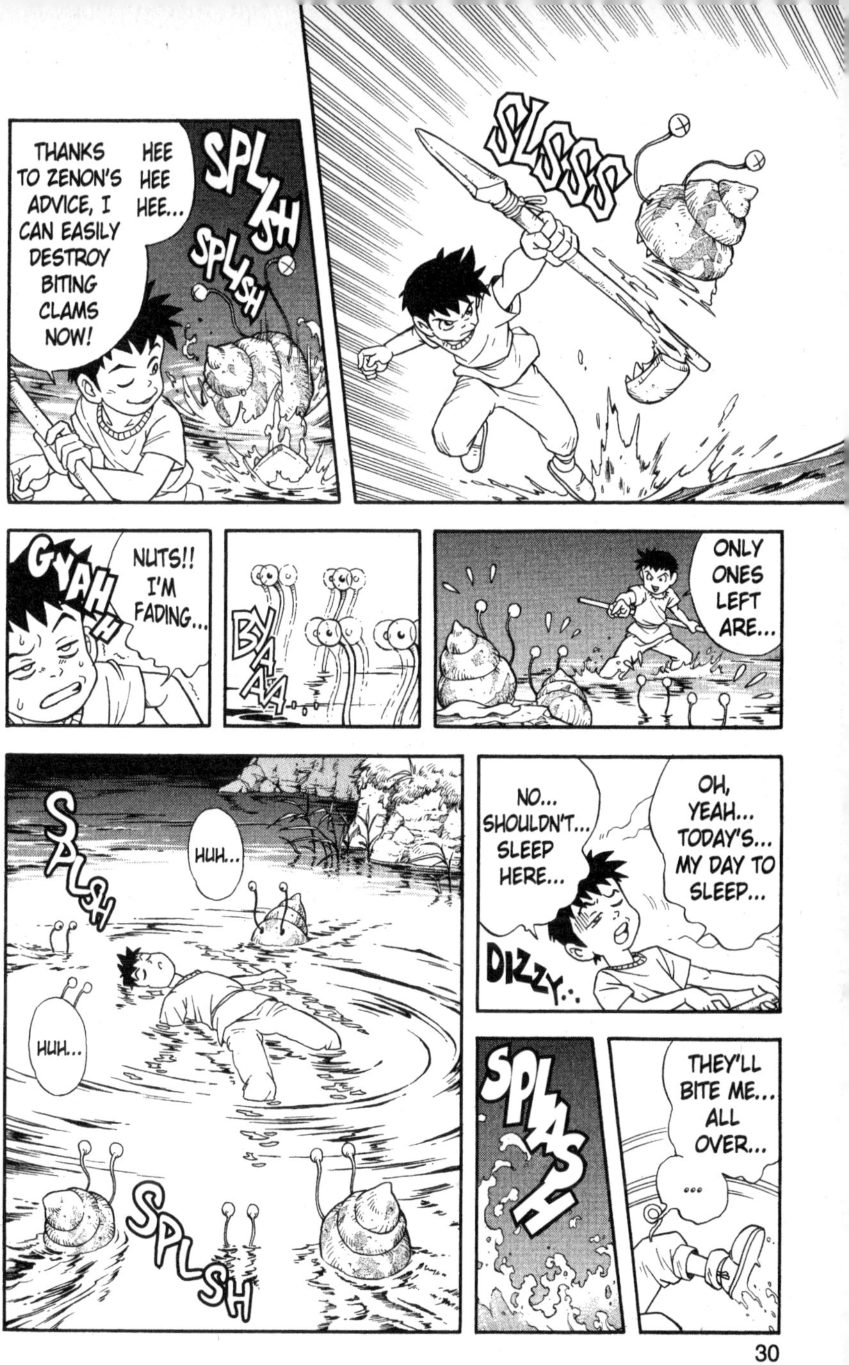
SLSSS
SPLASH
SPLASH
HEE HEE HEE...
THANKS TO ZENON'S ADVICE, I CAN EASILY DESTROY BITING CLAMS NOW!
ONLY ONES LEFT ARE...
BYAAA...
GYAHH
NUTS!! I'M FADING...
OH, YEAH... TODAY'S... MY DAY TO SLEEP...
NO... SHOULDN'T... SLEEP HERE...
DIZZY...
THEY'LL BITE ME... ALL OVER...
...
SPLASH
SPLSH
HUH...
HUH...
SPLSH

READ THIS WAY

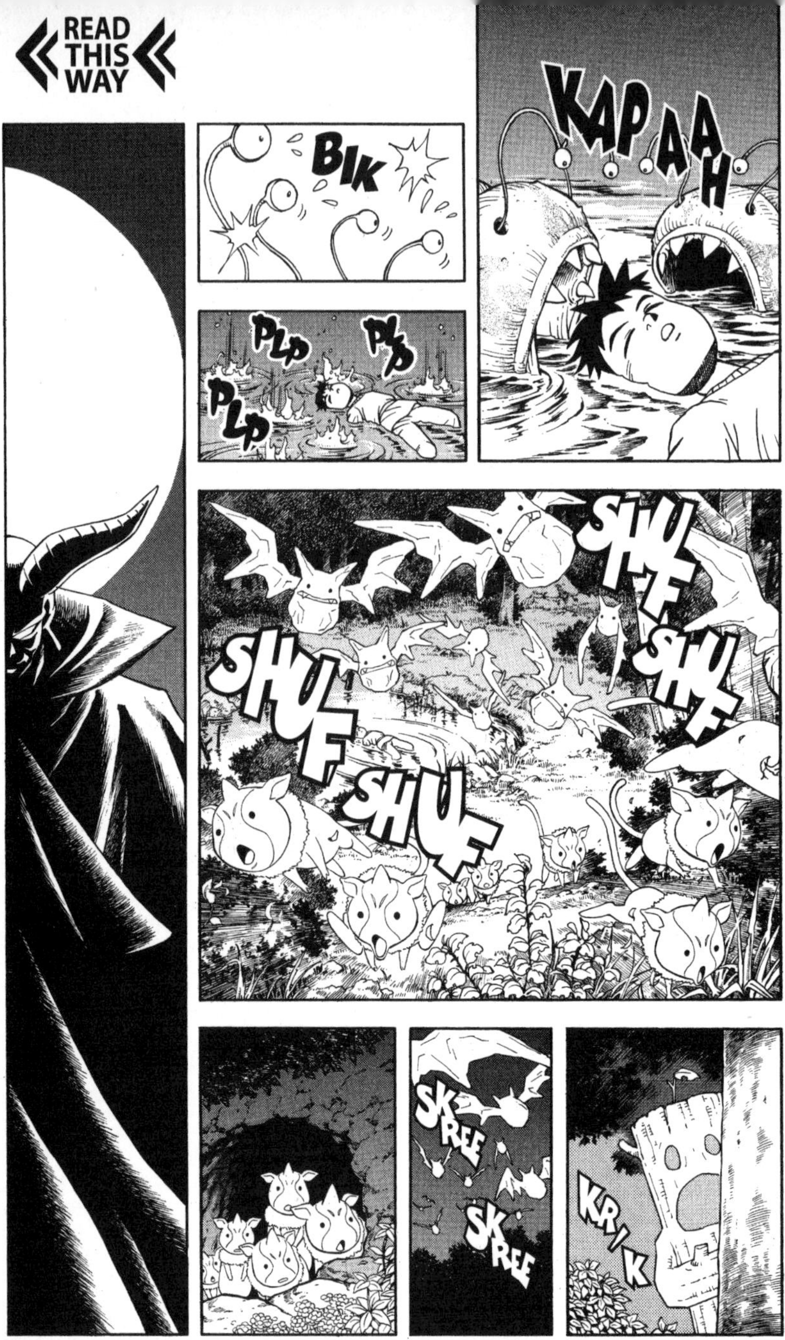
KAPAAH
BIK
PLP
PLP
PLP
SHUF
SHUF
SHUF
SHUF
KRIK
SKREE
SKREE

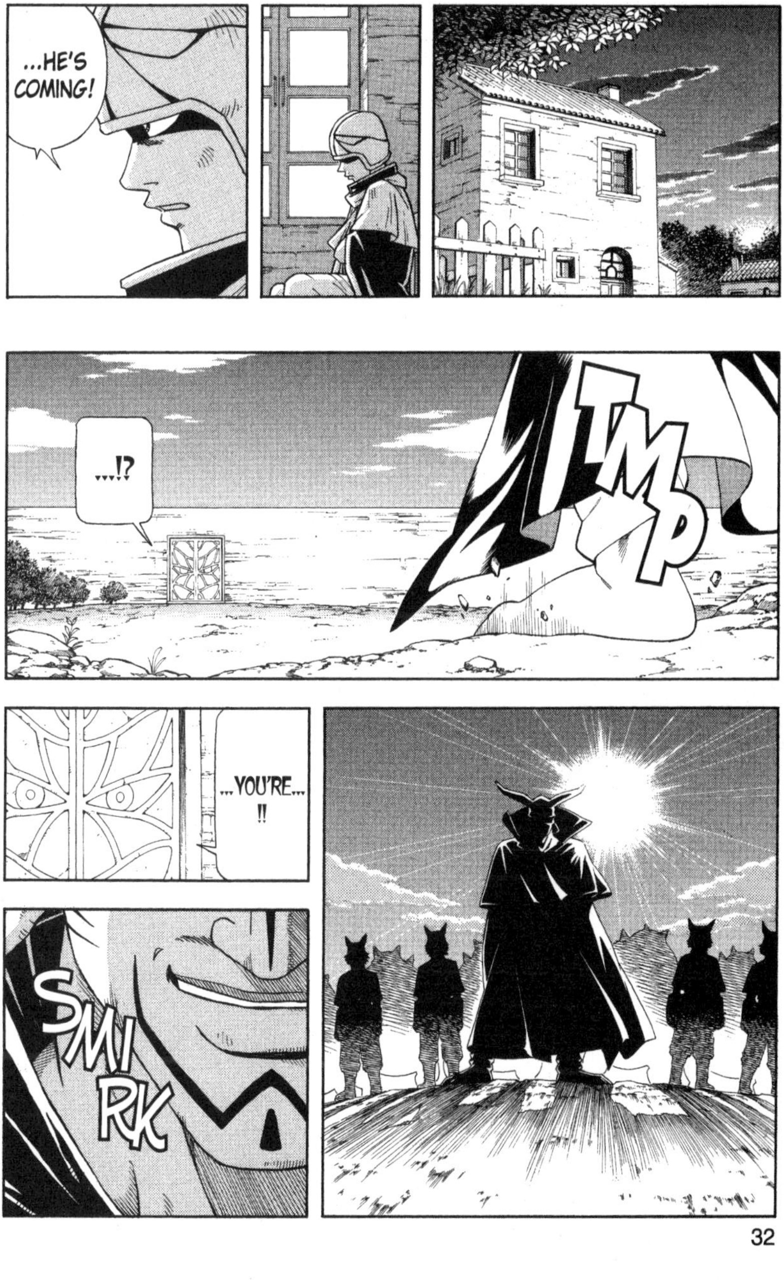
...HE'S COMING!
TMP
...!?
...YOU'RE... !!
SMIRK

READ THIS WAY

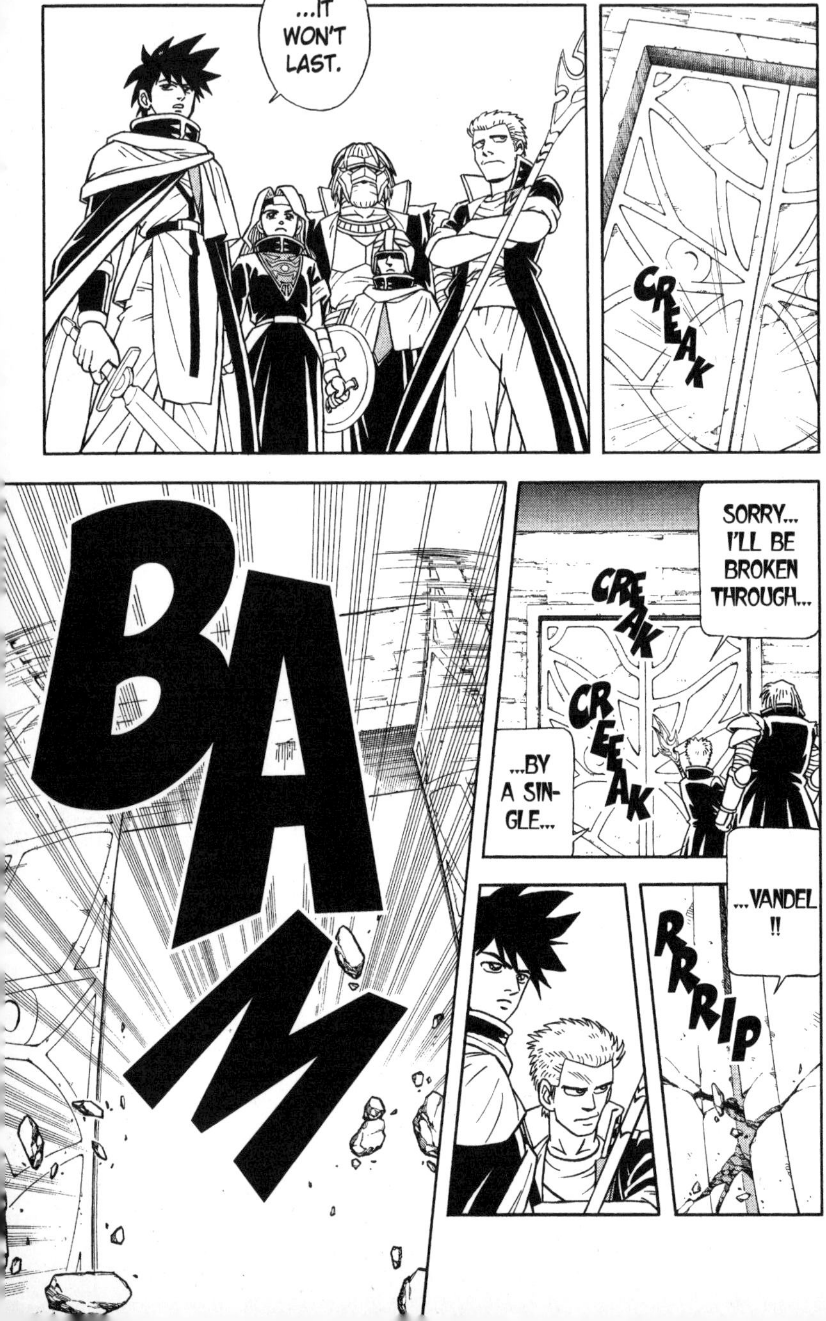
CREAK
...IT WON'T LAST.
SORRY... I'LL BE BROKEN THROUGH...
CREAK
CREEEAK
...BY A SINGLE...
...VANDEL!!
RRRIP
BAM

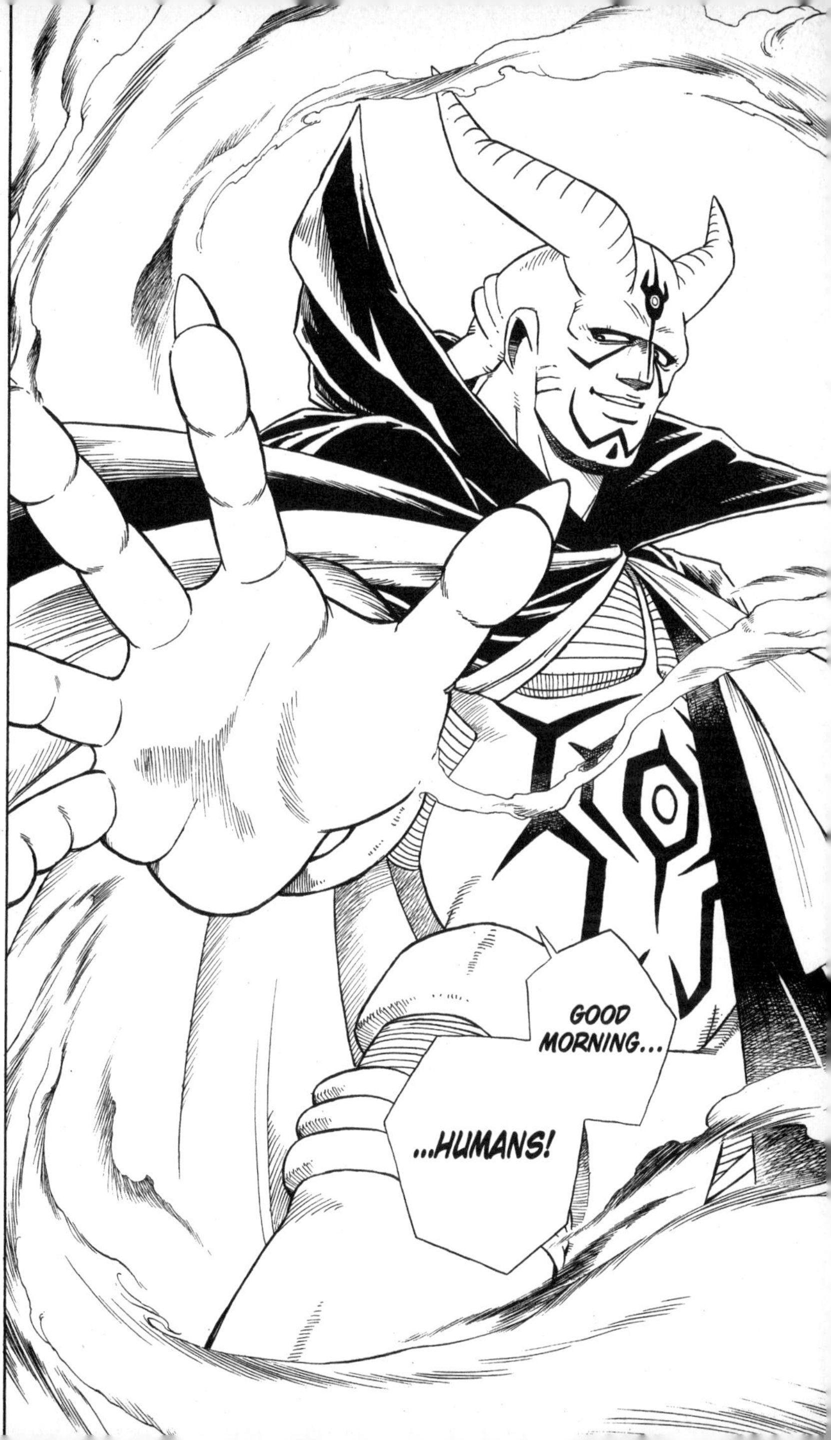
GOOD MORNING...
...HUMANS!

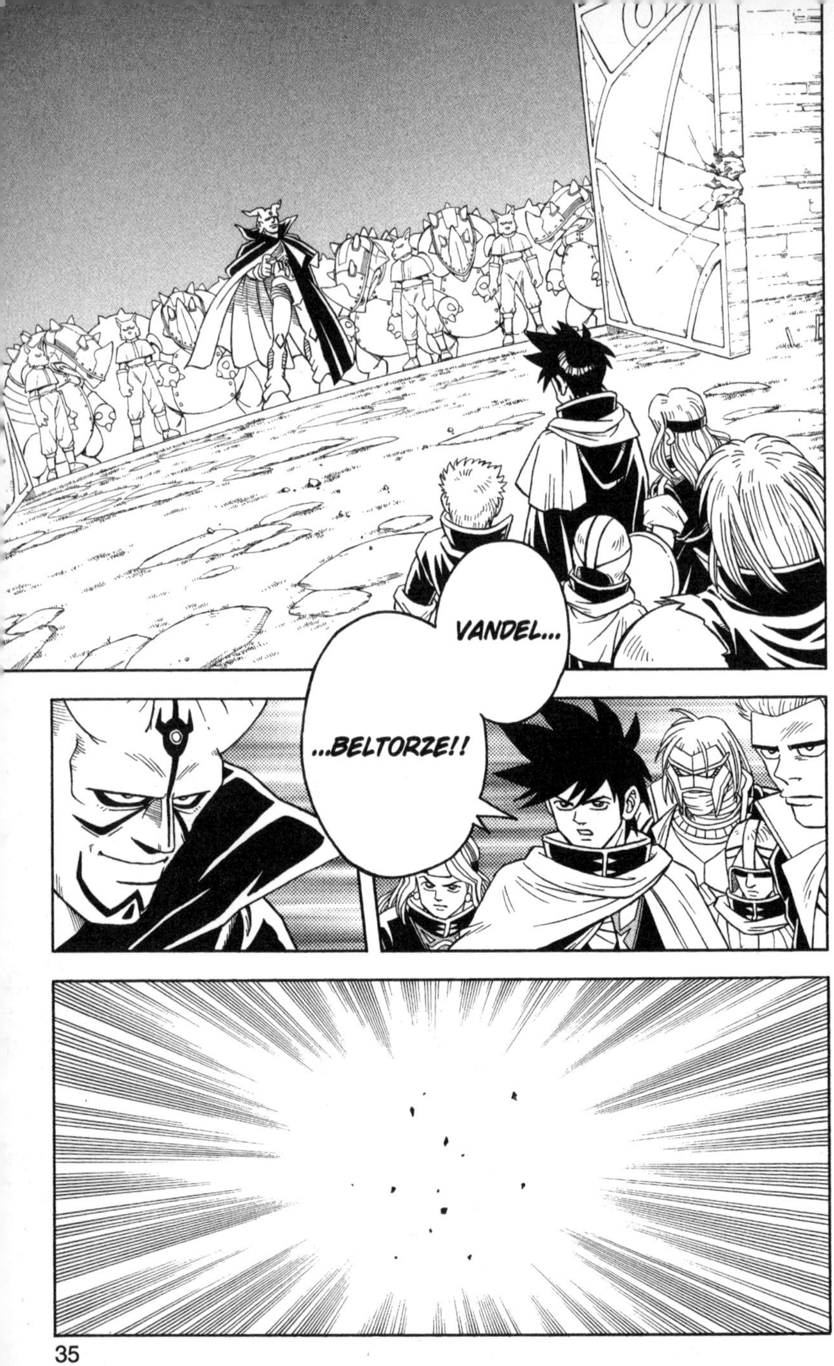
VANDEL...
...BELTORZE!!

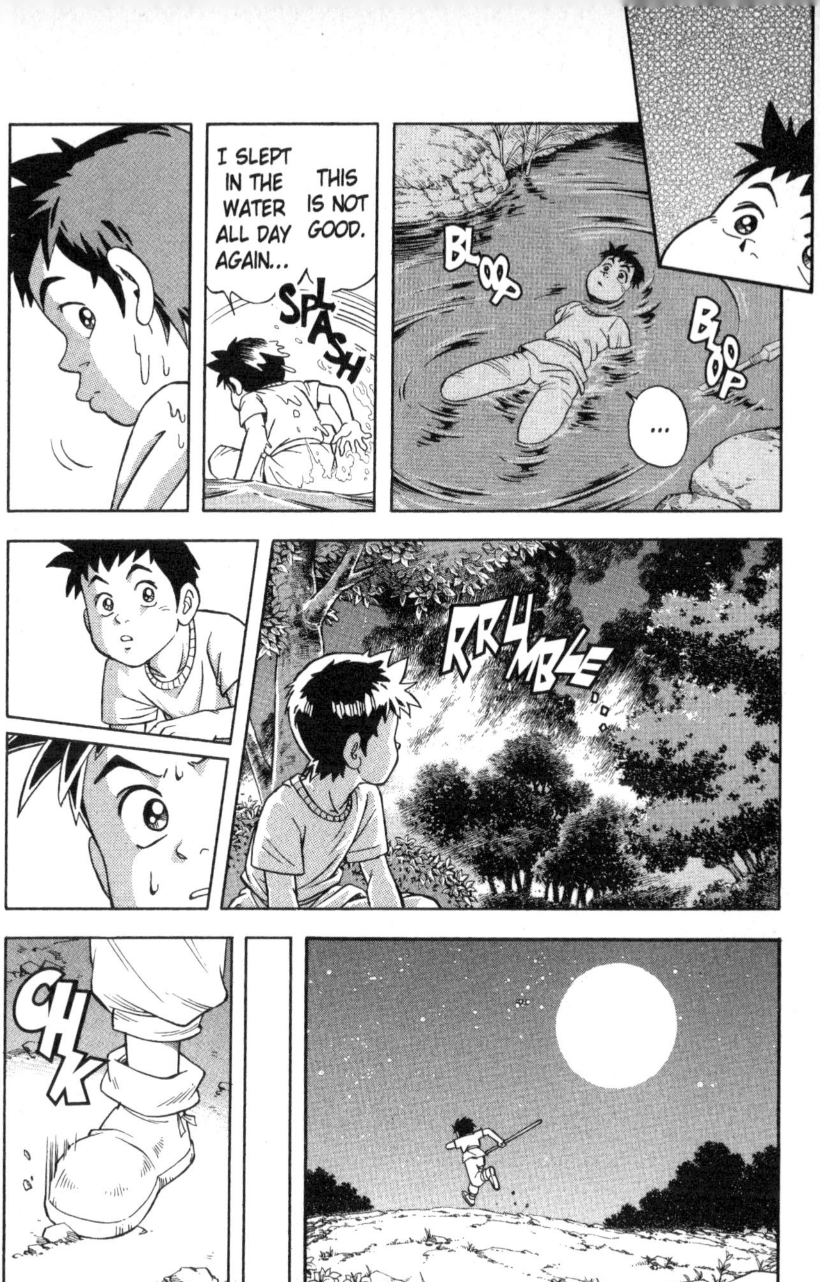
BLOOP
BLOOP
...
THIS IS NOT GOOD.
I SLEPT IN THE WATER ALL DAY AGAIN...
SPLASH
RRUMBLE
CHK

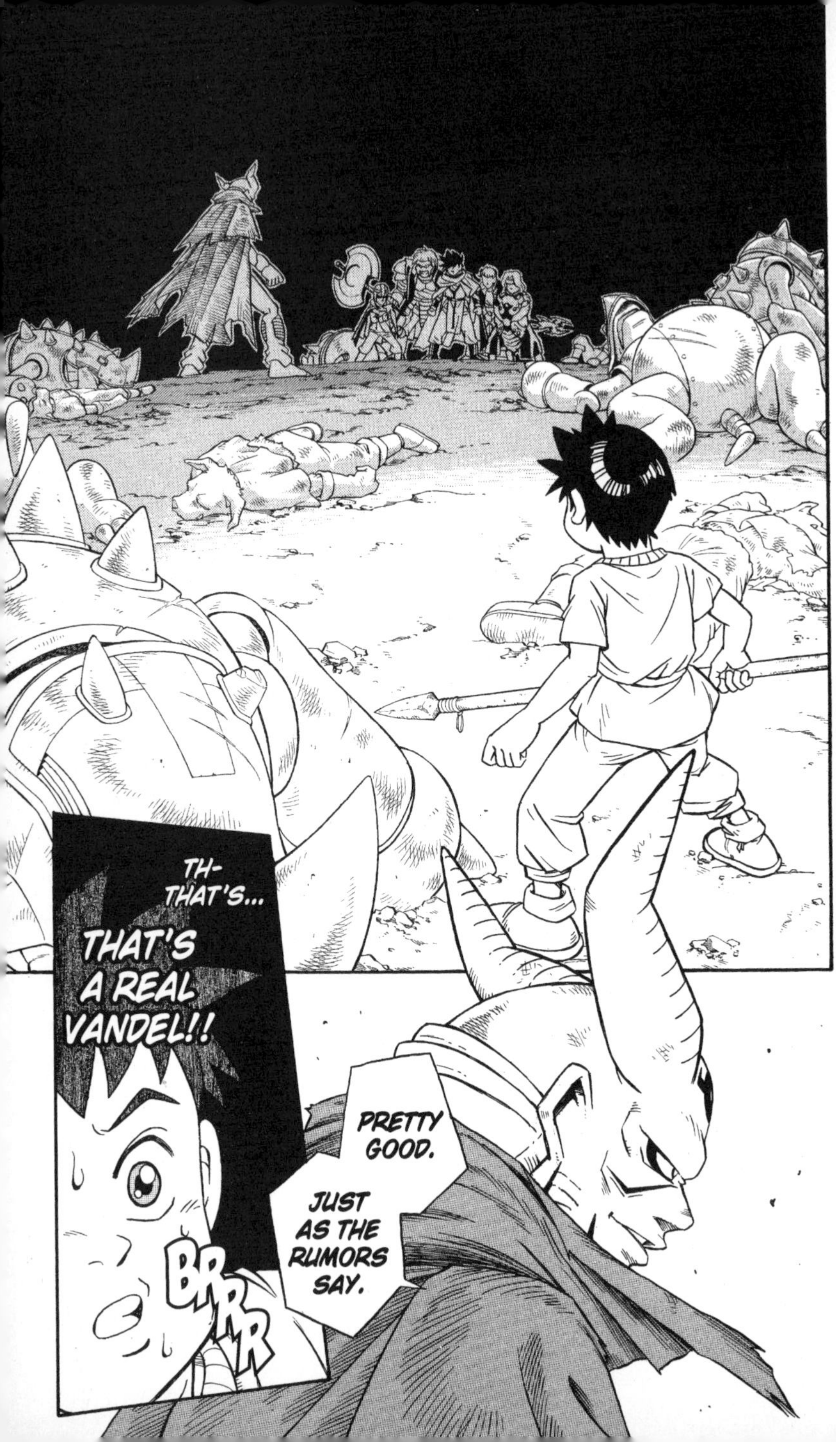
TH-
THAT'S...
THAT'S A REAL VANDEL!!
BRRR
PRETTY GOOD.
JUST AS THE RUMORS SAY.

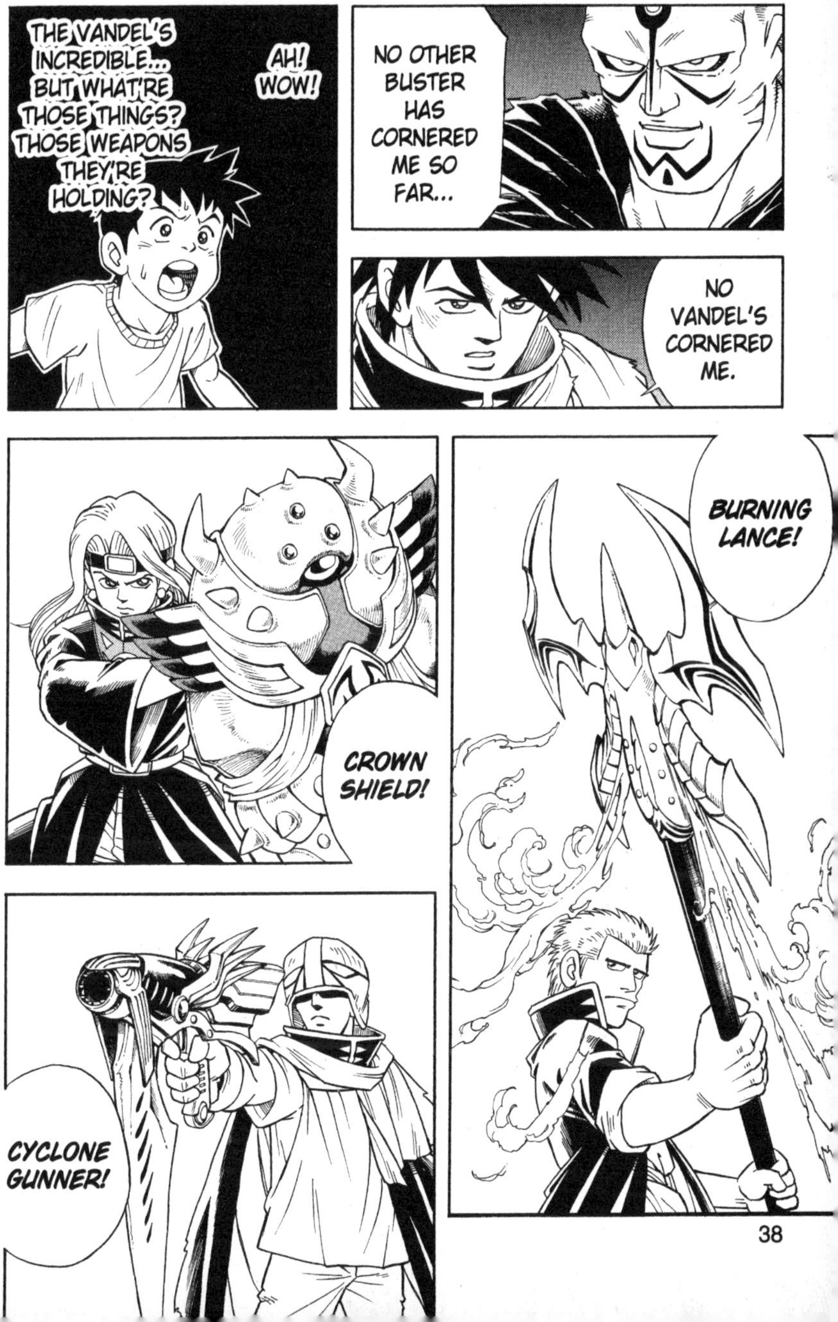
NO OTHER BUSTER HAS CORNERED ME SO FAR...
NO VANDEL'S CORNERED ME.
AH! WOW!
THE VANDEL'S INCREDIBLE... BUT WHAT'RE THOSE THINGS? THOSE WEAPONS THEY'RE HOLDING?
BURNING LANCE!
CROWN SHIELD!
CYCLONE GUNNER!

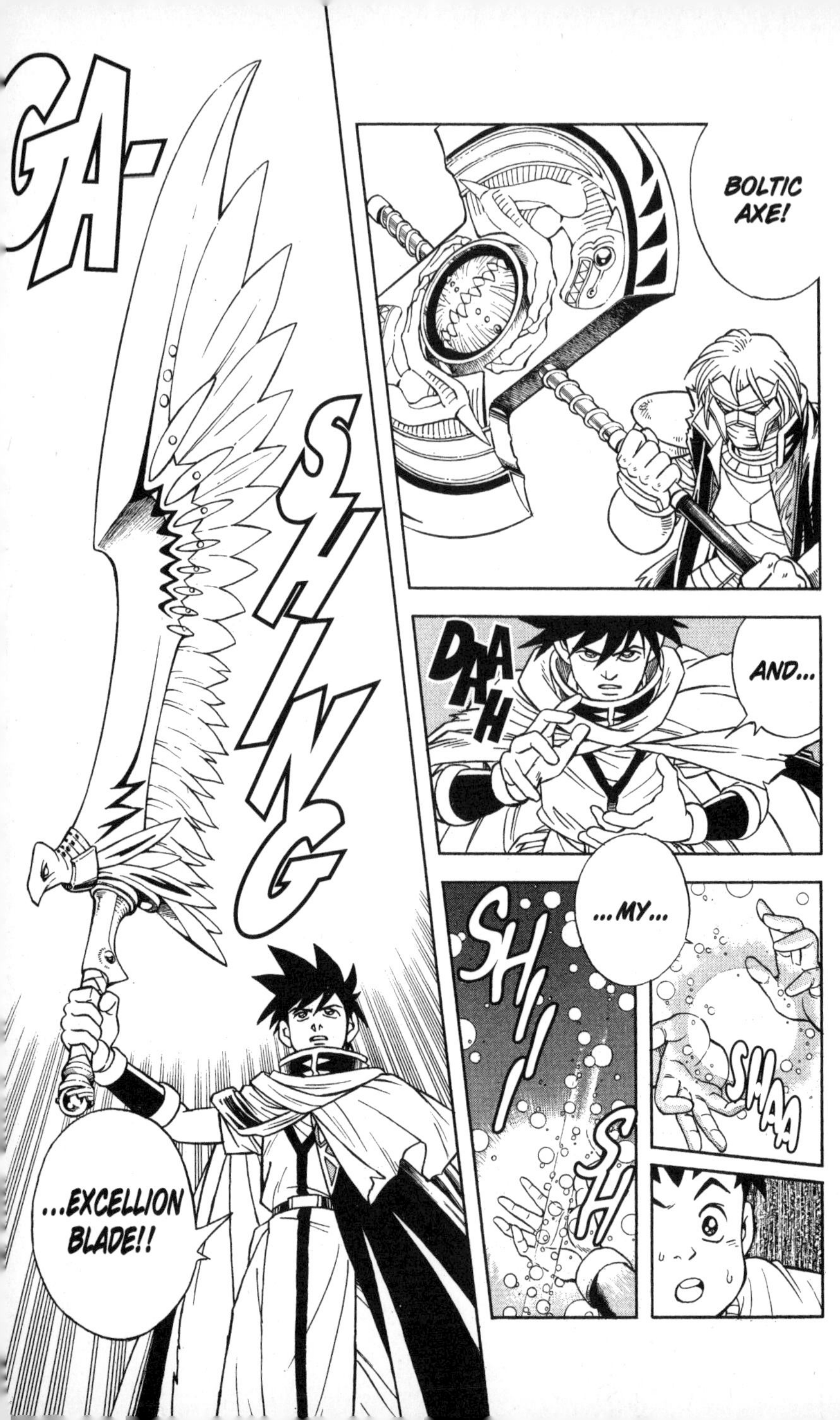
BOLTIC AXE!
AND...
DAAH
...MY...
SHAA
SHIIII SH
GA-SHING
...EXCELLION BLADE!!

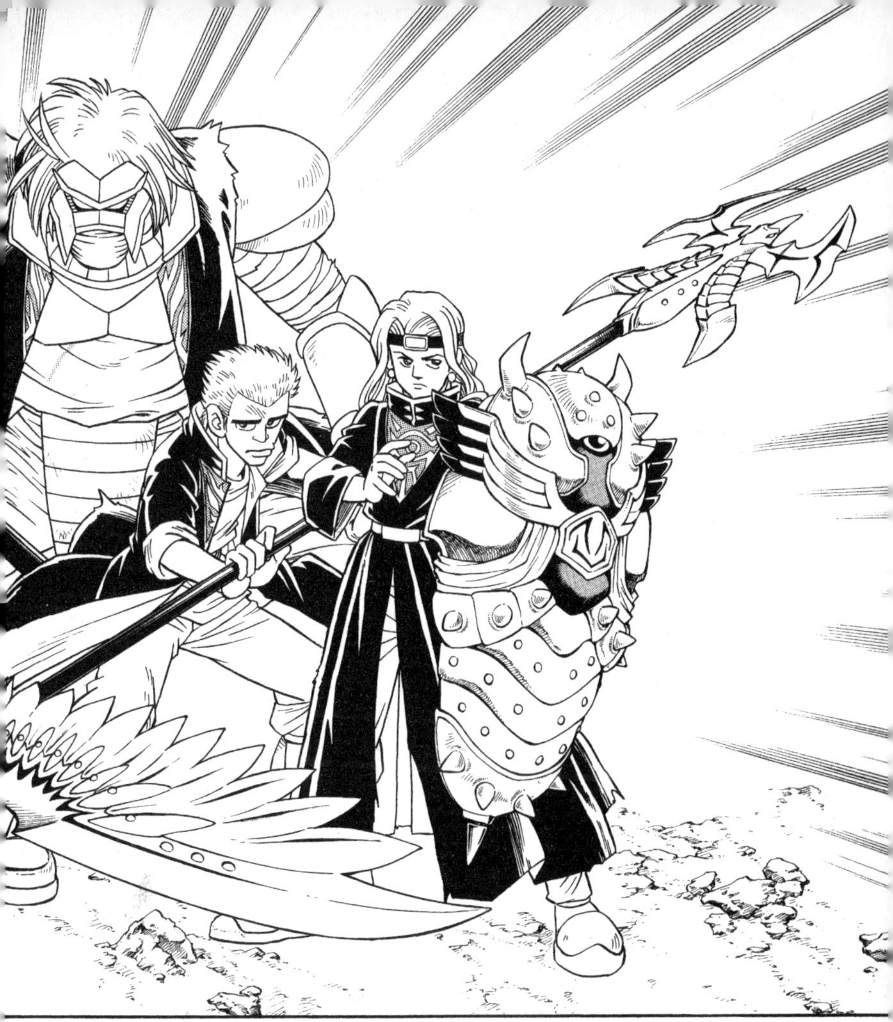

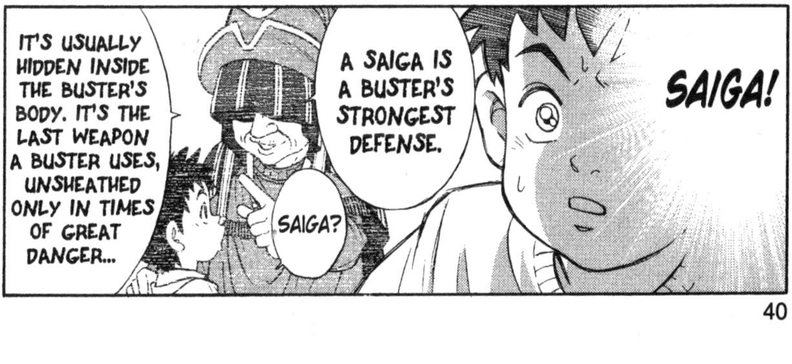
SAIGA!
A SAIGA IS A BUSTER'S STRONGEST DEFENSE.
SAIGA?
IT'S USUALLY HIDDEN INSIDE THE BUSTER'S BODY. IT'S THE LAST WEAPON A BUSTER USES, UNSHEATHED ONLY IN TIMES OF GREAT DANGER...

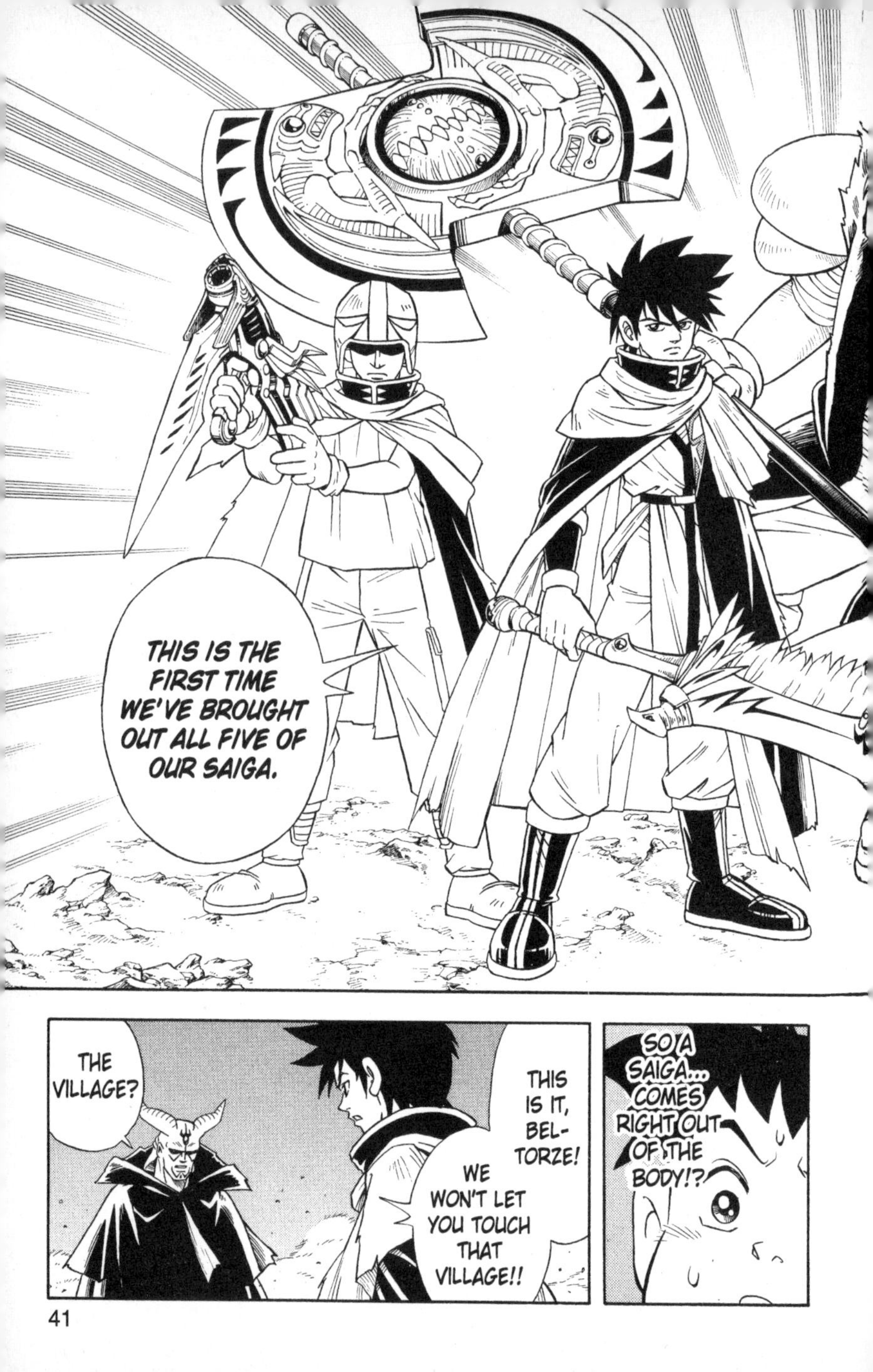
THIS IS THE FIRST TIME WE'VE BROUGHT OUT ALL FIVE OF OUR SAIGA.
SO A SAIGA... COMES RIGHT OUT OF THE BODY!?
THIS IS IT, BEL-TORZE!
THE VILLAGE?
WE WON'T LET YOU TOUCH THAT VILLAGE!!

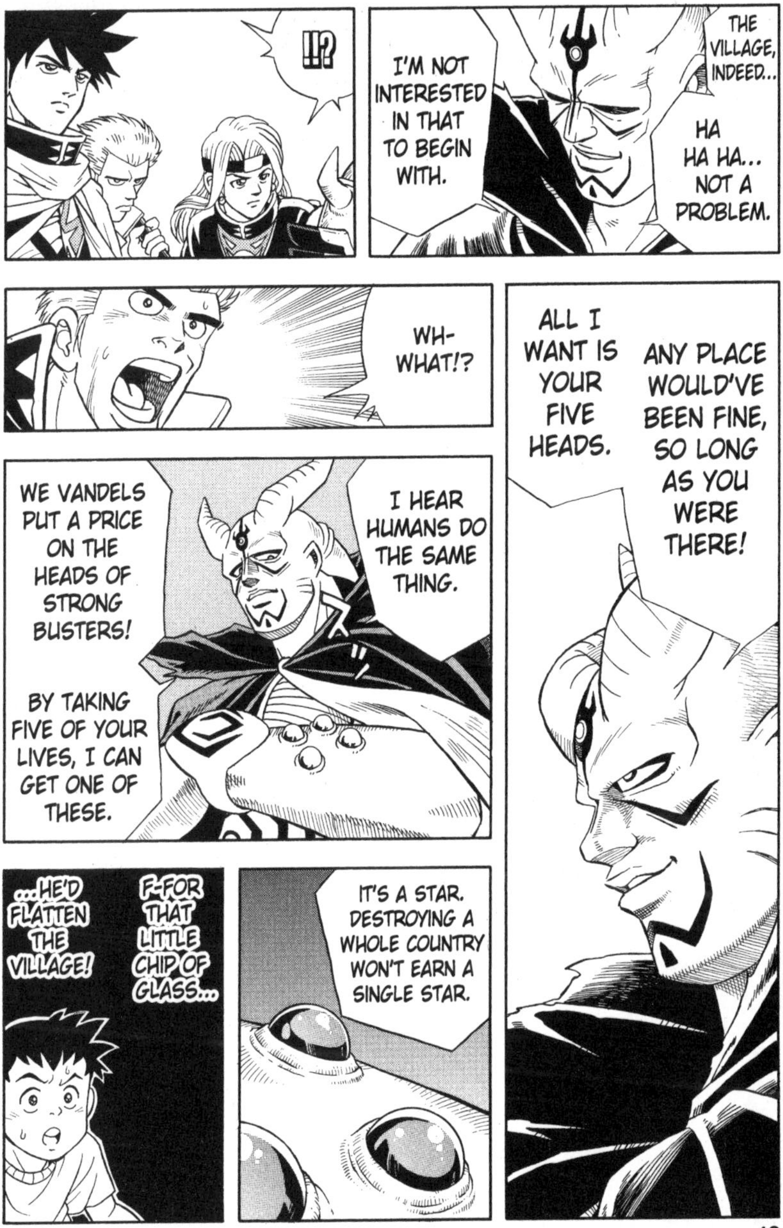
THE VILLAGE, INDEED...
HA HA HA... NOT A PROBLEM.
I'M NOT INTERESTED IN THAT TO BEGIN WITH.
!!?
ANY PLACE WOULD'VE BEEN FINE, SO LONG AS YOU WERE THERE!
ALL I WANT IS YOUR FIVE HEADS.
WH- WHAT!?
I HEAR HUMANS DO THE SAME THING.
WE VANDELS PUT A PRICE ON THE HEADS OF STRONG BUSTERS!
BY TAKING FIVE OF YOUR LIVES, I CAN GET ONE OF THESE.
IT'S A STAR. DESTROYING A WHOLE COUNTRY WON'T EARN A SINGLE STAR.
F-FOR THAT LITTLE CHIP OF GLASS...
...HE'D FLATTEN THE VILLAGE!

READ THIS WAY

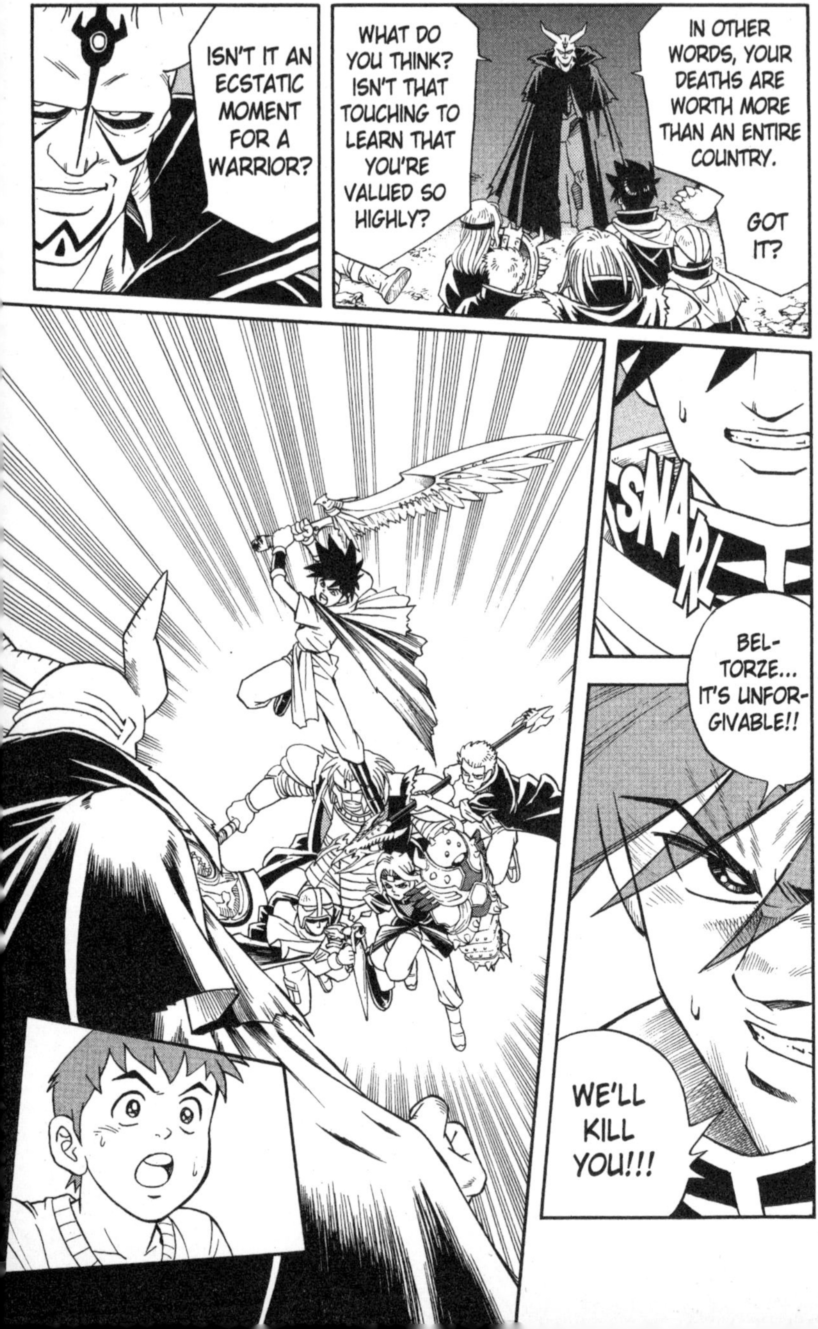
IN OTHER WORDS, YOUR DEATHS ARE WORTH MORE THAN AN ENTIRE COUNTRY.
GOT IT?
WHAT DO YOU THINK? ISN'T THAT TOUCHING TO LEARN THAT YOU'RE VALUED SO HIGHLY?
ISN'T IT AN ECSTATIC MOMENT FOR A WARRIOR?
SNARL
BEL-TORZE... IT'S UNFORGIVABLE!!
WE'LL KILL YOU!!!

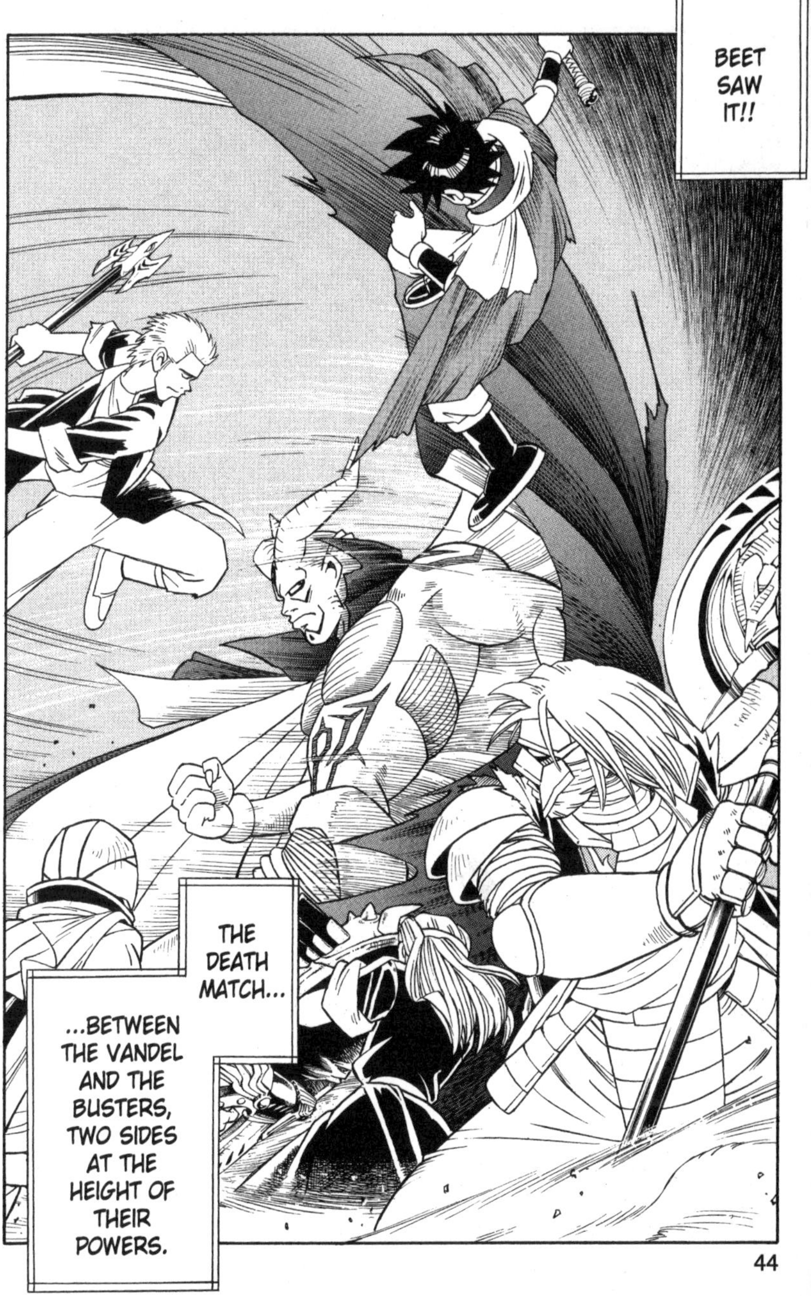
BEET SAW IT!!
THE DEATH MATCH...
...BETWEEN THE VANDEL AND THE BUSTERS, TWO SIDES AT THE HEIGHT OF THEIR POWERS.

READ THIS WAY

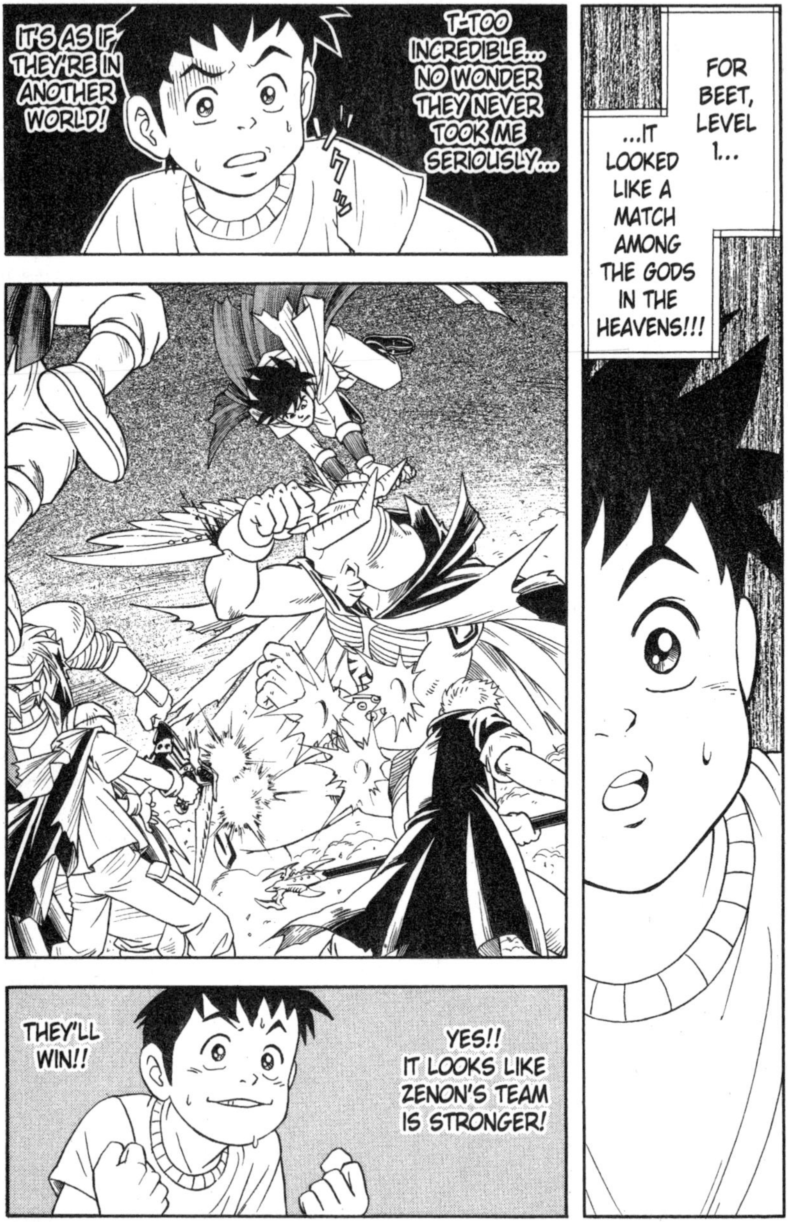
FOR BEET, LEVEL 1...
...IT LOOKED LIKE A MATCH AMONG THE GODS IN THE HEAVENS!!!
T-TOO INCREDIBLE... NO WONDER THEY NEVER TOOK ME SERIOUSLY...
IT'S AS IF THEY'RE IN ANOTHER WORLD!
YES!! IT LOOKS LIKE ZENON'S TEAM IS STRONGER!
THEY'LL WIN!!

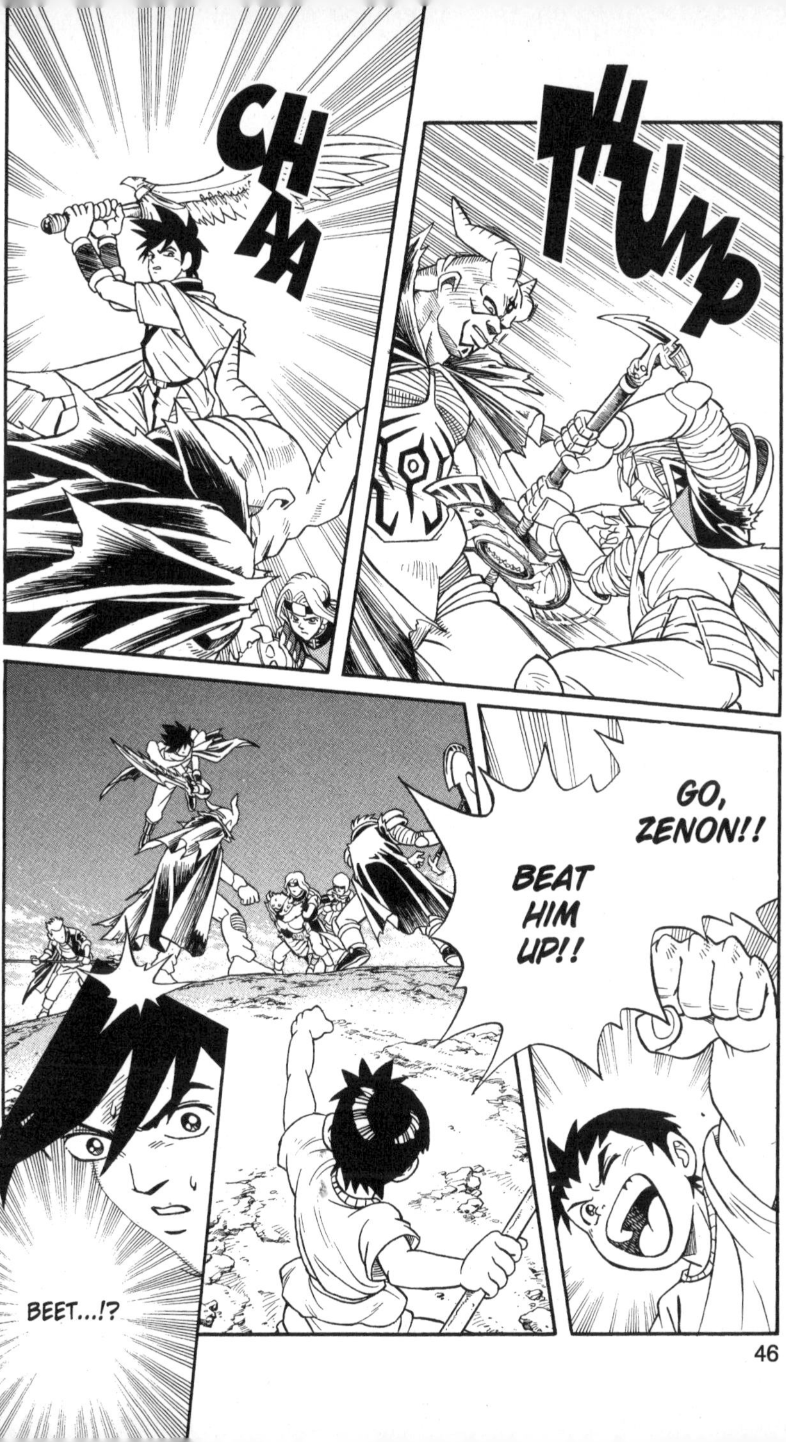
THUMP
CHAAA
GO, ZENON!!
BEAT HIM UP!!
BEET...!?

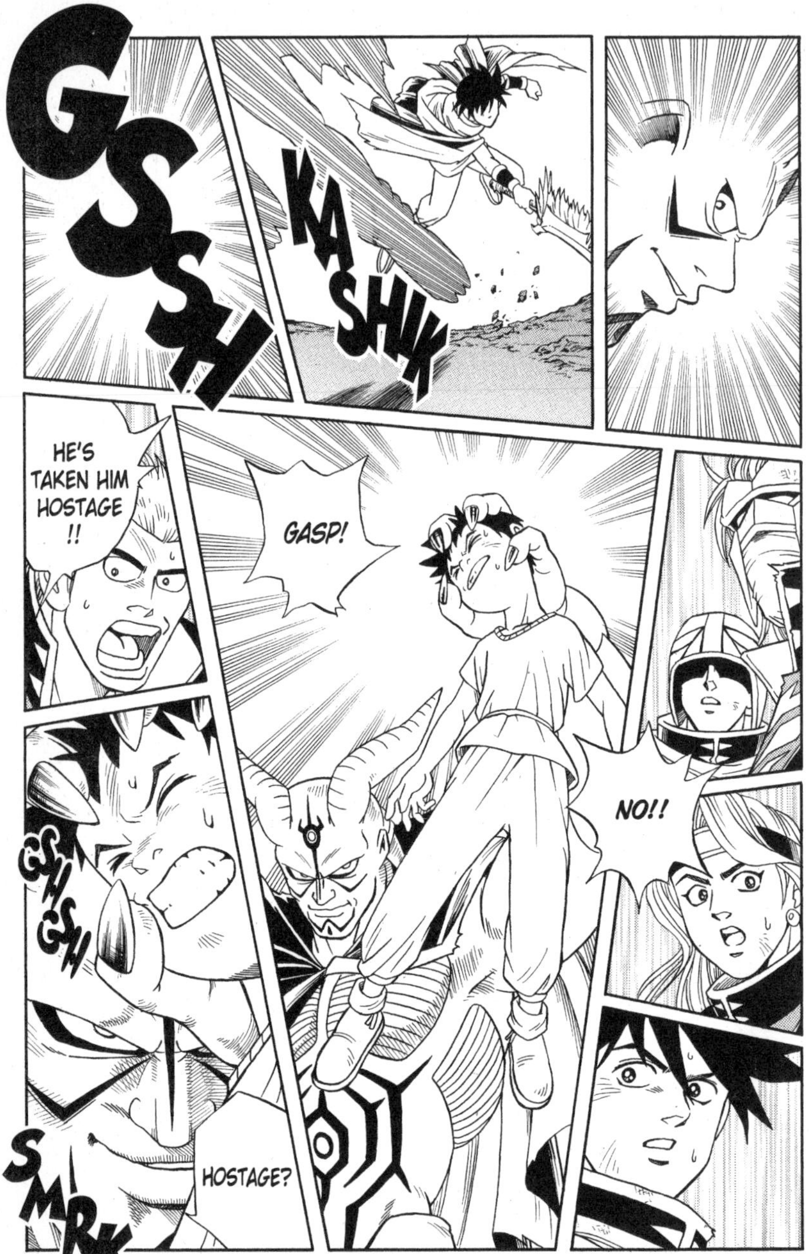
KASHUK
GSSH
NO!!
GASP!
HE'S TAKEN HIM HOSTAGE !!
GSH GSH
HOSTAGE?
SMRK

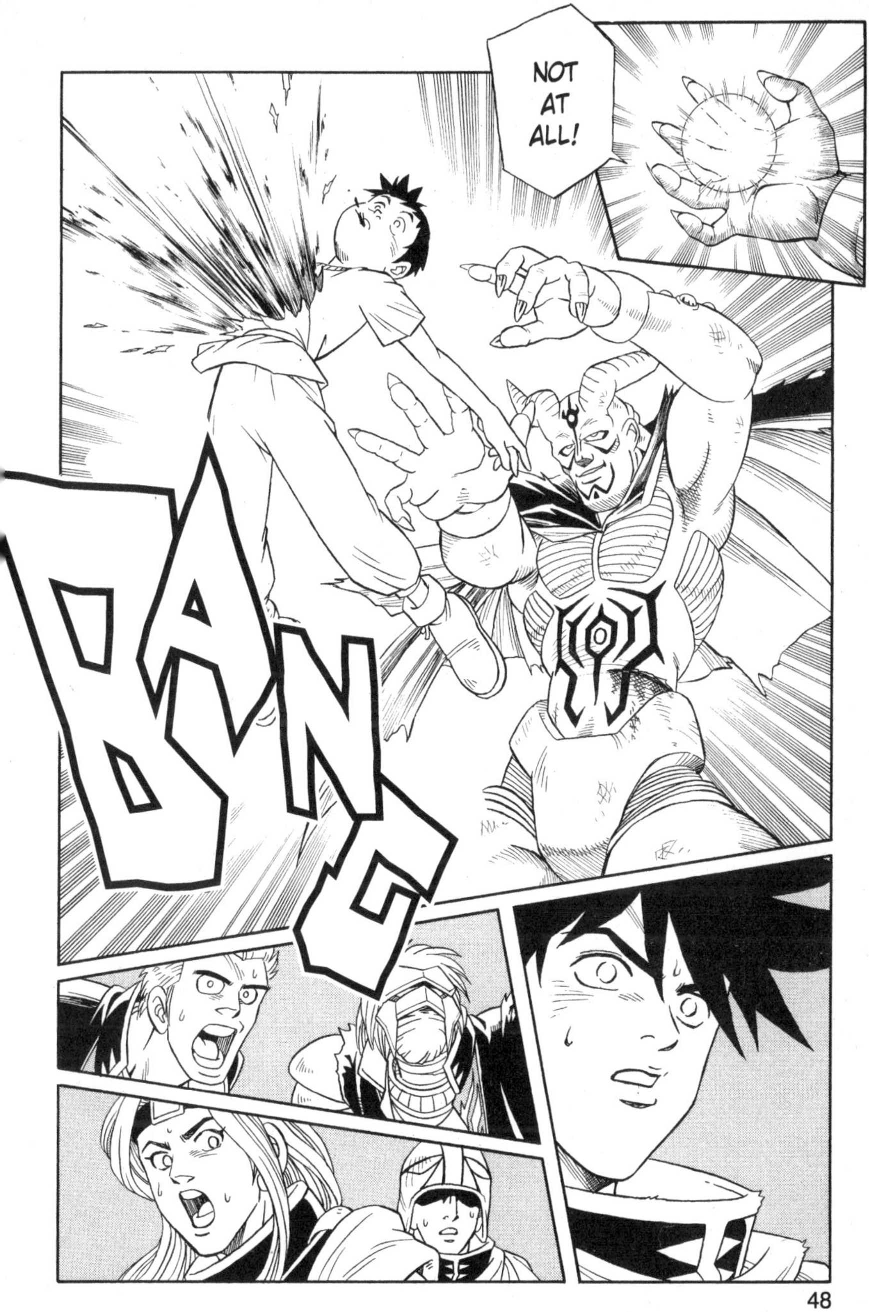
NOT AT ALL!
BANG

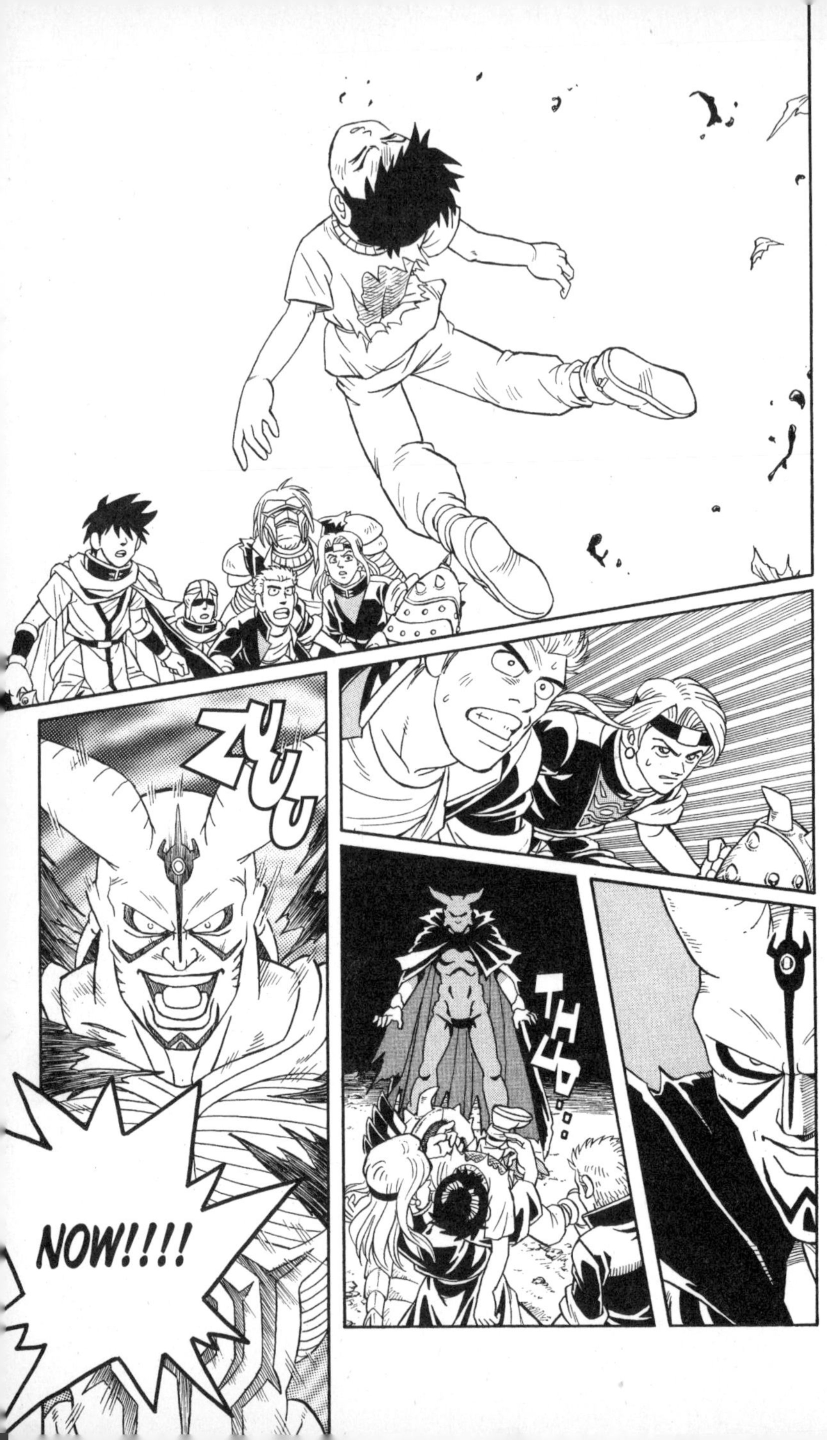
THUD...
ZUUU
NOW!!!!

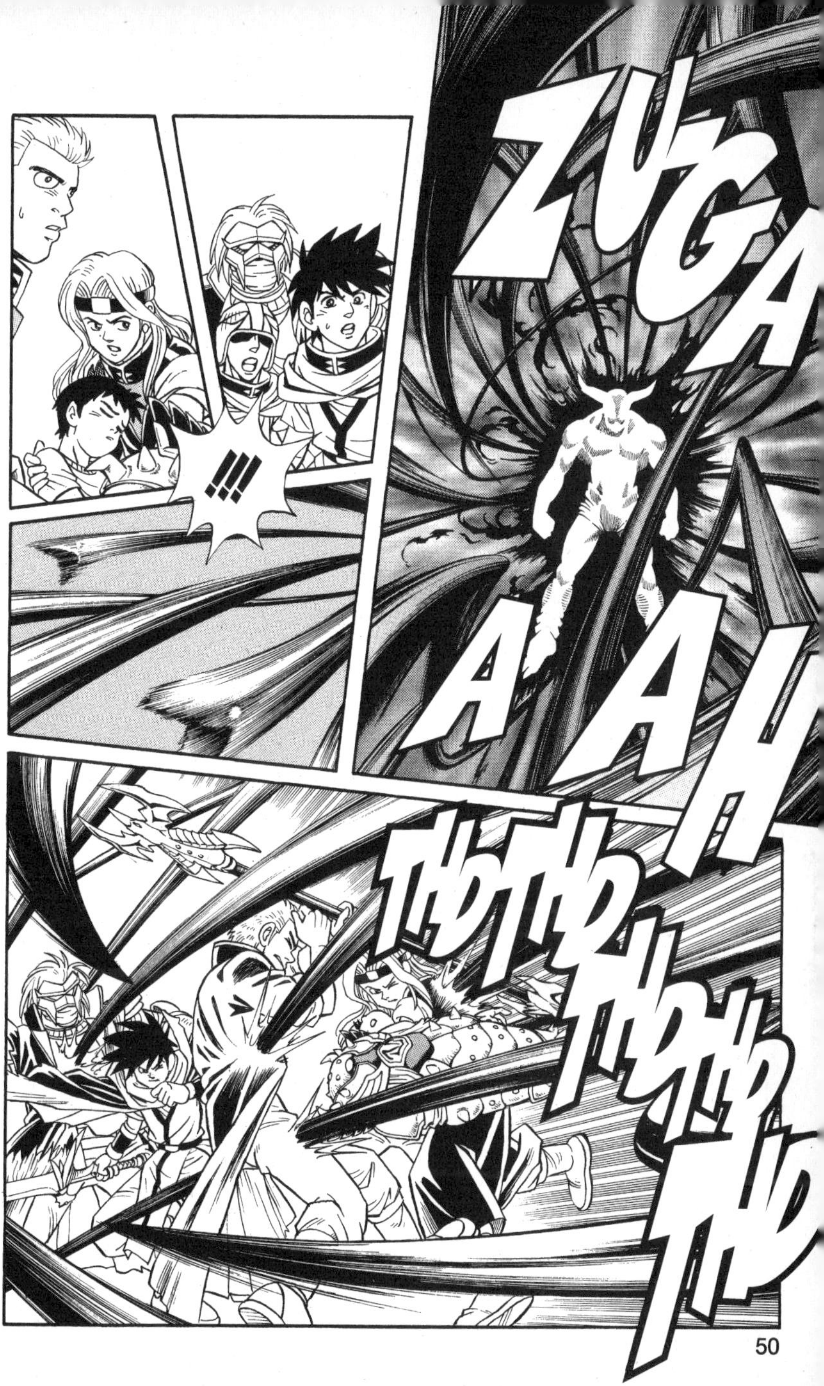
ZUGAAAH
!!!!
THD THD THD THD THD THD THD

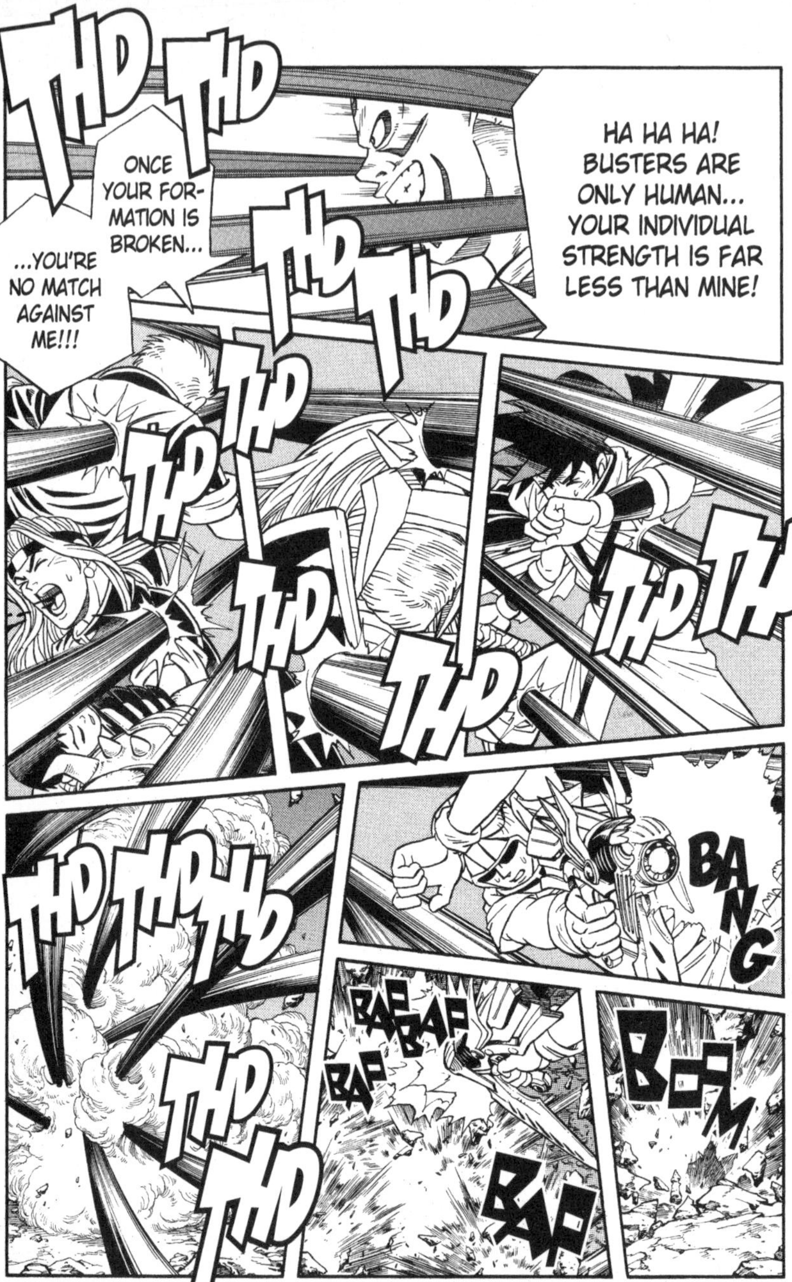
HA HA HA! BUSTERS ARE ONLY HUMAN... YOUR INDIVIDUAL STRENGTH IS FAR LESS THAN MINE!
THD THD
ONCE YOUR FOR-MATION IS BROKEN...
...YOU'RE NO MATCH AGAINST ME!!!
THD THD
THD THD
THD THD
THD THD
THD
BANG
THD THD THD
THD THD
BOOM
BAP BAP
BAP
BAP

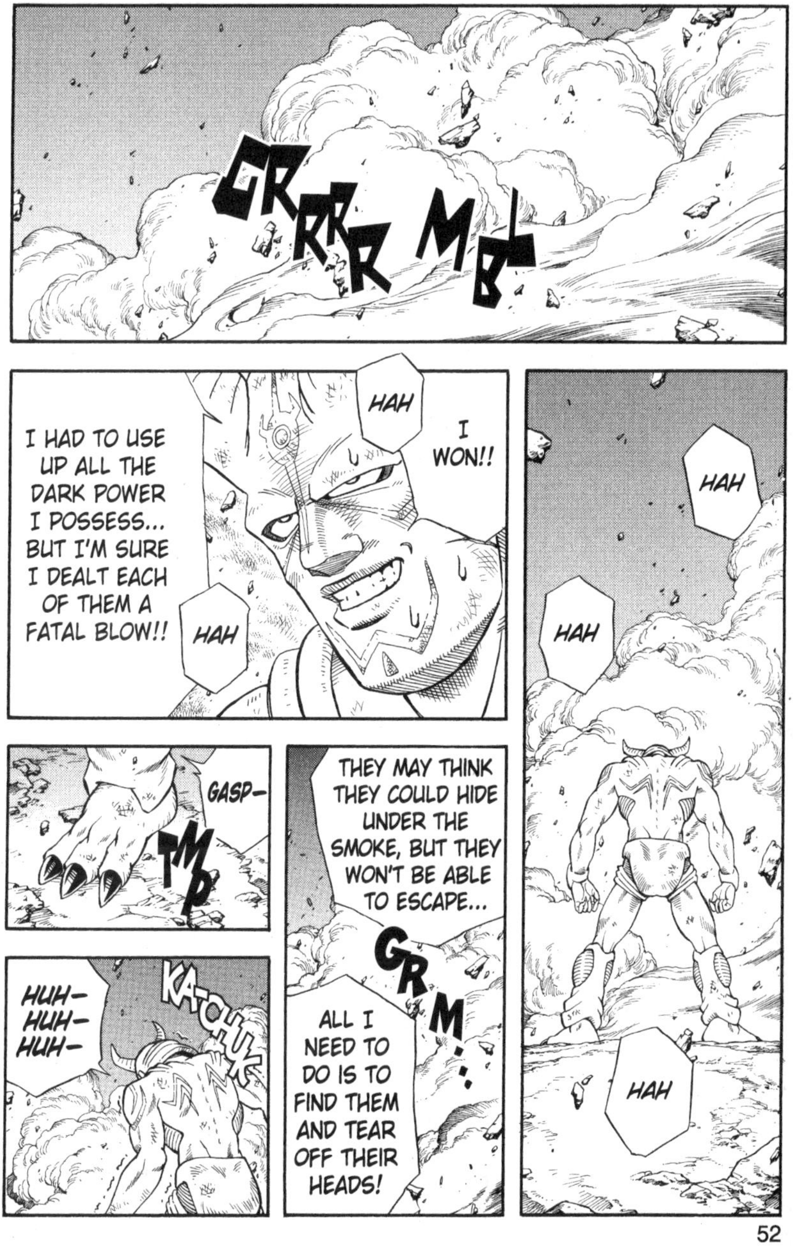
GRRRR MBL
HAH
HAH
HAH
HAH
I WON!!
I HAD TO USE UP ALL THE DARK POWER I POSSESS... BUT I'M SURE I DEALT EACH OF THEM A FATAL BLOW!!
HAH
THEY MAY THINK THEY COULD HIDE UNDER THE SMOKE, BUT THEY WON'T BE ABLE TO ESCAPE...
GRM..
ALL I NEED TO DO IS TO FIND THEM AND TEAR OFF THEIR HEADS!
GASP-
TMP
KA-CHUK
HUH- HUH- HUH-

READ THIS WAY

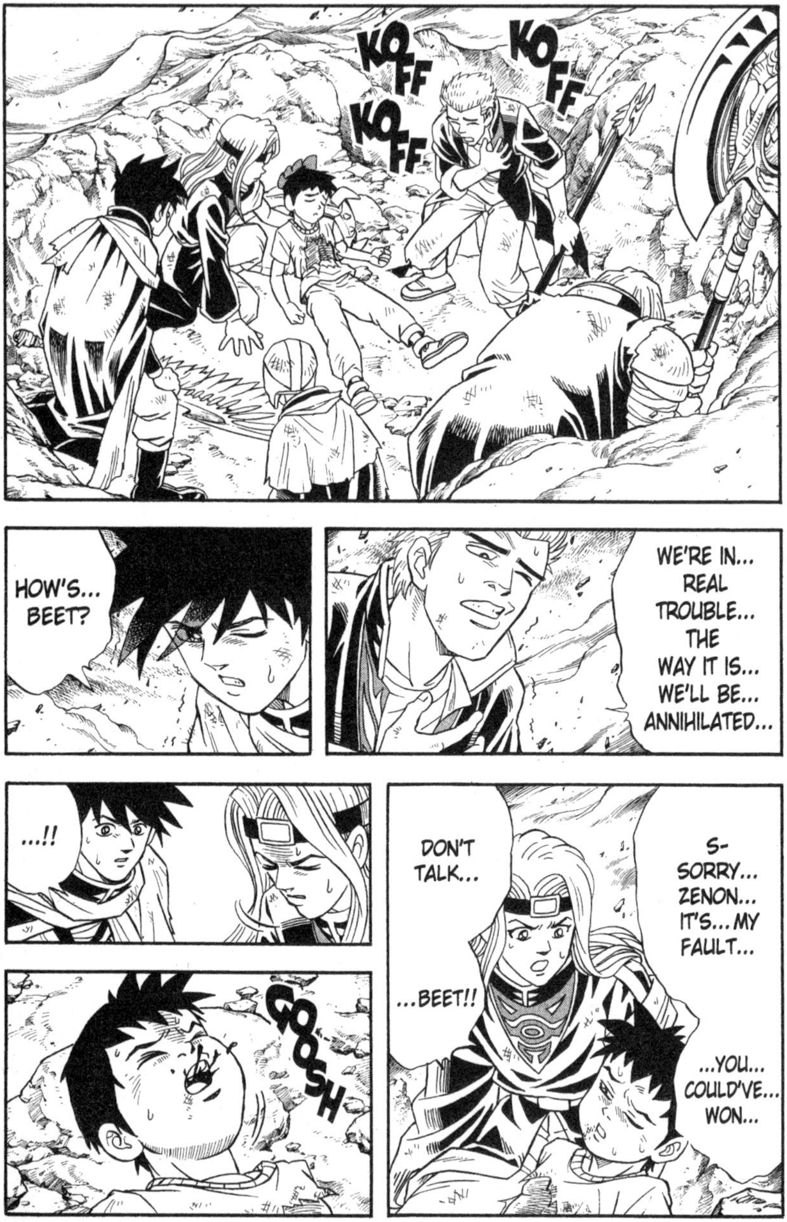
KOFF
KOFF
KOFF
WE'RE IN... REAL TROUBLE... THE WAY IT IS... WE'LL BE... ANNIHILATED...
HOW'S... BEET?
S- SORRY... ZENON... IT'S... MY FAULT...
DON'T TALK...
...YOU... COULD'VE... WON...
...BEET!!
...!!
GOOSH

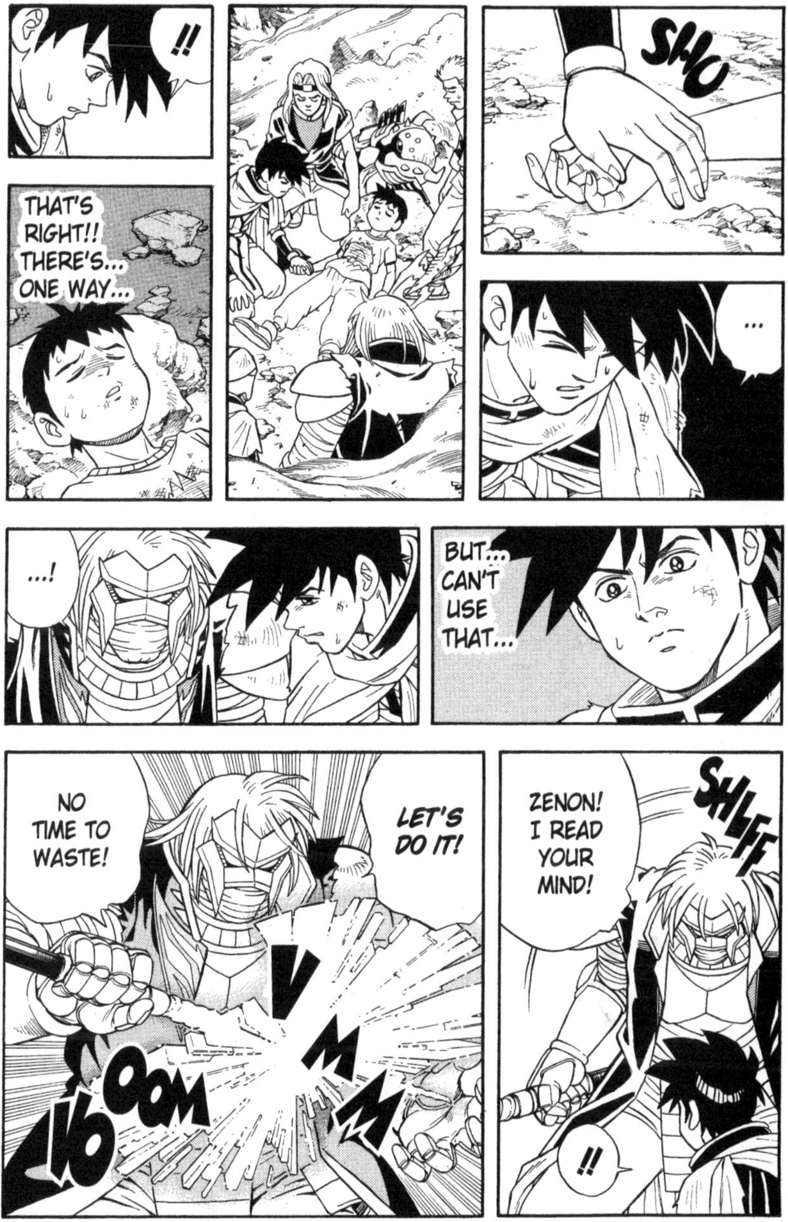
SHO
...
!!
THAT'S RIGHT!! THERE'S... ONE WAY...
BUT... CAN'T USE THAT...
...!
SHLFF
ZENON! I READ YOUR MIND!
!!
LET'S DO IT!
NO TIME TO WASTE!
VMMM
VOOOM

READ THIS WAY

SHUU
...OF COURSE!
WE'RE DYING... BUT IF WE POOL OUR ENERGY WITHIN SAIGA, WE CAN SAVE ONE LIFE...
VMMMM...
BUT YOU'LL ALL—
NO NEED TO FEEL THAT WAY, ZENON!
VUUUU...
YOU'VE SAVED EACH OF US AT LEAST ONCE BEFORE!
SHUUU
WE'LL GATHER OUR LIFE FORCES. USE THEM AS YOU WISH!

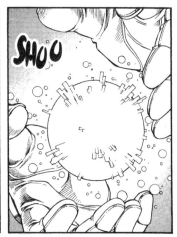

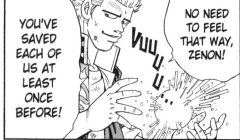

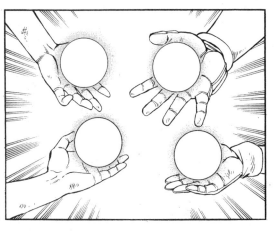

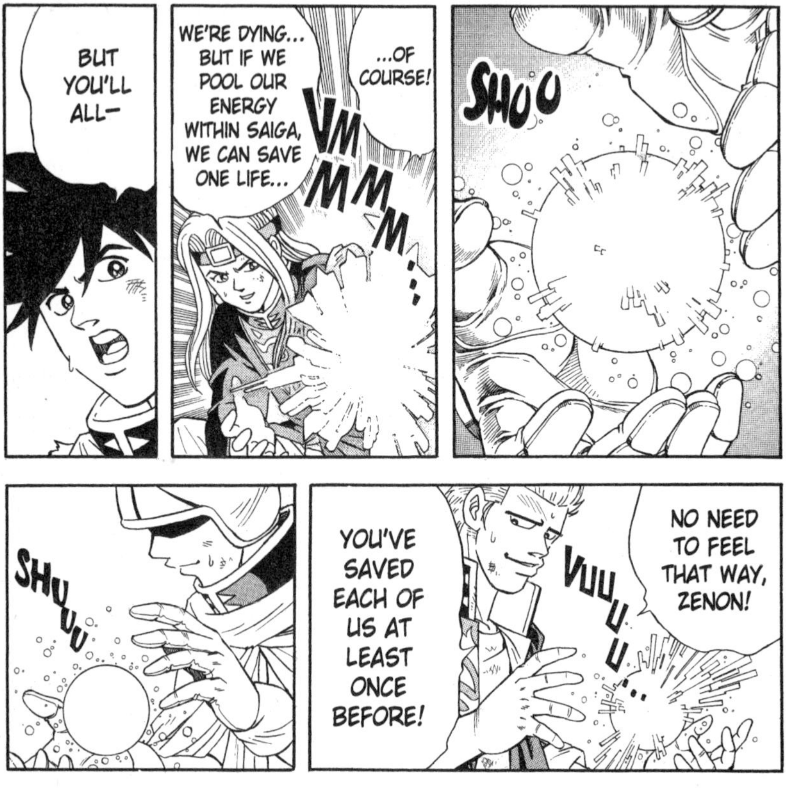

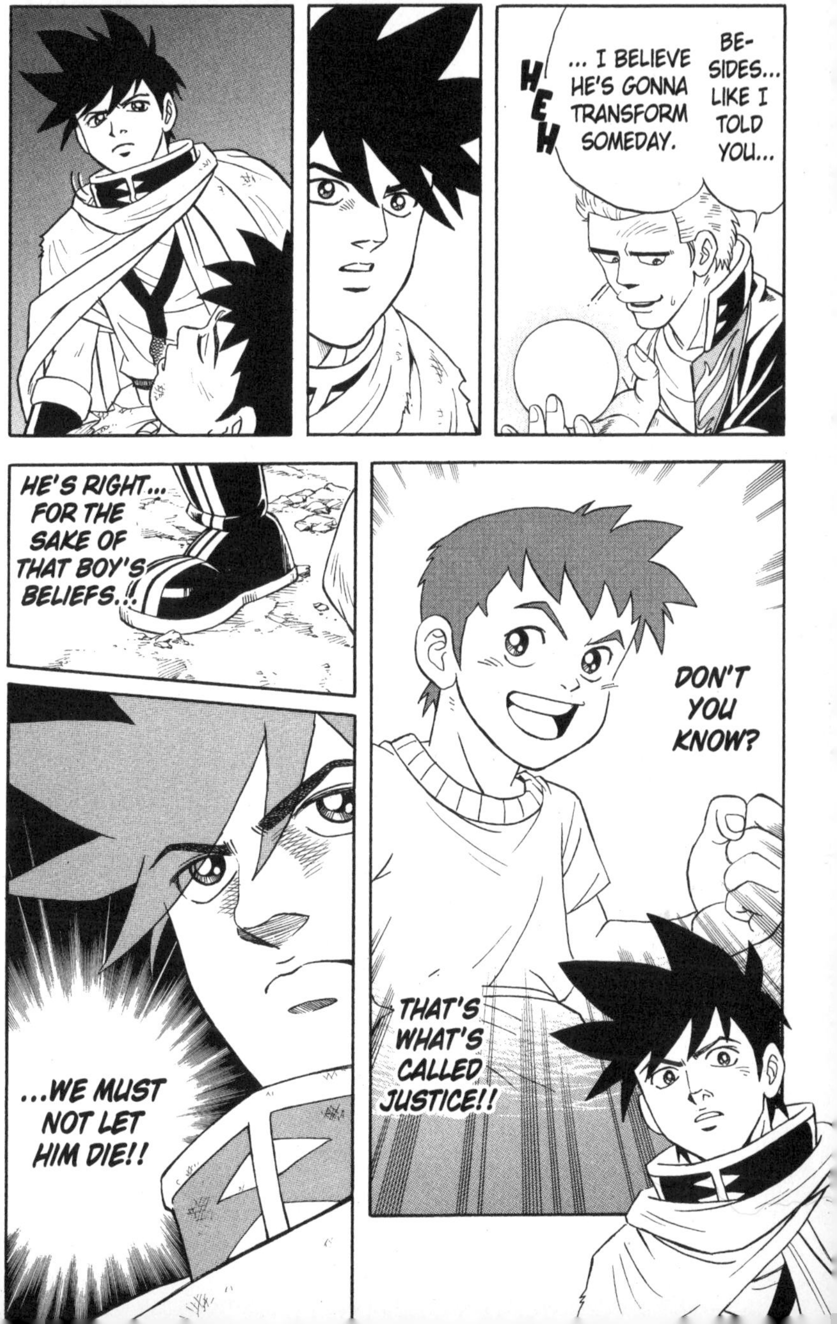
BE-SIDES... LIKE I TOLD YOU...
... I BELIEVE HE'S GONNA TRANSFORM SOMEDAY.
HEH
DON'T YOU KNOW?
THAT'S WHAT'S CALLED JUSTICE!!
HE'S RIGHT... FOR THE SAKE OF THAT BOY'S BELIEFS...!
...WE MUST NOT LET HIM DIE!!

READ THIS WAY

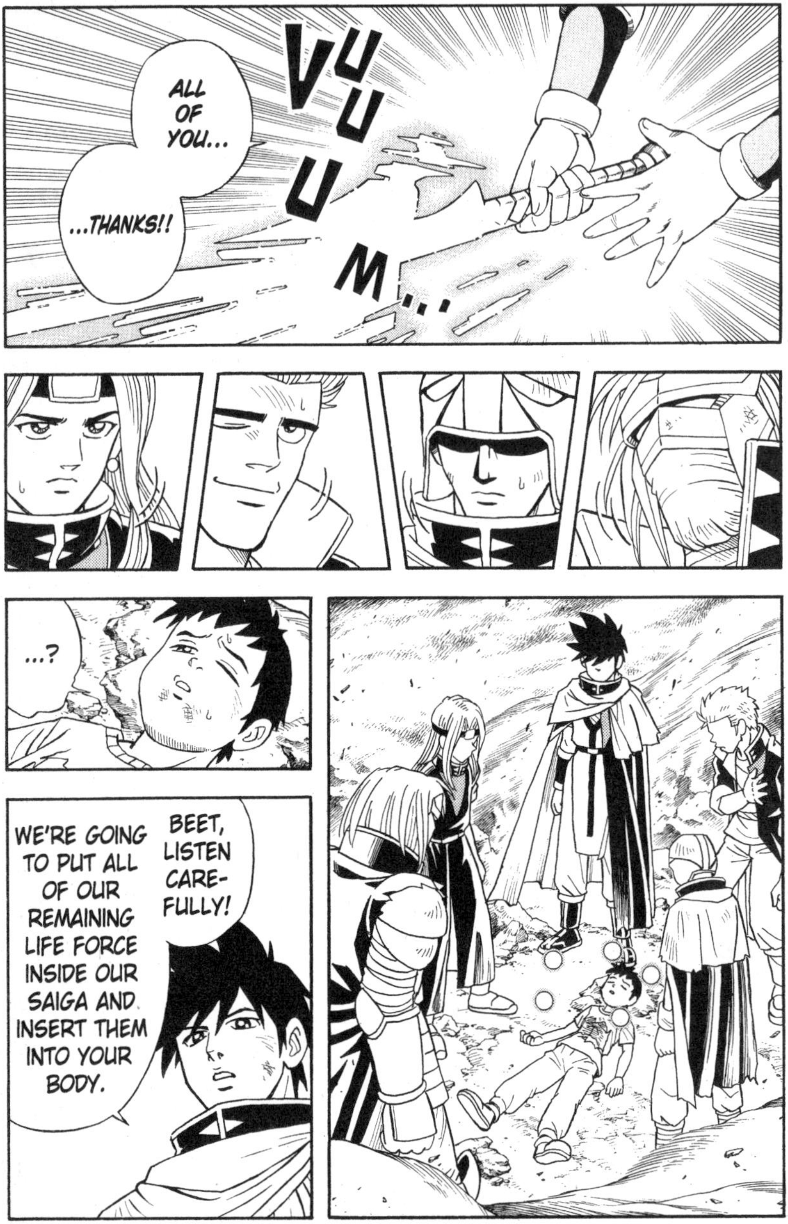
VUUUM...
ALL OF YOU...
...THANKS!!
...?
BEET, LISTEN CAREFULLY!
WE'RE GOING TO PUT ALL OF OUR REMAINING LIFE FORCE INSIDE OUR SAIGA AND INSERT THEM INTO YOUR BODY.

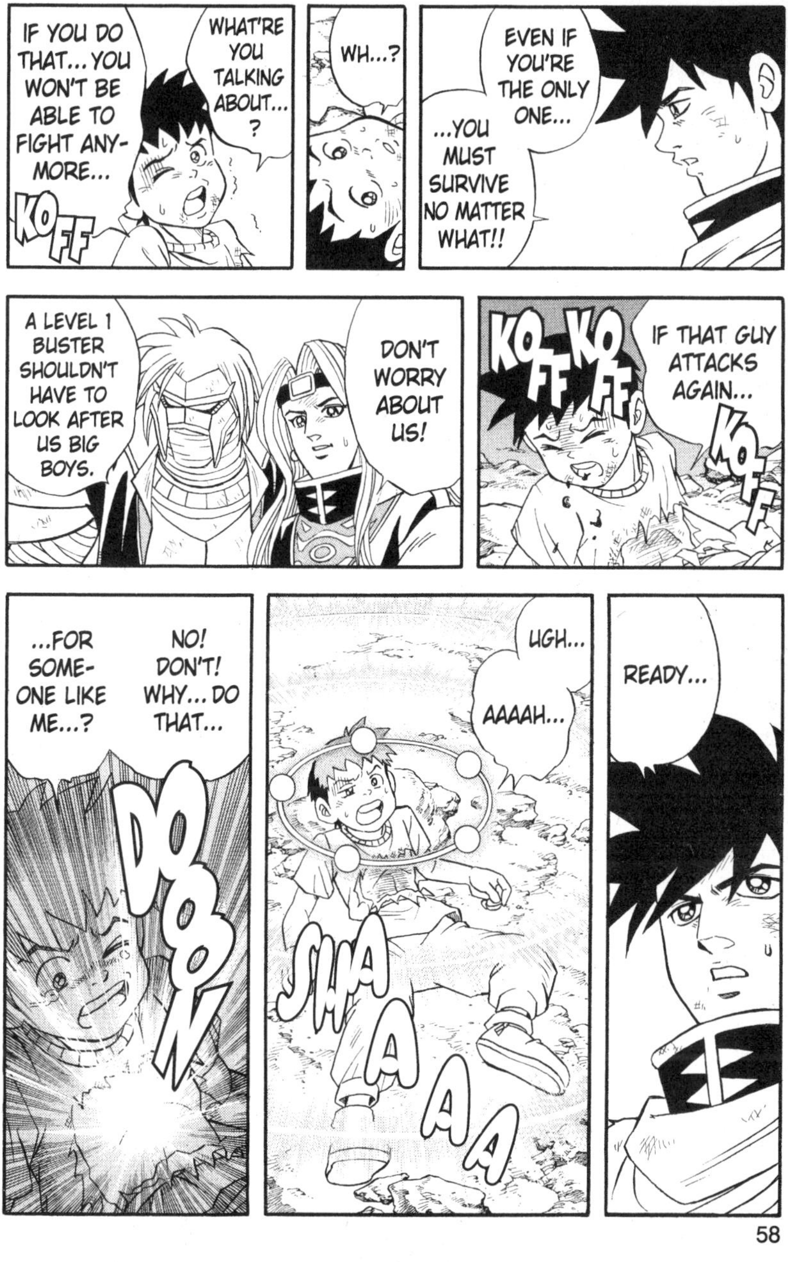
EVEN IF YOU'RE THE ONLY ONE...
...YOU MUST SURVIVE NO MATTER WHAT!!
WH...?
WHAT'RE YOU TALKING ABOUT...?
IF YOU DO THAT... YOU WON'T BE ABLE TO FIGHT ANY-MORE...
KOFF
IF THAT GUY ATTACKS AGAIN...
KOFF KOFF
KOFF
DON'T WORRY ABOUT US!
A LEVEL 1 BUSTER SHOULDN'T HAVE TO LOOK AFTER US BIG BOYS.
READY...
UGH...
AAAAH...
SHAAAAA
NO! DON'T! WHY... DO THAT...
...FOR SOME-ONE LIKE ME...?
DOOON

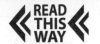

READ THIS WAY

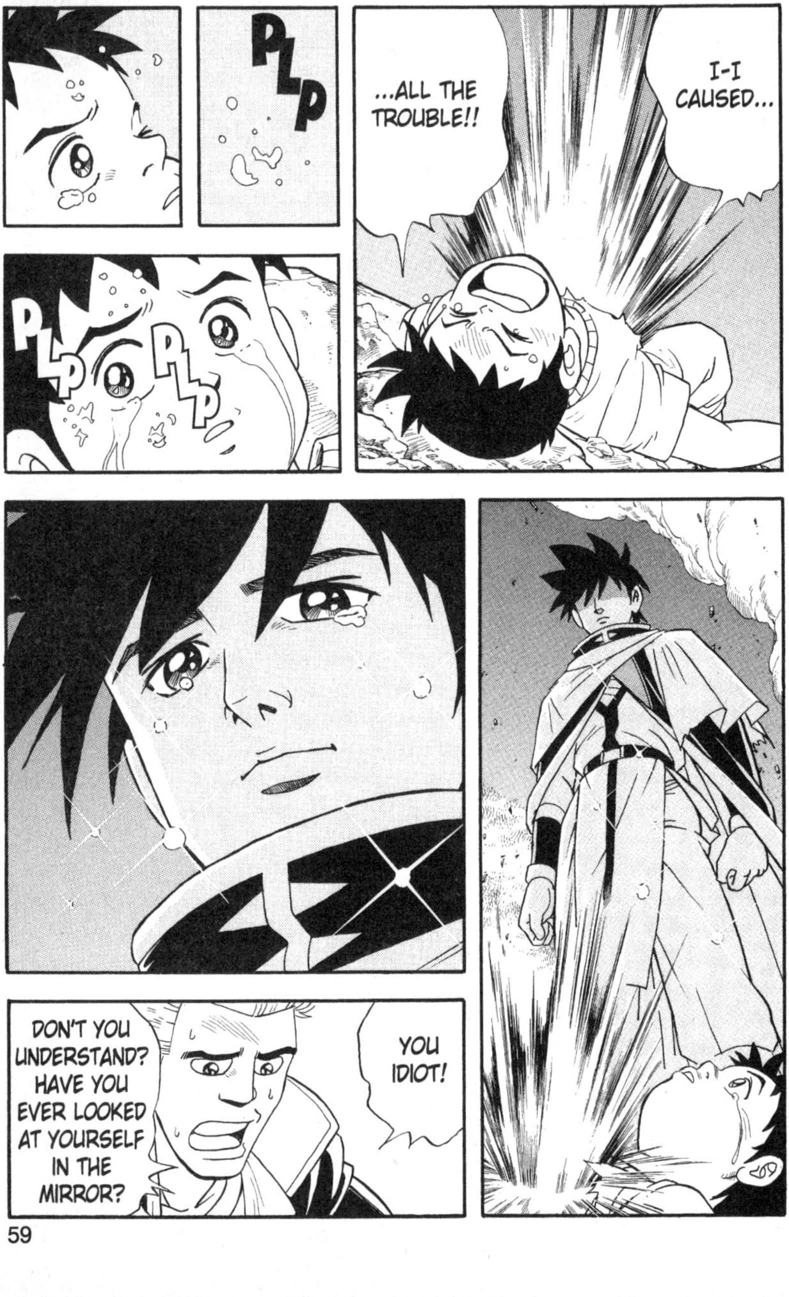
I-I CAUSED...
...ALL THE TROUBLE!!
PLP
PLP
PLP
YOU IDIOT!
DON'T YOU UNDERSTAND? HAVE YOU EVER LOOKED AT YOURSELF IN THE MIRROR?

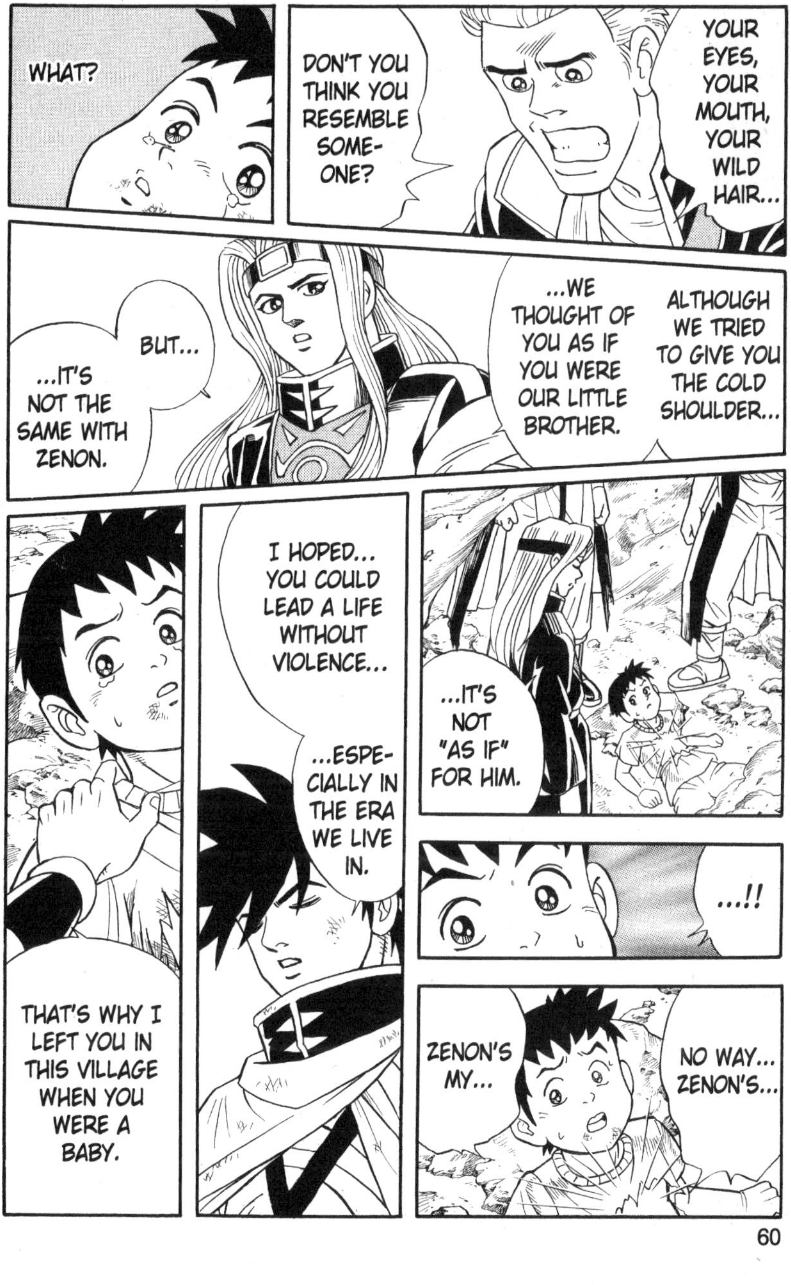
YOUR EYES, YOUR MOUTH, YOUR WILD HAIR...
DON'T YOU THINK YOU RESEMBLE SOME-ONE?
WHAT?
ALTHOUGH WE TRIED TO GIVE YOU THE COLD SHOULDER...
...WE THOUGHT OF YOU AS IF YOU WERE OUR LITTLE BROTHER.
BUT...
...IT'S NOT THE SAME WITH ZENON.
...IT'S NOT "AS IF" FOR HIM.
...!!
NO WAY... ZENON'S...
ZENON'S MY...
I HOPED... YOU COULD LEAD A LIFE WITHOUT VIOLENCE...
...ESPE-CIALLY IN THE ERA WE LIVE IN.
THAT'S WHY I LEFT YOU IN THIS VILLAGE WHEN YOU WERE A BABY.

READ THIS WAY

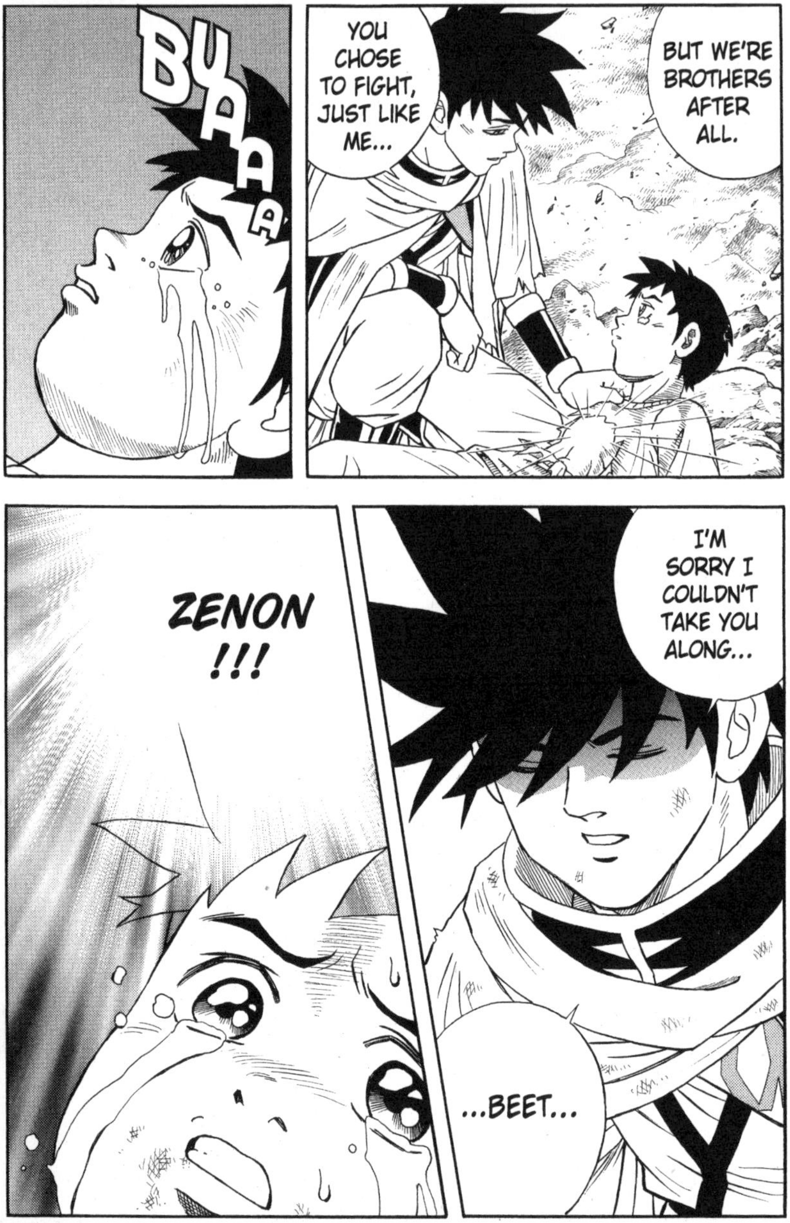
BUT WE'RE BROTHERS AFTER ALL.
YOU CHOSE TO FIGHT, JUST LIKE ME...
BUAAA
I'M SORRY I COULDN'T TAKE YOU ALONG...
...BEET...
ZENON !!!

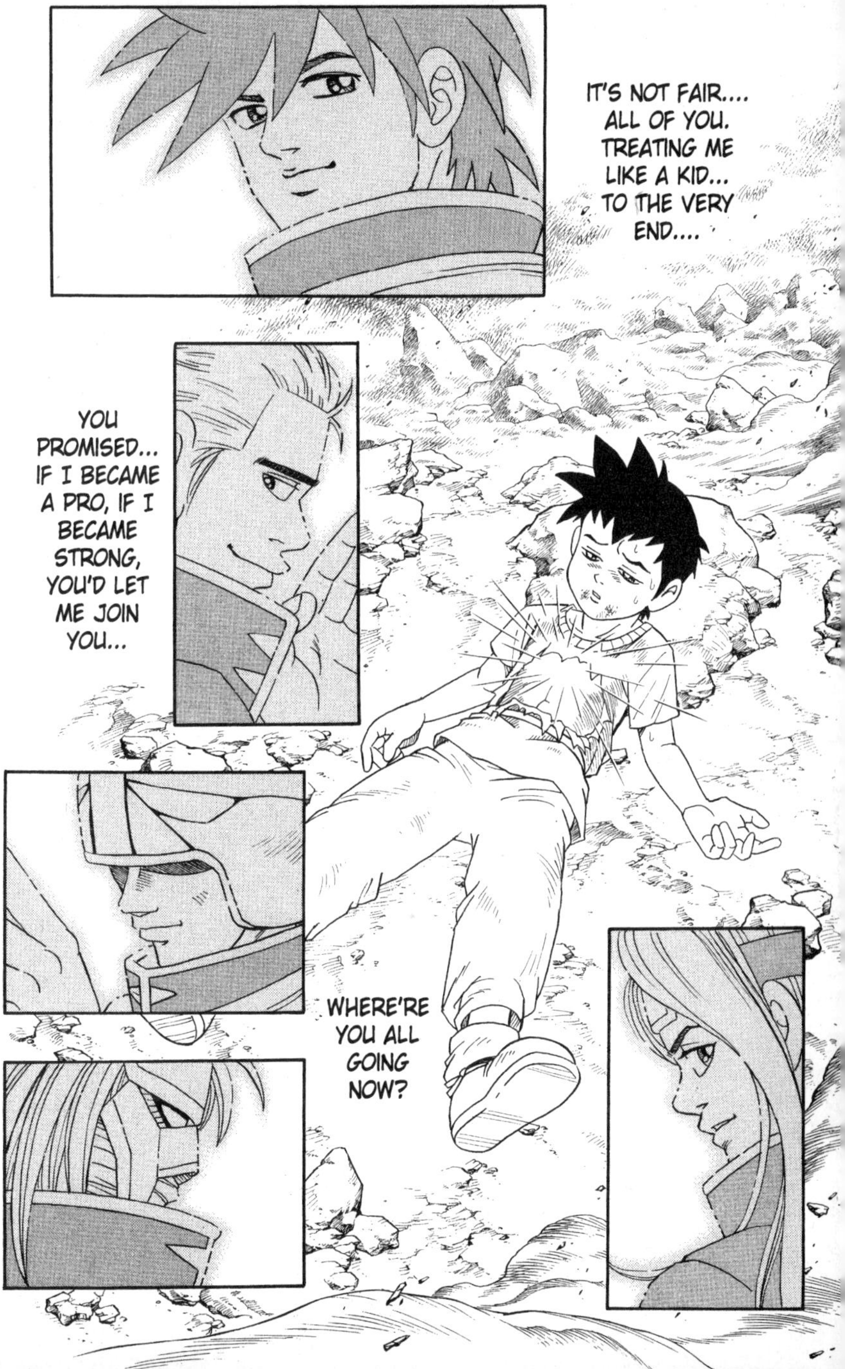
IT'S NOT FAIR.... ALL OF YOU. TREATING ME LIKE A KID... TO THE VERY END....
YOU PROMISED... IF I BECAME A PRO, IF I BECAME STRONG, YOU'D LET ME JOIN YOU...
WHERE'RE YOU ALL GOING NOW?

READ THIS WAY

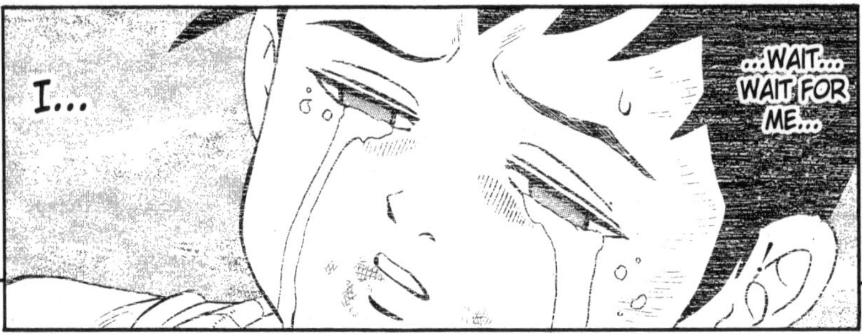
...WAIT... WAIT FOR ME...
I...

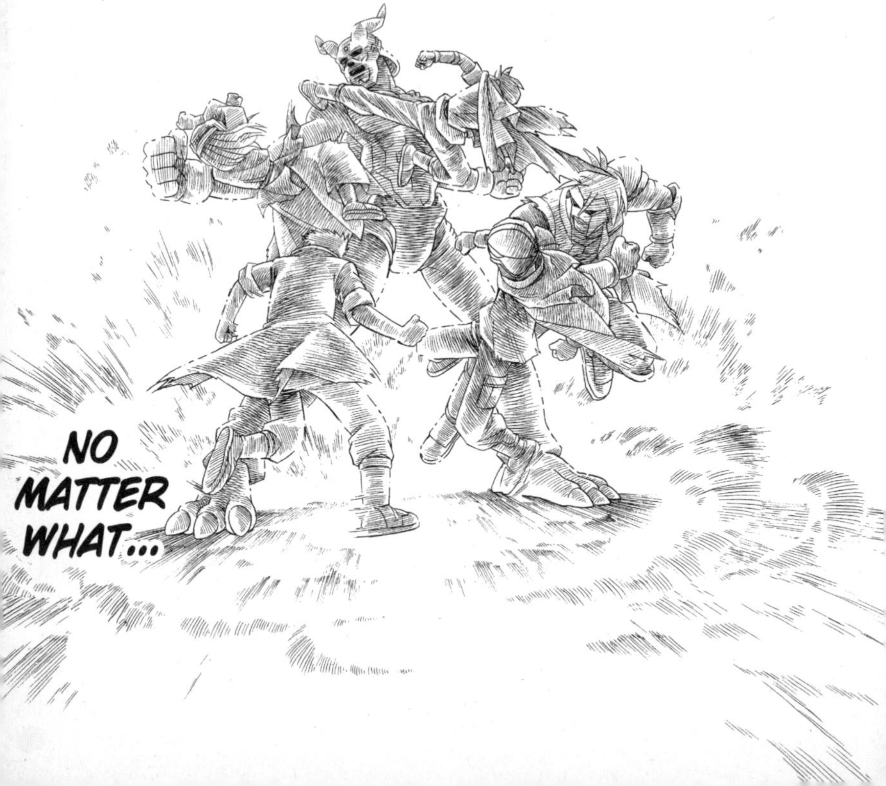
SOME-DAY...
NO MATTER WHAT...

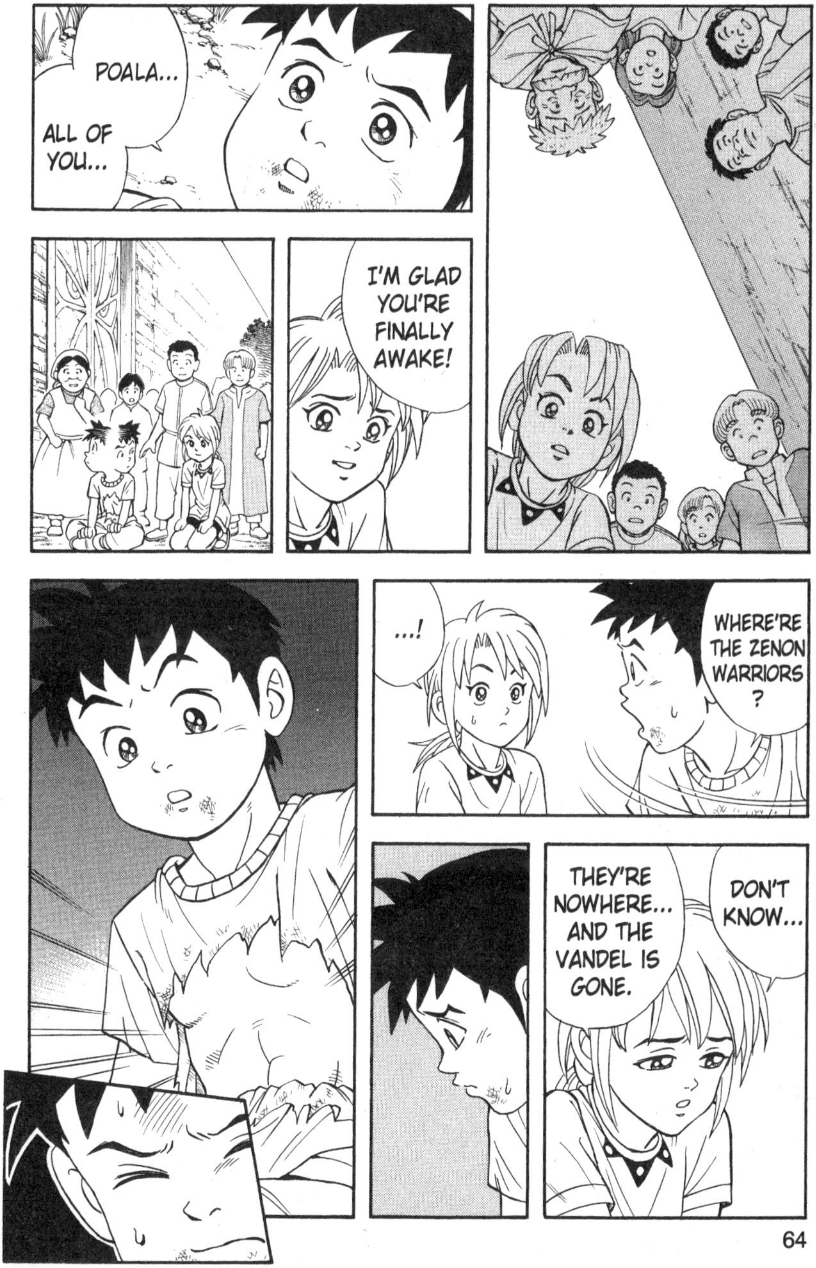
POALA...
ALL OF YOU...
I'M GLAD YOU'RE FINALLY AWAKE!
WHERE'RE THE ZENON WARRIORS?
...!
DON'T KNOW...
THEY'RE NOWHERE... AND THE VANDEL IS GONE.

READ THIS WAY

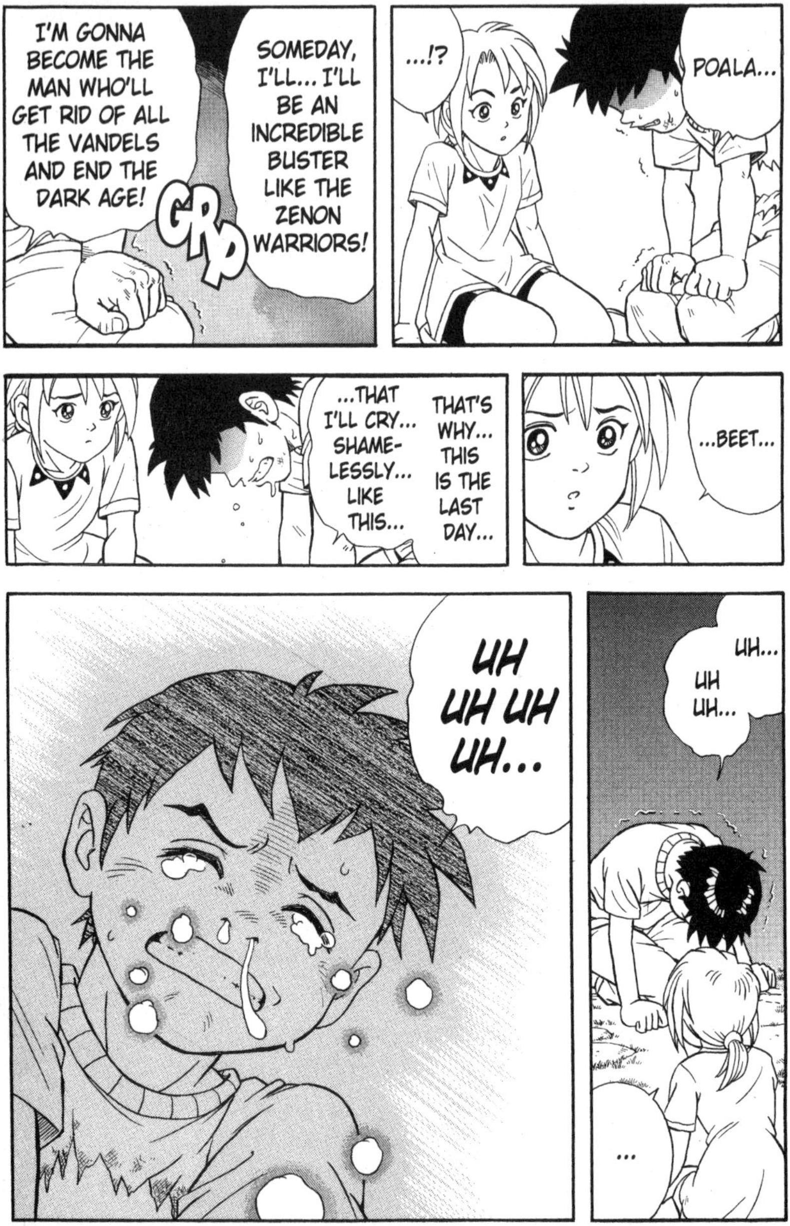
POALA...
...!?
SOMEDAY, I'LL... I'LL BE AN INCREDIBLE BUSTER LIKE THE ZENON WARRIORS!
GRP
I'M GONNA BECOME THE MAN WHO'LL GET RID OF ALL THE VANDELS AND END THE DARK AGE!
...BEET...
THAT'S WHY... THIS IS THE LAST DAY...
...THAT I'LL CRY... SHAME-LESSLY... LIKE THIS...
UH... UH UH...
...
UH UH UH UH...

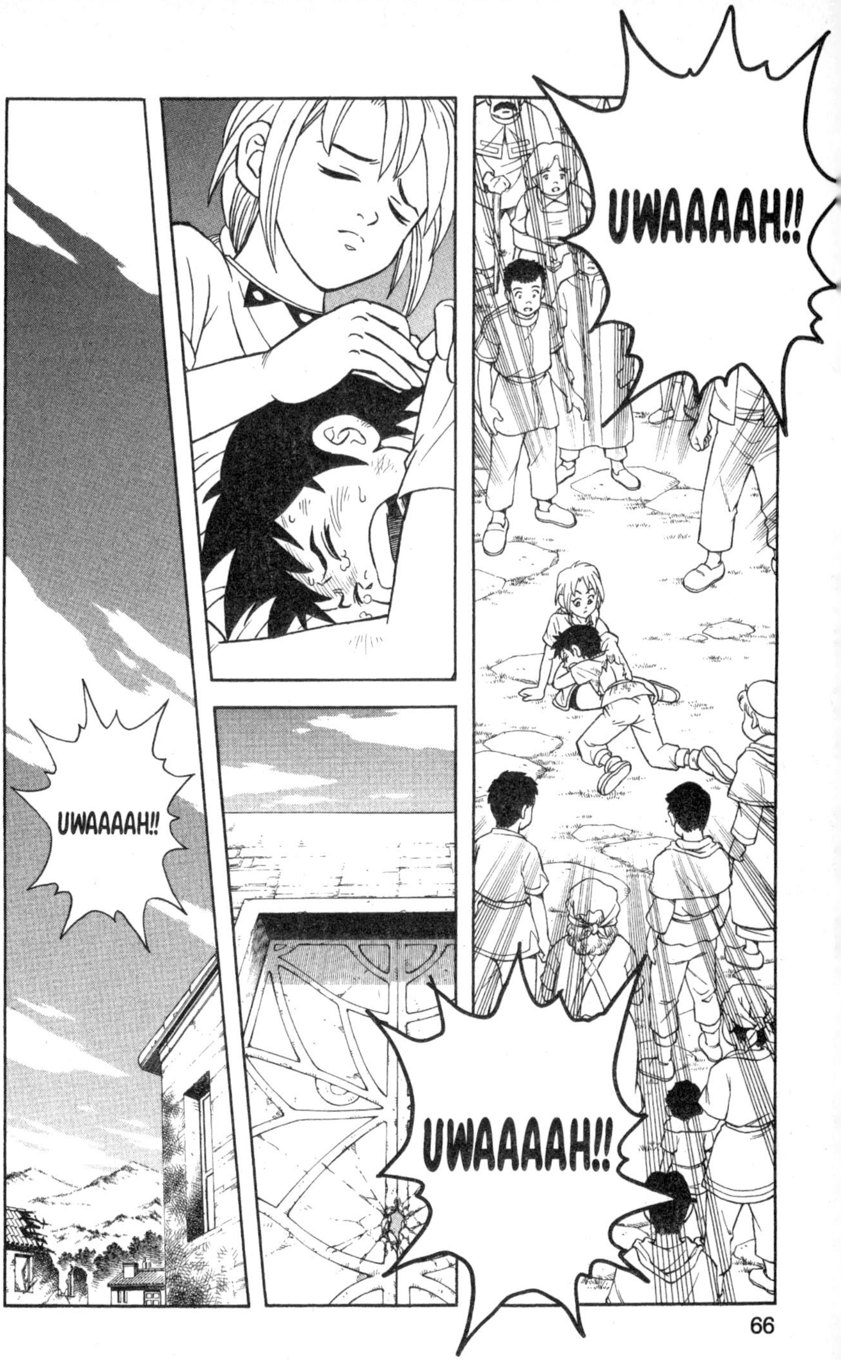
UWAAAAH!!
UWAAAAH!!
UWAAAAH!!

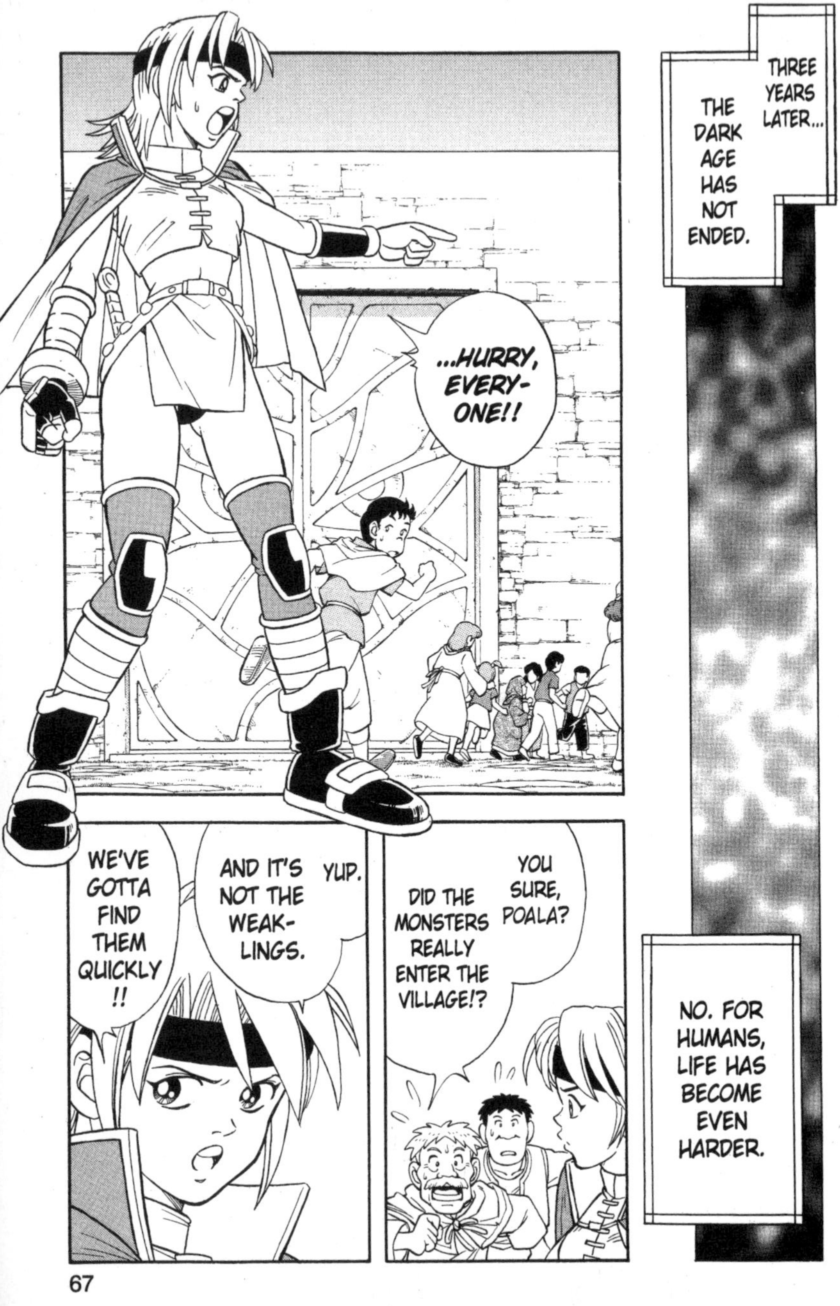
THREE YEARS LATER...
THE DARK AGE HAS NOT ENDED.
NO. FOR HUMANS, LIFE HAS BECOME EVEN HARDER.
...HURRY, EVERY-ONE!!
YOU SURE, POALA?
DID THE MONSTERS REALLY ENTER THE VILLAGE!?
YUP.
AND IT'S NOT THE WEAK-LINGS.
WE'VE GOTTA FIND THEM QUICKLY!!

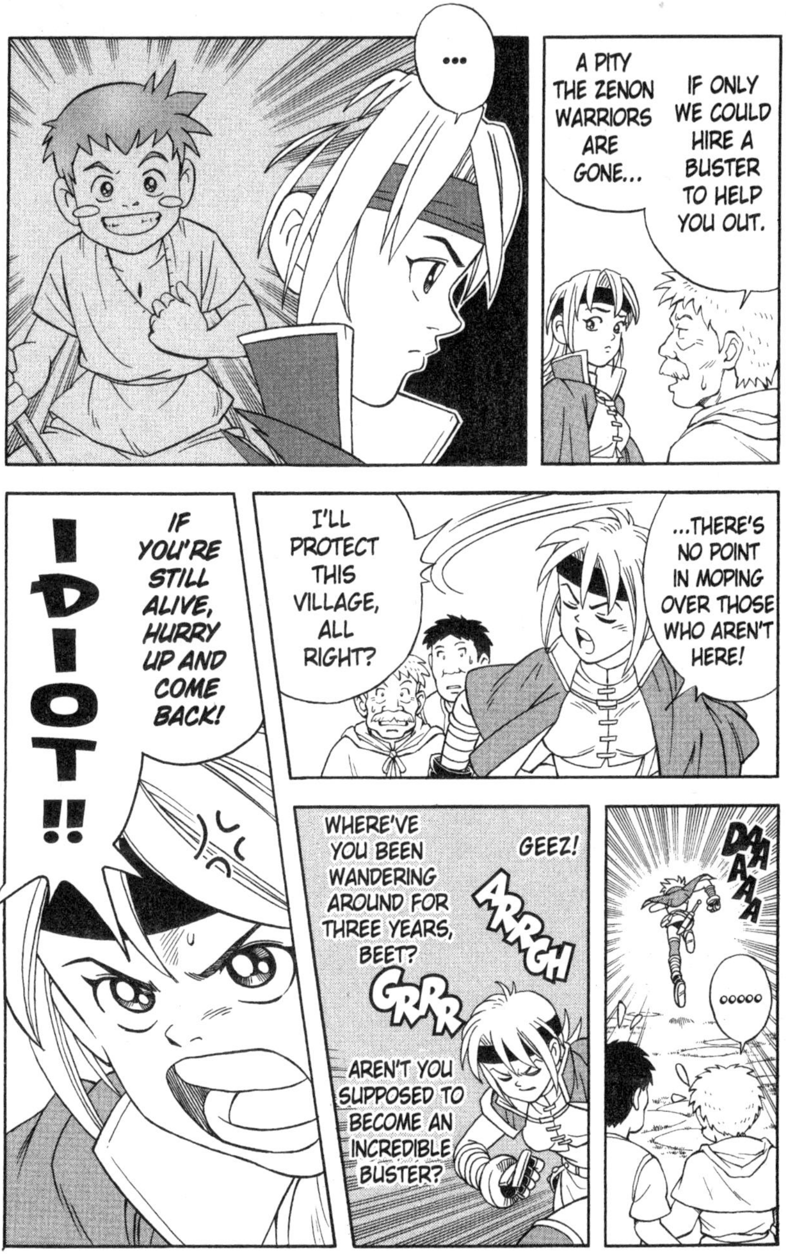
A PITY THE ZENON WARRIORS ARE GONE...
IF ONLY WE COULD HIRE A BUSTER TO HELP YOU OUT.
...
...THERE'S NO POINT IN MOPING OVER THOSE WHO AREN'T HERE!
I'LL PROTECT THIS VILLAGE, ALL RIGHT?
DAAAAA
ooooo
GEEZ!
WHERE'VE YOU BEEN WANDERING AROUND FOR THREE YEARS, BEET?
ARRRGH
GRRR
AREN'T YOU SUPPOSED TO BECOME AN INCREDIBLE BUSTER?
IF YOU'RE STILL ALIVE, HURRY UP AND COME BACK!
IDIOT!!

READ THIS WAY

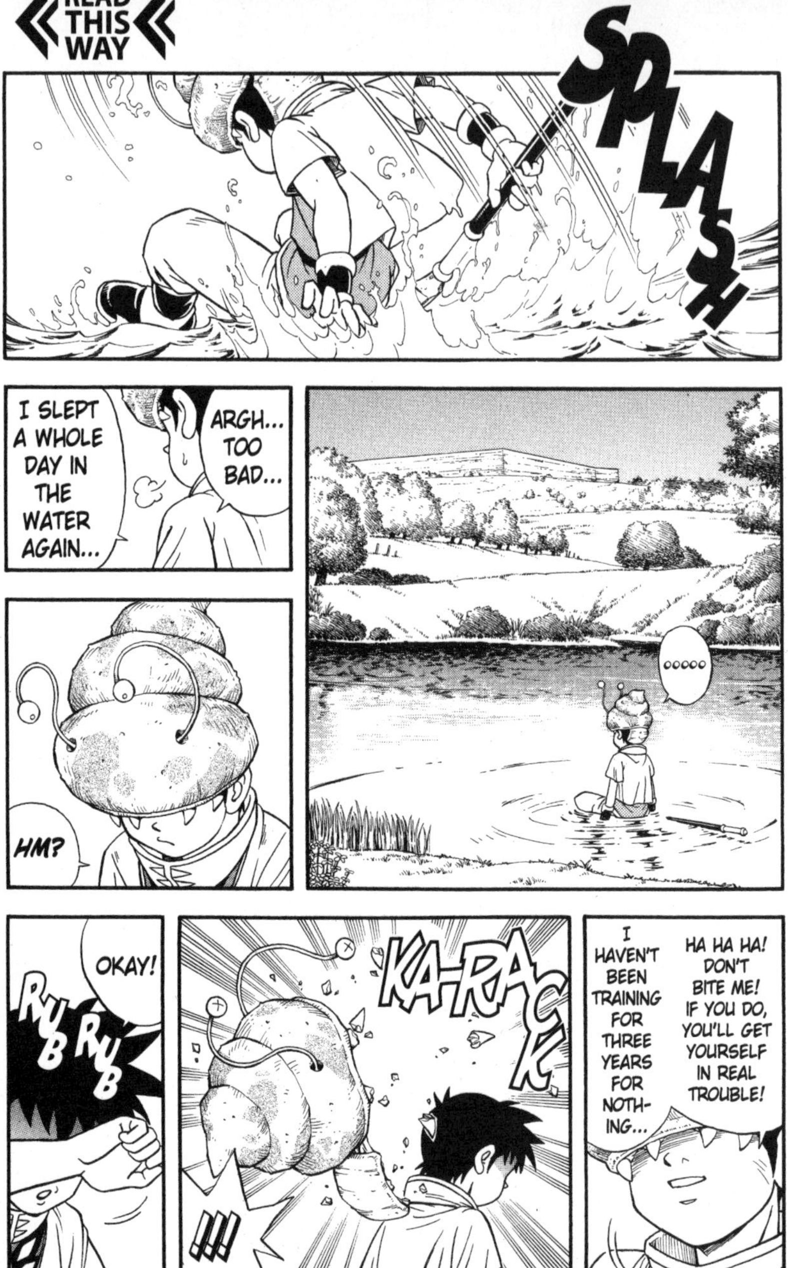

SPLASH
.....
ARGH... TOO BAD...
I SLEPT A WHOLE DAY IN THE WATER AGAIN...
HM?
HA HA HA! DON'T BITE ME! IF YOU DO, YOU'LL GET YOURSELF IN REAL TROUBLE!
I HAVEN'T BEEN TRAINING FOR THREE YEARS FOR NOTHING...
KA-RACK
!!!
OKAY!
RUB RUB

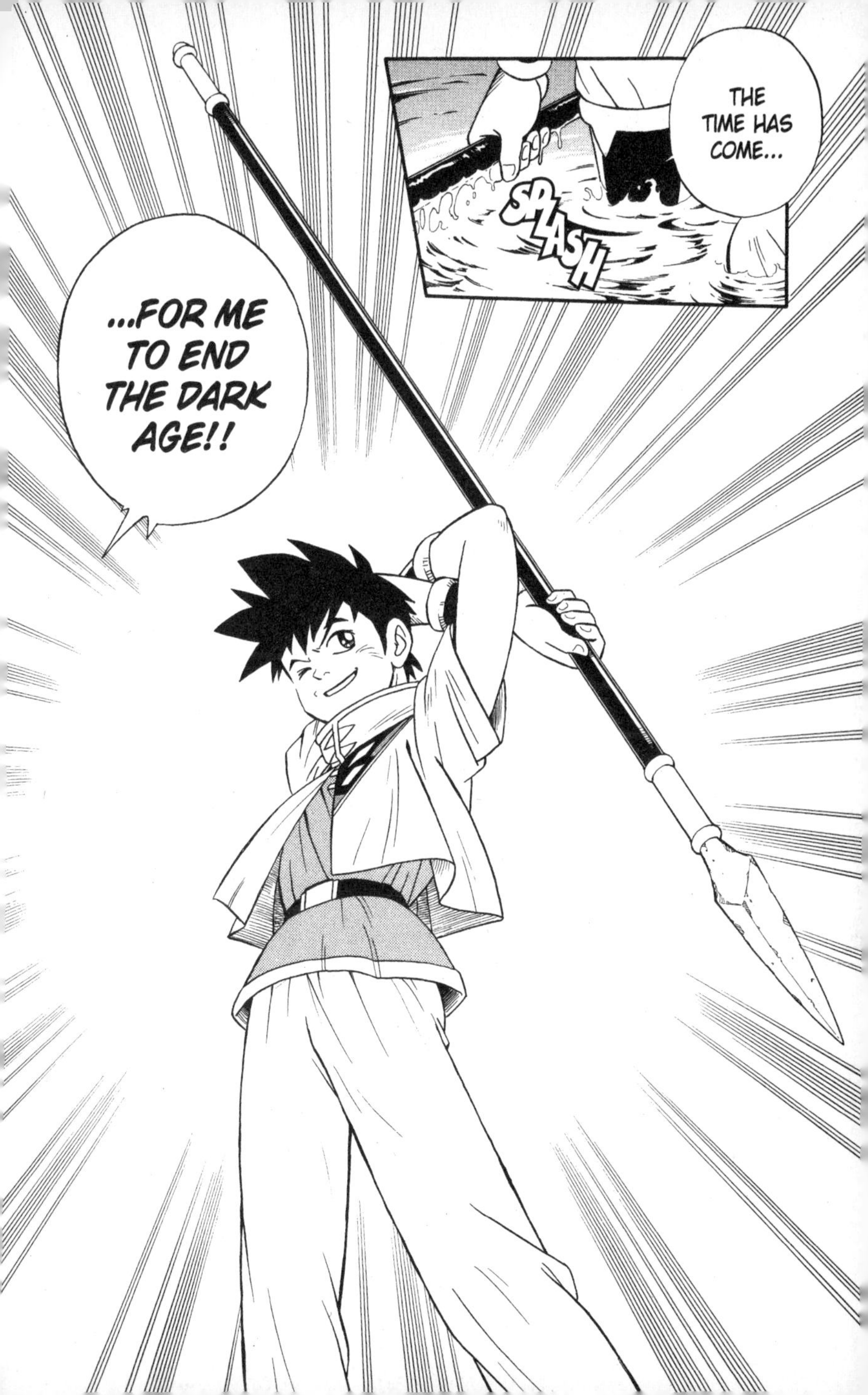
THE TIME HAS COME...
SPLASH
...FOR ME TO END THE DARK AGE!!

Chapter 2: He Who Returned!

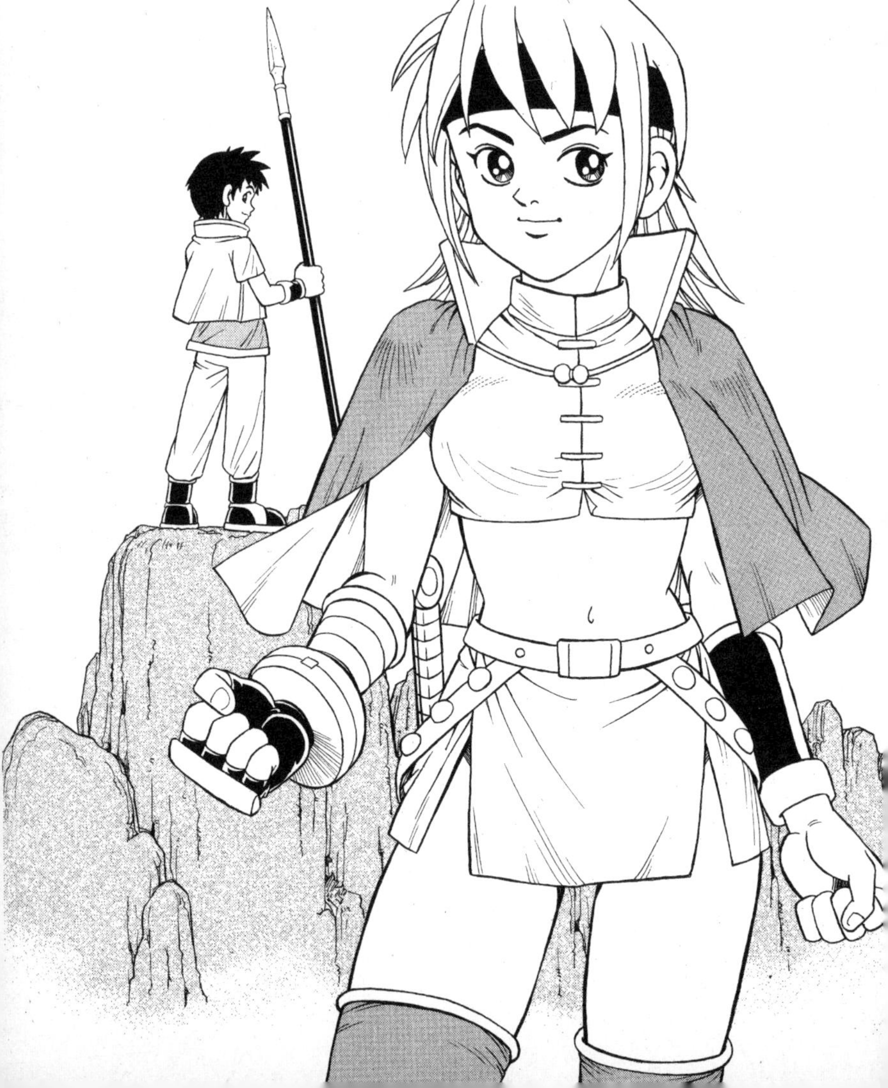

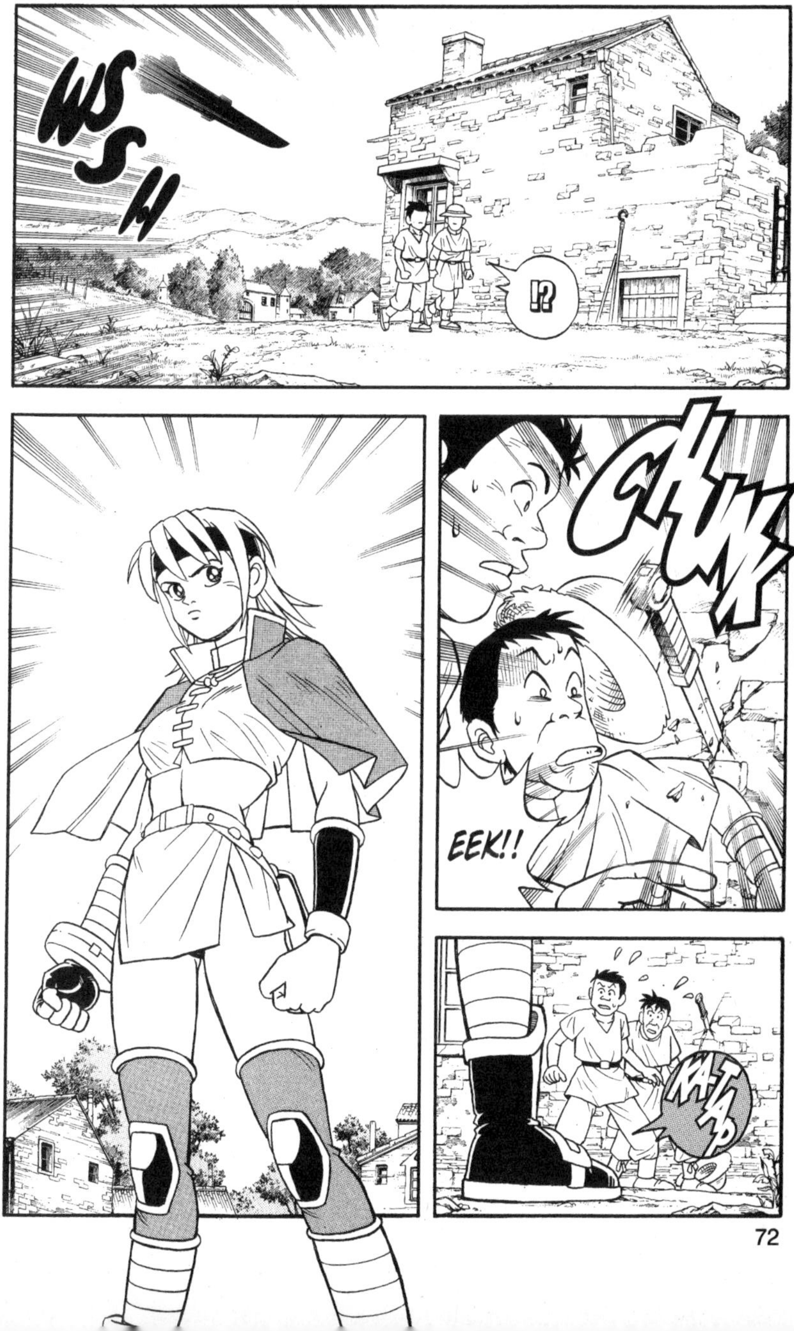
!?
WSSH
CHUK
EEK!!
KA-TAP

READ THIS WAY

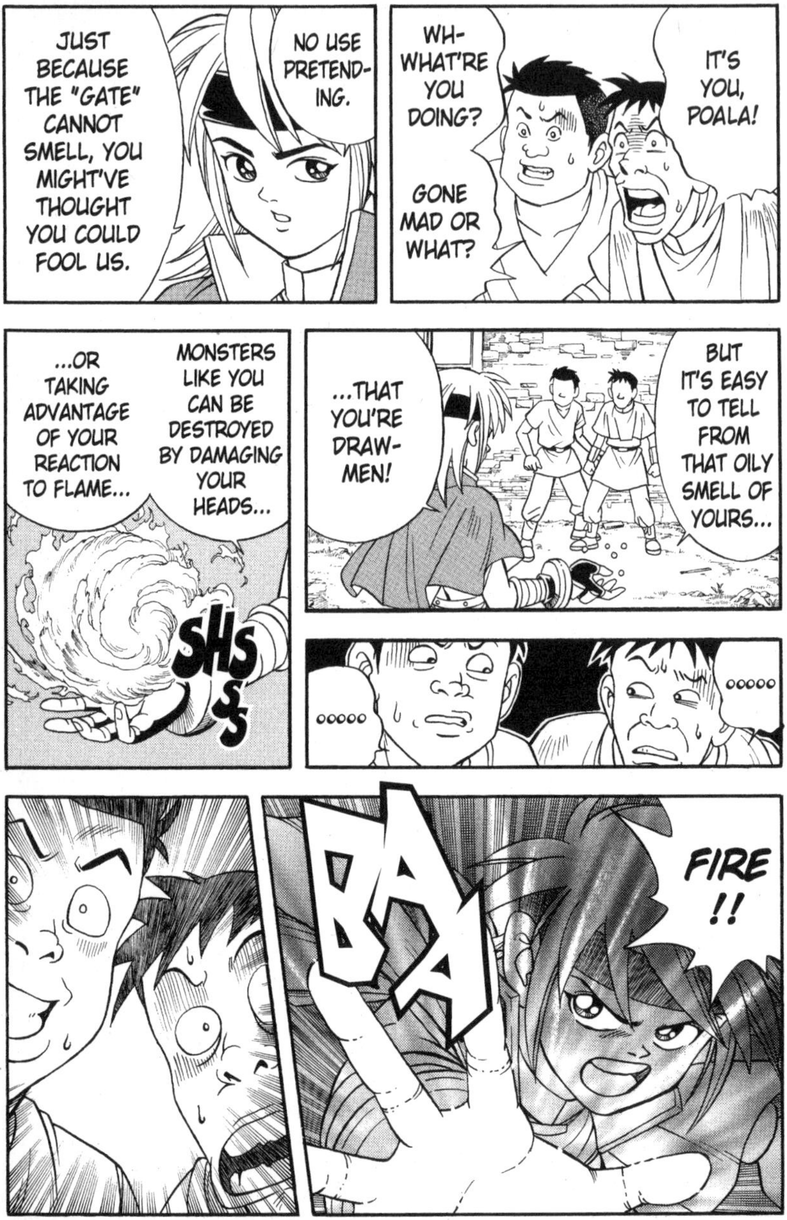
IT'S YOU, POALA!
WH- WHAT'RE YOU DOING?
GONE MAD OR WHAT?
NO USE PRETEND-ING.
JUST BECAUSE THE "GATE" CANNOT SMELL, YOU MIGHT'VE THOUGHT YOU COULD FOOL US.
BUT IT'S EASY TO TELL FROM THAT OILY SMELL OF YOURS...
...THAT YOU'RE DRAW-MEN!
ooooo
ooooo
MONSTERS LIKE YOU CAN BE DESTROYED BY DAMAGING YOUR HEADS...
...OR TAKING ADVANTAGE OF YOUR REACTION TO FLAME...
SHSSSS
FIRE !!
BA

FWOOOSH
WHOA !!
FSH FSH
GLOOP
DOOON
SHA
KA-CHING

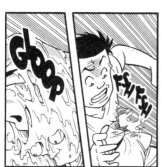

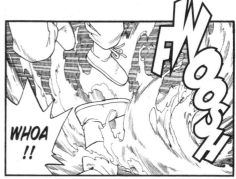

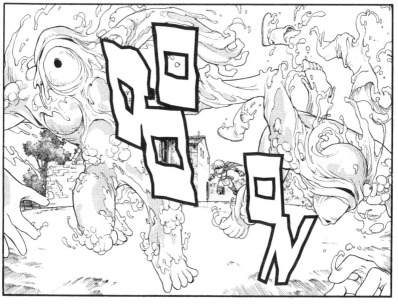

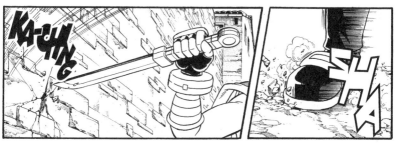

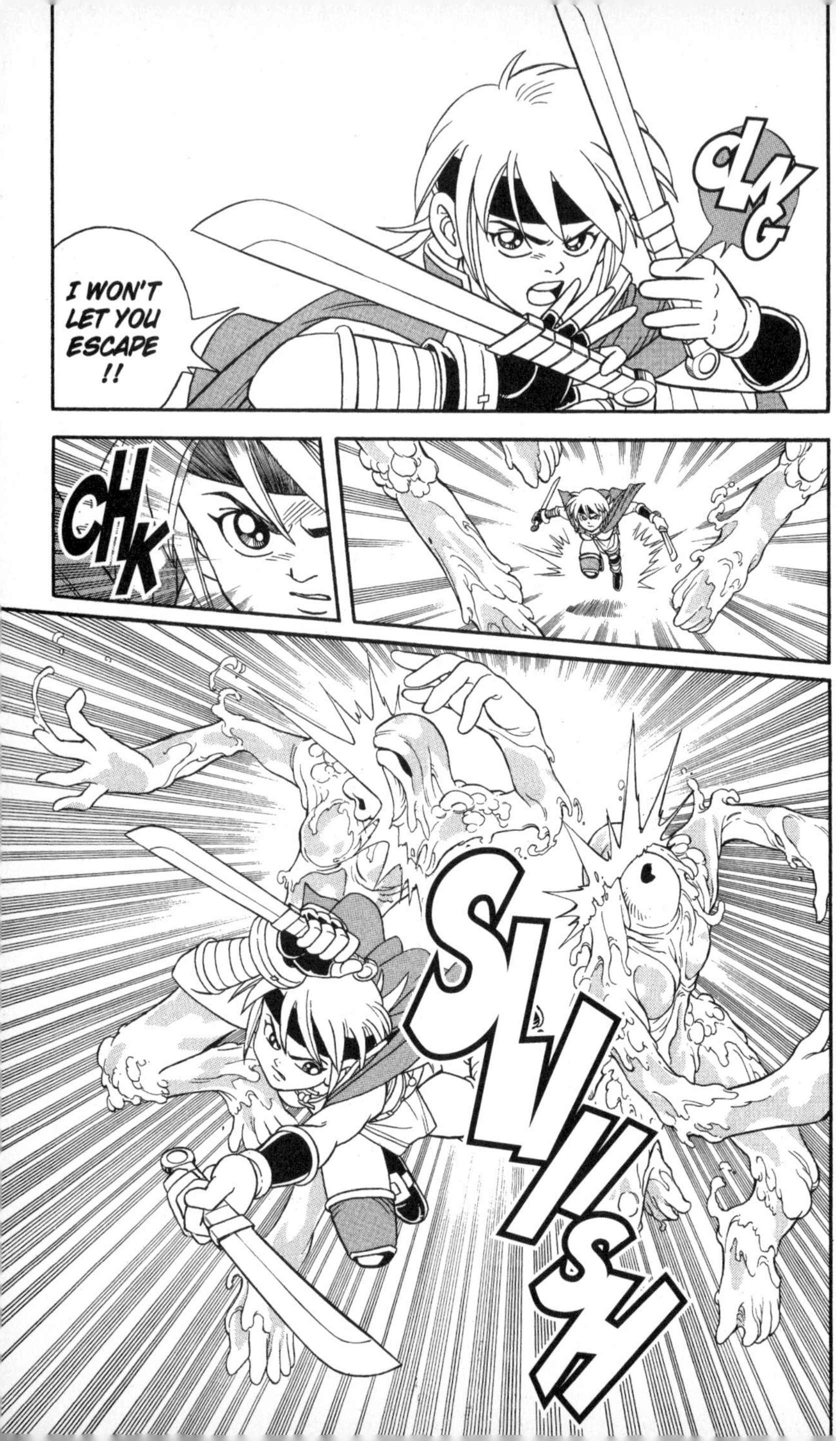
CLNG
I WON'T LET YOU ESCAPE !!
CHK
SWISH

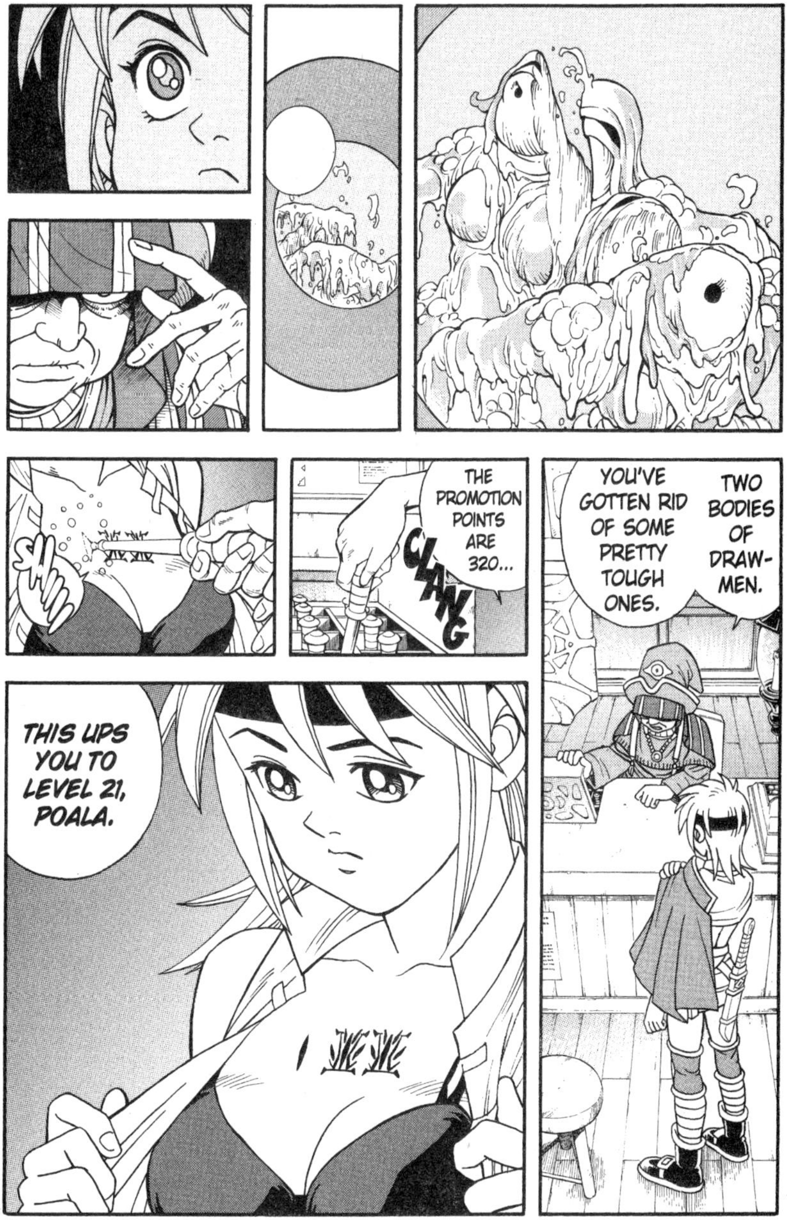
TWO BODIES OF DRAW-MEN.
YOU'VE GOTTEN RID OF SOME PRETTY TOUGH ONES.
THE PROMOTION POINTS ARE 320...
CLANG
SHW
THIS UPS YOU TO LEVEL 21, POALA.

READ THIS WAY

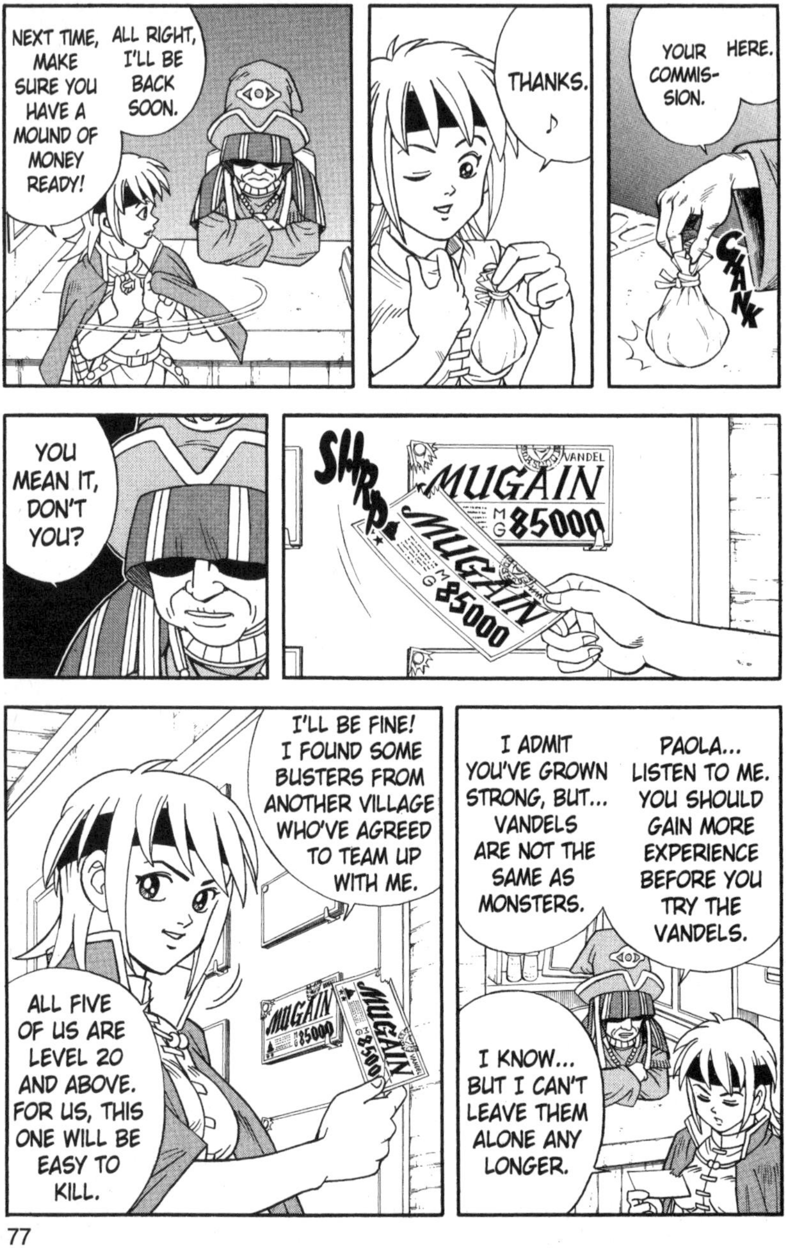
HERE.
YOUR COMMISSION.
CHANK
THANKS. ♪
ALL RIGHT, I'LL BE BACK SOON.
NEXT TIME, MAKE SURE YOU HAVE A MOUND OF MONEY READY!
VANDEL
MUGAIN
MG 85000
SHRIP
MUGAIN
MG 85000
YOU MEAN IT, DON'T YOU?
PAOLA... LISTEN TO ME. YOU SHOULD GAIN MORE EXPERIENCE BEFORE YOU TRY THE VANDELS.
I ADMIT YOU'VE GROWN STRONG, BUT... VANDELS ARE NOT THE SAME AS MONSTERS.
I KNOW... BUT I CAN'T LEAVE THEM ALONE ANY LONGER.
I'LL BE FINE! I FOUND SOME BUSTERS FROM ANOTHER VILLAGE WHO'VE AGREED TO TEAM UP WITH ME.
ALL FIVE OF US ARE LEVEL 20 AND ABOVE. FOR US, THIS ONE WILL BE EASY TO KILL.
MUGAIN
MG 85000
MUGAIN
MG 85000
VANDEL

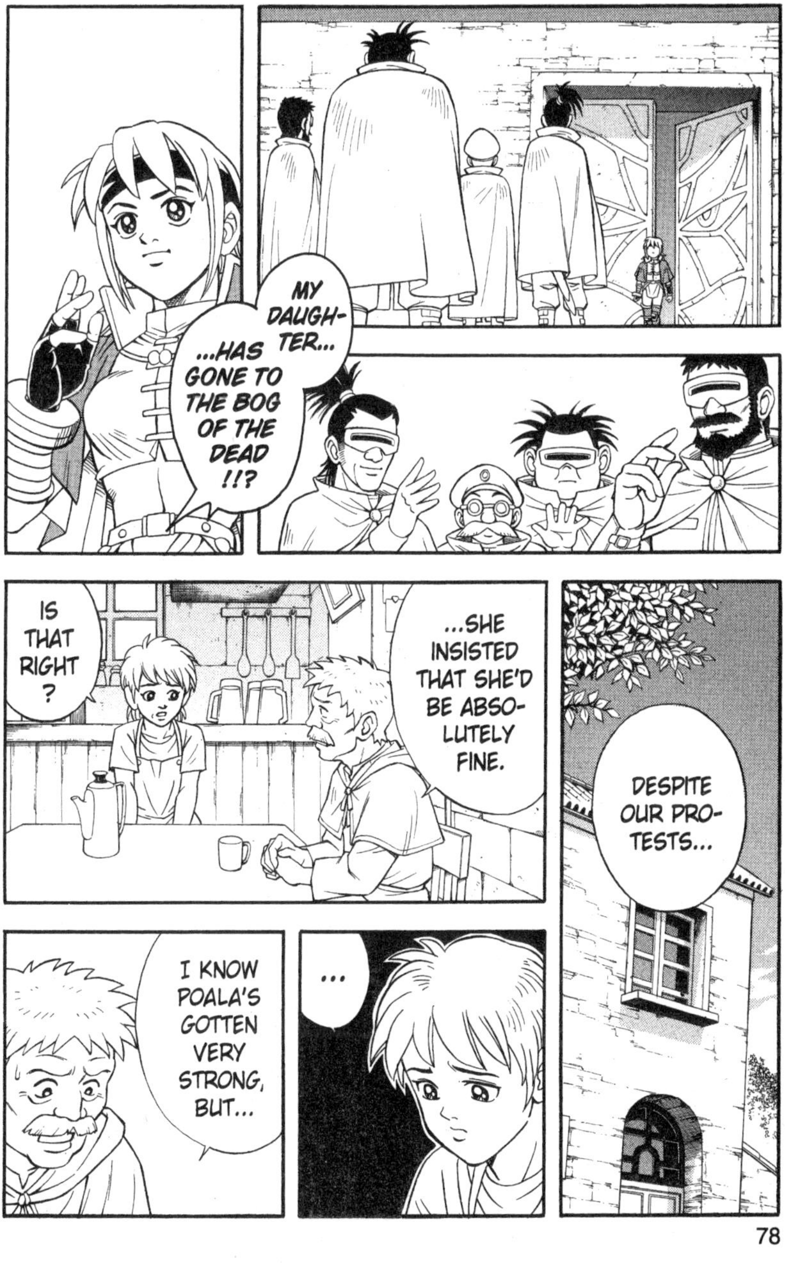
MY DAUGHTER...
...HAS GONE TO THE BOG OF THE DEAD!!?
DESPITE OUR PROTESTS...
...SHE INSISTED THAT SHE'D BE ABSOLUTELY FINE.
IS THAT RIGHT?
...
I KNOW POALA'S GOTTEN VERY STRONG, BUT...

READ THIS WAY

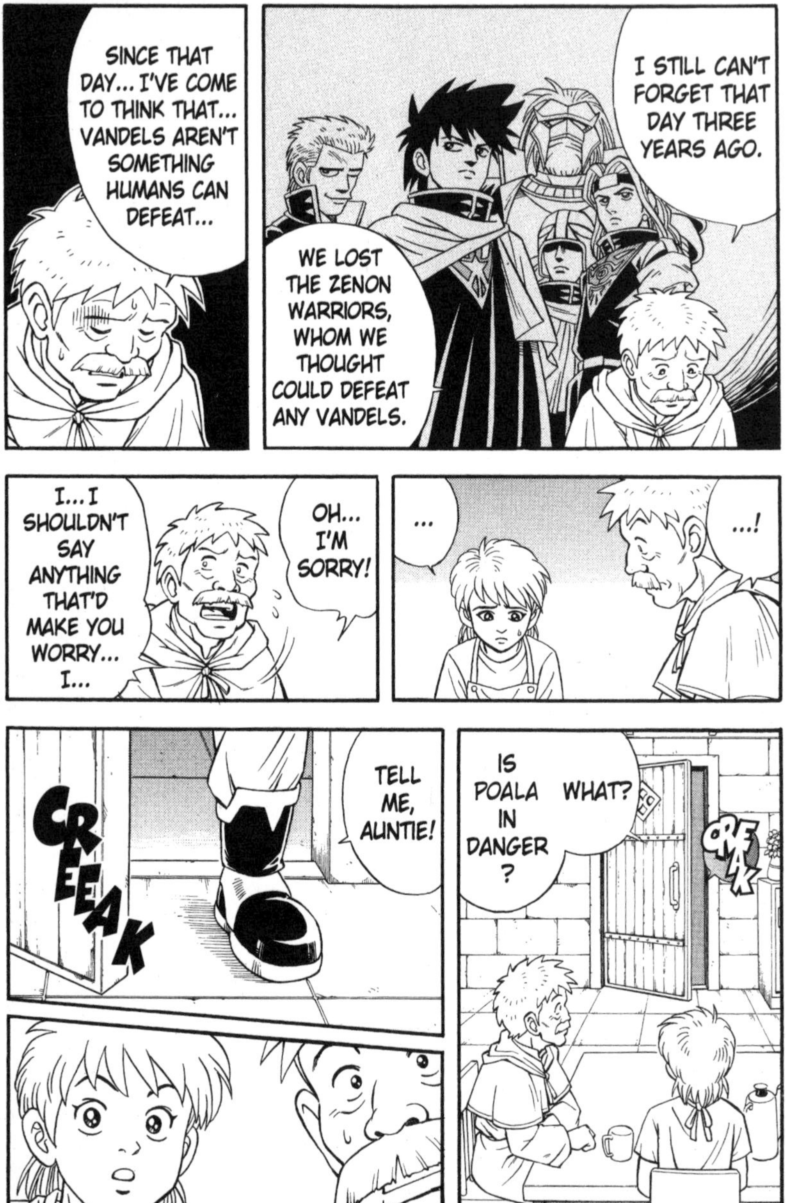

I STILL CAN'T FORGET THAT DAY THREE YEARS AGO.
WE LOST THE ZENON WARRIORS, WHOM WE THOUGHT COULD DEFEAT ANY VANDELS.
SINCE THAT DAY... I'VE COME TO THINK THAT... VANDELS AREN'T SOMETHING HUMANS CAN DEFEAT...
...!
...
OH... I'M SORRY!
I... I SHOULDN'T SAY ANYTHING THAT'D MAKE YOU WORRY... I...
WHAT?
IS POALA IN DANGER?
CREAK
TELL ME, AUNTIE!
CREEEAK

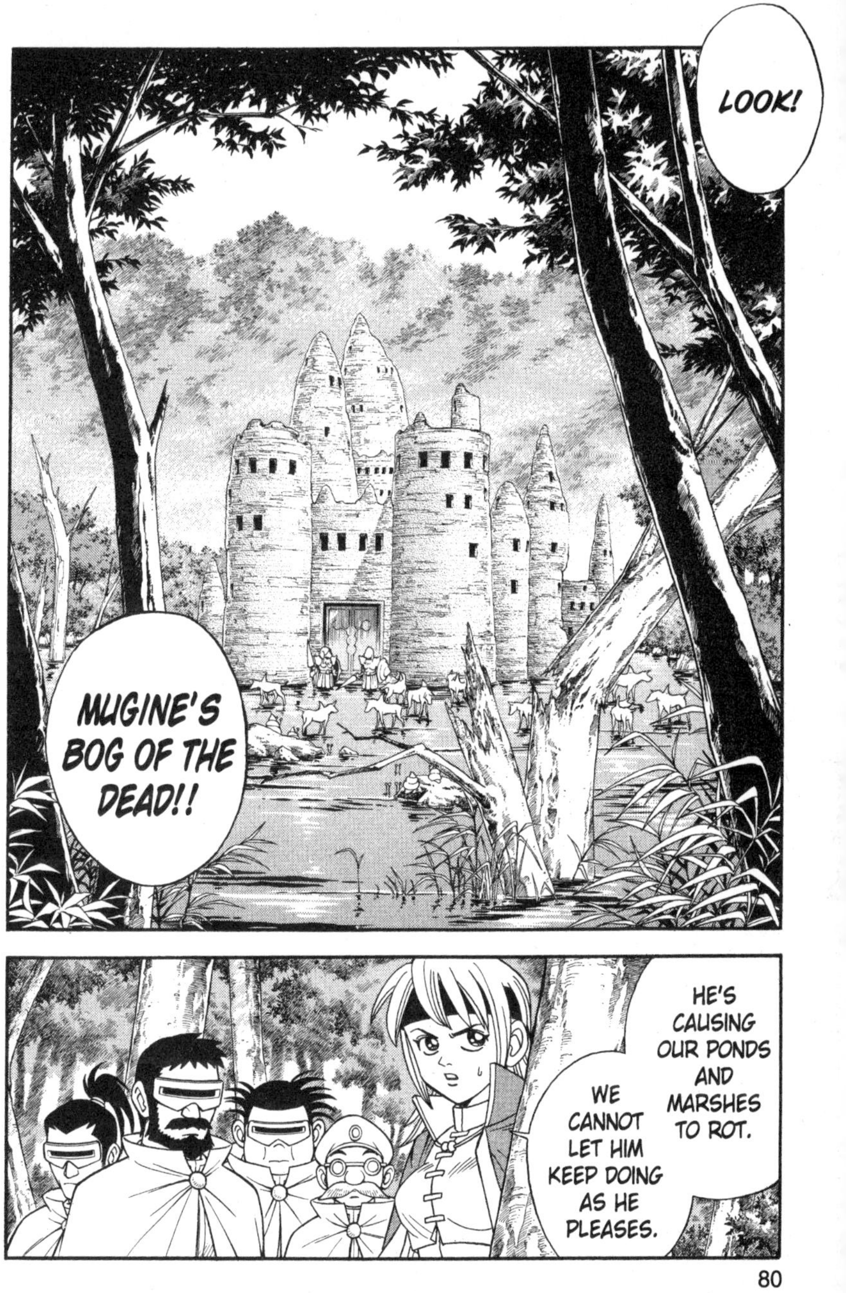
LOOK!
MUGINE'S BOG OF THE DEAD!!
HE'S CAUSING OUR PONDS AND MARSHES TO ROT.
WE CANNOT LET HIM KEEP DOING AS HE PLEASES.

READ THIS WAY

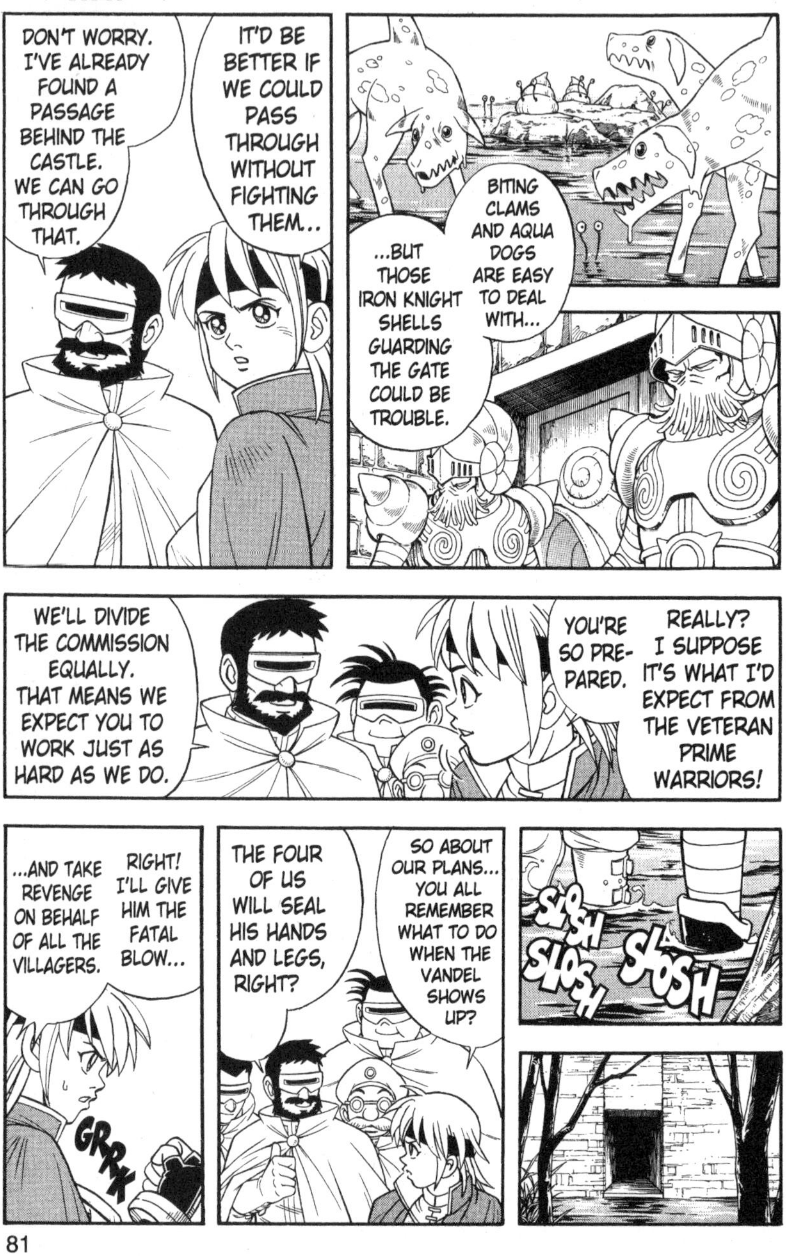

BITING CLAMS AND AQUA DOGS ARE EASY TO DEAL WITH...
...BUT THOSE IRON KNIGHT SHELLS GUARDING THE GATE COULD BE TROUBLE.
IT'D BE BETTER IF WE COULD PASS THROUGH WITHOUT FIGHTING THEM...
DON'T WORRY. I'VE ALREADY FOUND A PASSAGE BEHIND THE CASTLE. WE CAN GO THROUGH THAT.
REALLY? I SUPPOSE IT'S WHAT I'D EXPECT FROM THE VETERAN PRIME WARRIORS!
YOU'RE SO PRE-PARED.
WE'LL DIVIDE THE COMMISSION EQUALLY. THAT MEANS WE EXPECT YOU TO WORK JUST AS HARD AS WE DO.
SLOSH
SLOSH
SLOSH
SO ABOUT OUR PLANS... YOU ALL REMEMBER WHAT TO DO WHEN THE VANDEL SHOWS UP?
THE FOUR OF US WILL SEAL HIS HANDS AND LEGS, RIGHT?
RIGHT! I'LL GIVE HIM THE FATAL BLOW...
...AND TAKE REVENGE ON BEHALF OF ALL THE VILLAGERS.
GRRK

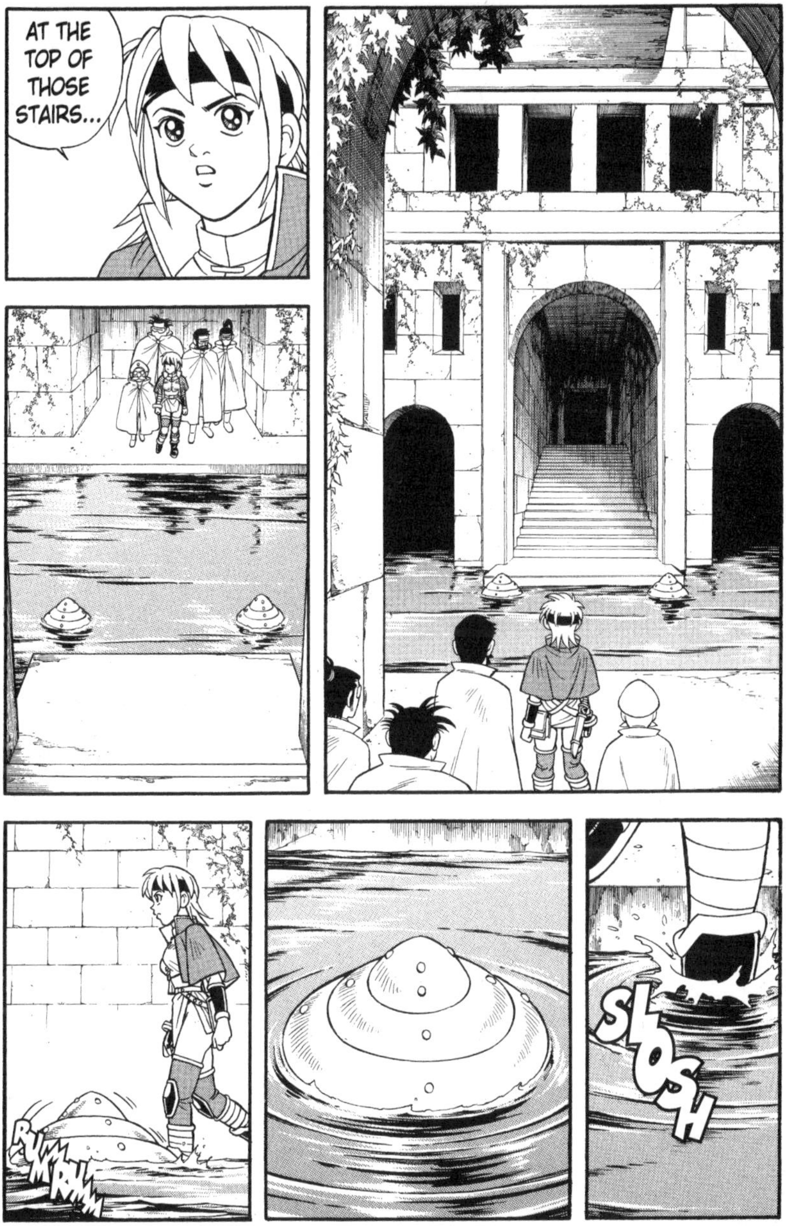
AT THE TOP OF THOSE STAIRS...
SLOSH
RUMM RUMM

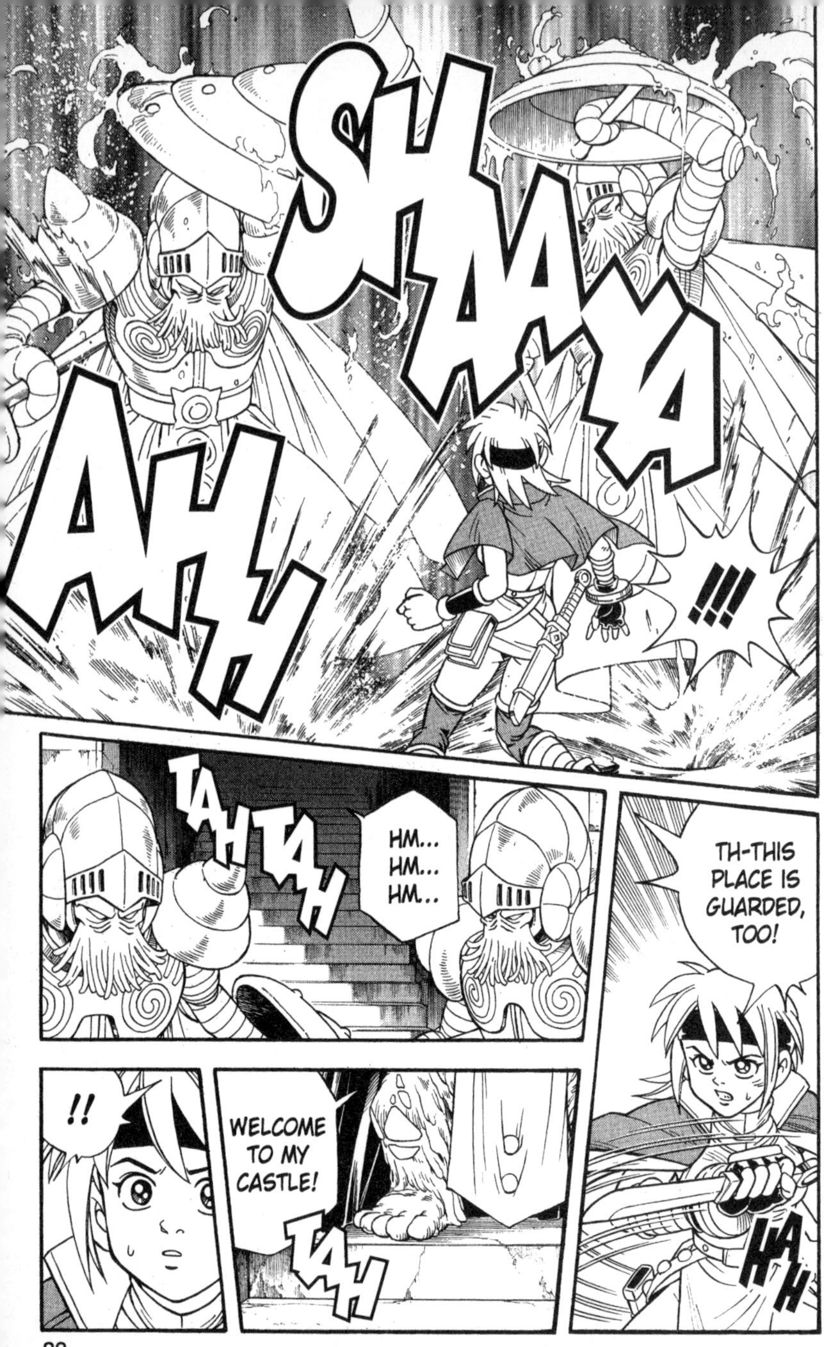
SHAAYA
AHHH
!!!!
TH-THIS PLACE IS GUARDED, TOO!
HAH
HM... HM... HM..
TAH TAH
WELCOME TO MY CASTLE!
TAH
!!

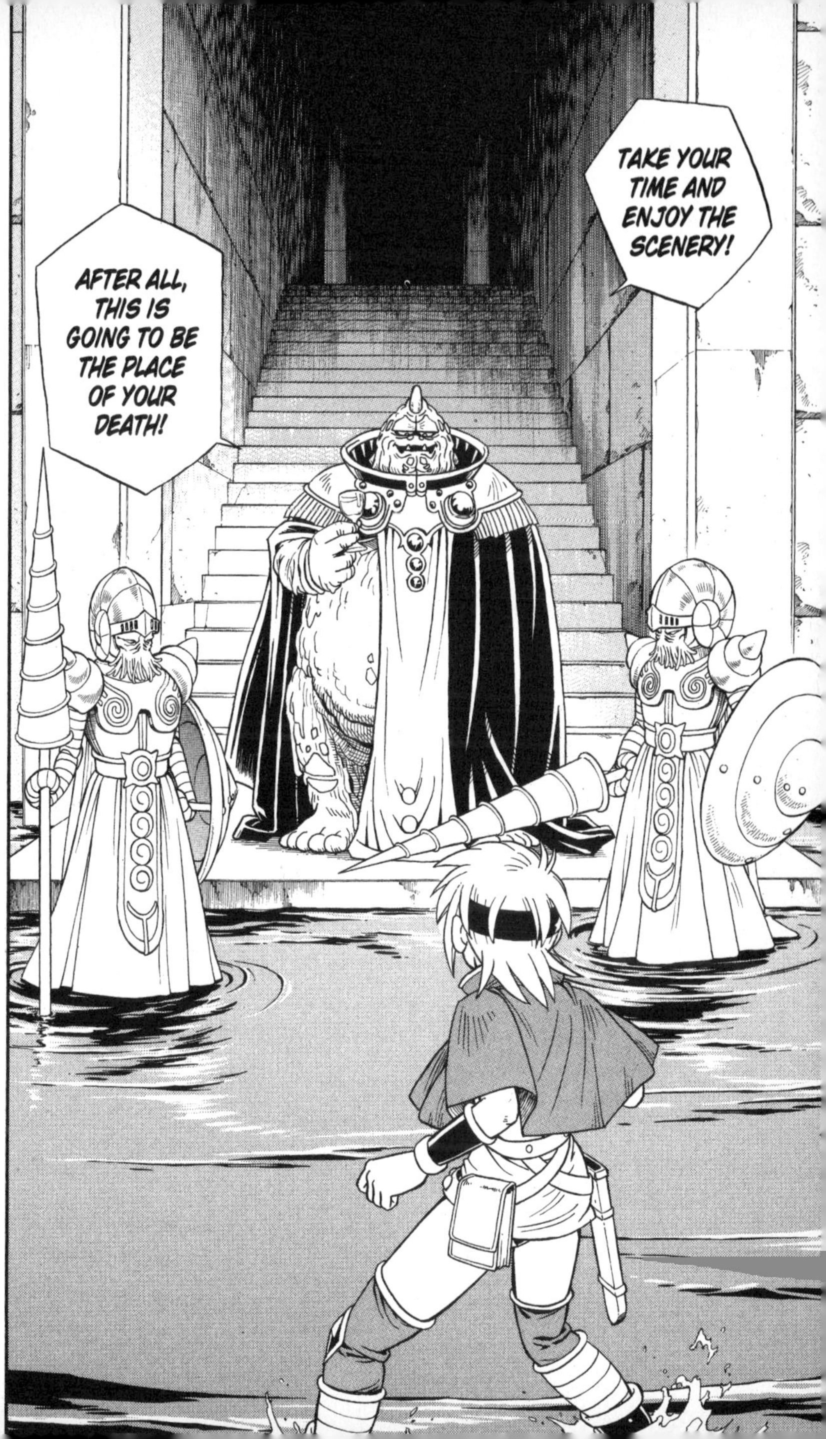
TAKE YOUR TIME AND ENJOY THE SCENERY!
AFTER ALL, THIS IS GOING TO BE THE PLACE OF YOUR DEATH!

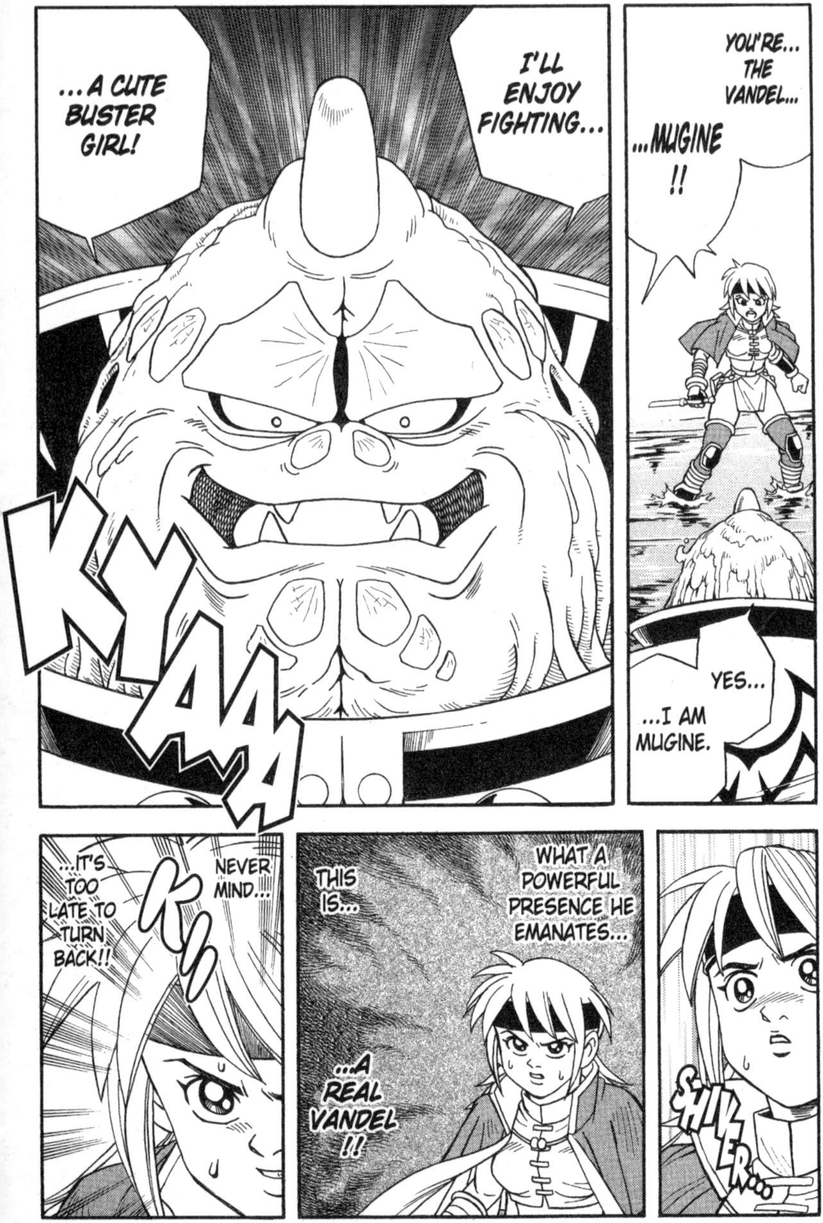
YOU'RE... THE VANDEL...
...MUGINE !!
YES...
...I AM MUGINE.
I'LL ENJOY FIGHTING...
...A CUTE BUSTER GIRL!
KYAAA
SHIVER...
WHAT A POWERFUL PRESENCE HE EMANATES...
THIS IS...
...A REAL VANDEL !!
NEVER MIND...
...IT'S TOO LATE TO TURN BACK!!
KII

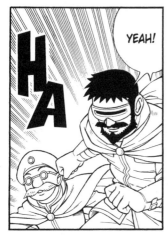

EVERYONE! WE'VE GOT NO CHOICE BUT TO FIGHT NOW!!
LET'S FOLLOW THE PLAN!!
YEAH!
HA
!!
GRAB
GRP
GRAB
WH-WHAT'RE YOU DOING?!
YOU'RE TO SEAL THE HANDS AND THE LEGS OF THE VANDEL...
GLOOP
!!!

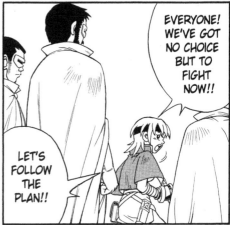

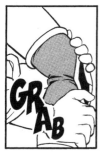

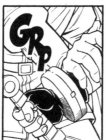

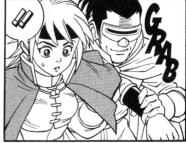

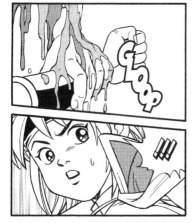

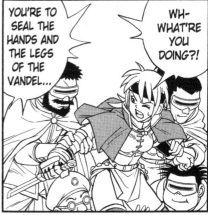

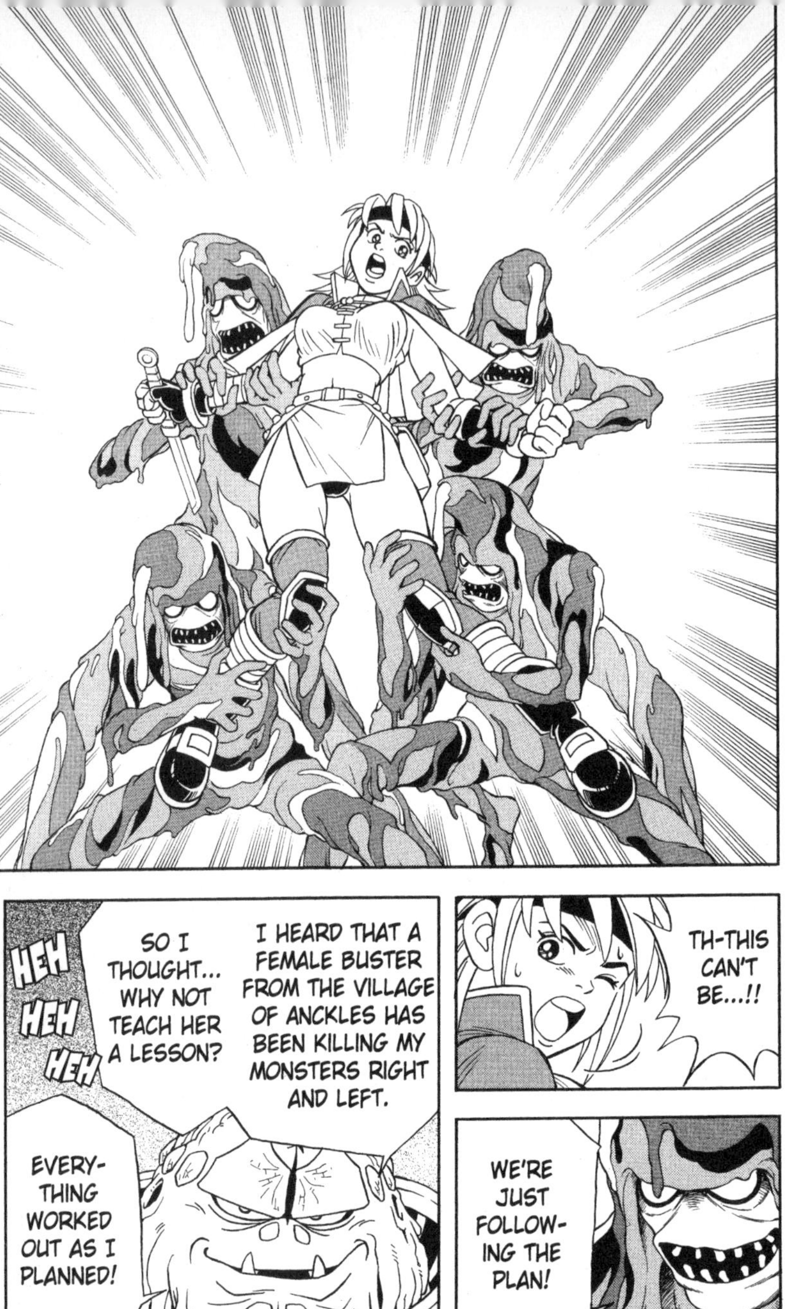
TH-THIS CAN'T BE...!!
WE'RE JUST FOLLOWING THE PLAN!
I HEARD THAT A FEMALE BUSTER FROM THE VILLAGE OF ANCKLES HAS BEEN KILLING MY MONSTERS RIGHT AND LEFT.
SO I THOUGHT... WHY NOT TEACH HER A LESSON?
HEH HEH HEH
EVERY-THING WORKED OUT AS I PLANNED!

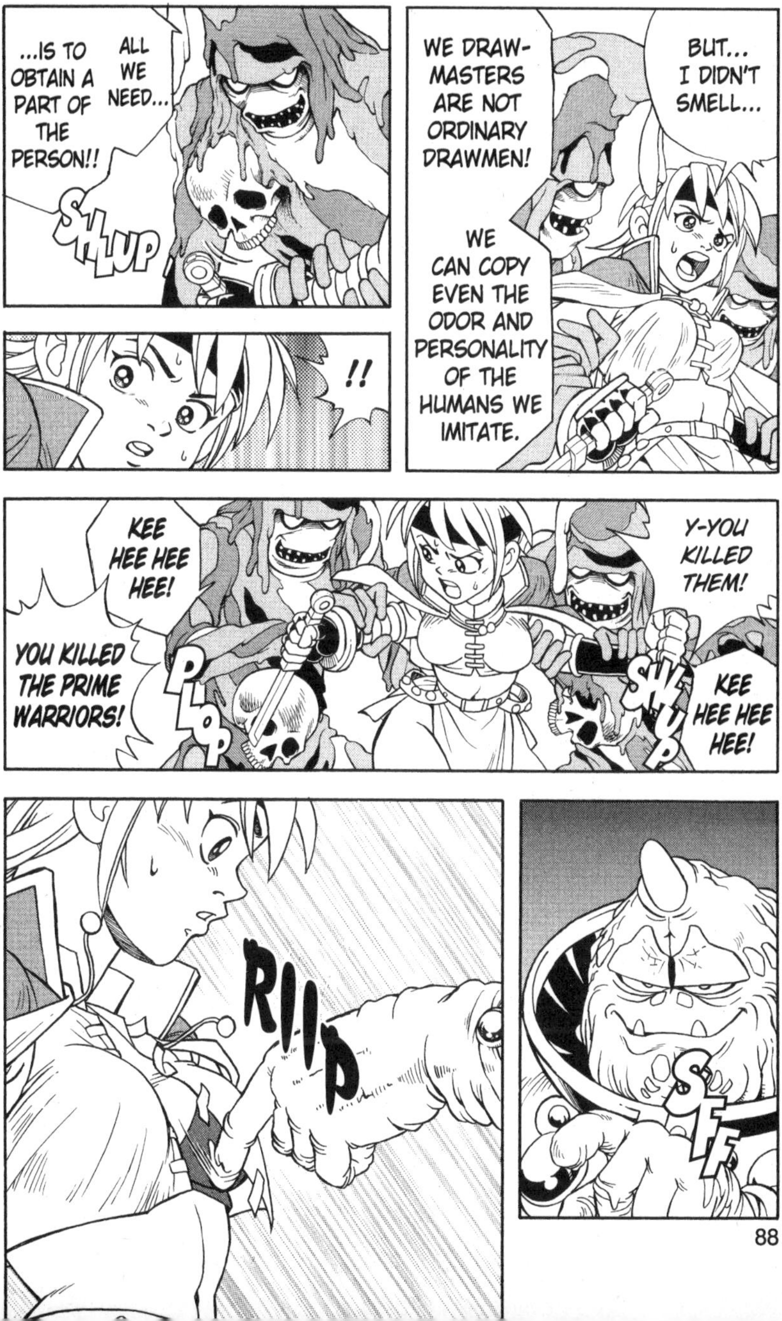
BUT... I DIDN'T SMELL...
WE DRAW-MASTERS ARE NOT ORDINARY DRAWMEN!
WE CAN COPY EVEN THE ODOR AND PERSONALITY OF THE HUMANS WE IMITATE.
ALL WE NEED...
...IS TO OBTAIN A PART OF THE PERSON!!
SHLUP
!!
Y-YOU KILLED THEM!
KEE HEE HEE HEE!
SHLUP
KEE HEE HEE HEE!
YOU KILLED THE PRIME WARRIORS!
PLOP
SFF
RIIP

READ THIS WAY

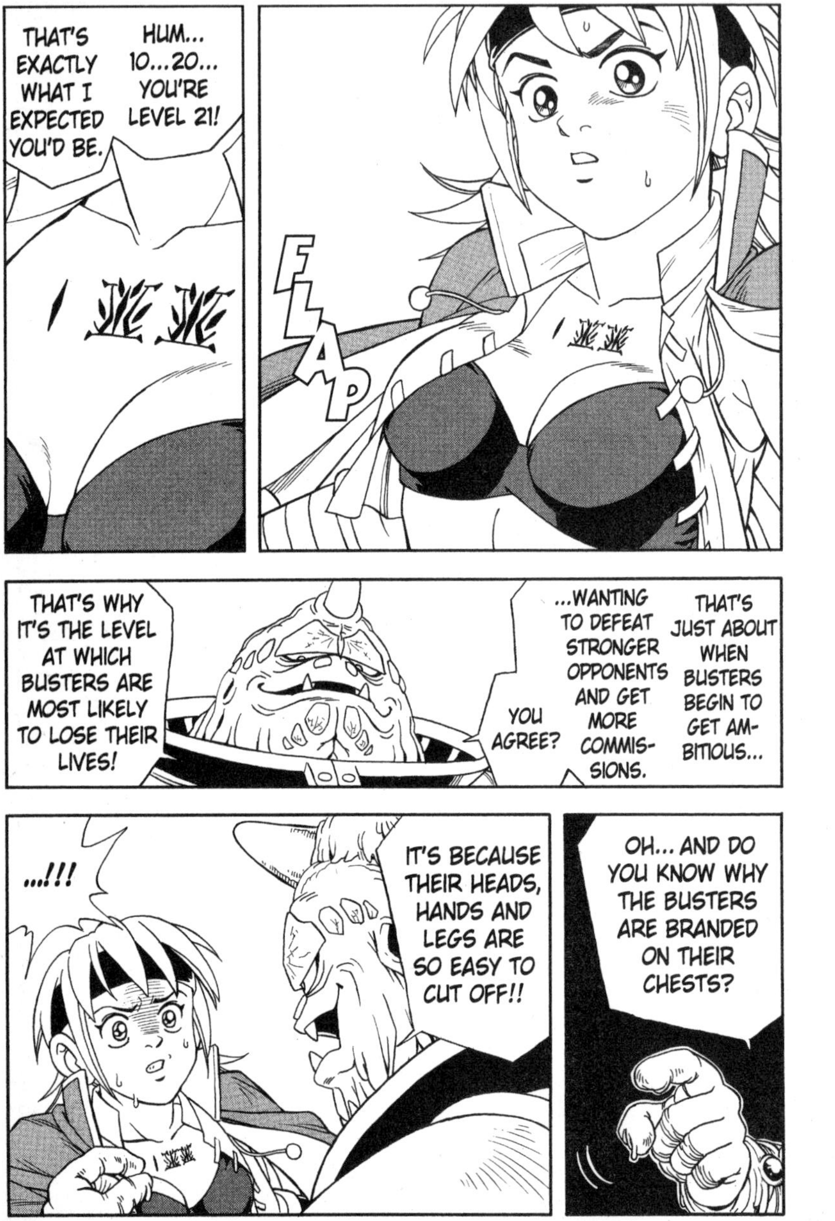
FLAP
HUM... 10...20... YOU'RE LEVEL 21!
THAT'S EXACTLY WHAT I EXPECTED YOU'D BE.
THAT'S JUST ABOUT WHEN BUSTERS BEGIN TO GET AM-BITIOUS...
...WANTING TO DEFEAT STRONGER OPPONENTS AND GET MORE COMMIS-SIONS.
YOU AGREE?
THAT'S WHY IT'S THE LEVEL AT WHICH BUSTERS ARE MOST LIKELY TO LOSE THEIR LIVES!
OH... AND DO YOU KNOW WHY THE BUSTERS ARE BRANDED ON THEIR CHESTS?
IT'S BECAUSE THEIR HEADS, HANDS AND LEGS ARE SO EASY TO CUT OFF!!
...!!!

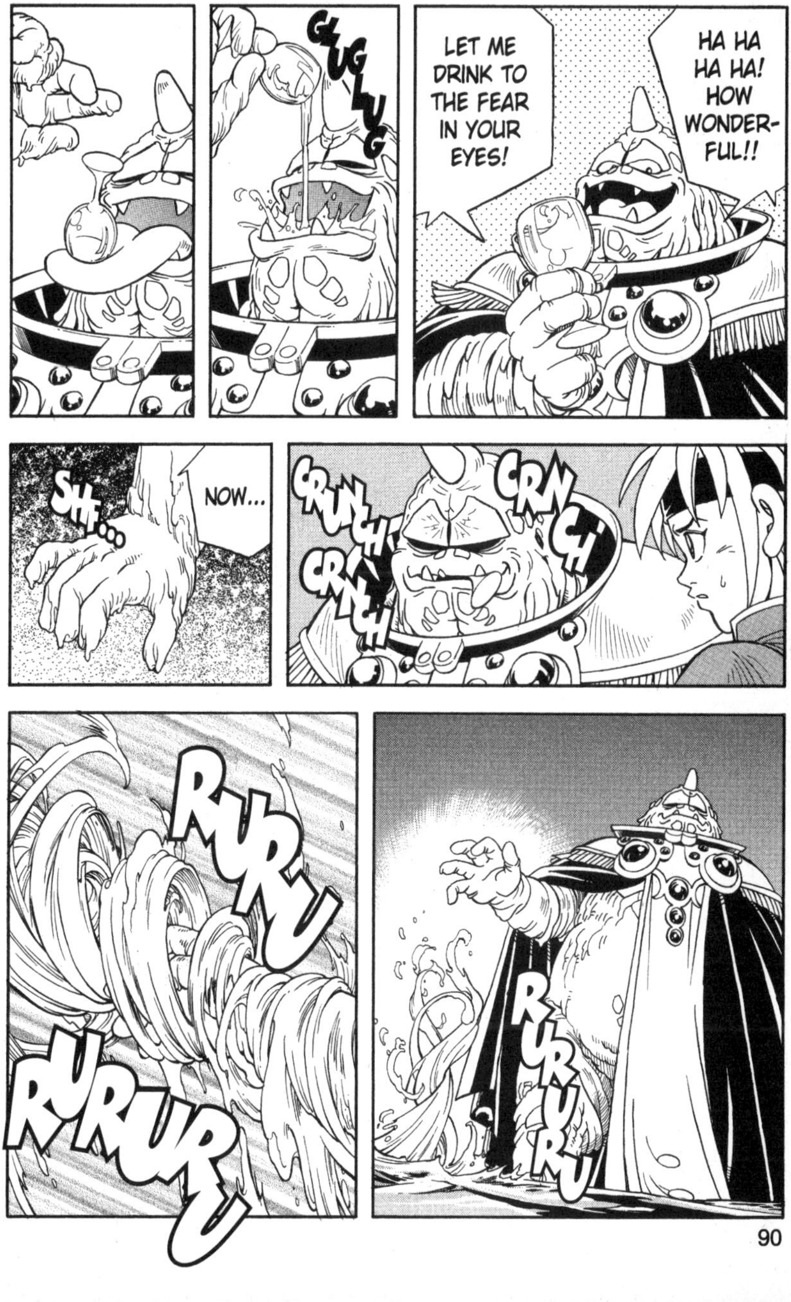
HA HA HA HA! HOW WONDER-FUL!!
LET ME DRINK TO THE FEAR IN YOUR EYES!
GLUGLUG
CRNCH
CRUNCH
CRNCH
NOW...
SHF...
RURURURU
RURU
RURURU

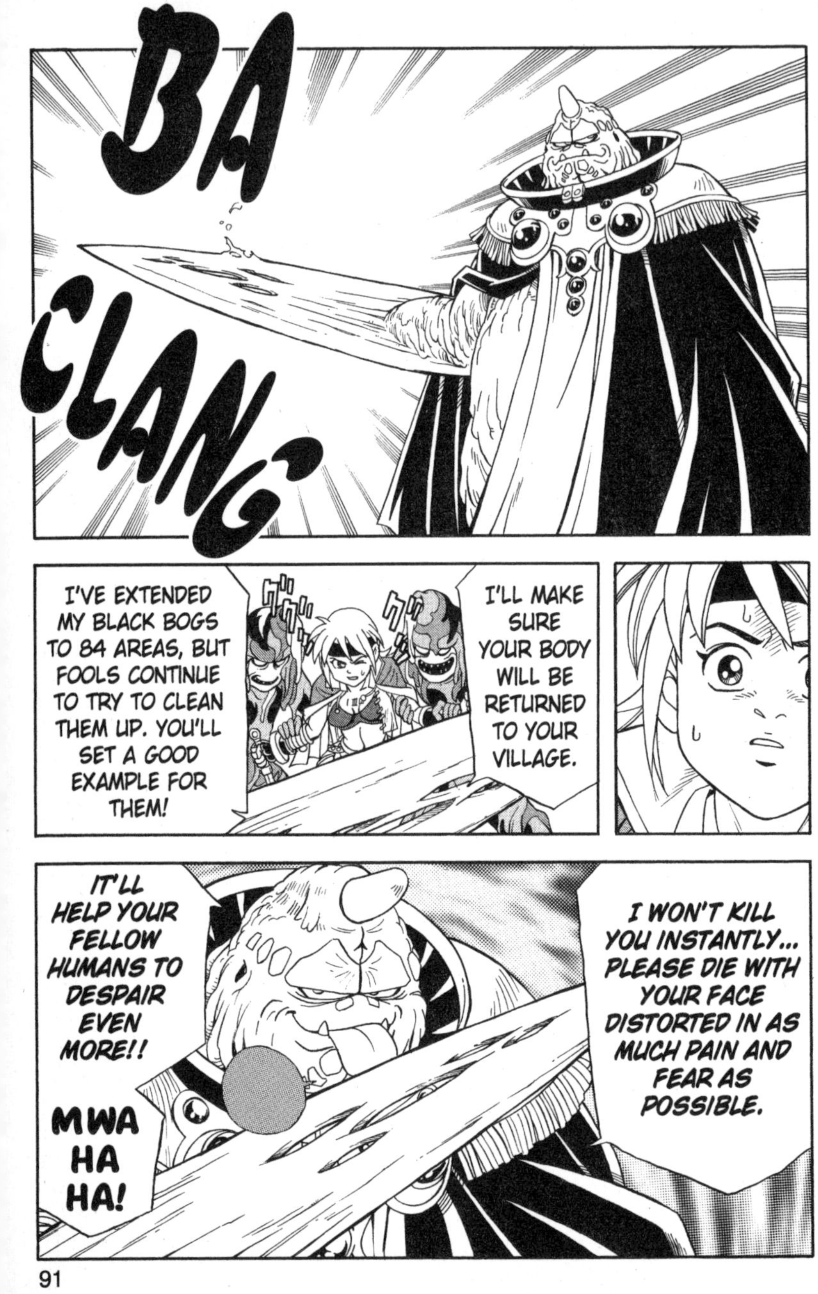
BA
CLANG
I'LL MAKE SURE YOUR BODY WILL BE RETURNED TO YOUR VILLAGE.
I'VE EXTENDED MY BLACK BOGS TO 84 AREAS, BUT FOOLS CONTINUE TO TRY TO CLEAN THEM UP. YOU'LL SET A GOOD EXAMPLE FOR THEM!
I WON'T KILL YOU INSTANTLY... PLEASE DIE WITH YOUR FACE DISTORTED IN AS MUCH PAIN AND FEAR AS POSSIBLE.
IT'LL HELP YOUR FELLOW HUMANS TO DESPAIR EVEN MORE!!
MWA HA HA!

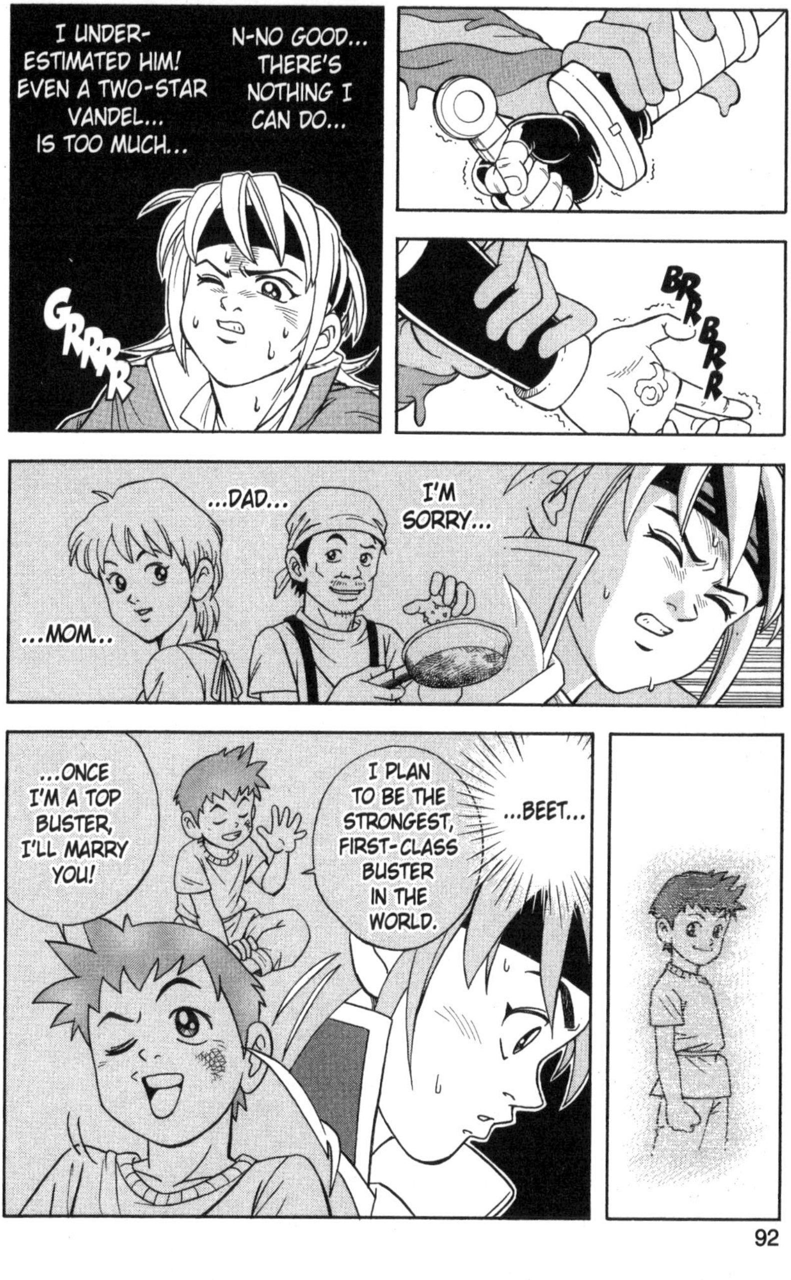
BRRRBRRR
N-NO GOOD... THERE'S NOTHING I CAN DO...
I UNDER-ESTIMATED HIM! EVEN A TWO-STAR VANDEL... IS TOO MUCH...
GRRRR
I'M SORRY...
...DAD...
...MOM...
...BEET...
I PLAN TO BE THE STRONGEST, FIRST-CLASS BUSTER IN THE WORLD.
...ONCE I'M A TOP BUSTER, I'LL MARRY YOU!

READ THIS WAY

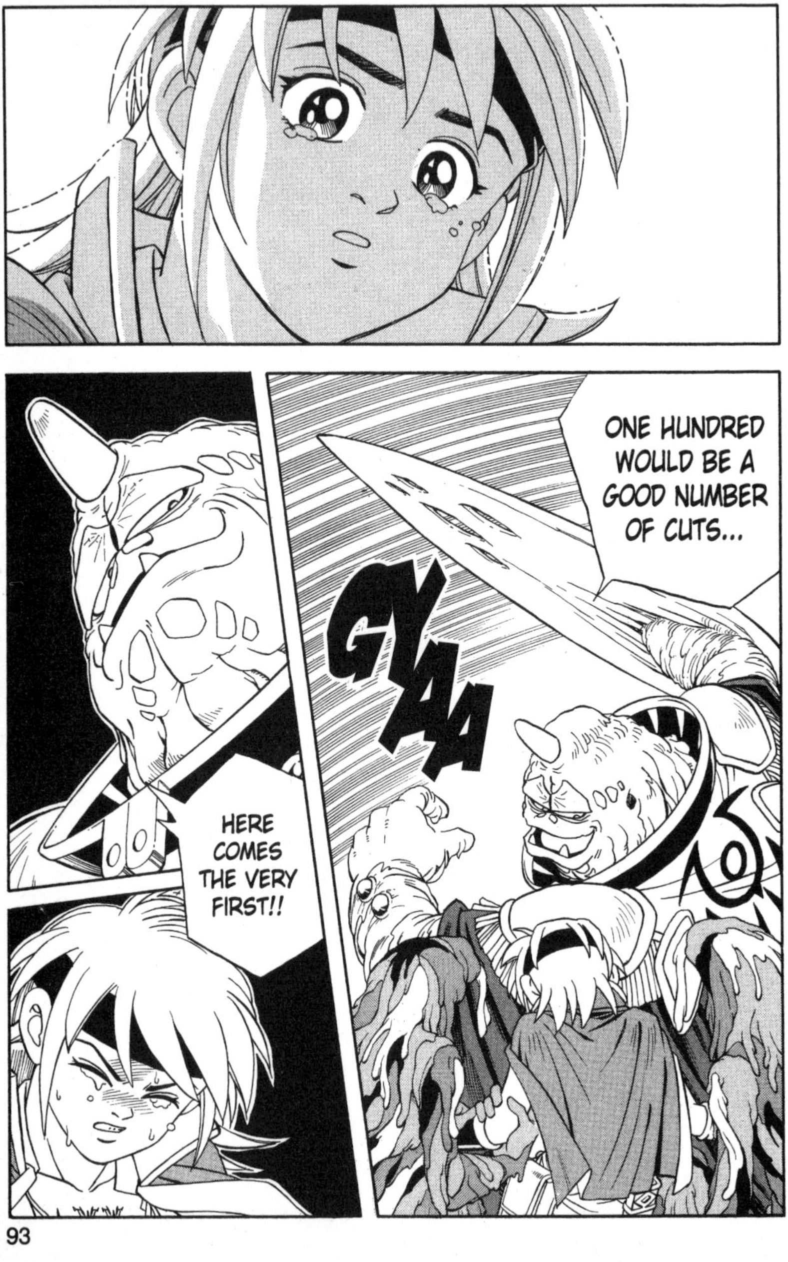
ONE HUNDRED WOULD BE A GOOD NUMBER OF CUTS...
GYAAA
HERE COMES THE VERY FIRST!!

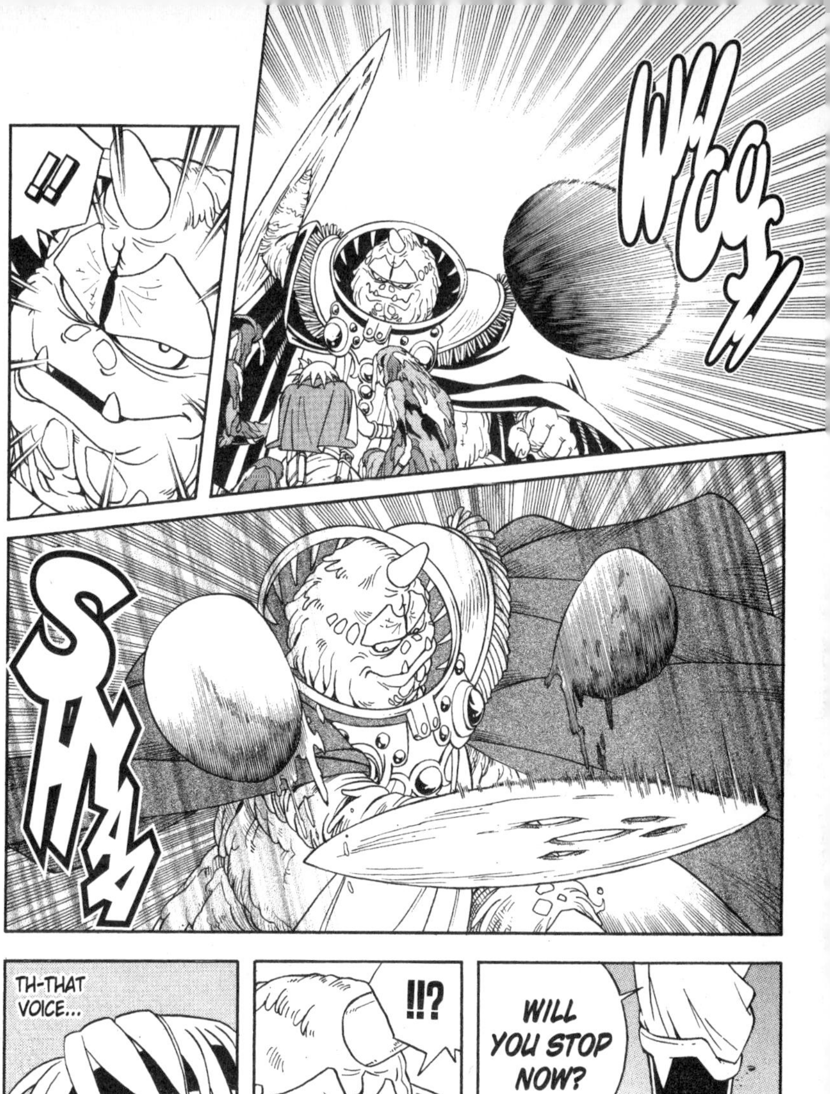
WHOOSH
!!
SHAA
WILL YOU STOP NOW?
TAK
!!?
TH-THAT VOICE...

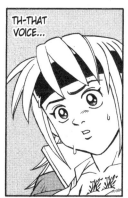

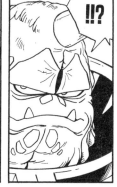

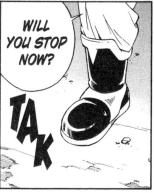

READ THIS WAY

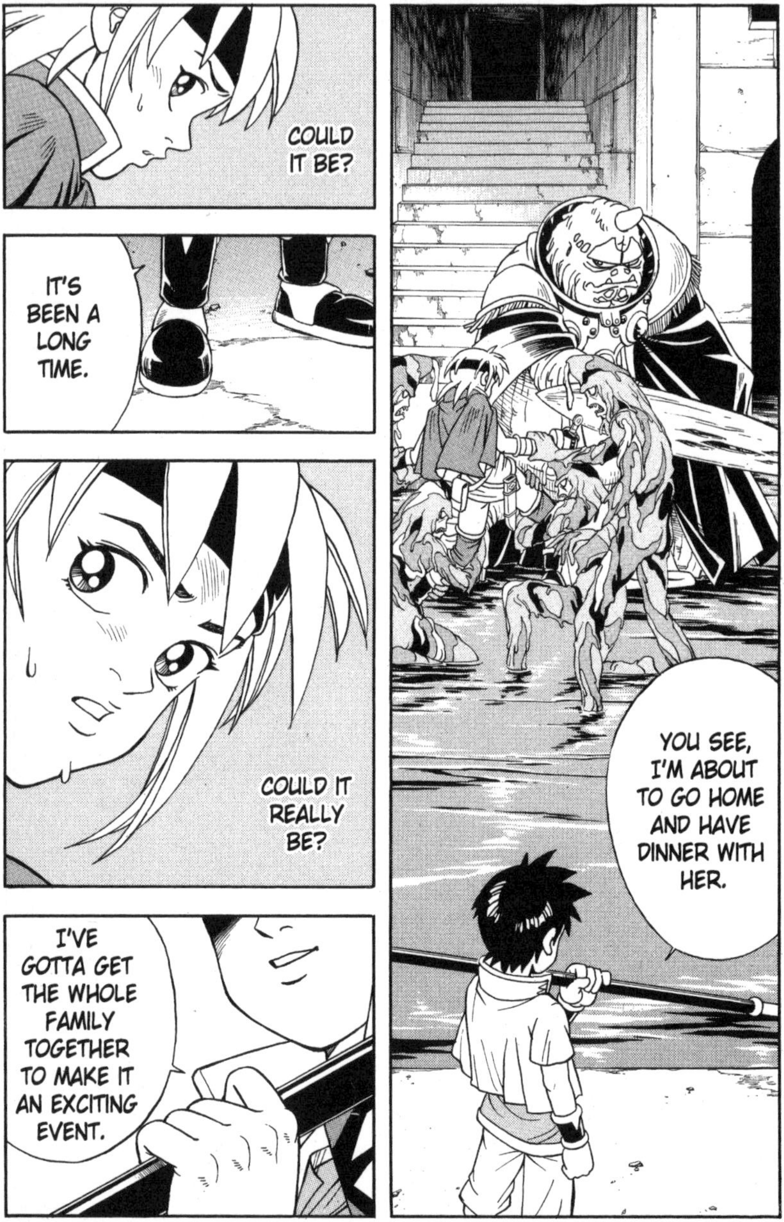
YOU SEE, I'M ABOUT TO GO HOME AND HAVE DINNER WITH HER.
COULD IT BE?
IT'S BEEN A LONG TIME.
COULD IT REALLY BE?
I'VE GOTTA GET THE WHOLE FAMILY TOGETHER TO MAKE IT AN EXCITING EVENT.

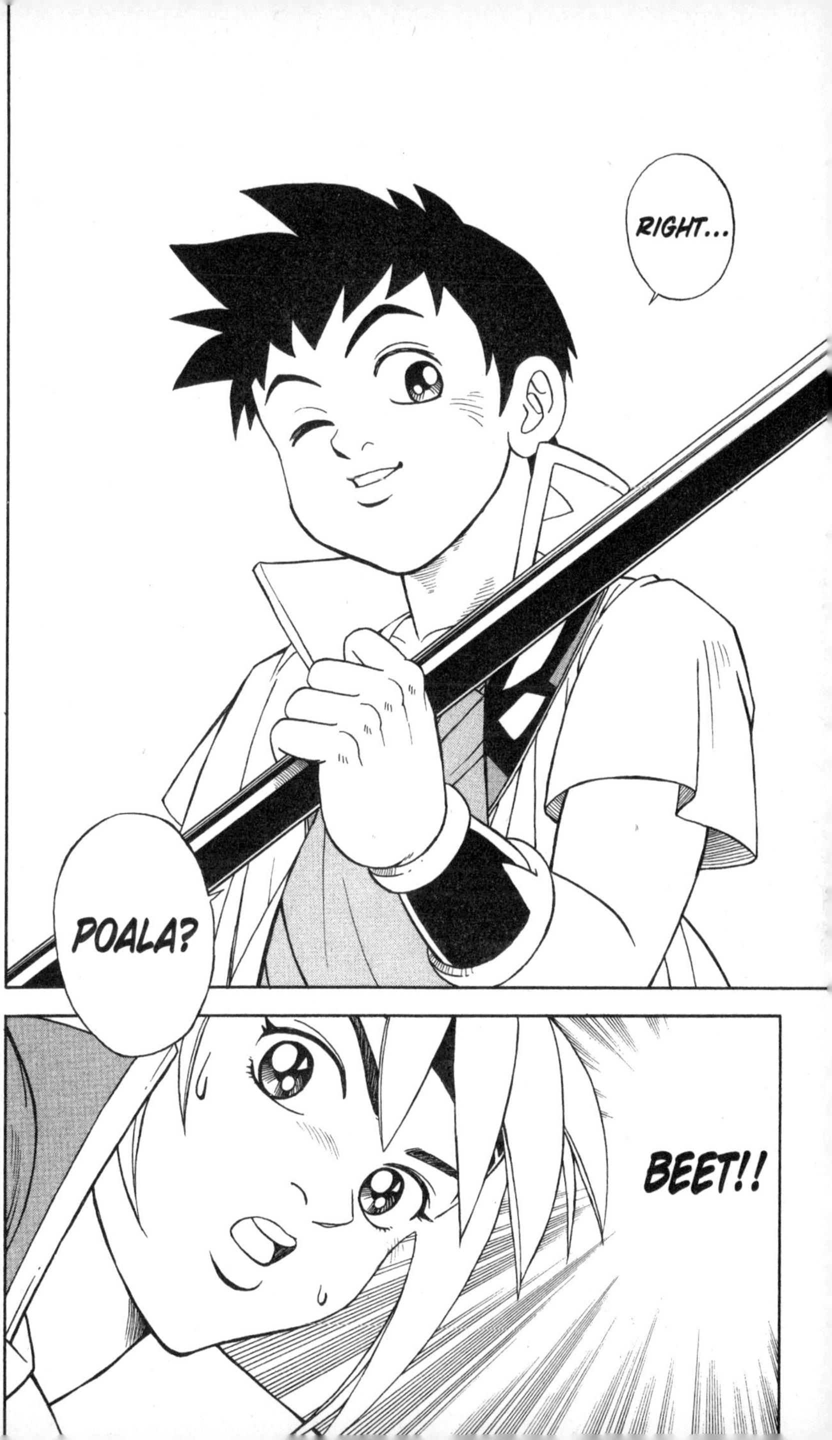
RIGHT...
POALA?
BEET!!

READ THIS WAY

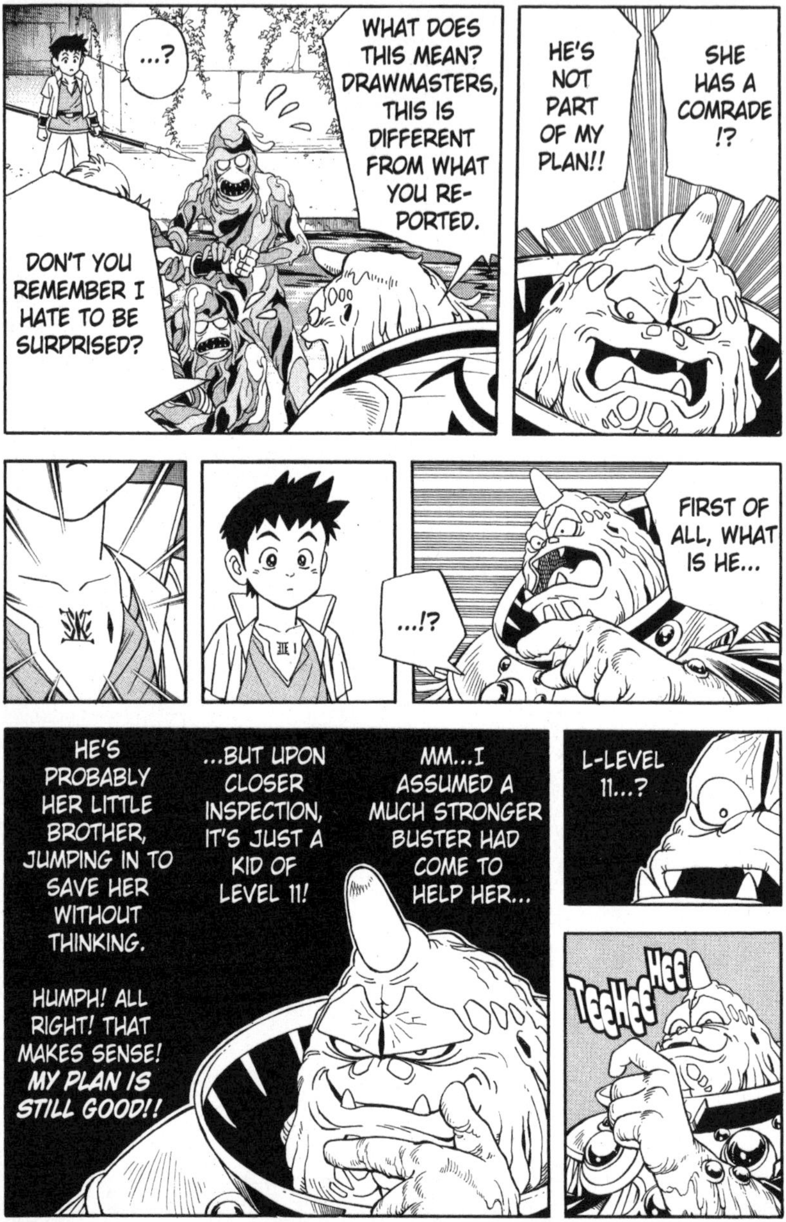
SHE HAS A COMRADE!?
HE'S NOT PART OF MY PLAN!!
WHAT DOES THIS MEAN? DRAWMASTERS, THIS IS DIFFERENT FROM WHAT YOU RE-PORTED.
...?
DON'T YOU REMEMBER I HATE TO BE SURPRISED?
FIRST OF ALL, WHAT IS HE...
...!?
L-LEVEL 11...?
TEEHEEHEE
MM...I ASSUMED A MUCH STRONGER BUSTER HAD COME TO HELP HER...
...BUT UPON CLOSER INSPECTION, IT'S JUST A KID OF LEVEL 11!
HE'S PROBABLY HER LITTLE BROTHER, JUMPING IN TO SAVE HER WITHOUT THINKING.
HUMPH! ALL RIGHT! THAT MAKES SENSE! MY PLAN IS STILL GOOD!!

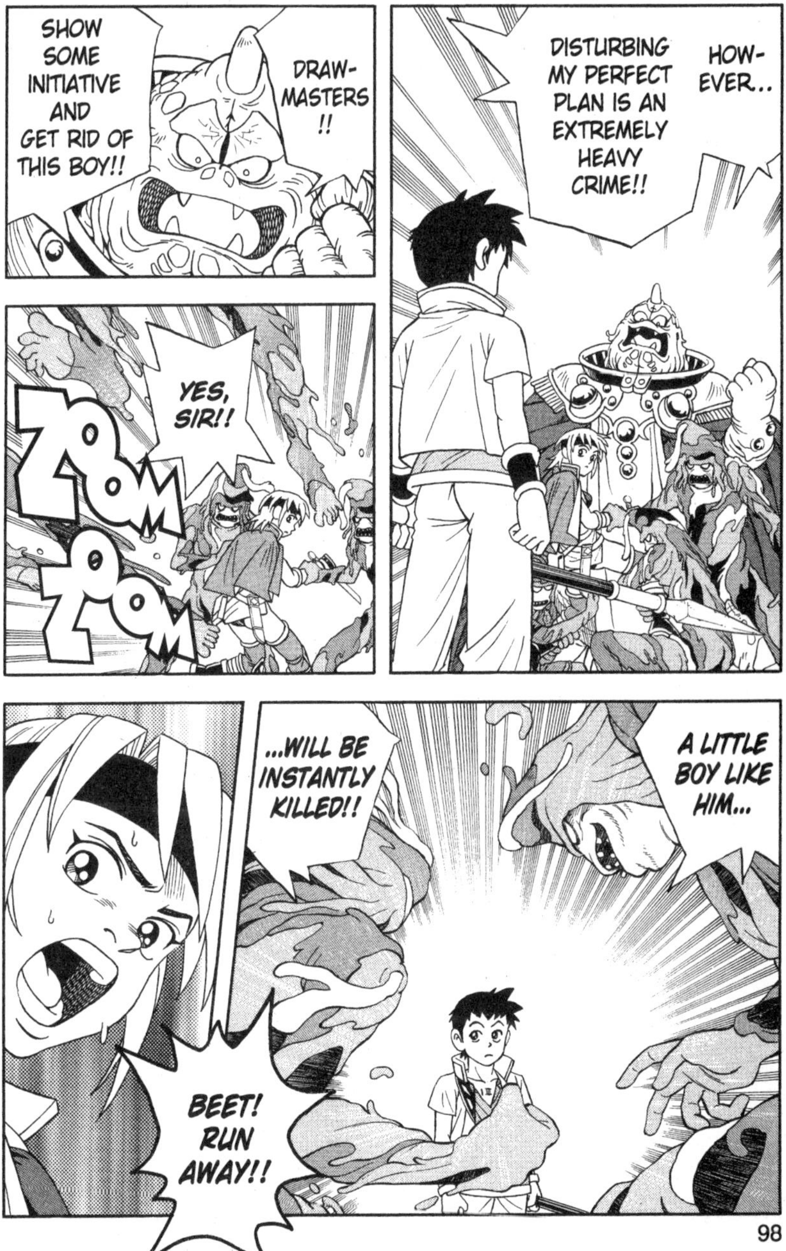
HOW-EVER...
DISTURBING MY PERFECT PLAN IS AN EXTREMELY HEAVY CRIME!!
DRAW-MASTERS!!
SHOW SOME INITIATIVE AND GET RID OF THIS BOY!!
YES, SIR!!
ZOOM
ZOOM
A LITTLE BOY LIKE HIM...
...WILL BE INSTANTLY KILLED!!
BEET! RUN AWAY!!

READ THIS WAY

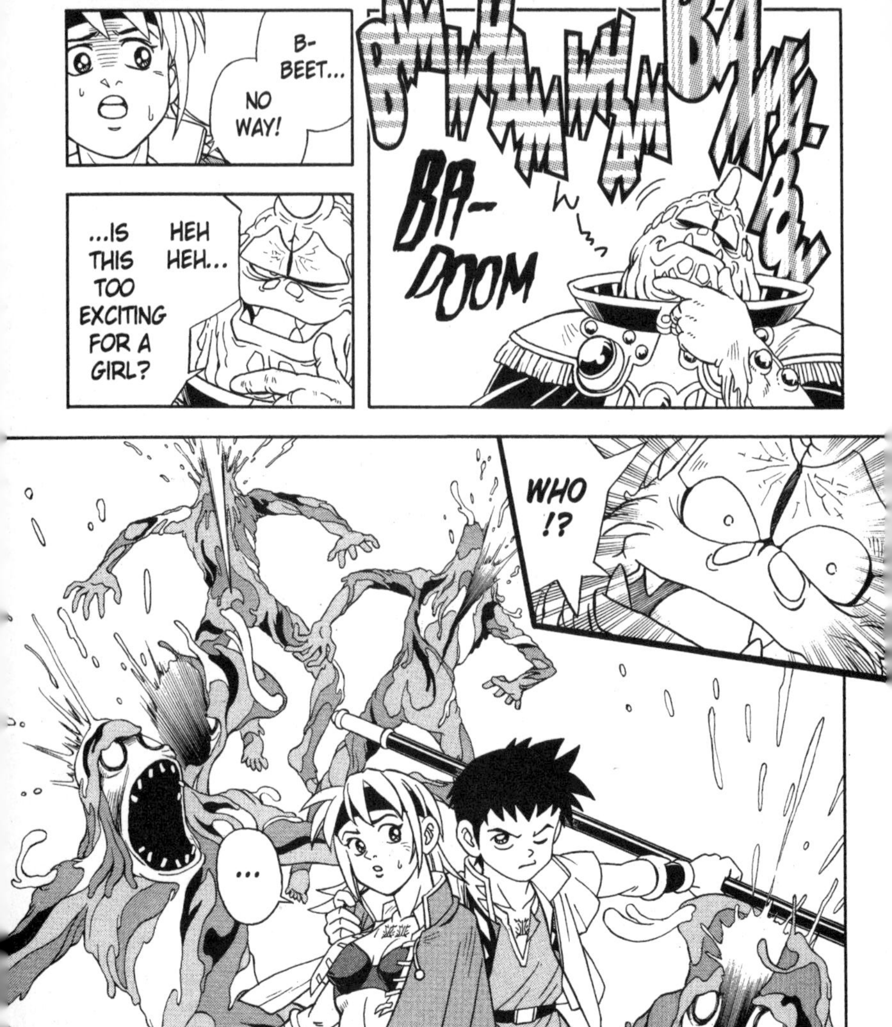
BA- DOOM
B- BEET...
NO WAY!
HEH HEH...
...IS THIS TOO EXCITING FOR A GIRL?
WHO !?
...

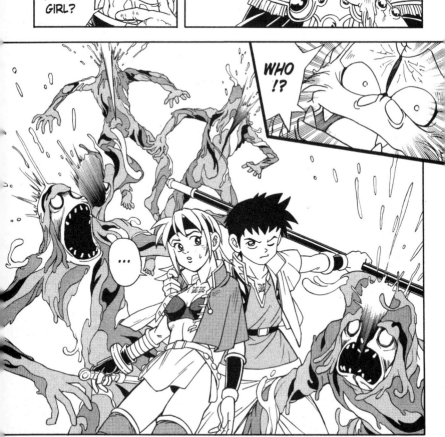

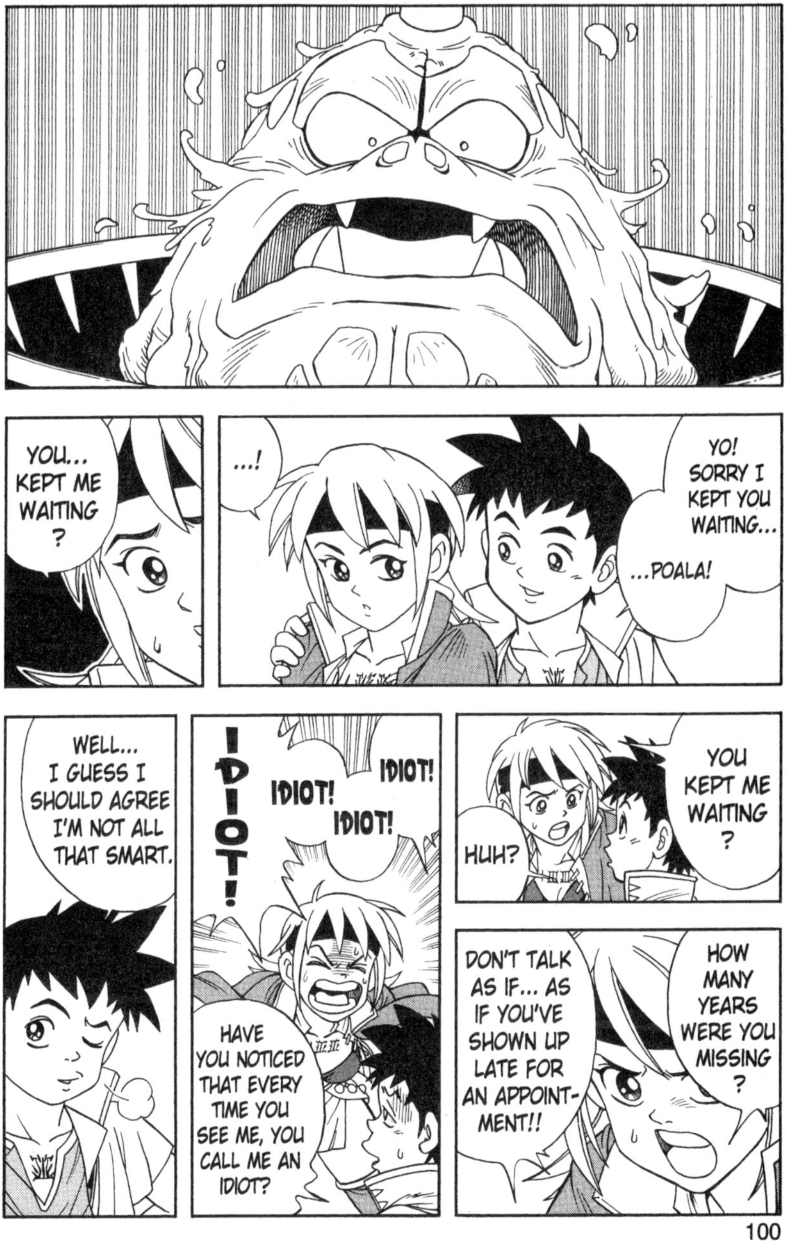
YO! SORRY I KEPT YOU WAITING...
...POALA!
...!
YOU... KEPT ME WAITING?
YOU KEPT ME WAITING?
HUH?
HOW MANY YEARS WERE YOU MISSING?
DON'T TALK AS IF... AS IF YOU'VE SHOWN UP LATE FOR AN APPOINT-MENT!!
IDIOT!
IDIOT!
IDIOT!
IDIOT!
HAVE YOU NOTICED THAT EVERY TIME YOU SEE ME, YOU CALL ME AN IDIOT?
WELL... I GUESS I SHOULD AGREE I'M NOT ALL THAT SMART.

READ THIS WAY

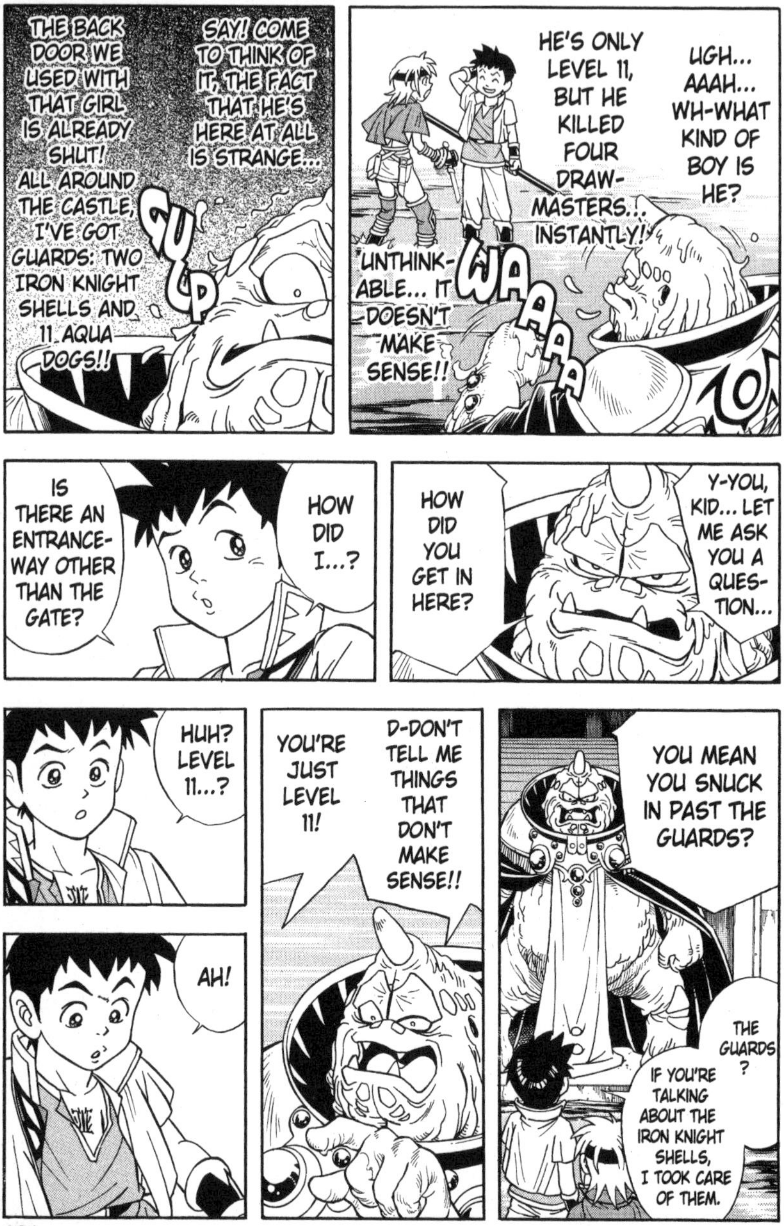
UGH... AAAH... WH-WHAT KIND OF BOY IS HE?
HE'S ONLY LEVEL 11, BUT HE KILLED FOUR DRAW-MASTERS... INSTANTLY!
WAAAAA
UNTHINKABLE... IT DOESN'T MAKE SENSE!!
SAY! COME TO THINK OF IT, THE FACT THAT HE'S HERE AT ALL IS STRANGE...
THE BACK DOOR WE USED WITH THAT GIRL IS ALREADY SHUT! ALL AROUND THE CASTLE, I'VE GOT GUARDS: TWO IRON KNIGHT SHELLS AND 11 AQUA DOGS!!
GULP
Y-YOU, KID... LET ME ASK YOU A QUESTION...
HOW DID YOU GET IN HERE?
HOW DID I...?
IS THERE AN ENTRANCEWAY OTHER THAN THE GATE?
YOU MEAN YOU SNUCK IN PAST THE GUARDS?
THE GUARDS?
IF YOU'RE TALKING ABOUT THE IRON KNIGHT SHELLS, I TOOK CARE OF THEM.
D-DON'T TELL ME THINGS THAT DON'T MAKE SENSE!!
YOU'RE JUST LEVEL 11!
HUH? LEVEL 11...?
AH!

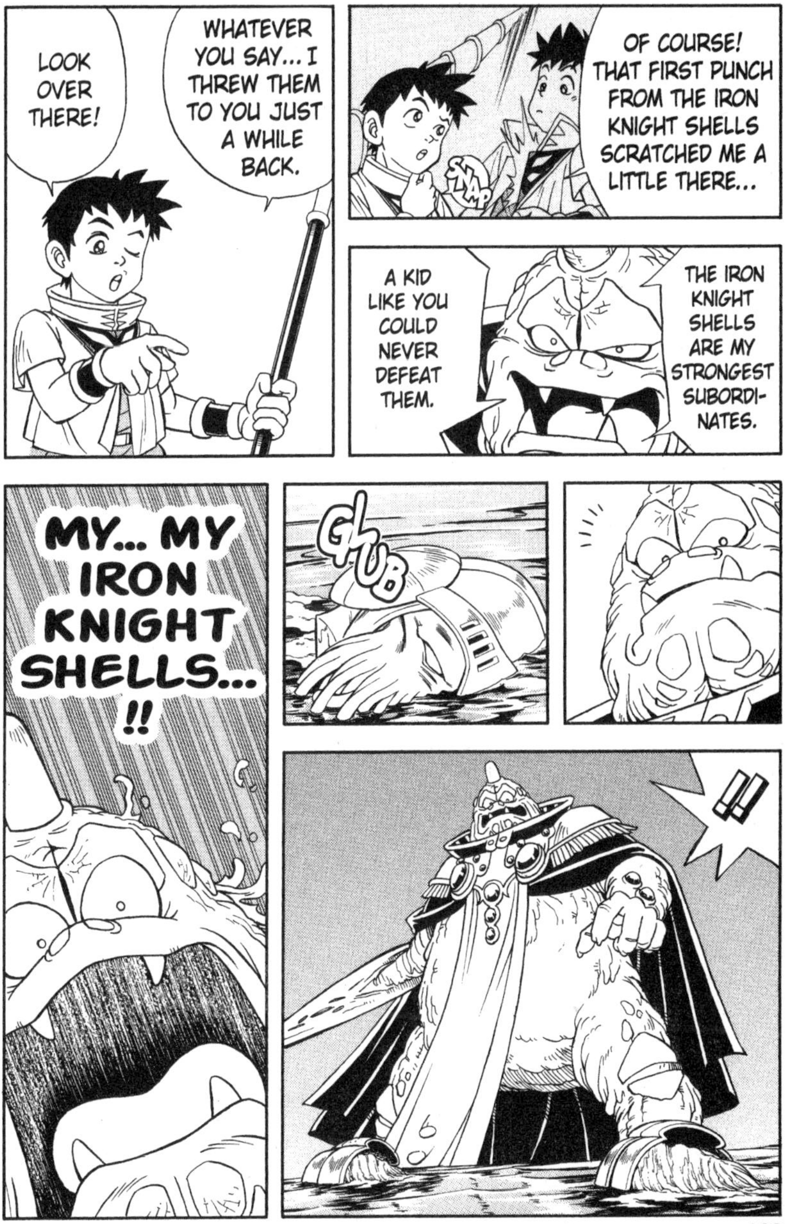

OF COURSE! THAT FIRST PUNCH FROM THE IRON KNIGHT SHELLS SCRATCHED ME A LITTLE THERE...
SNAP
THE IRON KNIGHT SHELLS ARE MY STRONGEST SUBORDI-NATES.
A KID LIKE YOU COULD NEVER DEFEAT THEM.
WHATEVER YOU SAY... I THREW THEM TO YOU JUST A WHILE BACK.
LOOK OVER THERE!
GLUB
!!
MY... MY IRON KNIGHT SHELLS... !!

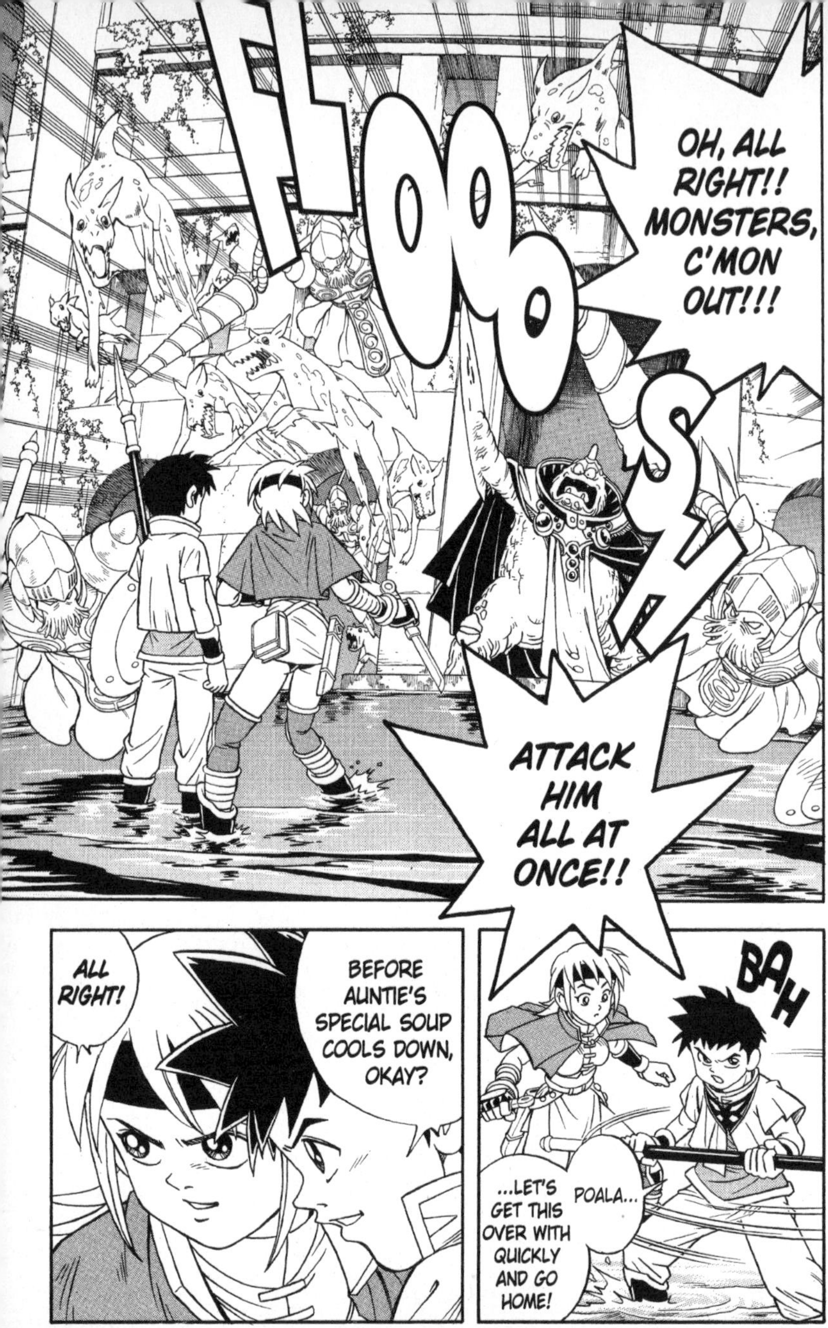
OH, ALL RIGHT!! MONSTERS, C'MON OUT!!!
FLOOOSH
ATTACK HIM ALL AT ONCE!!
BAH
POALA...
...LET'S GET THIS OVER WITH QUICKLY AND GO HOME!
BEFORE AUNTIE'S SPECIAL SOUP COOLS DOWN, OKAY?
ALL RIGHT!

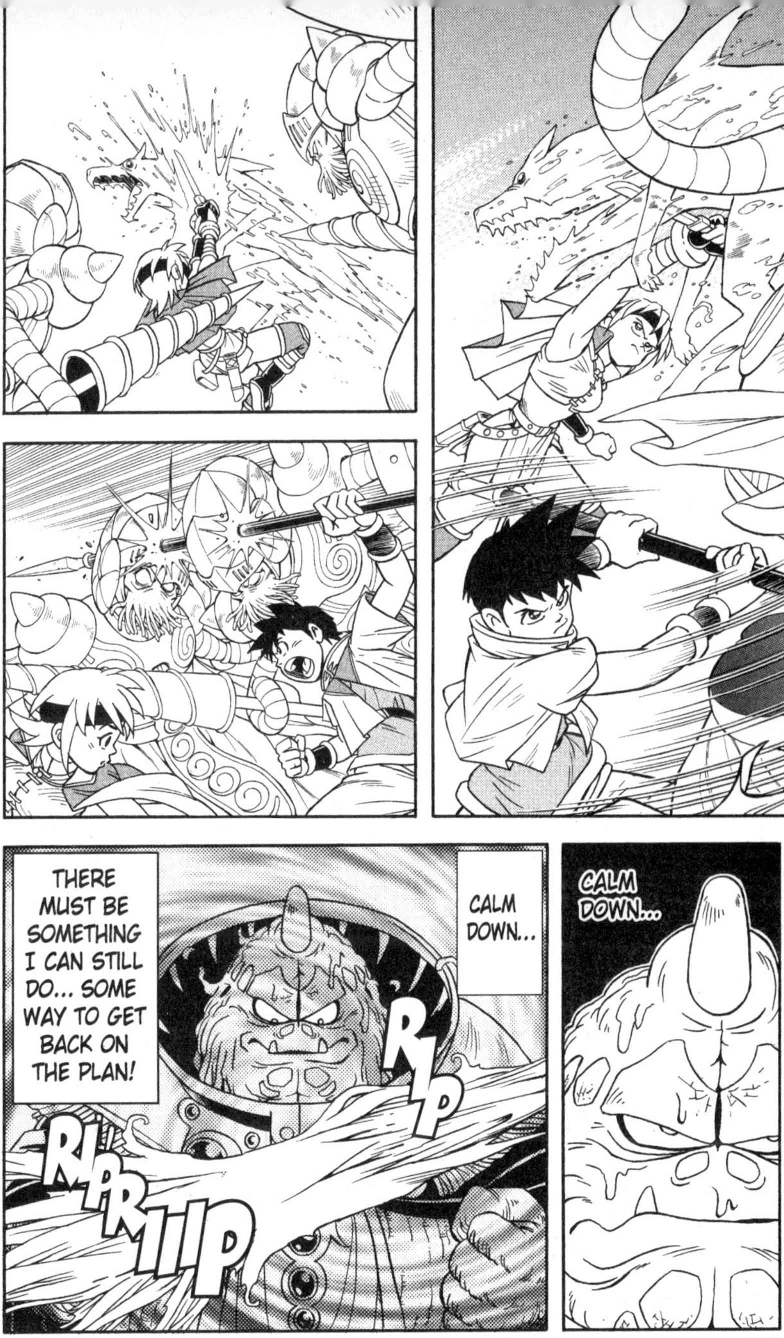
CALM DOWN...
CALM DOWN...
THERE MUST BE SOMETHING I CAN STILL DO... SOME WAY TO GET BACK ON THE PLAN!
RIP
RIPRIIIP

READ THIS WAY

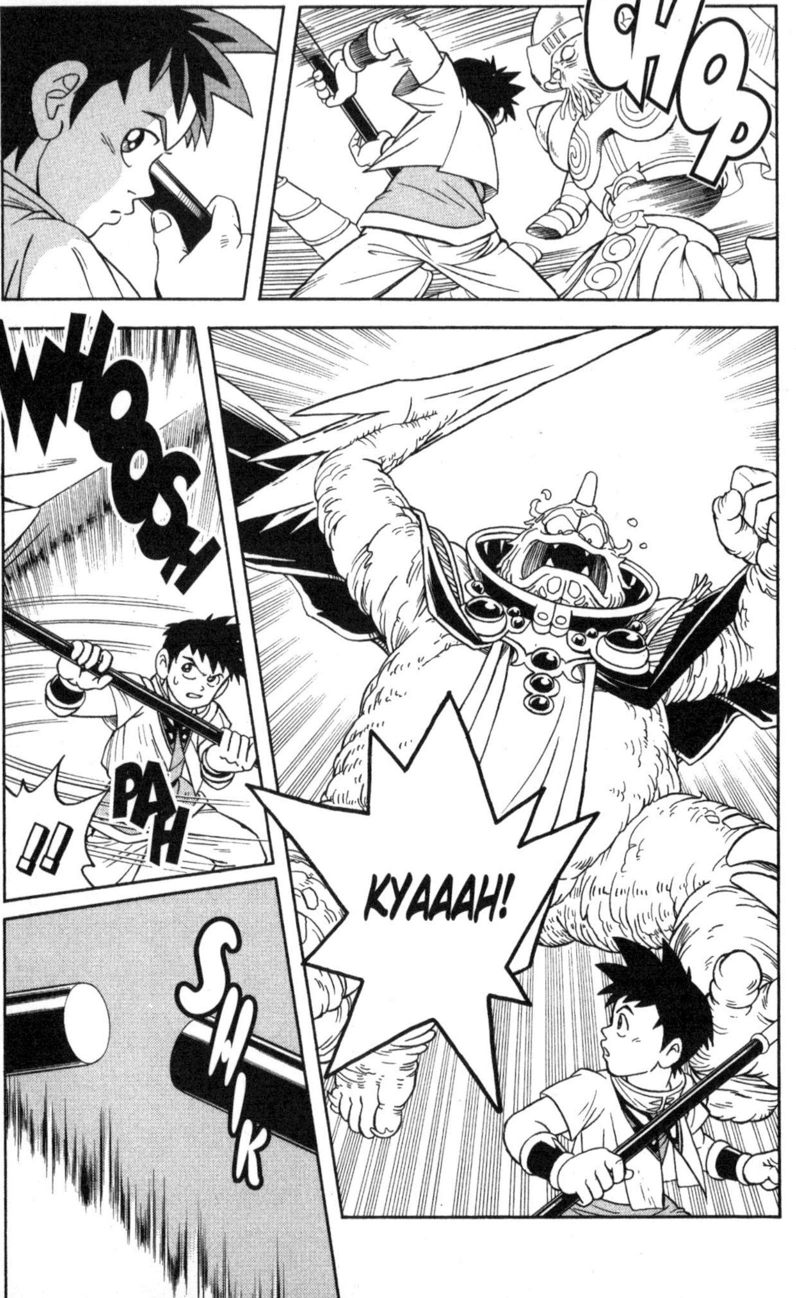
CHOP
KYAAAH!
WHOOSH
PAH!!
SHWIK

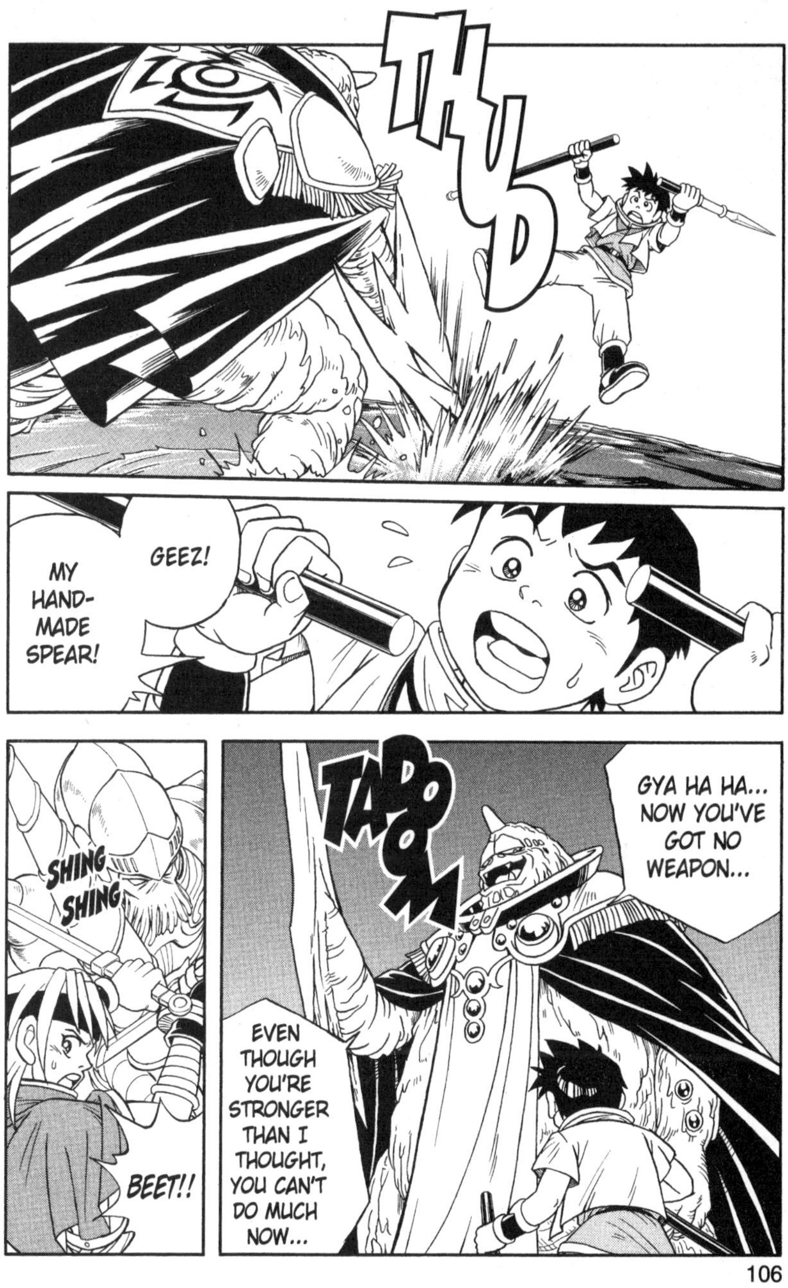
THUD
GEEZ!
MY HAND-MADE SPEAR!
TADOOM
GYA HA HA... NOW YOU'VE GOT NO WEAPON...
EVEN THOUGH YOU'RE STRONGER THAN I THOUGHT, YOU CAN'T DO MUCH NOW...
SHING SHING
BEET!!

READ THIS WAY

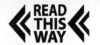

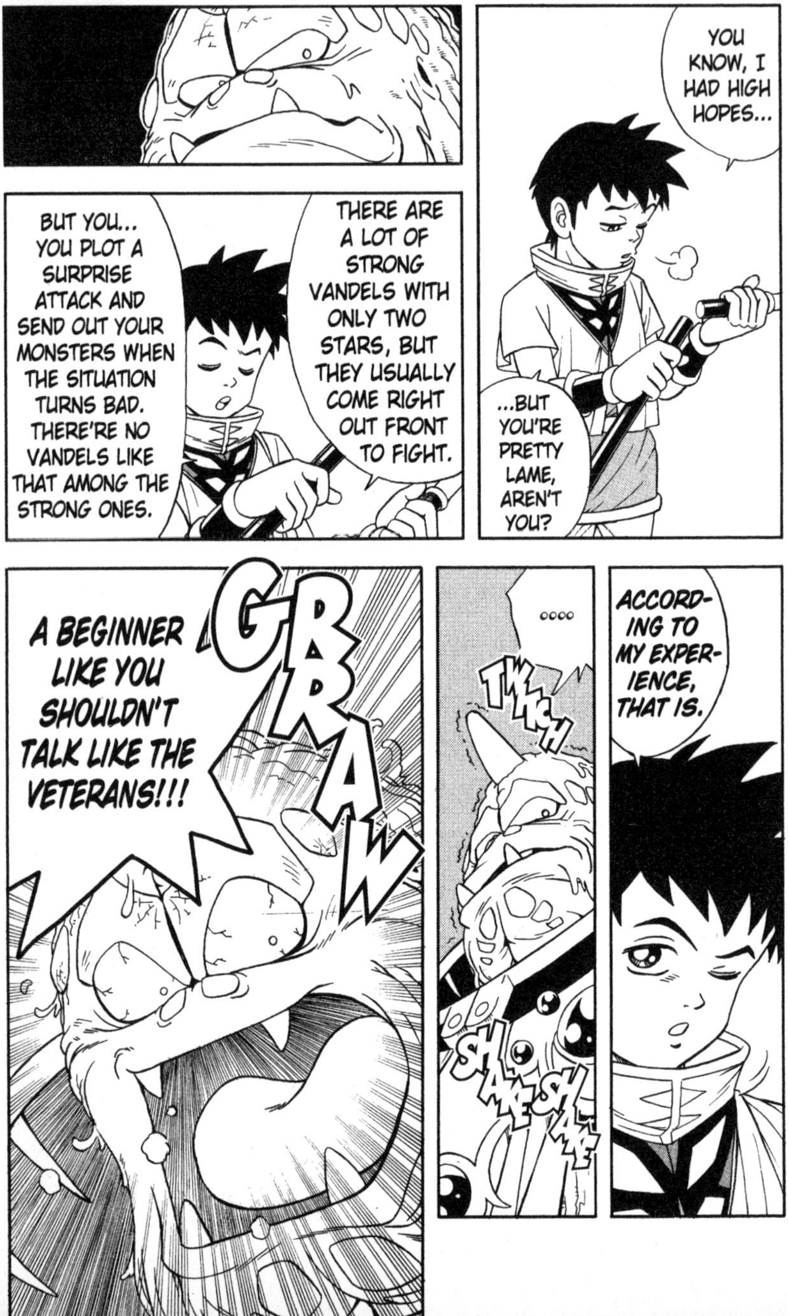
YOU KNOW, I HAD HIGH HOPES...
...BUT YOU'RE PRETTY LAME, AREN'T YOU?
THERE ARE A LOT OF STRONG VANDELS WITH ONLY TWO STARS, BUT THEY USUALLY COME RIGHT OUT FRONT TO FIGHT.
BUT YOU... YOU PLOT A SURPRISE ATTACK AND SEND OUT YOUR MONSTERS WHEN THE SITUATION TURNS BAD. THERE'RE NO VANDELS LIKE THAT AMONG THE STRONG ONES.
ACCORDING TO MY EXPERIENCE, THAT IS.
....
TWITCH
SHAKE SHAKE
GRAW
A BEGINNER LIKE YOU SHOULDN'T TALK LIKE THE VETERANS!!!

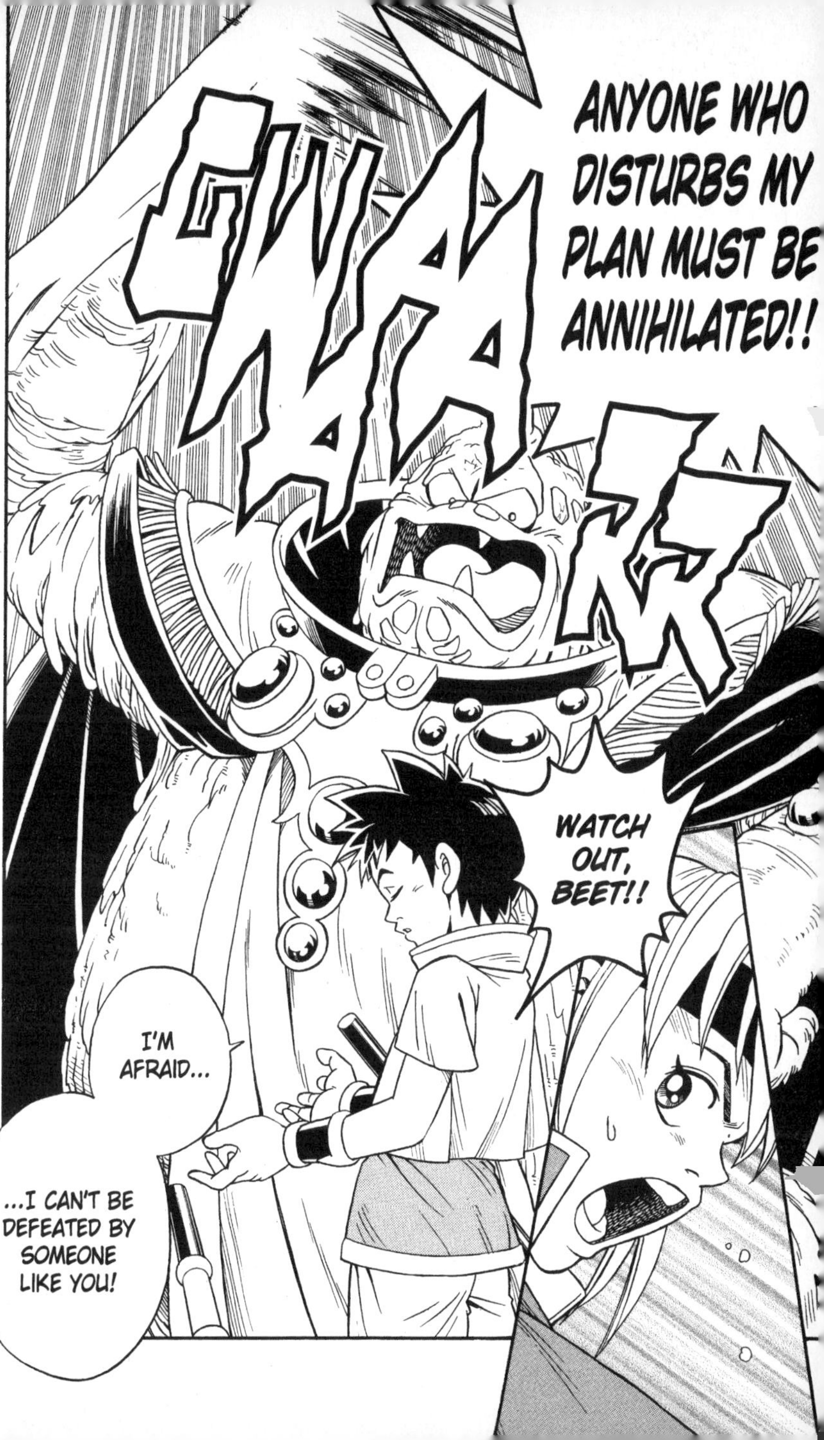
ANYONE WHO DISTURBS MY PLAN MUST BE ANNIHILATED!!
WATCH OUT, BEET!!
I'M AFRAID...
...I CAN'T BE DEFEATED BY SOMEONE LIKE YOU!

READ THIS WAY

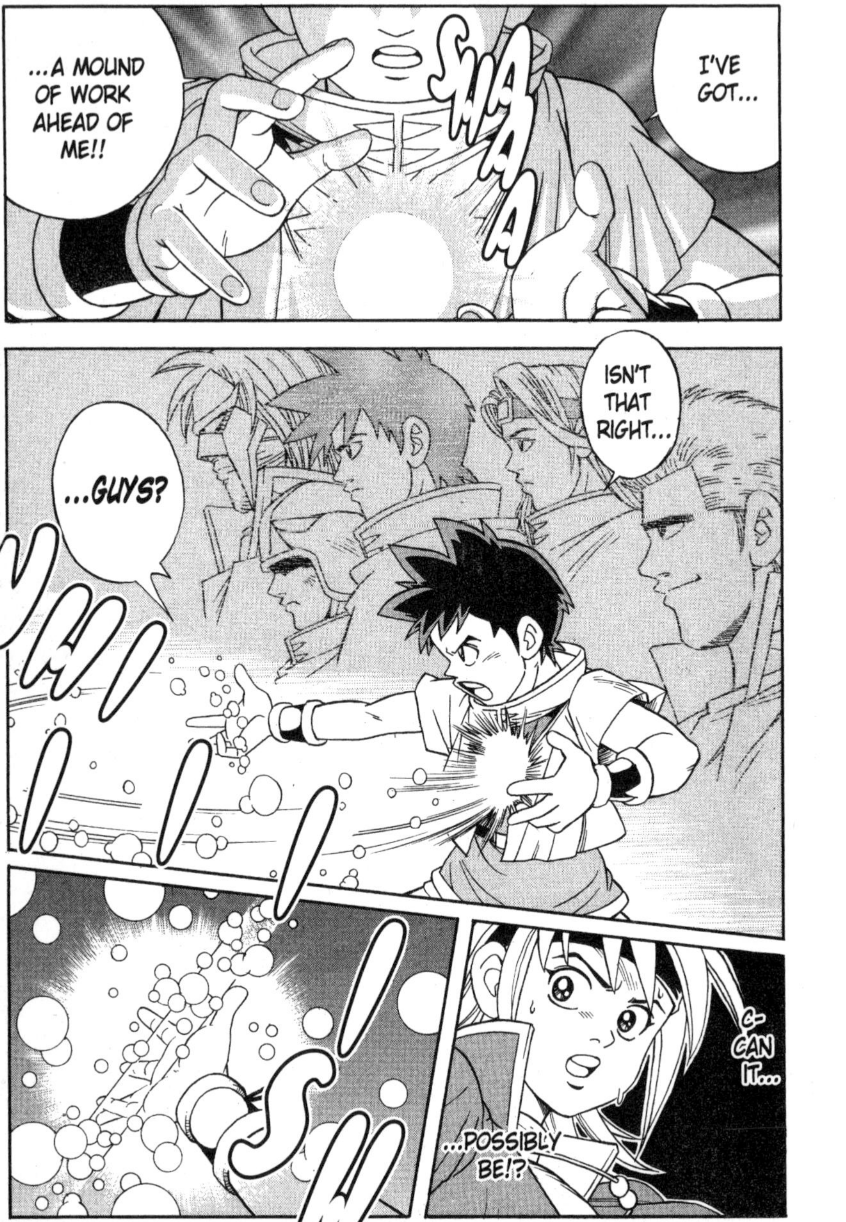

I'VE GOT...
...A MOUND OF WORK AHEAD OF ME!!
SHAAAA
ISN'T THAT RIGHT...
...GUYS?
WHIIIIIII
C-CAN IT...
...POSSIBLY BE!?
SH

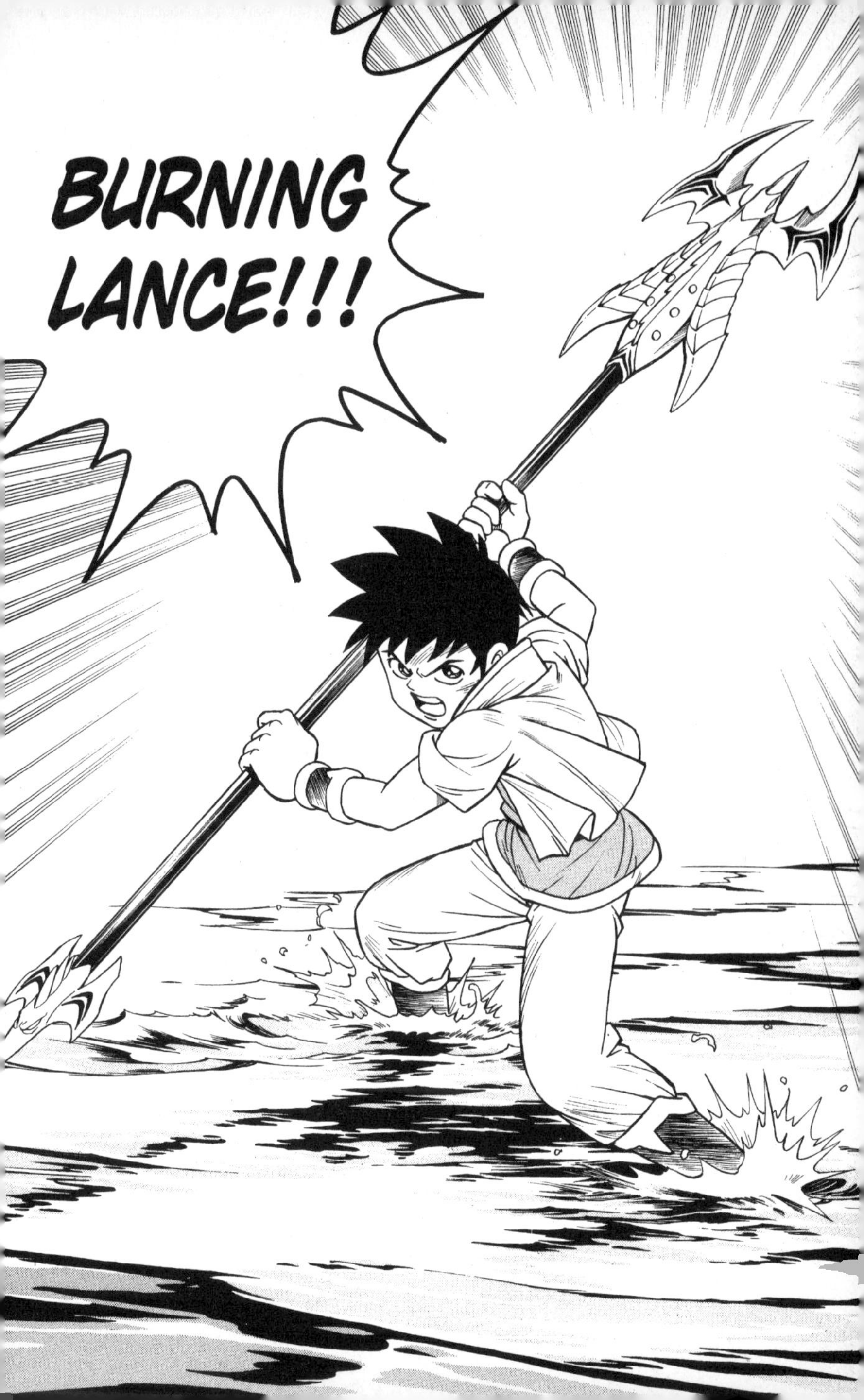
BURNING LANCE!!!

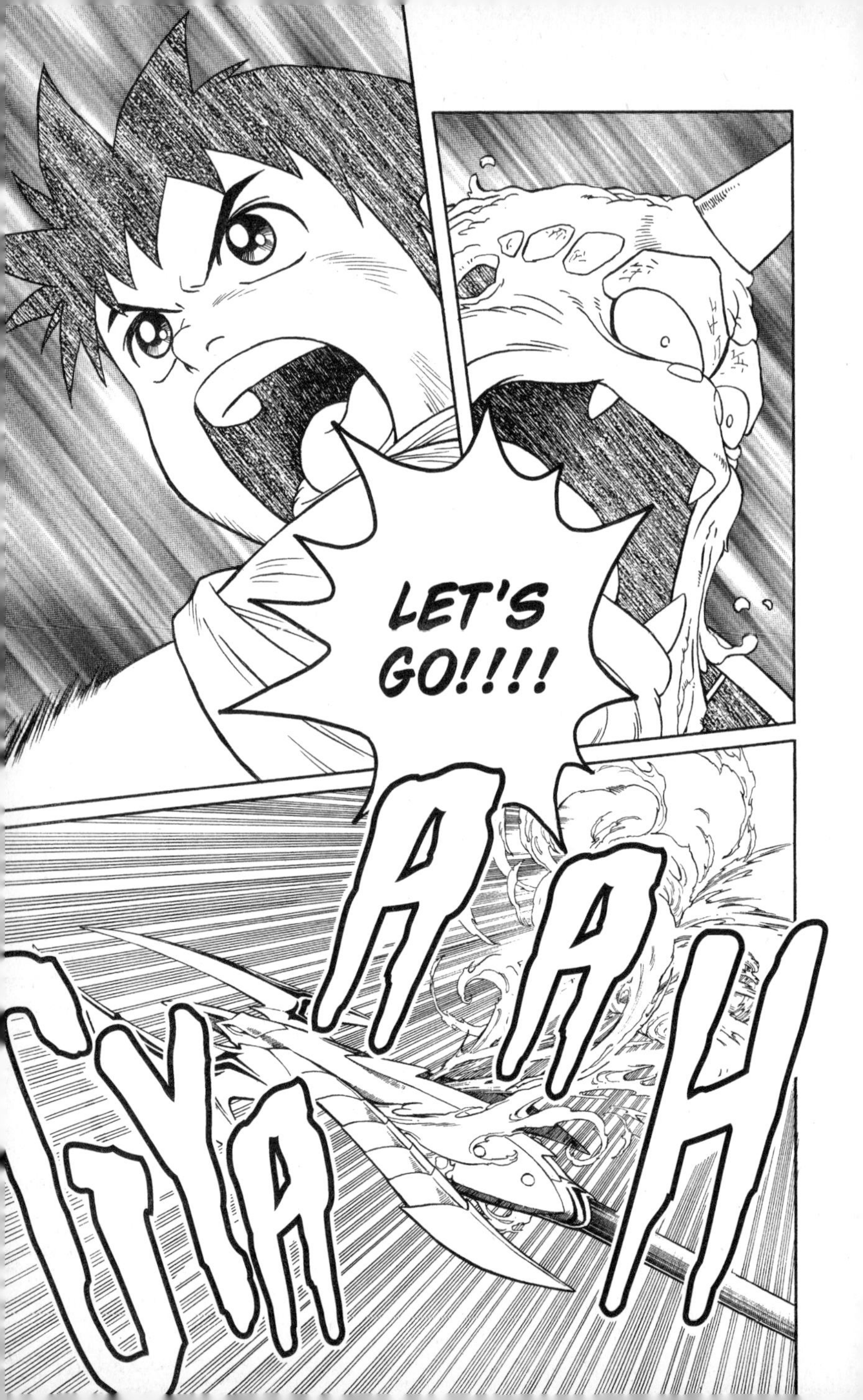
LET'S GO!!!!
YAAAH

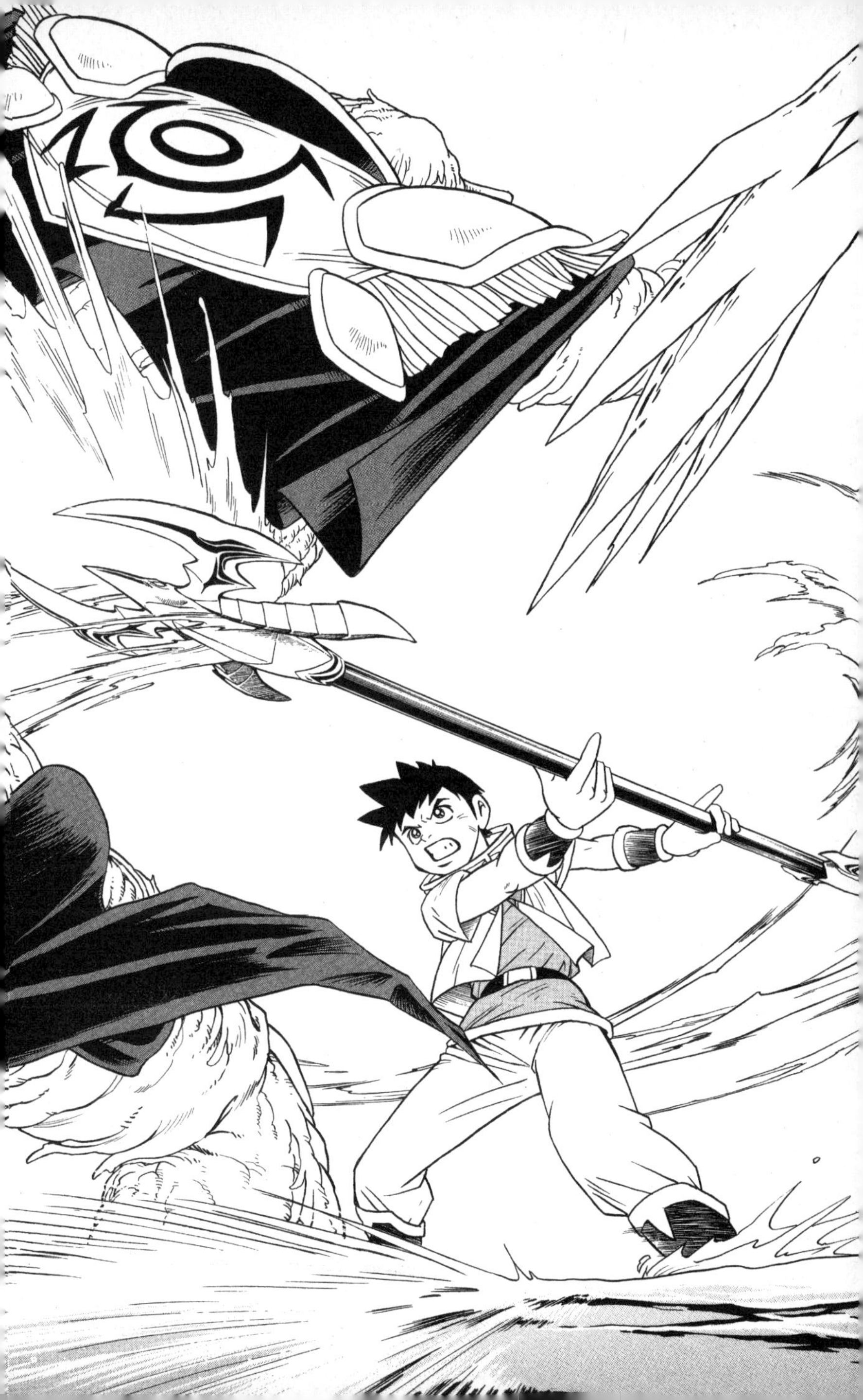

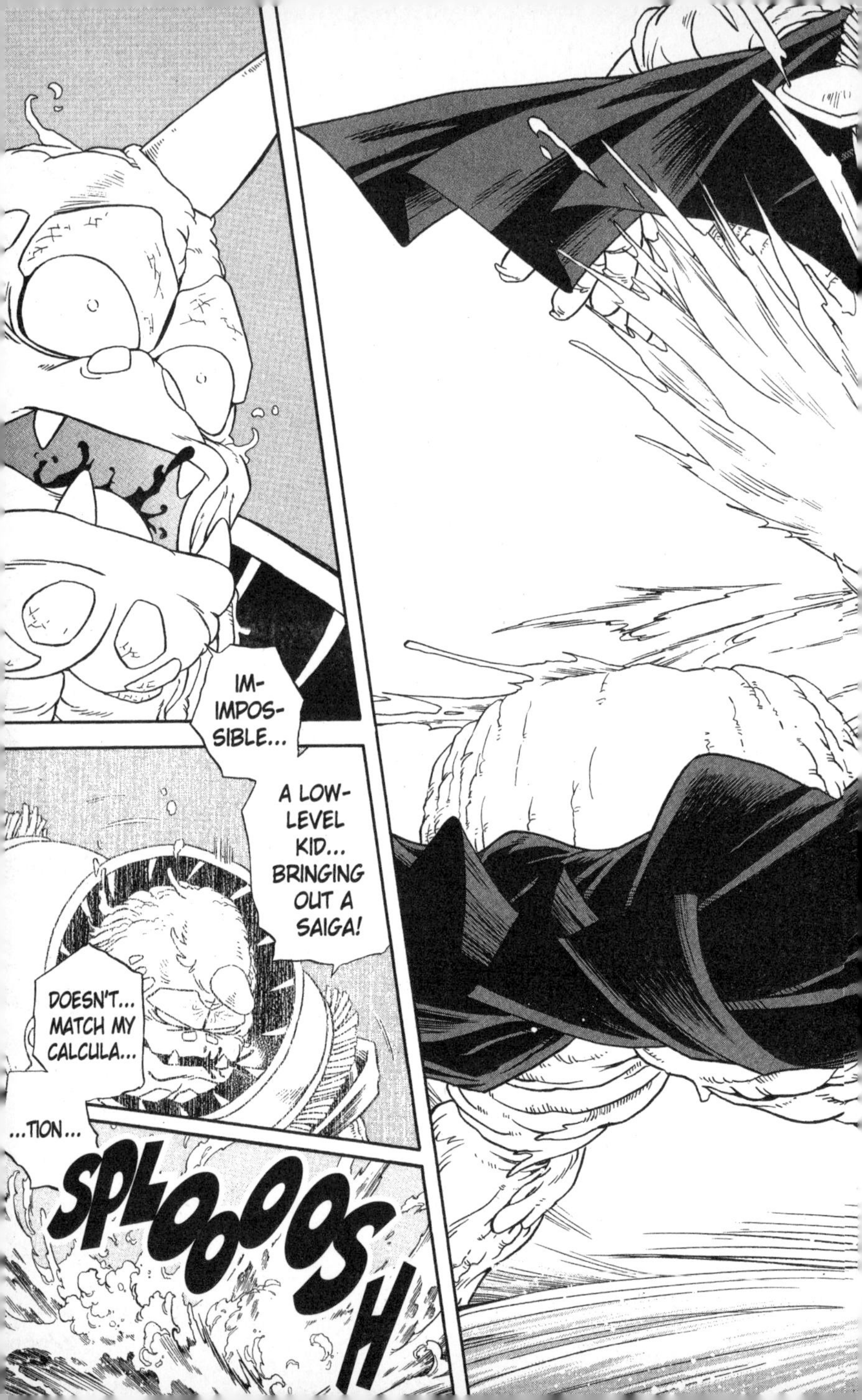
IM-IMPOSSIBLE...
A LOW-LEVEL KID... BRINGING OUT A SAIGA!
DOESN'T... MATCH MY CALCULA...
...TION...
SPLOOOOSH

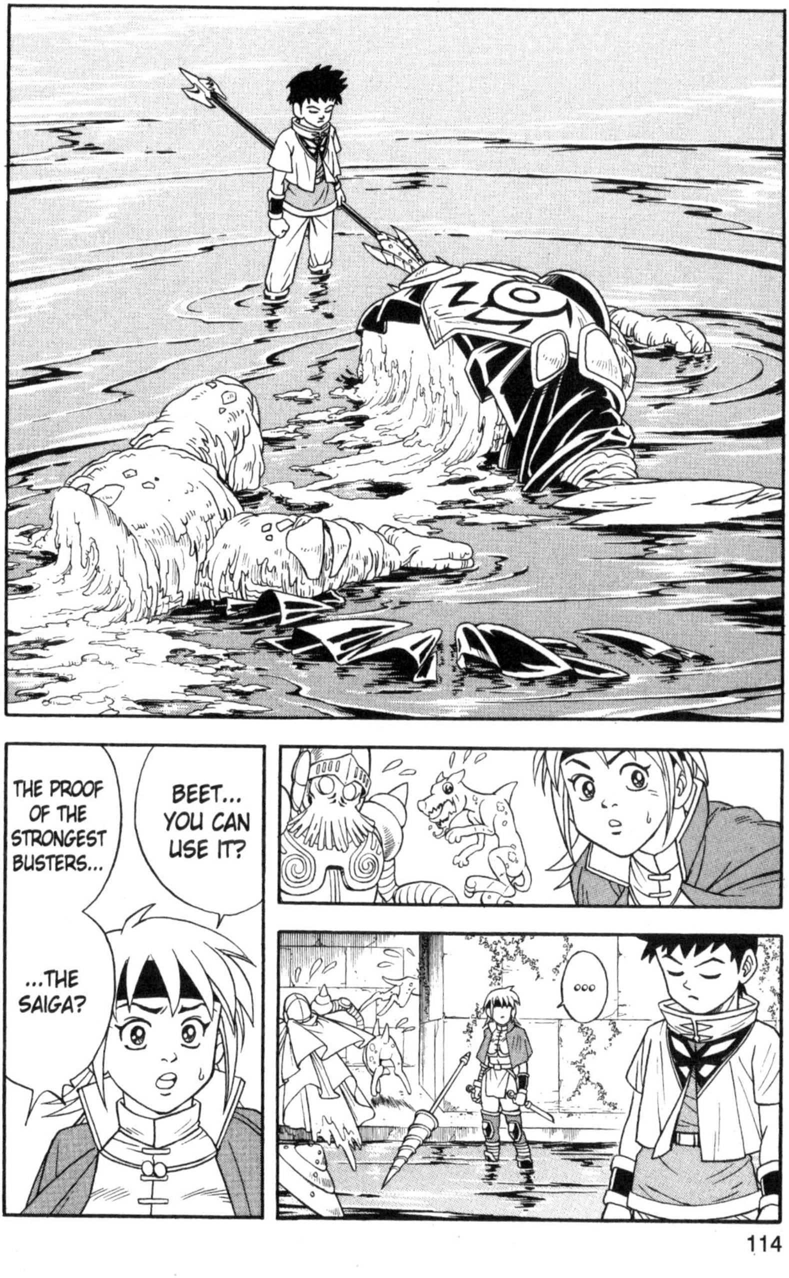
...
BEET... YOU CAN USE IT?
THE PROOF OF THE STRONGEST BUSTERS...
...THE SAIGA?

READ THIS WAY

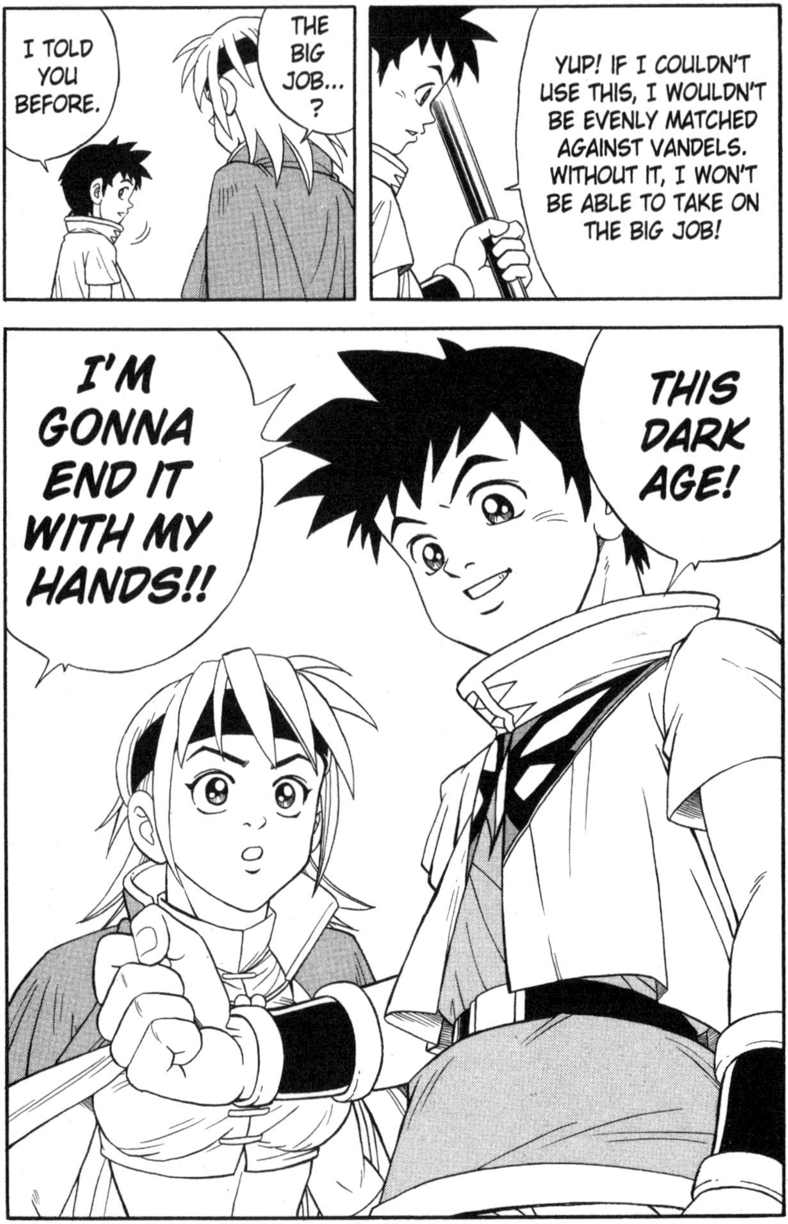
YUP! IF I COULDN'T USE THIS, I WOULDN'T BE EVENLY MATCHED AGAINST VANDELS. WITHOUT IT, I WON'T BE ABLE TO TAKE ON THE BIG JOB!
THE BIG JOB... ?
I TOLD YOU BEFORE.
THIS DARK AGE!
I'M GONNA END IT WITH MY HANDS!!

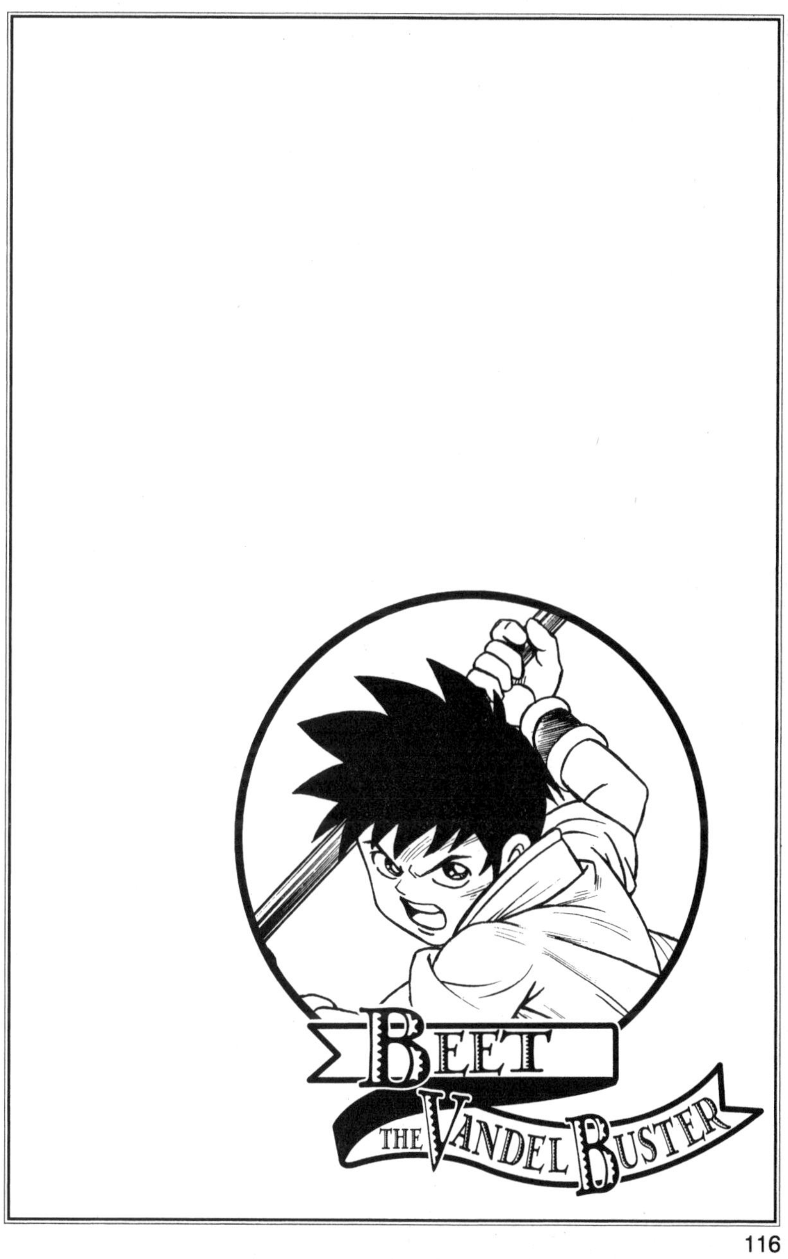
BEET
THE VANDEL BUSTER

Chapter 3: The Time of Departure!

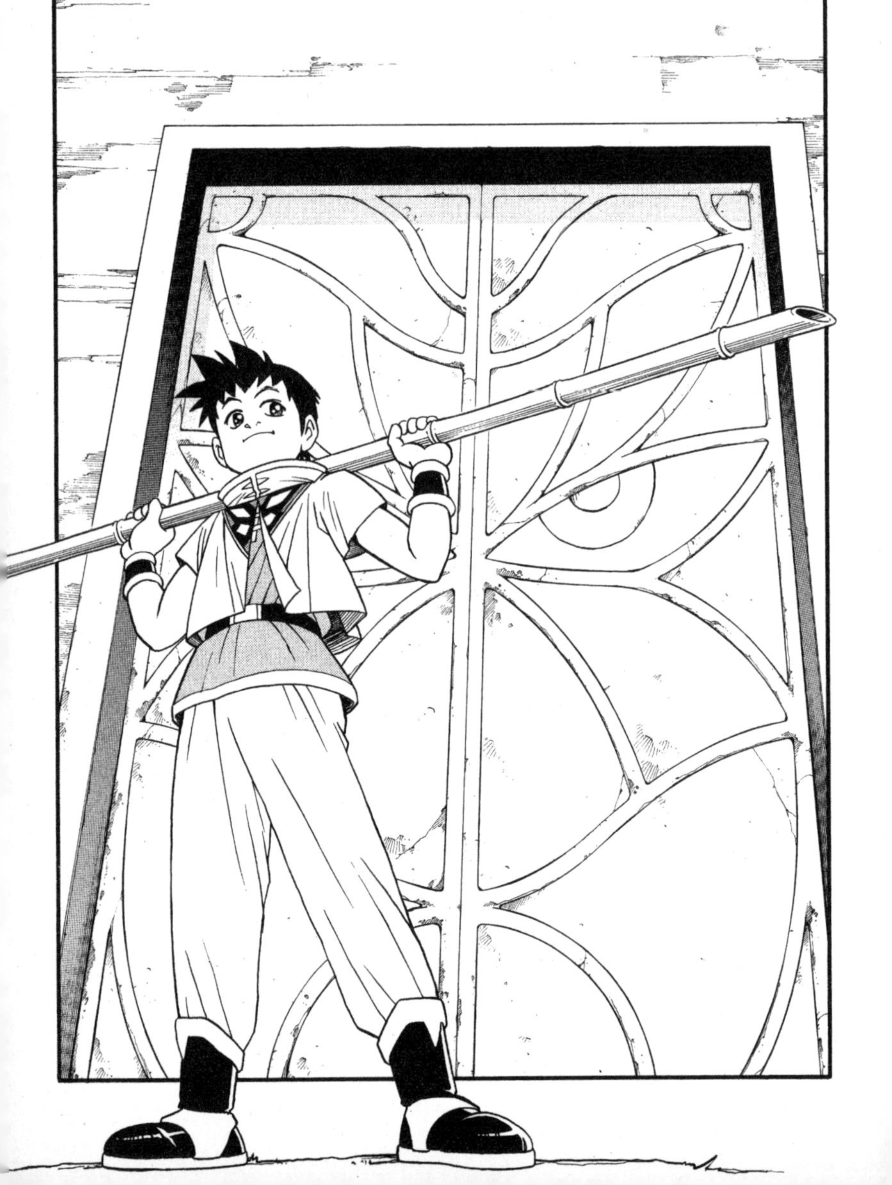

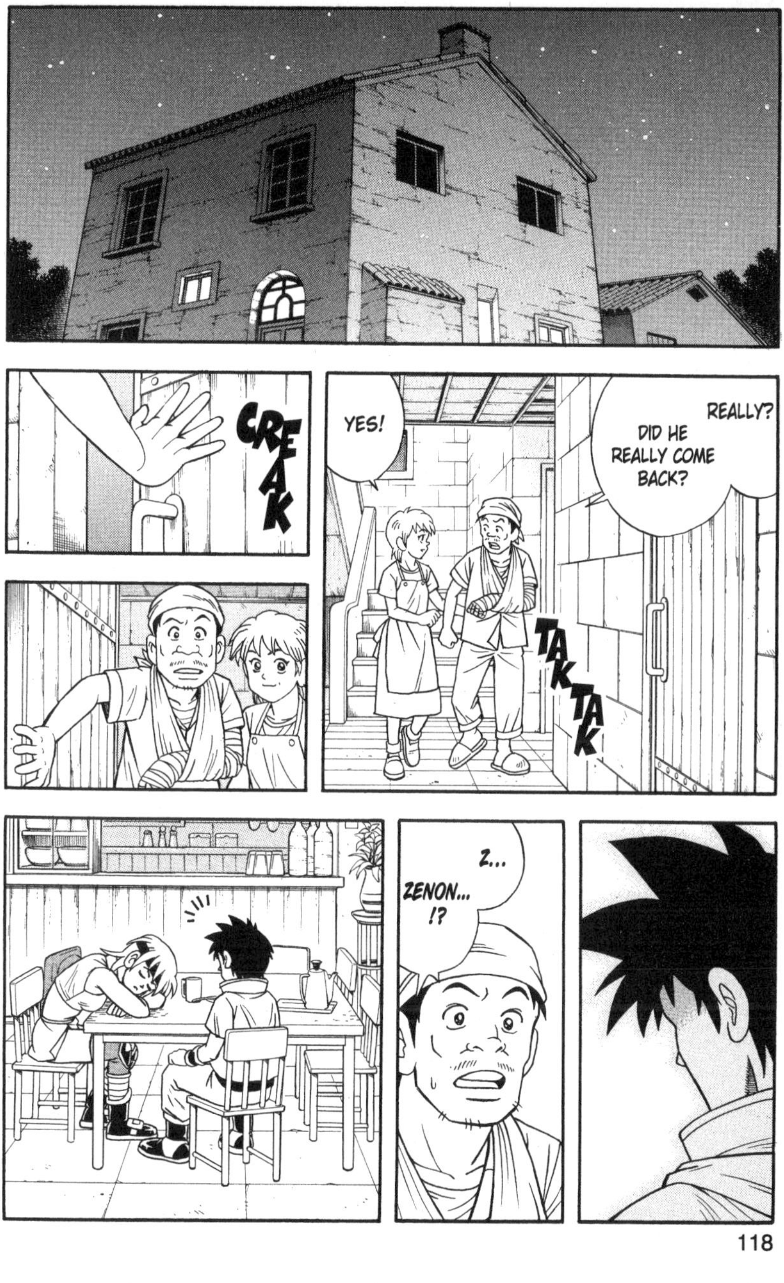

REALLY?
DID HE REALLY COME BACK?
YES!
TAK TAK
CREAK
Z...
ZENON... !?

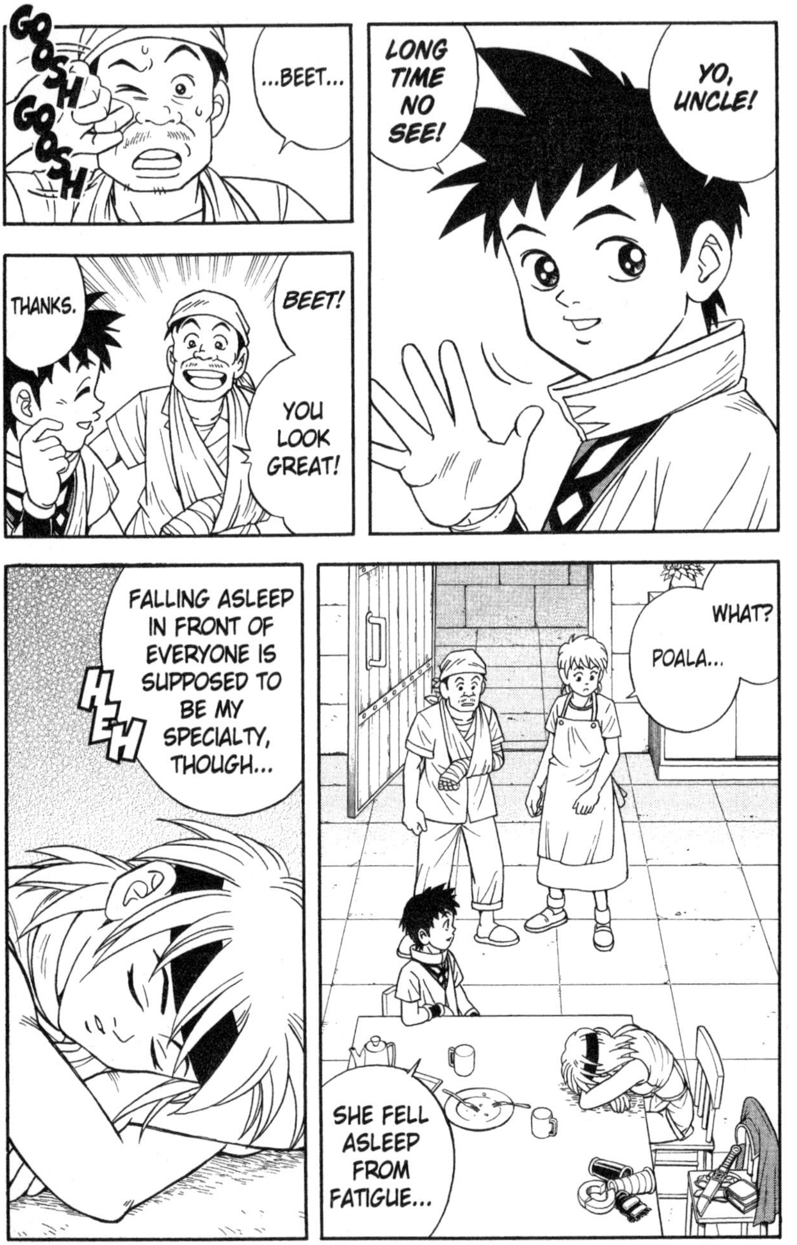
YO, UNCLE!
LONG TIME NO SEE!
...BEET...
GOOSH GOOSH
BEET!
YOU LOOK GREAT!
THANKS.
WHAT?
POALA...
SHE FELL ASLEEP FROM FATIGUE...
FALLING ASLEEP IN FRONT OF EVERYONE IS SUPPOSED TO BE MY SPECIALTY, THOUGH...
HEH

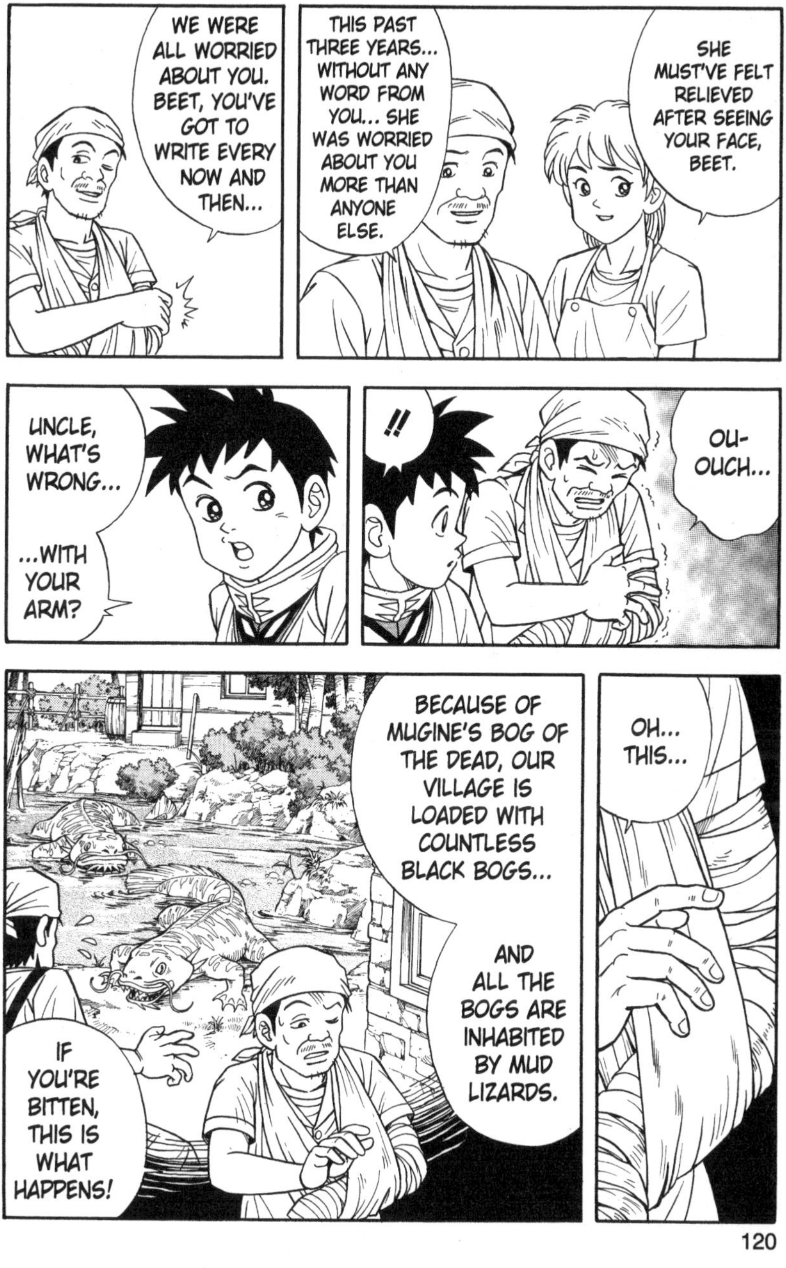
SHE MUST'VE FELT RELIEVED AFTER SEEING YOUR FACE, BEET.
THIS PAST THREE YEARS... WITHOUT ANY WORD FROM YOU... SHE WAS WORRIED ABOUT YOU MORE THAN ANYONE ELSE.
WE WERE ALL WORRIED ABOUT YOU. BEET, YOU'VE GOT TO WRITE EVERY NOW AND THEN...
OU-OUCH...
!!
UNCLE, WHAT'S WRONG...
...WITH YOUR ARM?
OH... THIS...
BECAUSE OF MUGINE'S BOG OF THE DEAD, OUR VILLAGE IS LOADED WITH COUNTLESS BLACK BOGS...
AND ALL THE BOGS ARE INHABITED BY MUD LIZARDS.
IF YOU'RE BITTEN, THIS IS WHAT HAPPENS!

READ THIS WAY

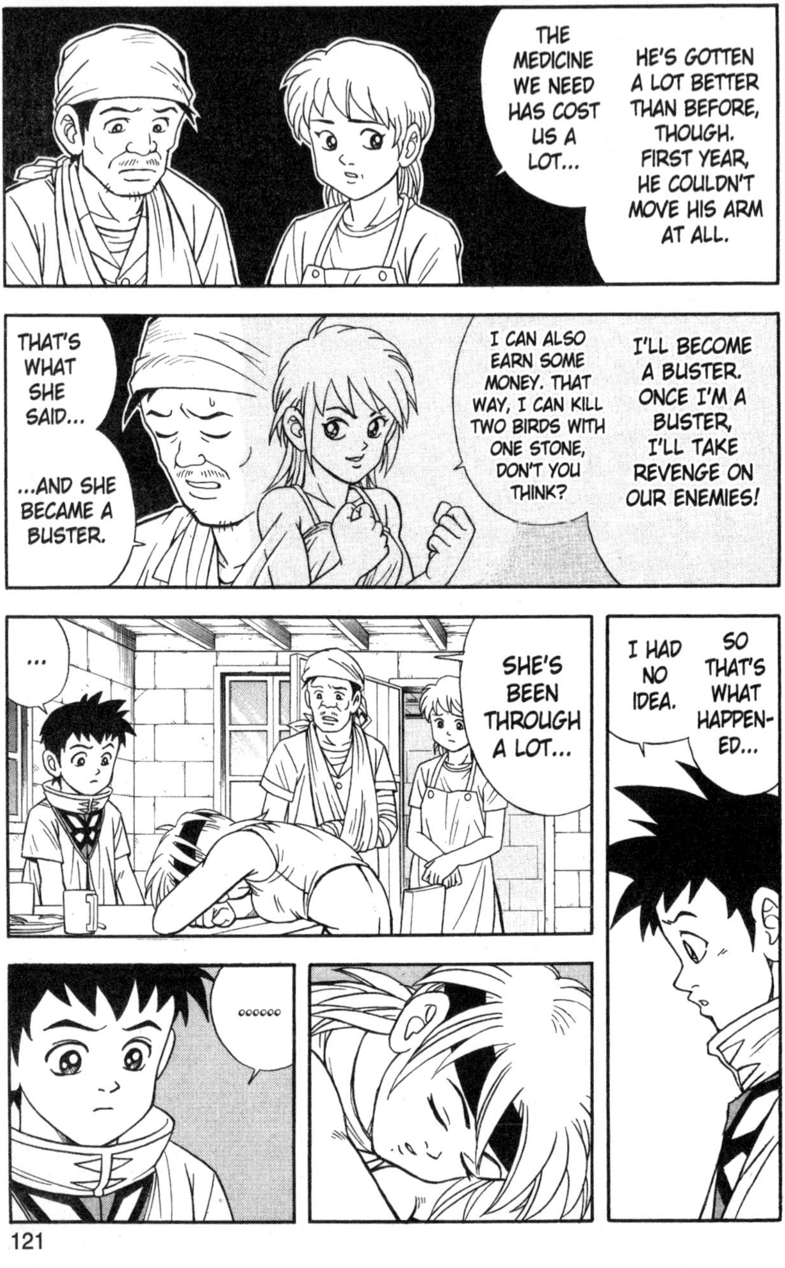

HE'S GOTTEN A LOT BETTER THAN BEFORE, THOUGH. FIRST YEAR, HE COULDN'T MOVE HIS ARM AT ALL.
THE MEDICINE WE NEED HAS COST US A LOT...
I'LL BECOME A BUSTER. ONCE I'M A BUSTER, I'LL TAKE REVENGE ON OUR ENEMIES!
I CAN ALSO EARN SOME MONEY. THAT WAY, I CAN KILL TWO BIRDS WITH ONE STONE, DON'T YOU THINK?
THAT'S WHAT SHE SAID...
...AND SHE BECAME A BUSTER.
SO THAT'S WHAT HAPPENED...
I HAD NO IDEA.
SHE'S BEEN THROUGH A LOT...
...
......

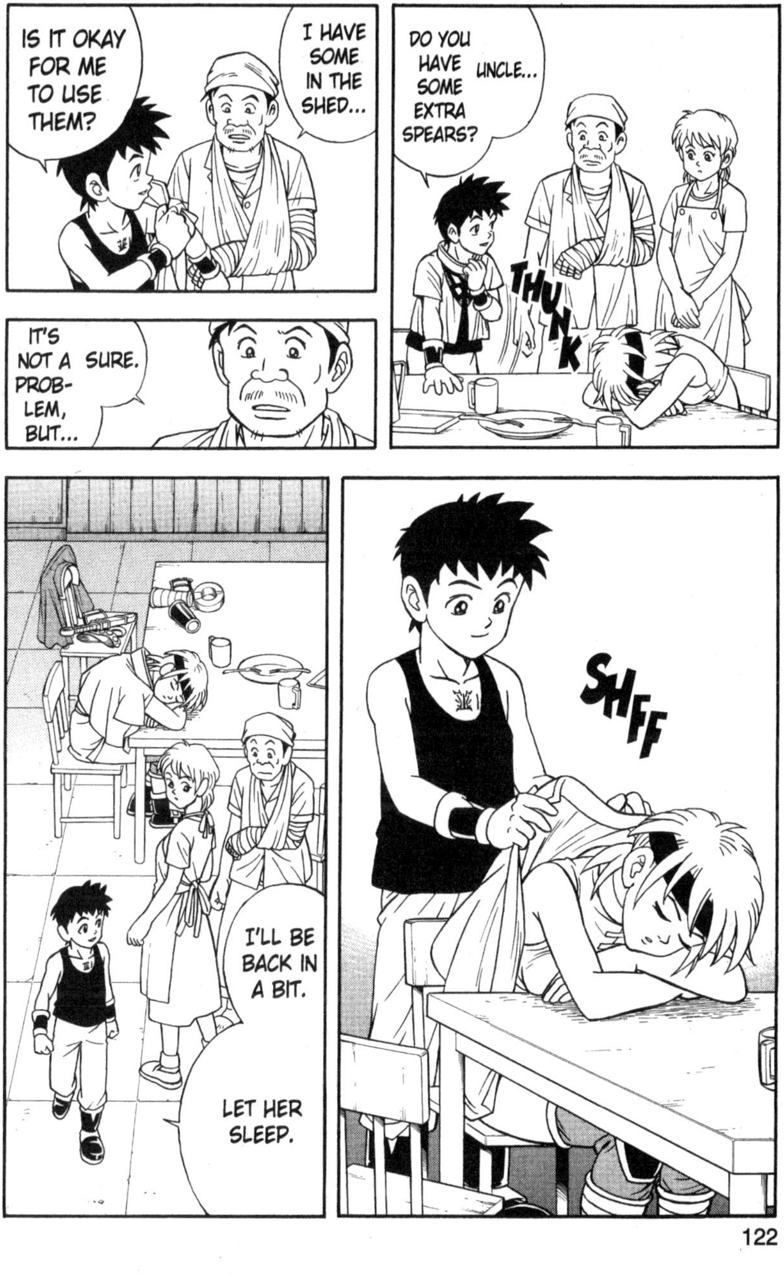
UNCLE...
DO YOU HAVE SOME EXTRA SPEARS?
THUNK
I HAVE SOME IN THE SHED...
IS IT OKAY FOR ME TO USE THEM?
SURE.
IT'S NOT A PROBLEM, BUT...
SHFF
I'LL BE BACK IN A BIT.
LET HER SLEEP.

READ THIS WAY

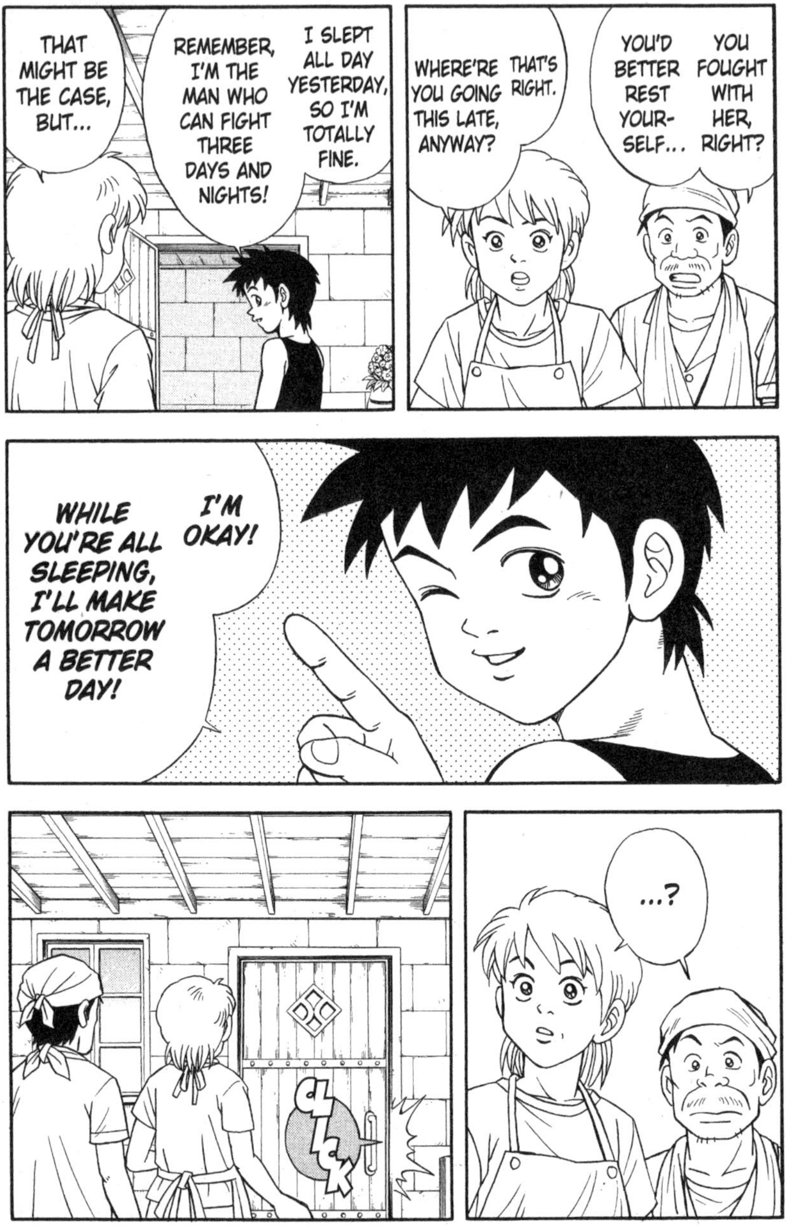
YOU FOUGHT WITH HER, RIGHT?
YOU'D BETTER REST YOURSELF...
THAT'S RIGHT.
WHERE'RE YOU GOING THIS LATE, ANYWAY?
I SLEPT ALL DAY YESTERDAY, SO I'M TOTALLY FINE.
REMEMBER, I'M THE MAN WHO CAN FIGHT THREE DAYS AND NIGHTS!
THAT MIGHT BE THE CASE, BUT...
I'M OKAY!
WHILE YOU'RE ALL SLEEPING, I'LL MAKE TOMORROW A BETTER DAY!
...?
CLICK

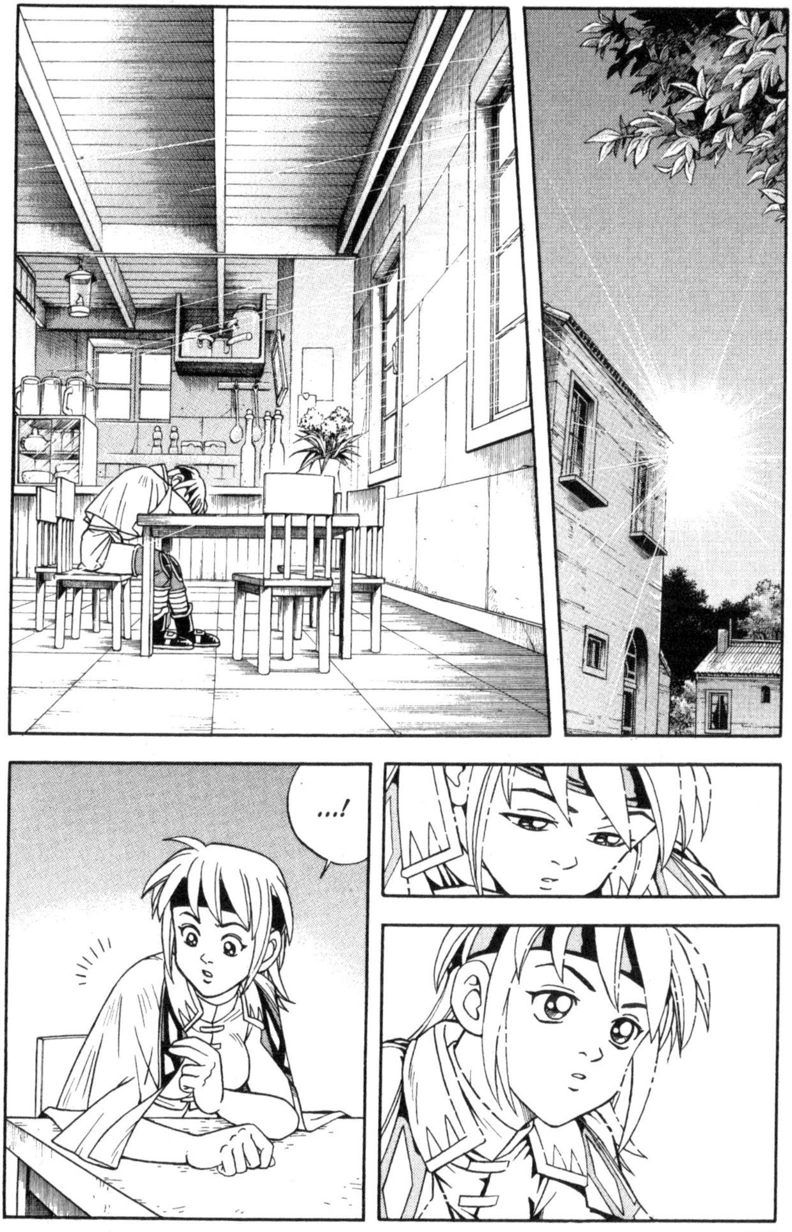
...!

READ THIS WAY

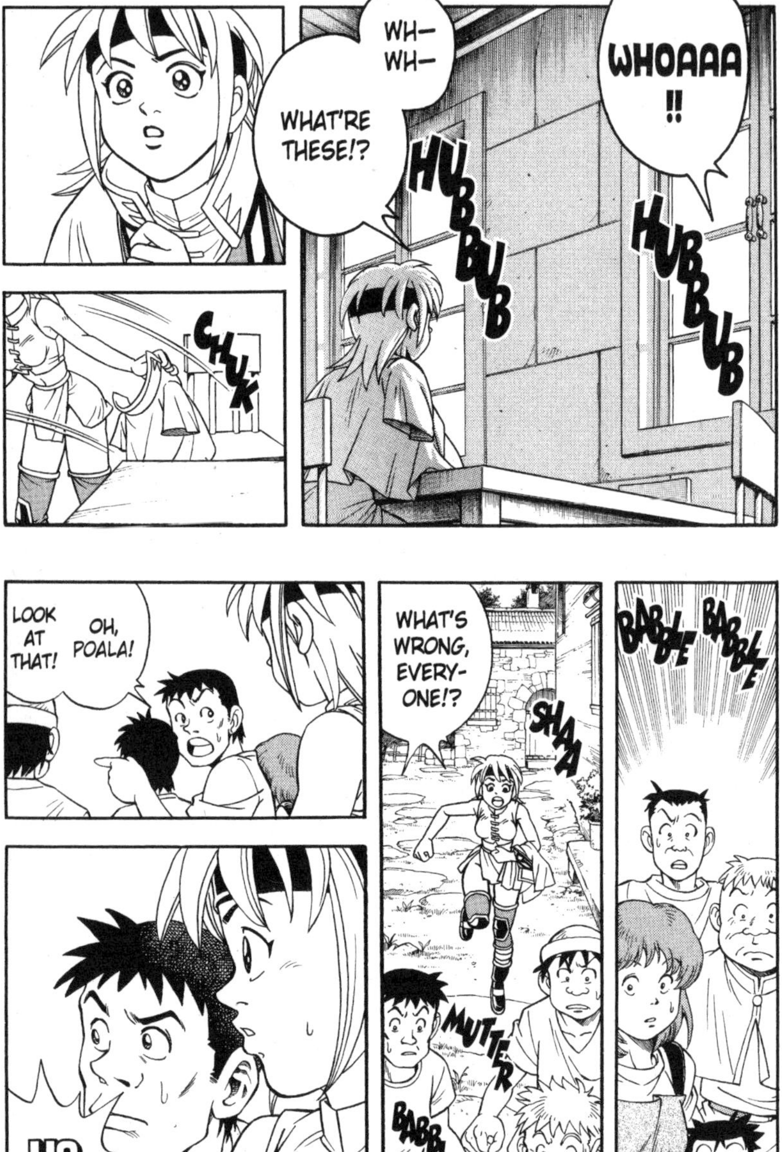

WHOAAA!!
HUBBUB
WH— WH—
WHAT'RE THESE!?
HUBBUB
CHUK
BABBLE BABBLE
WHAT'S WRONG, EVERYONE!?
SHAAA
MUTTER
BABBLE
OH, POALA!
LOOK AT THAT!
!!?

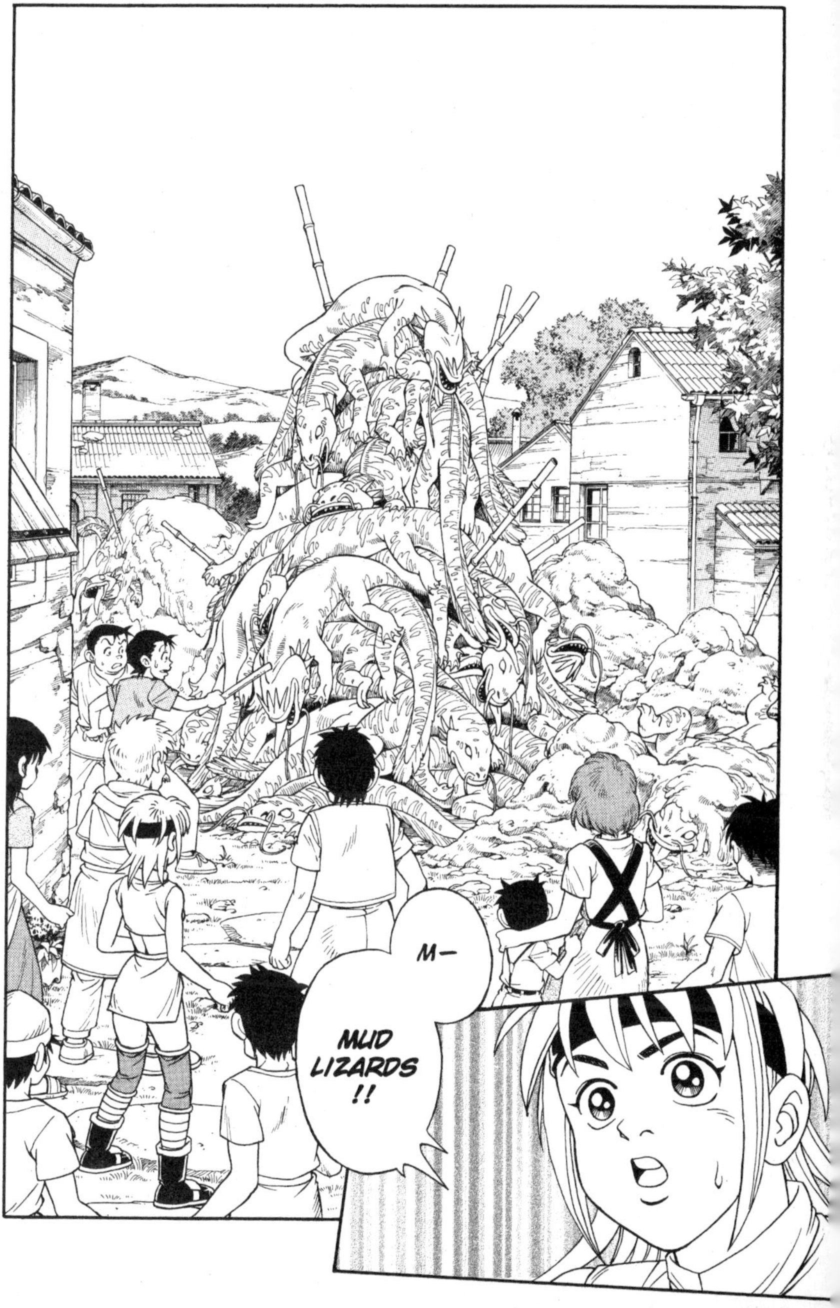
M—
MUD LIZARDS !!

READ THIS WAY

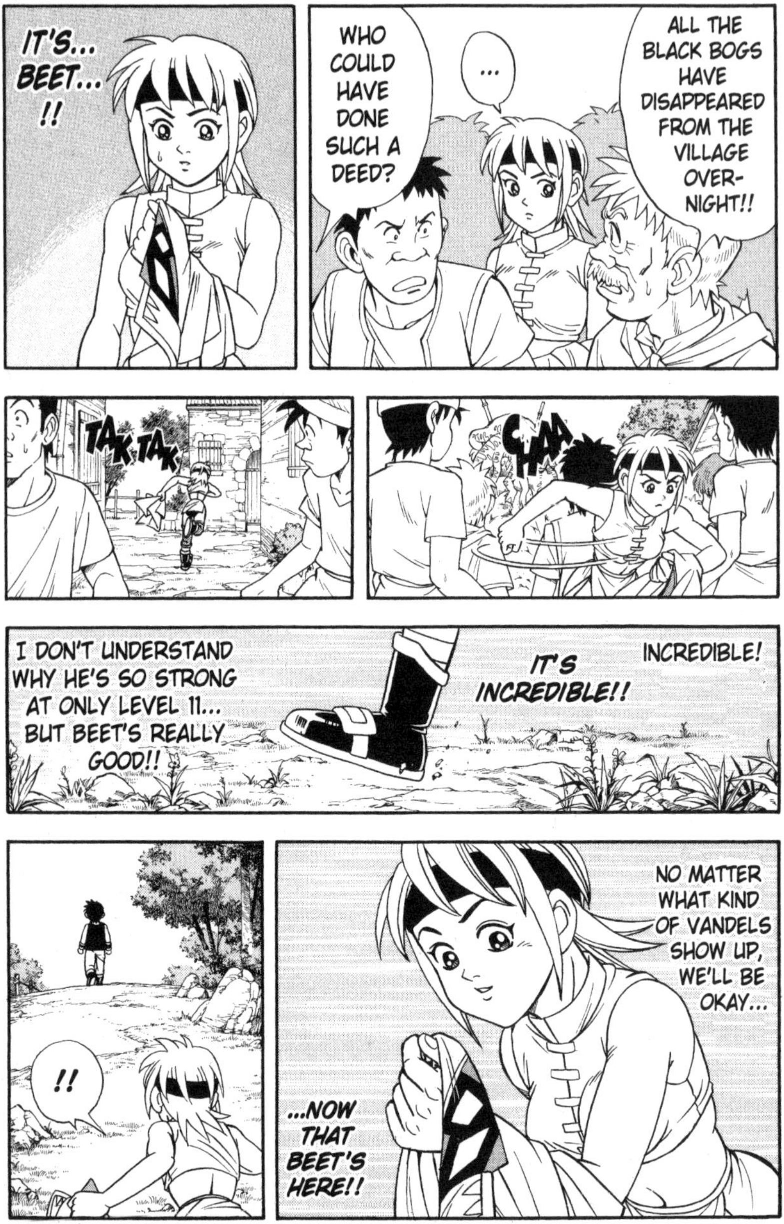
ALL THE BLACK BOGS HAVE DISAPPEARED FROM THE VILLAGE OVER-NIGHT!!
...
WHO COULD HAVE DONE SUCH A DEED?
IT'S... BEET... !!
TAK TAK
INCREDIBLE!
IT'S INCREDIBLE!!
I DON'T UNDERSTAND WHY HE'S SO STRONG AT ONLY LEVEL 11... BUT BEET'S REALLY GOOD!!
NO MATTER WHAT KIND OF VANDELS SHOW UP, WE'LL BE OKAY...
...NOW THAT BEET'S HERE!!
!!

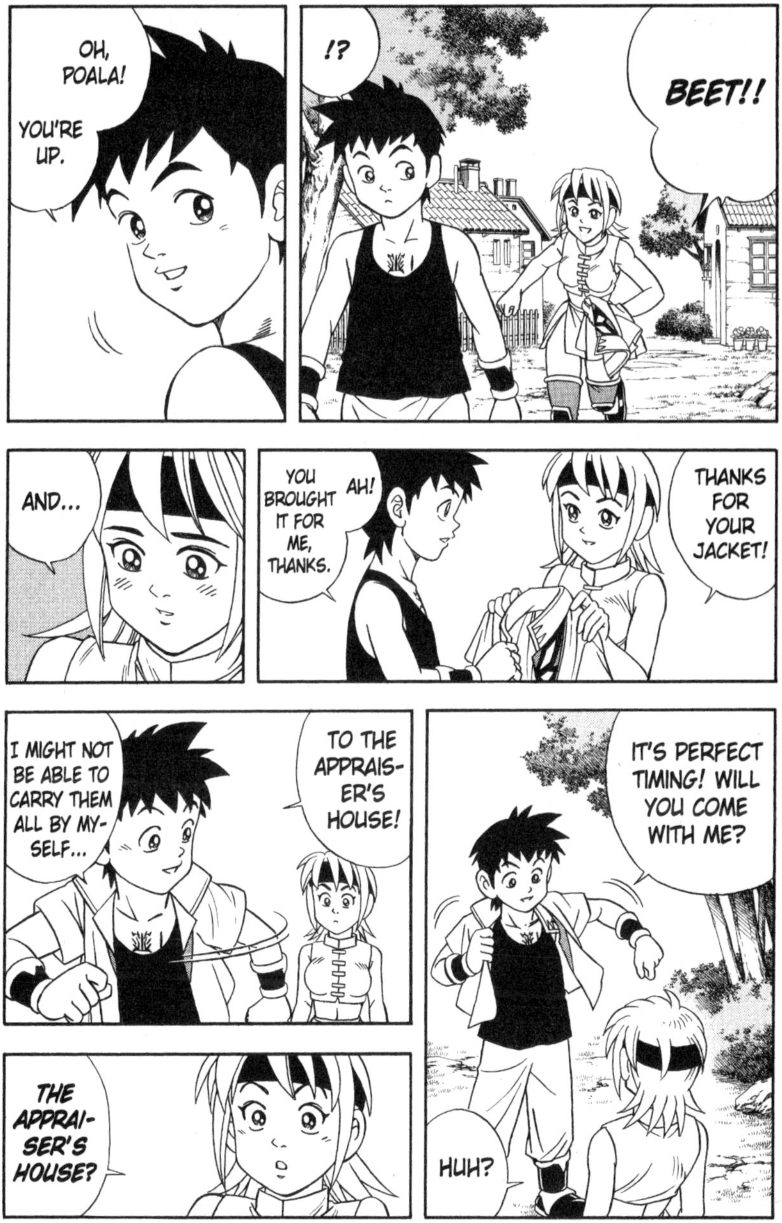
BEET!!
!?
OH, POALA!
YOU'RE UP.
THANKS FOR YOUR JACKET!
AH!
YOU BROUGHT IT FOR ME, THANKS.
AND...
IT'S PERFECT TIMING! WILL YOU COME WITH ME?
HUH?
TO THE APPRAISER'S HOUSE!
I MIGHT NOT BE ABLE TO CARRY THEM ALL BY MYSELF...
THE APPRAISER'S HOUSE?

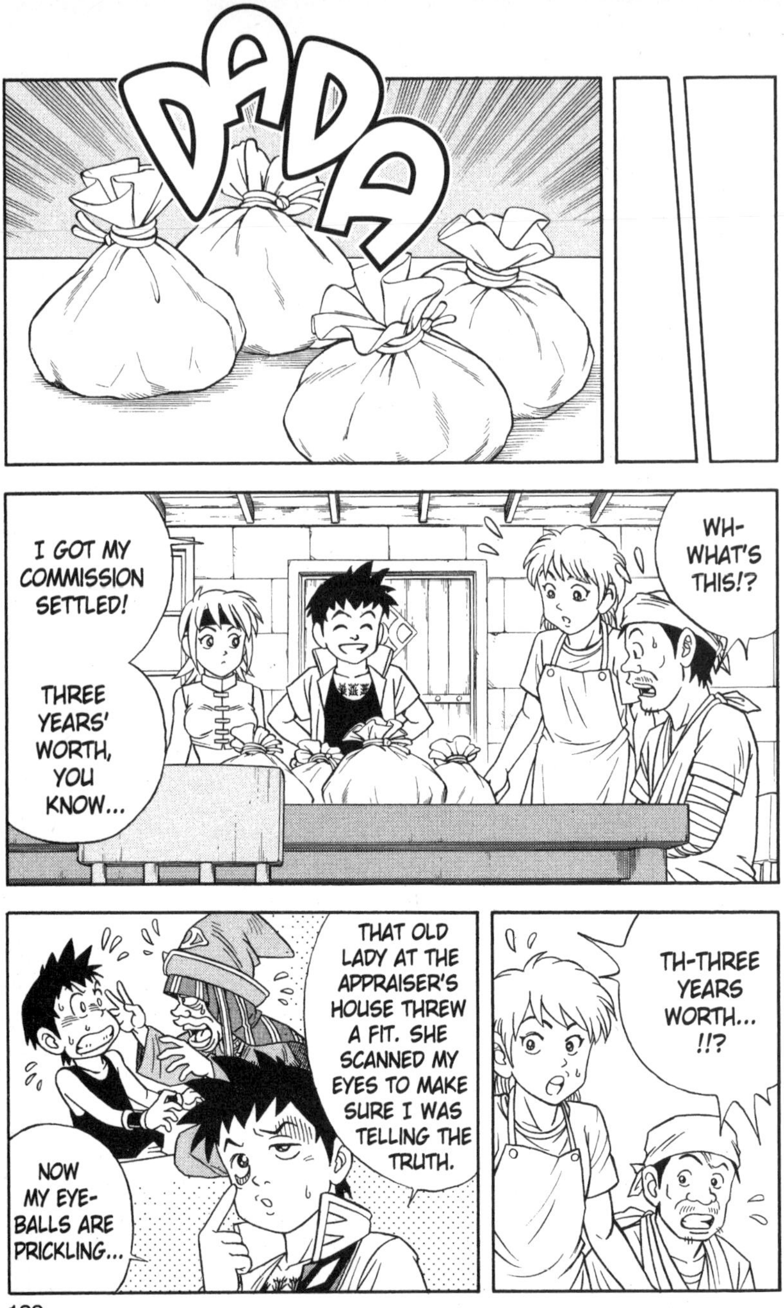
DADA
WH-WHAT'S THIS!?
I GOT MY COMMISSION SETTLED!
THREE YEARS' WORTH, YOU KNOW...
TH-THREE YEARS WORTH...!!?
THAT OLD LADY AT THE APPRAISER'S HOUSE THREW A FIT. SHE SCANNED MY EYES TO MAKE SURE I WAS TELLING THE TRUTH.
NOW MY EYE-BALLS ARE PRICKLING...

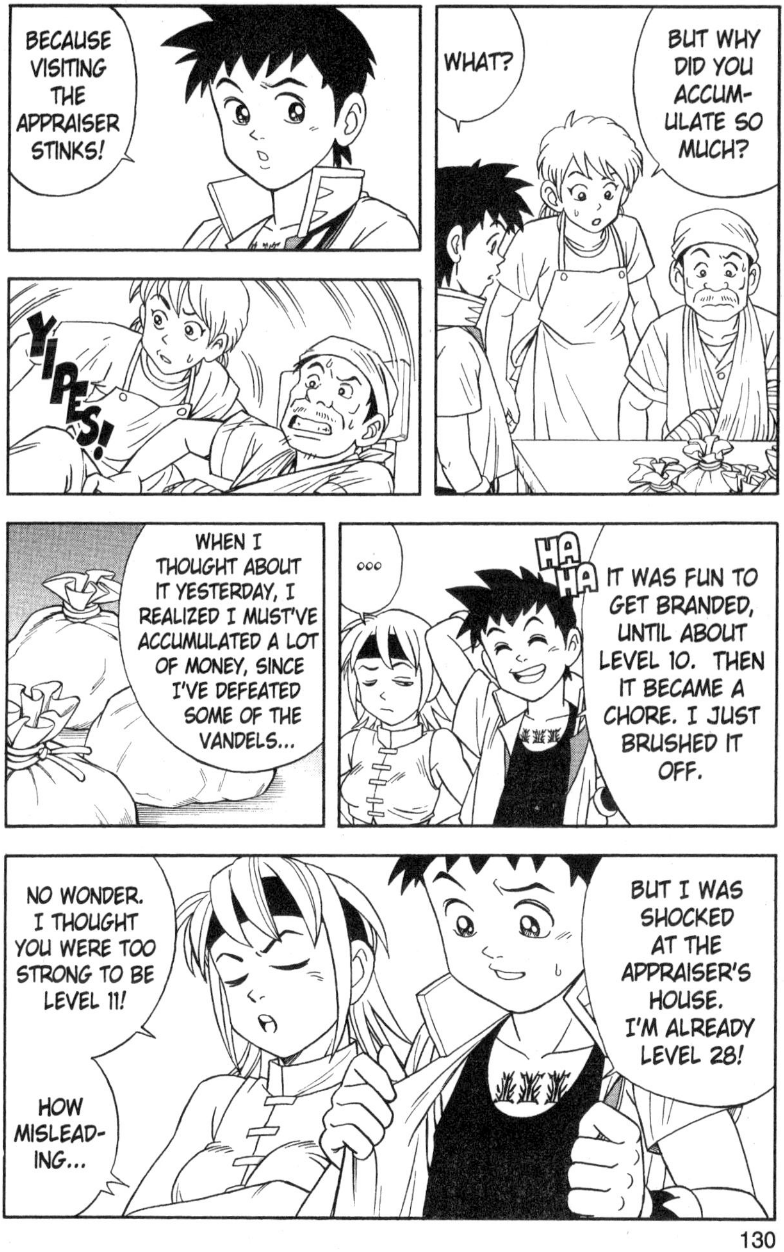
BUT WHY DID YOU ACCUM-ULATE SO MUCH?
WHAT?
BECAUSE VISITING THE APPRAISER STINKS!
YIPES!
HA HA
IT WAS FUN TO GET BRANDED, UNTIL ABOUT LEVEL 10. THEN IT BECAME A CHORE. I JUST BRUSHED IT OFF.
...
WHEN I THOUGHT ABOUT IT YESTERDAY, I REALIZED I MUST'VE ACCUMULATED A LOT OF MONEY, SINCE I'VE DEFEATED SOME OF THE VANDELS...
BUT I WAS SHOCKED AT THE APPRAISER'S HOUSE. I'M ALREADY LEVEL 28!
NO WONDER. I THOUGHT YOU WERE TOO STRONG TO BE LEVEL 11!
HOW MISLEAD-ING...

READ THIS WAY

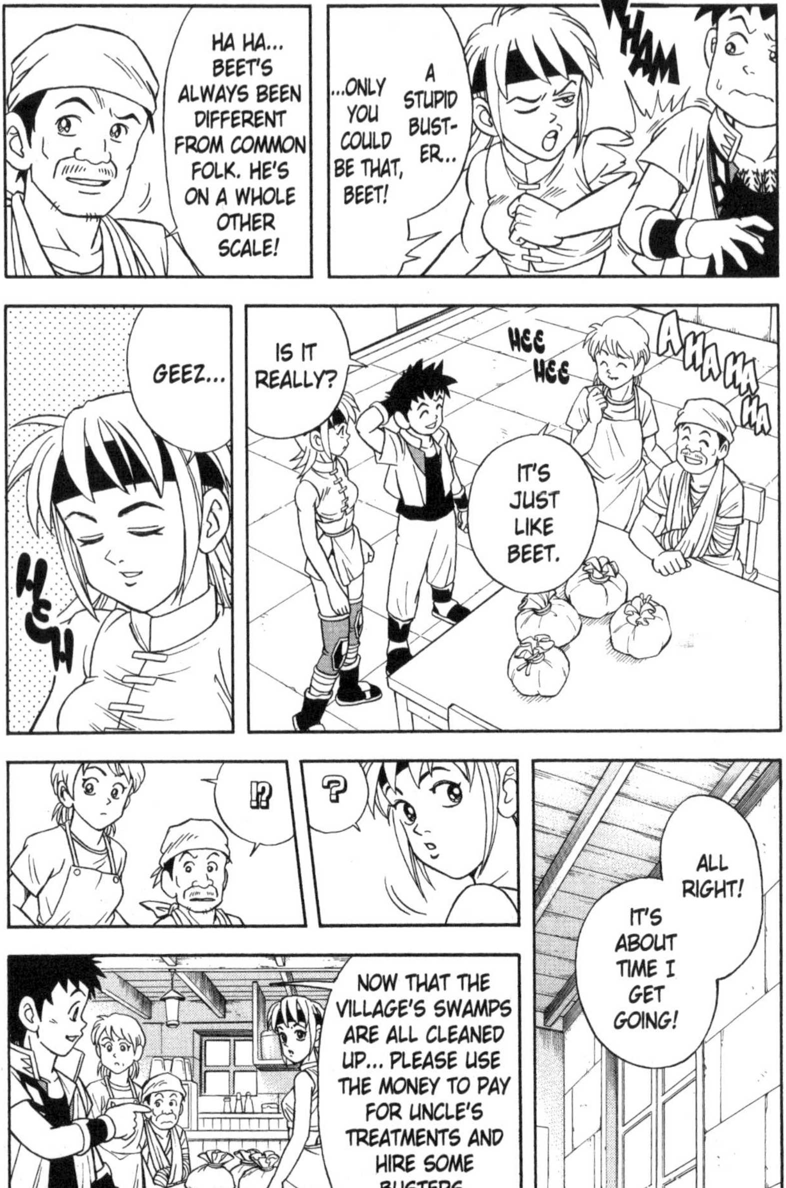

WHAM
A STUPID BUSTER...
...ONLY YOU COULD BE THAT, BEET!
HA HA... BEET'S ALWAYS BEEN DIFFERENT FROM COMMON FOLK. HE'S ON A WHOLE OTHER SCALE!
AHAHAHAHA
HEE HEE
IS IT REALLY?
IT'S JUST LIKE BEET.
GEEZ...
HEH
ALL RIGHT! IT'S ABOUT TIME I GET GOING!
?
!?
NOW THAT THE VILLAGE'S SWAMPS ARE ALL CLEANED UP... PLEASE USE THE MONEY TO PAY FOR UNCLE'S TREATMENTS AND HIRE SOME BUSTERS.

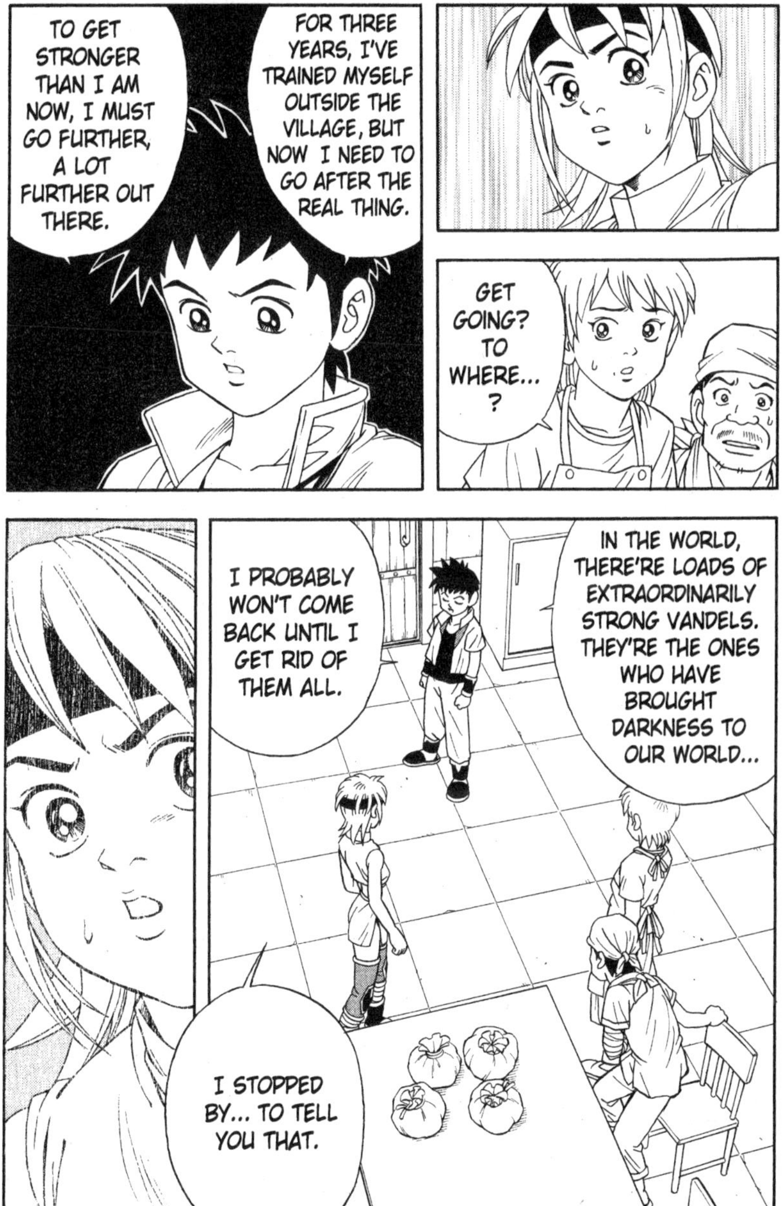
GET GOING? TO WHERE... ?
FOR THREE YEARS, I'VE TRAINED MYSELF OUTSIDE THE VILLAGE, BUT NOW I NEED TO GO AFTER THE REAL THING.
TO GET STRONGER THAN I AM NOW, I MUST GO FURTHER, A LOT FURTHER OUT THERE.
IN THE WORLD, THERE'RE LOADS OF EXTRAORDINARILY STRONG VANDELS. THEY'RE THE ONES WHO HAVE BROUGHT DARKNESS TO OUR WORLD...
I PROBABLY WON'T COME BACK UNTIL I GET RID OF THEM ALL.
I STOPPED BY... TO TELL YOU THAT.

READ THIS WAY

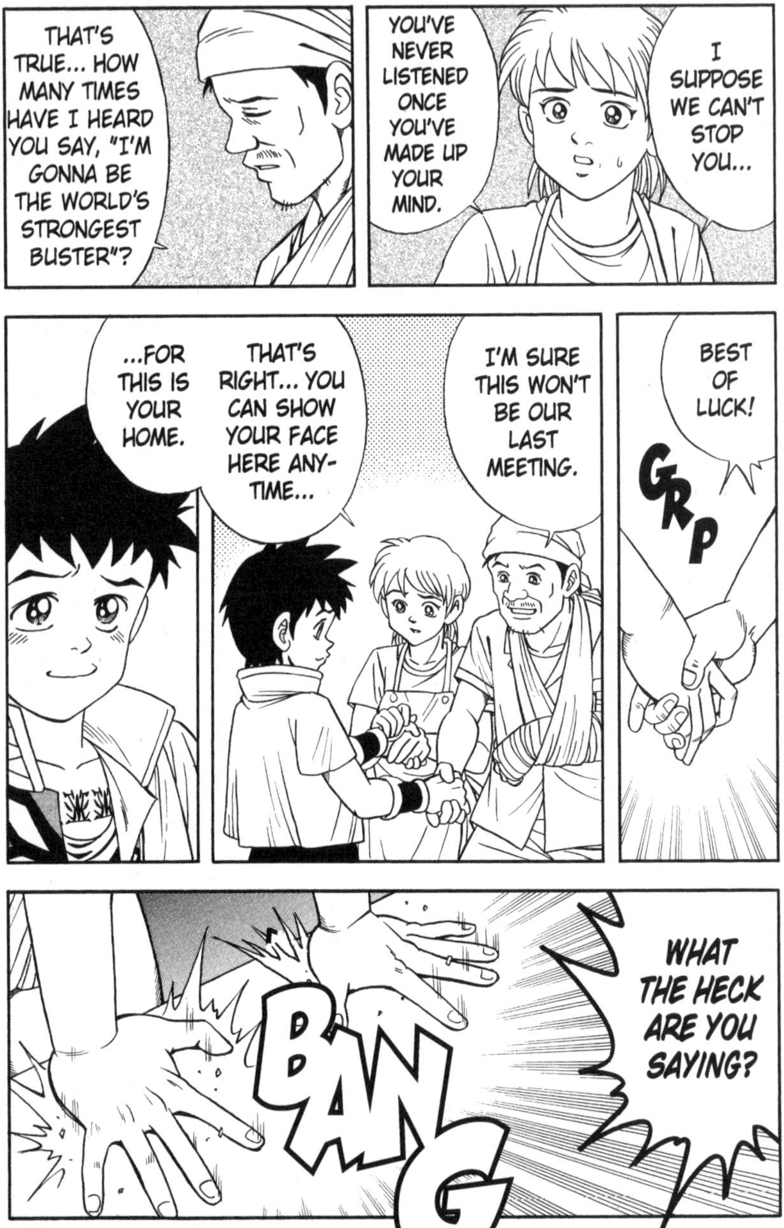
I SUPPOSE WE CAN'T STOP YOU...
YOU'VE NEVER LISTENED ONCE YOU'VE MADE UP YOUR MIND.
THAT'S TRUE... HOW MANY TIMES HAVE I HEARD YOU SAY, "I'M GONNA BE THE WORLD'S STRONGEST BUSTER"?
BEST OF LUCK!
GRP
I'M SURE THIS WON'T BE OUR LAST MEETING.
THAT'S RIGHT... YOU CAN SHOW YOUR FACE HERE ANY-TIME...
...FOR THIS IS YOUR HOME.
WHAT THE HECK ARE YOU SAYING?
BANG

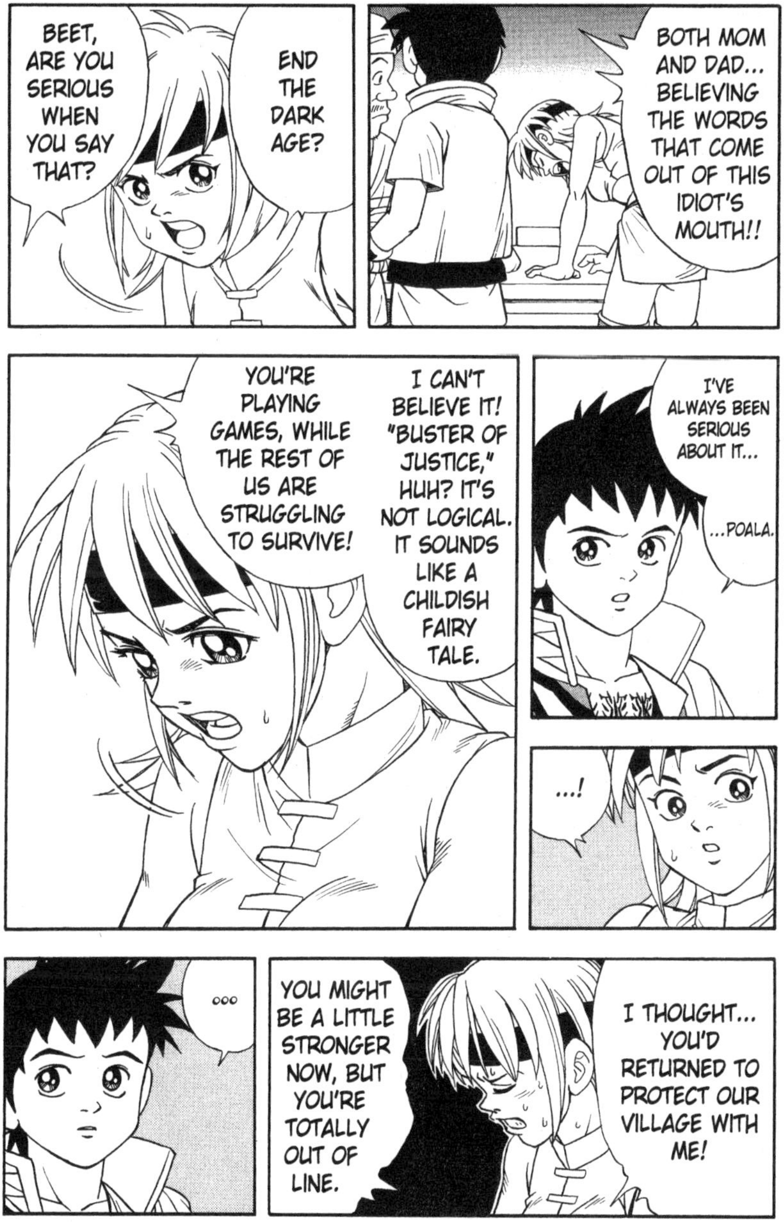
BOTH MOM AND DAD... BELIEVING THE WORDS THAT COME OUT OF THIS IDIOT'S MOUTH!!
END THE DARK AGE?
BEET, ARE YOU SERIOUS WHEN YOU SAY THAT?
I'VE ALWAYS BEEN SERIOUS ABOUT IT...
...POALA.
...!
I CAN'T BELIEVE IT! "BUSTER OF JUSTICE," HUH? IT'S NOT LOGICAL. IT SOUNDS LIKE A CHILDISH FAIRY TALE.
YOU'RE PLAYING GAMES, WHILE THE REST OF US ARE STRUGGLING TO SURVIVE!
I THOUGHT... YOU'D RETURNED TO PROTECT OUR VILLAGE WITH ME!
YOU MIGHT BE A LITTLE STRONGER NOW, BUT YOU'RE TOTALLY OUT OF LINE.
...

READ THIS WAY

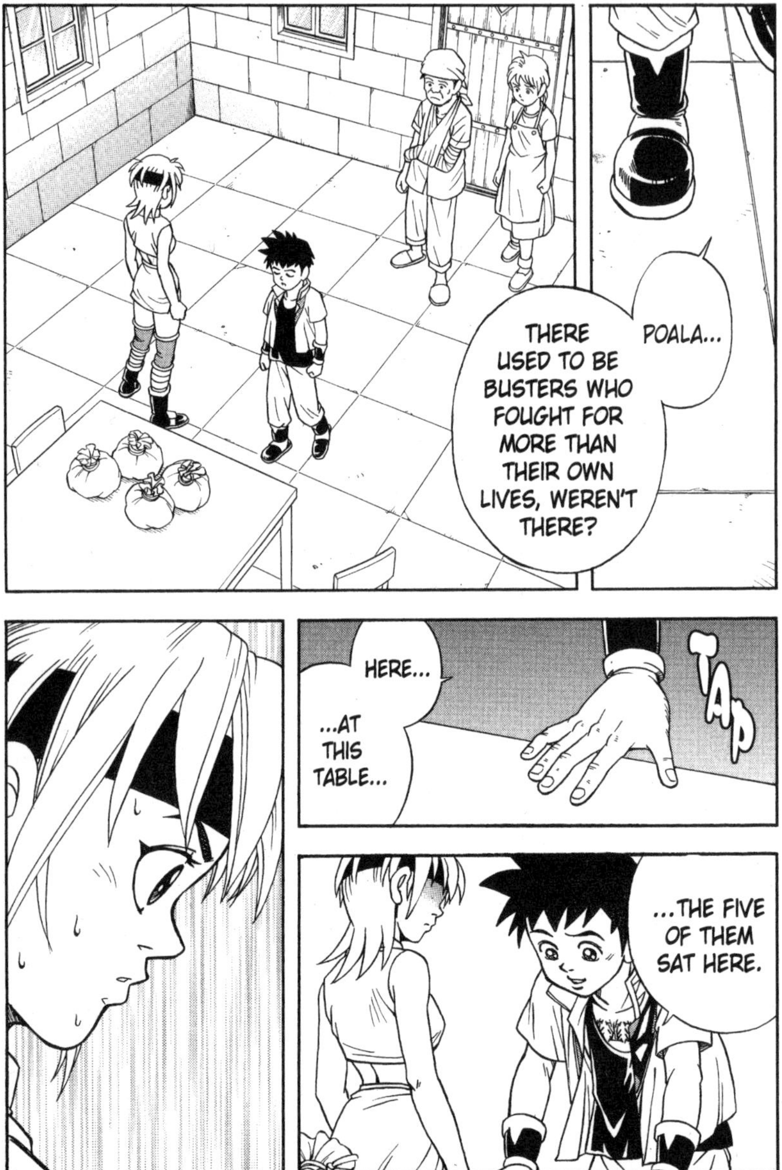
POALA...
THERE USED TO BE BUSTERS WHO FOUGHT FOR MORE THAN THEIR OWN LIVES, WEREN'T THERE?
HERE...
...AT THIS TABLE...
TAP
...THE FIVE OF THEM SAT HERE.

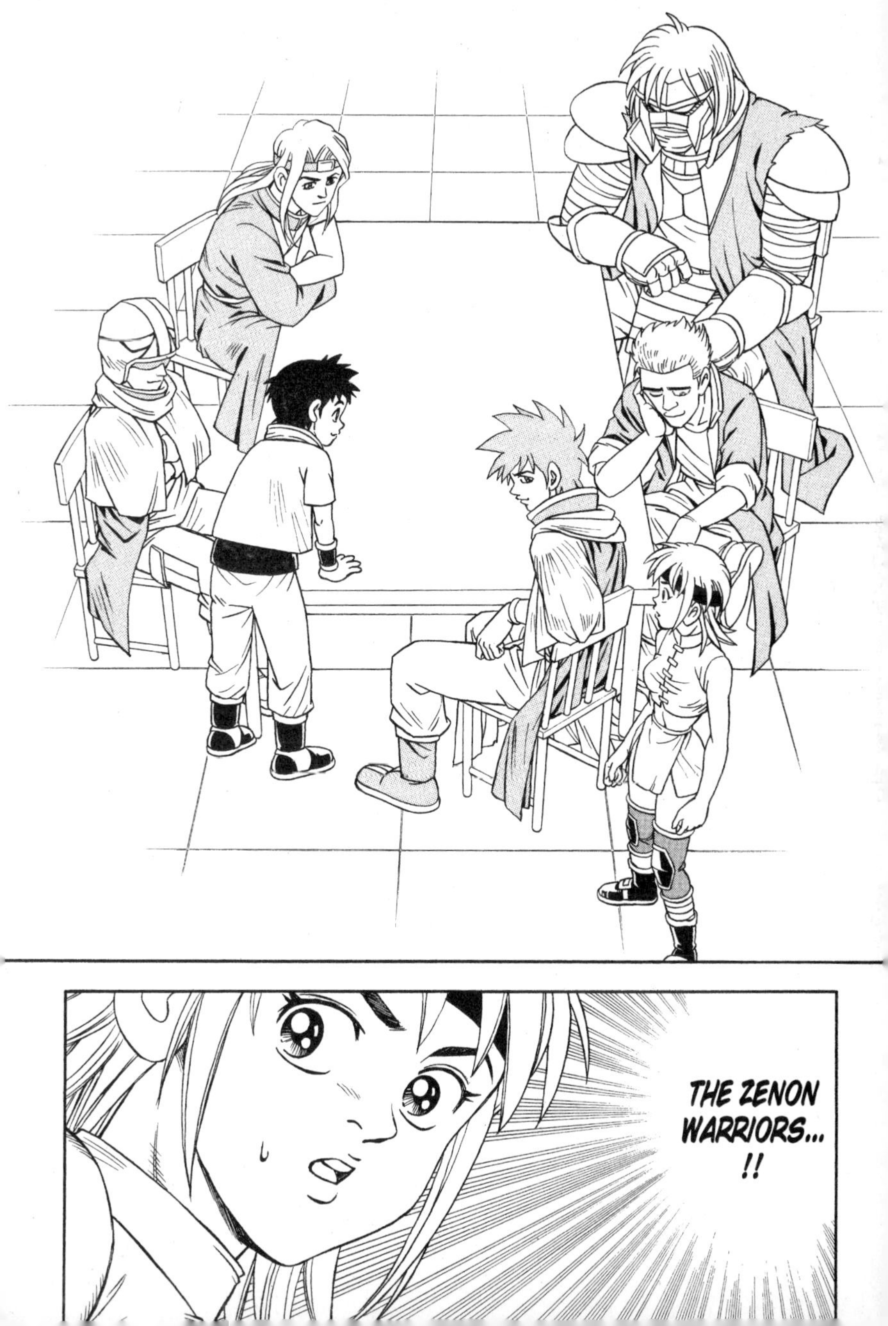
THE ZENON WARRIORS... !!

READ THIS WAY

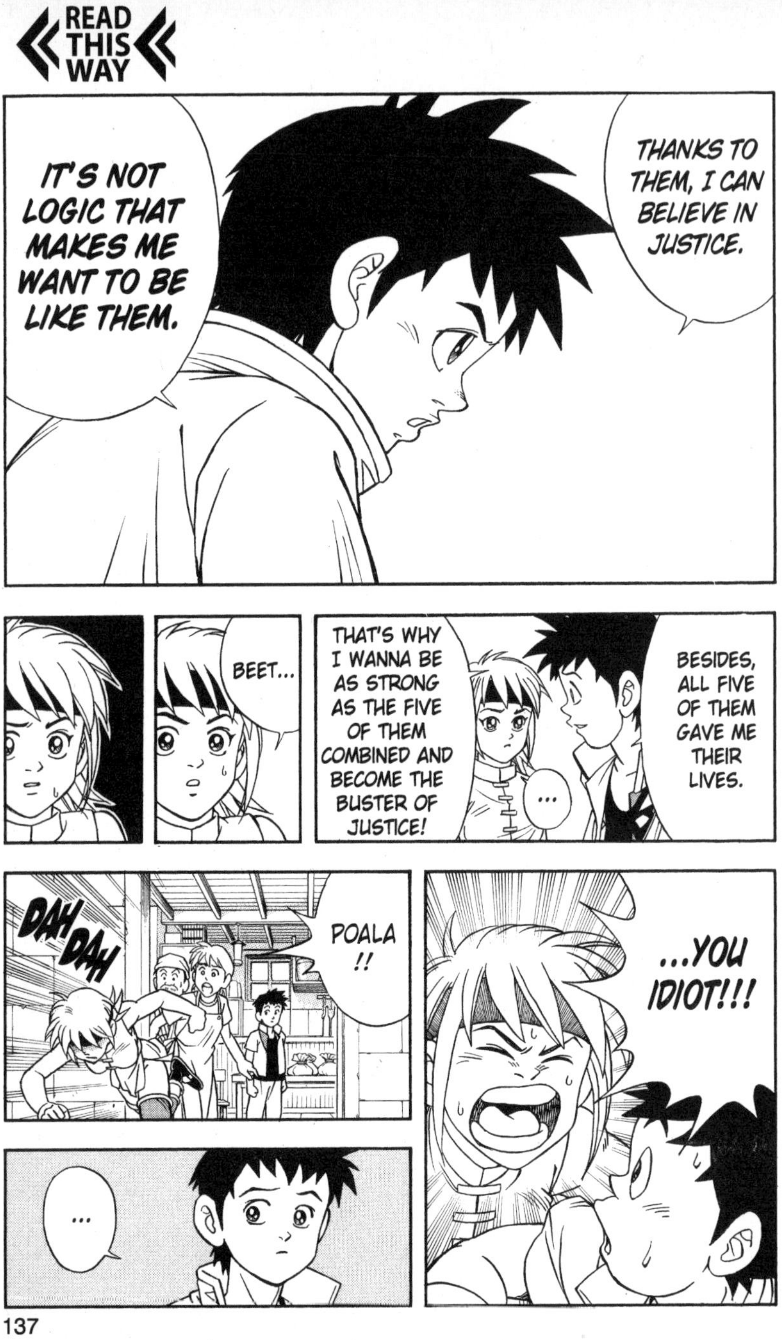
THANKS TO THEM, I CAN BELIEVE IN JUSTICE.
IT'S NOT LOGIC THAT MAKES ME WANT TO BE LIKE THEM.
BESIDES, ALL FIVE OF THEM GAVE ME THEIR LIVES.
...
THAT'S WHY I WANNA BE AS STRONG AS THE FIVE OF THEM COMBINED AND BECOME THE BUSTER OF JUSTICE!
BEET...
...YOU IDIOT!!!
POALA !!
DAH DAH
...

READ THIS WAY

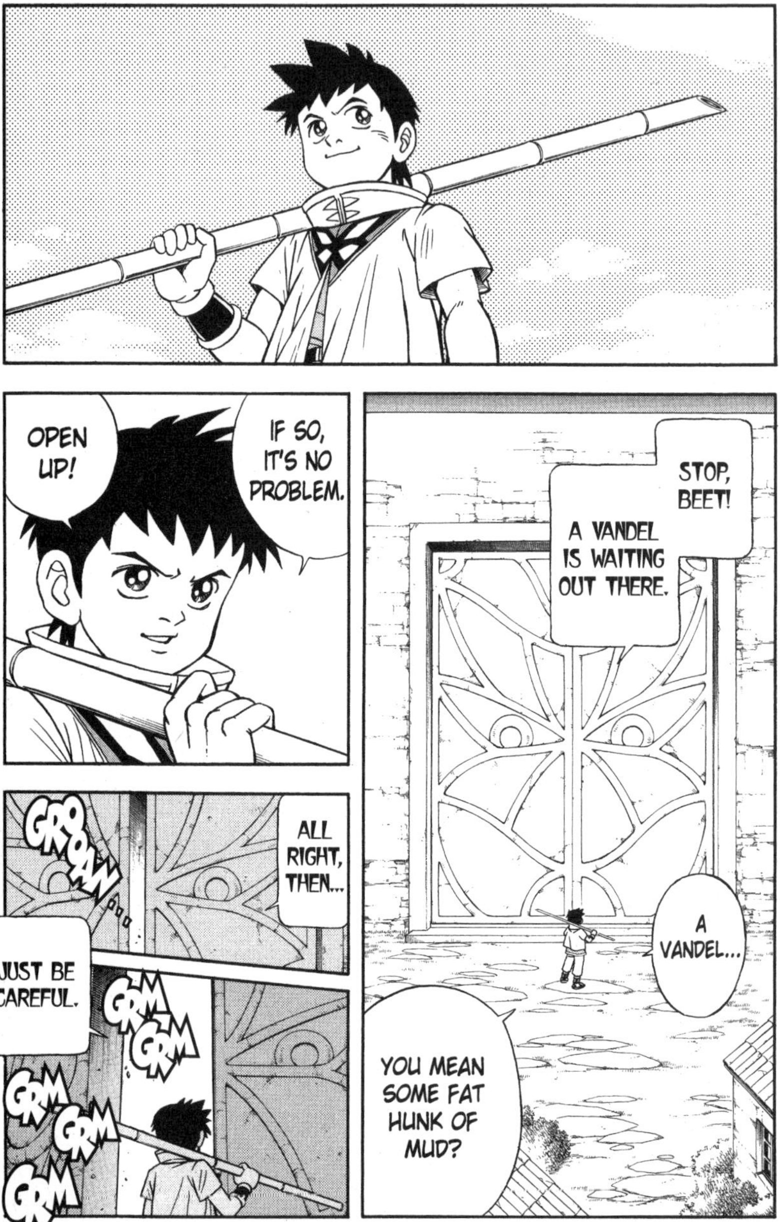

STOP, BEET!
A VANDEL IS WAITING OUT THERE.
A VANDEL...
YOU MEAN SOME FAT HUNK OF MUD?
IF SO, IT'S NO PROBLEM.
OPEN UP!
ALL RIGHT, THEN...
GROAAN...
JUST BE CAREFUL.
GRM GRM GRM
GRM GRM
GRM

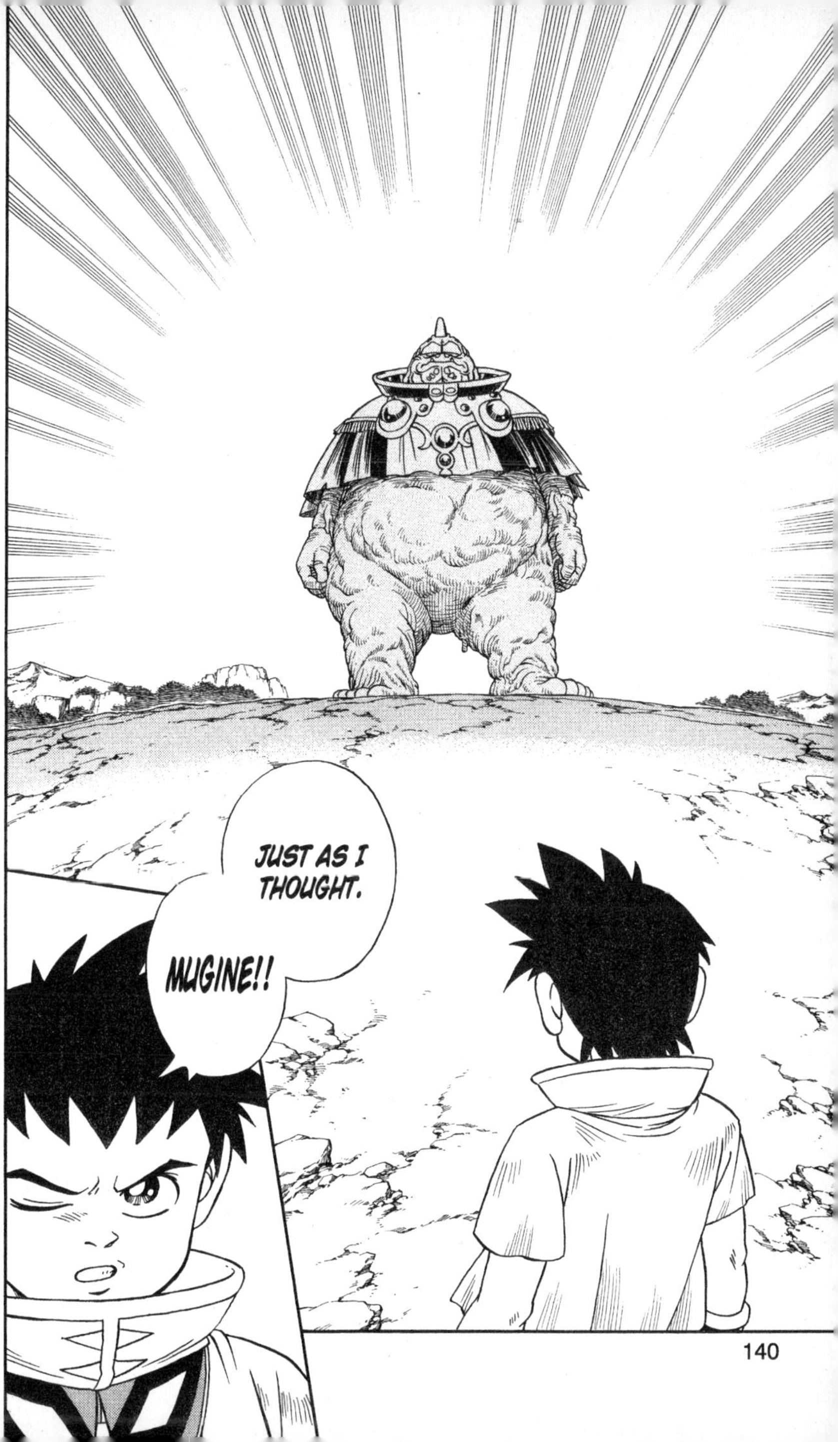
JUST AS I THOUGHT.
MUGINE!!

READ THIS WAY

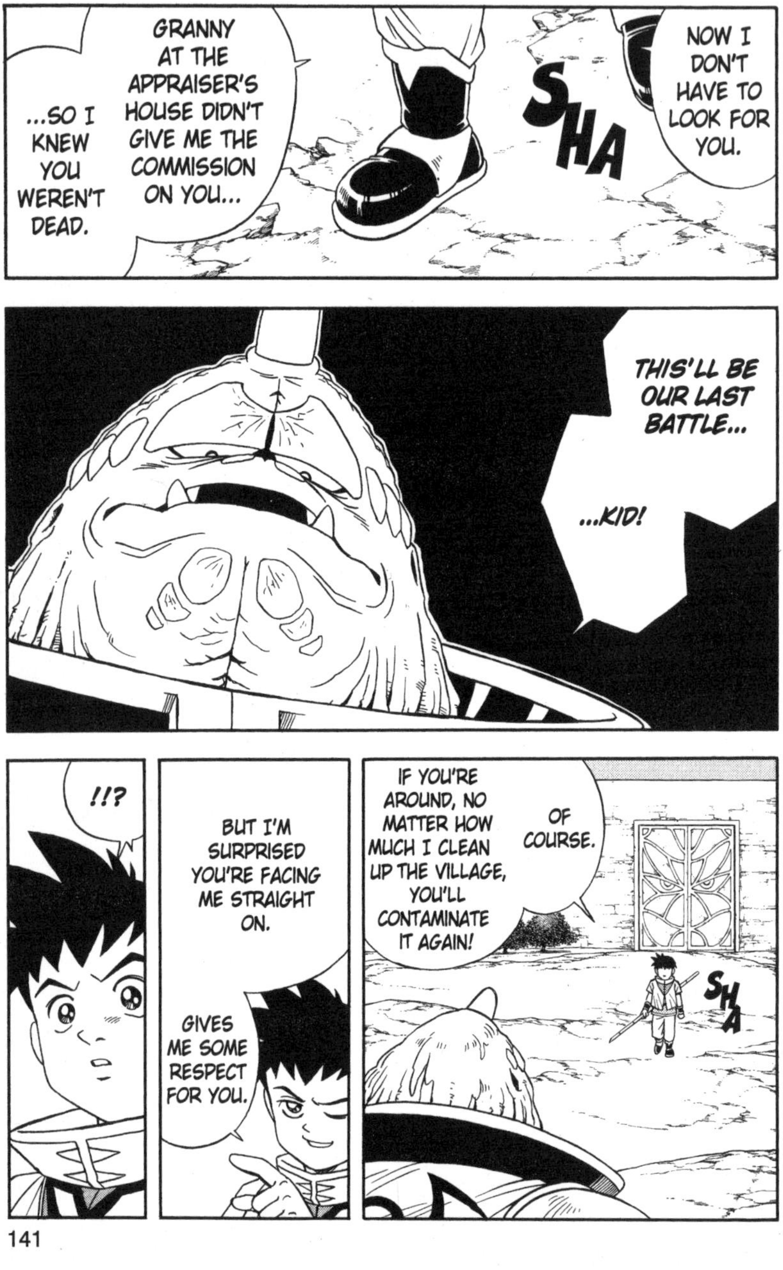
NOW I DON'T HAVE TO LOOK FOR YOU.
SHA
GRANNY AT THE APPRAISER'S HOUSE DIDN'T GIVE ME THE COMMISSION ON YOU...
...SO I KNEW YOU WEREN'T DEAD.
THIS'LL BE OUR LAST BATTLE...
...KID!
OF COURSE.
IF YOU'RE AROUND, NO MATTER HOW MUCH I CLEAN UP THE VILLAGE, YOU'LL CONTAMINATE IT AGAIN!
SHA
BUT I'M SURPRISED YOU'RE FACING ME STRAIGHT ON.
GIVES ME SOME RESPECT FOR YOU.
!!?

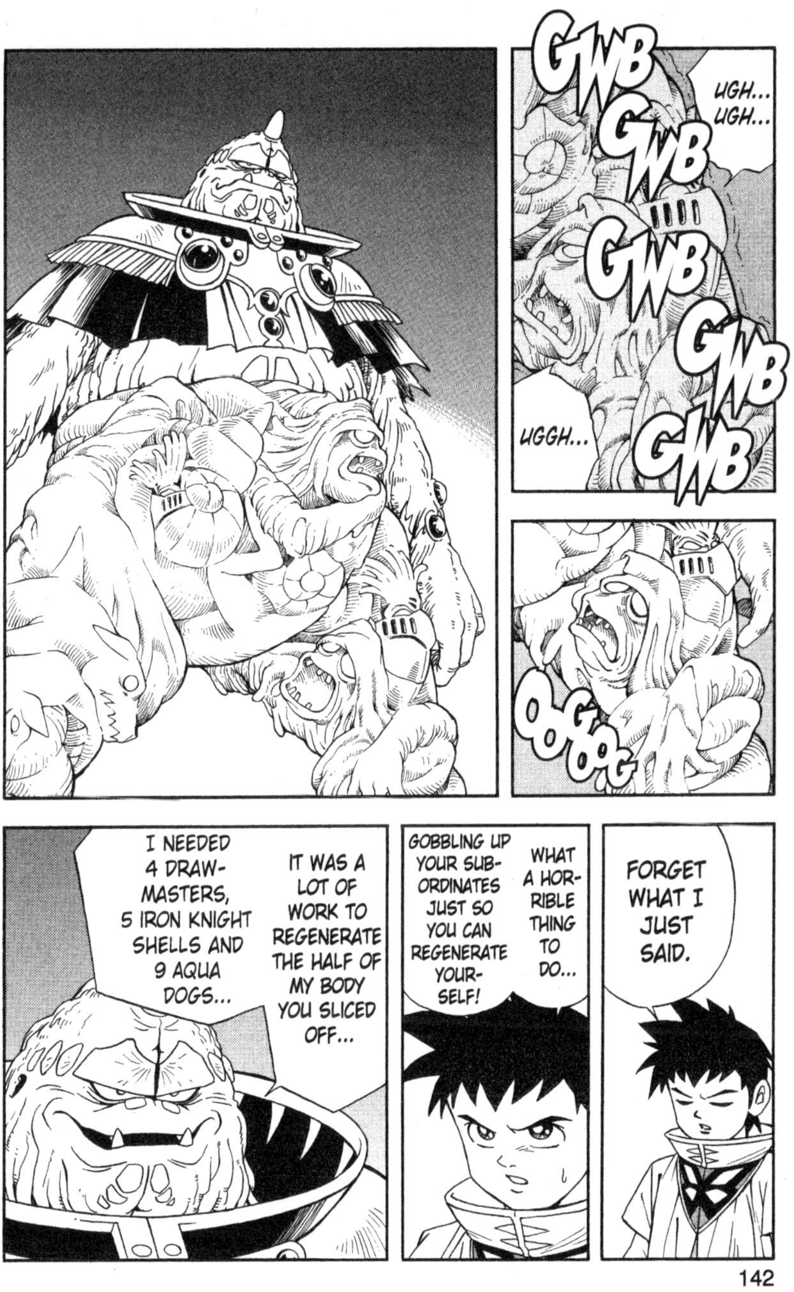
UGH... UGH...
GWB
GWB
GWB
GWB
GWB
UGGH...
OOGOOG
FORGET WHAT I JUST SAID.
WHAT A HORRIBLE THING TO DO...
GOBBLING UP YOUR SUBORDINATES JUST SO YOU CAN REGENERATE YOURSELF!
IT WAS A LOT OF WORK TO REGENERATE THE HALF OF MY BODY YOU SLICED OFF...
I NEEDED 4 DRAW-MASTERS, 5 IRON KNIGHT SHELLS AND 9 AQUA DOGS...

READ THIS WAY

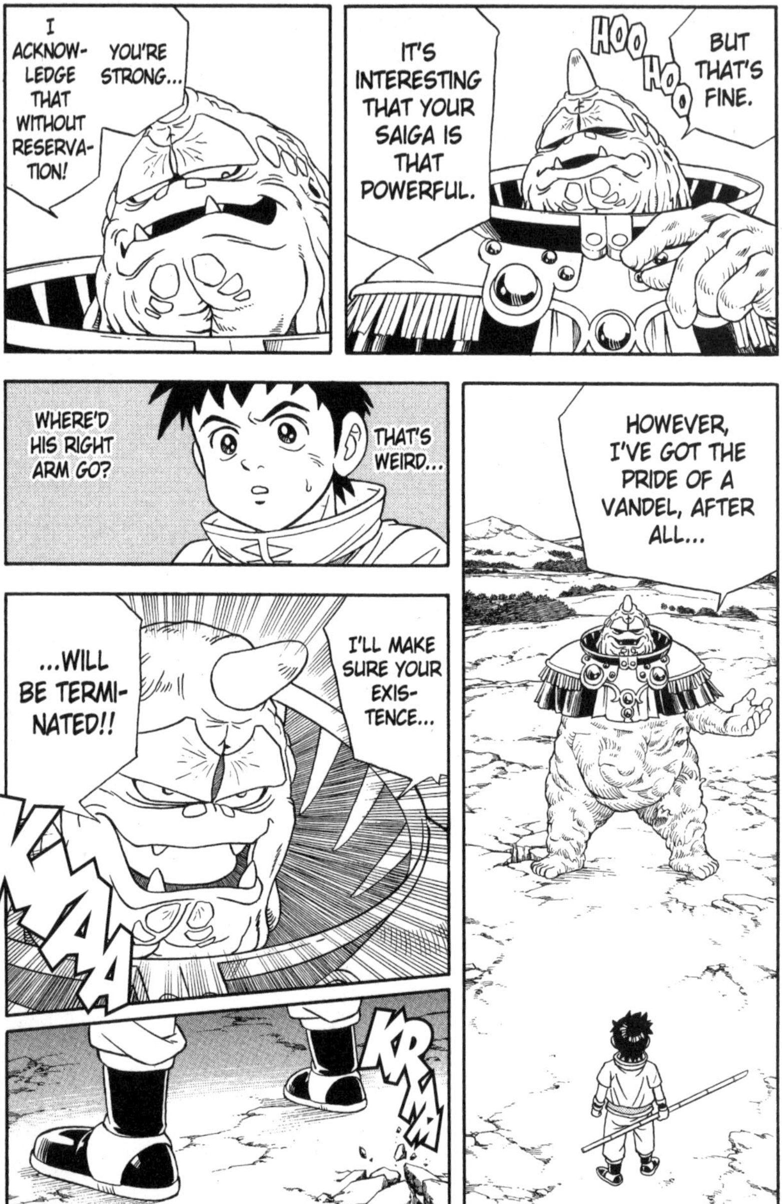
HOO HOO
BUT THAT'S FINE.
IT'S INTERESTING THAT YOUR SAIGA IS THAT POWERFUL.
YOU'RE STRONG...
I ACKNOWLEDGE THAT WITHOUT RESERVATION!
HOWEVER, I'VE GOT THE PRIDE OF A VANDEL, AFTER ALL...
THAT'S WEIRD...
WHERE'D HIS RIGHT ARM GO?
I'LL MAKE SURE YOUR EXISTENCE...
...WILL BE TERMINATED!!
KWAA
KRMM

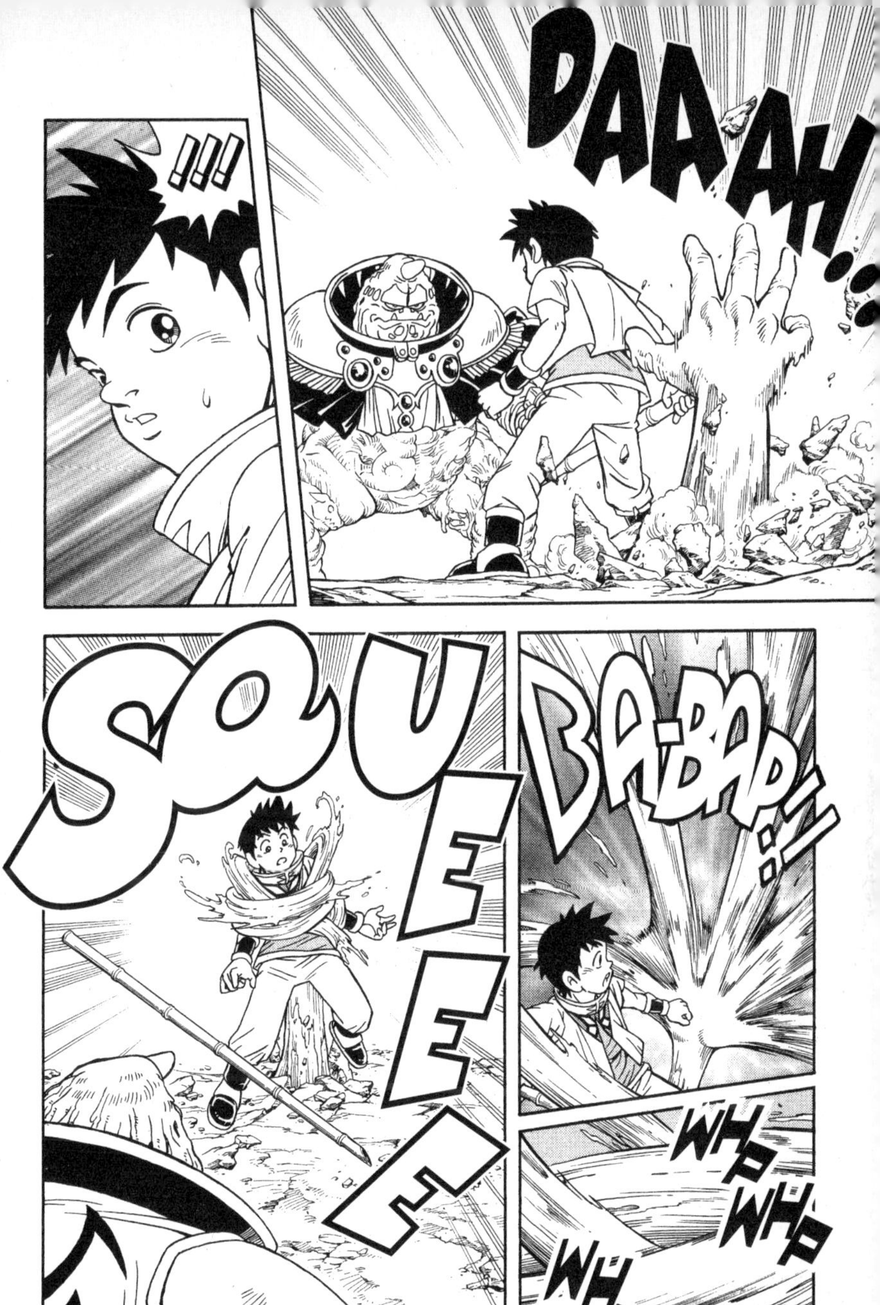
DAAAH...
!!!
BA-BAP!!
WHP
WHP
WHP
SQUEEEE

HEH HEH HEH

EVEN IF YOUR SAIGA'S STRONG, YOU PROBABLY CAN'T USE IT WITHOUT YOUR HANDS, RIGHT?

C'MON...

UGH UGH UGH

OO-OOPS!!

...!!

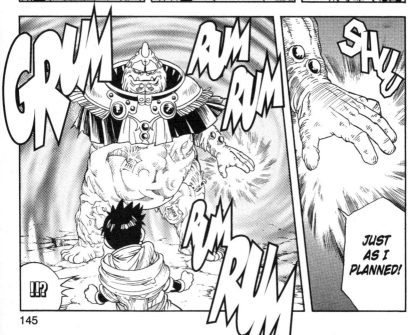

GRUM

RUM RUM

SHU

RUM RUM

!!?

JUST AS I PLANNED!

145

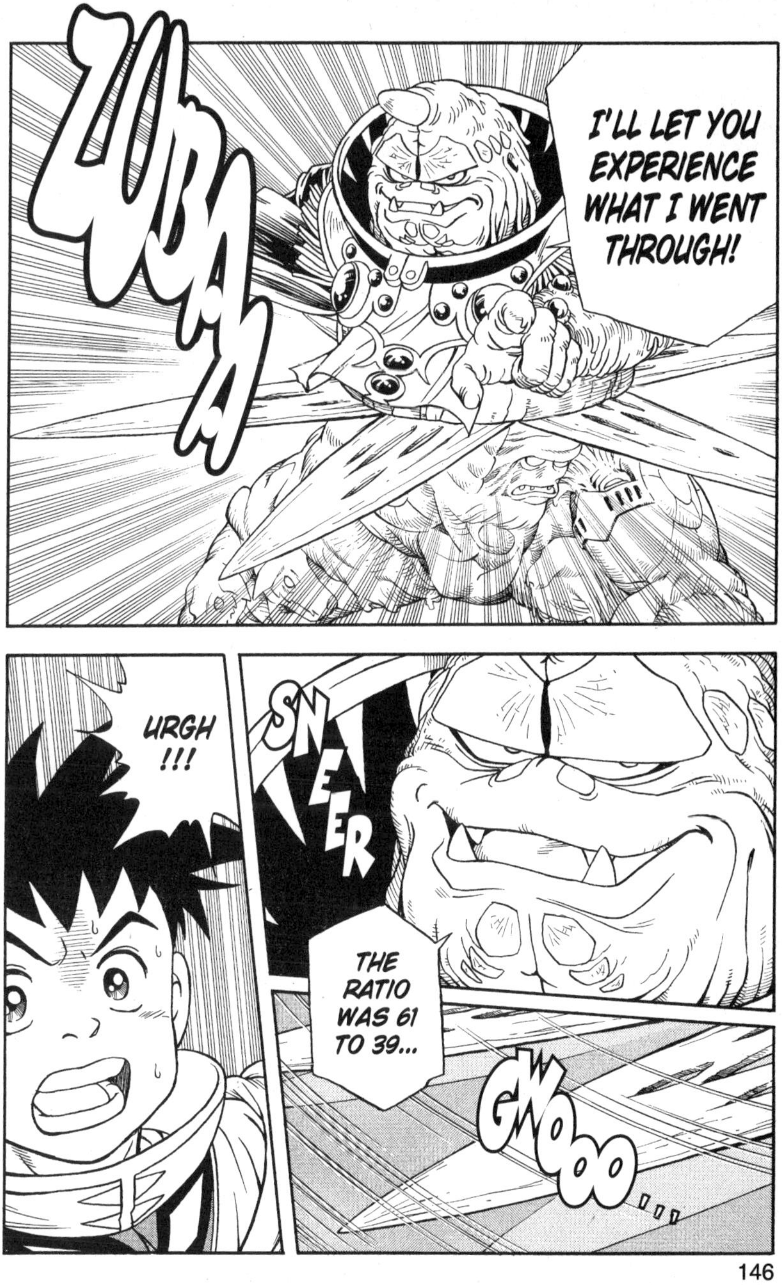
I'LL LET YOU EXPERIENCE WHAT I WENT THROUGH!
ZUBAAA
SNEER
THE RATIO WAS 61 TO 39...
GWOOO...
URGH !!!

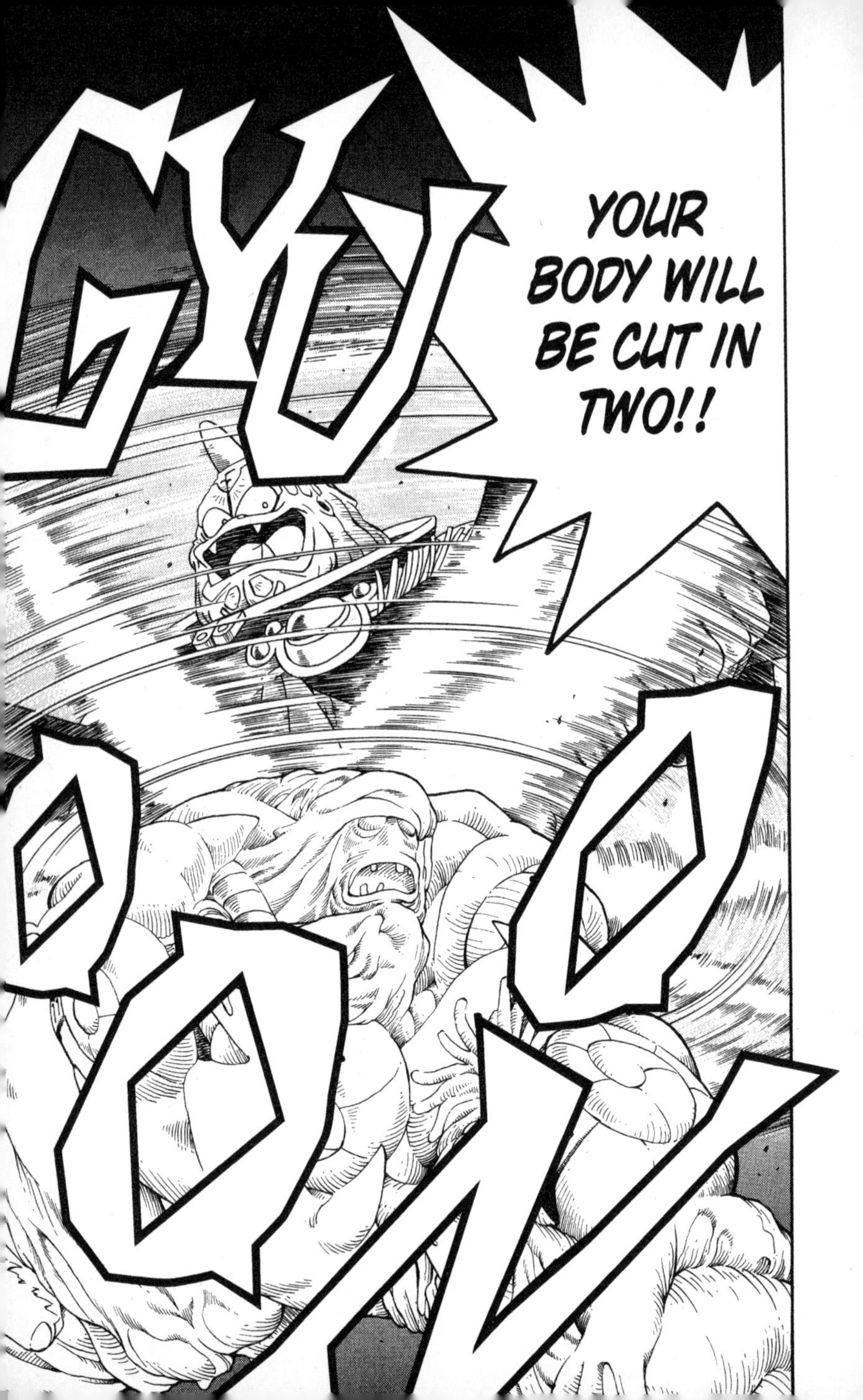
CYU
YOUR BODY WILL BE CUT IN TWO!!
OOON

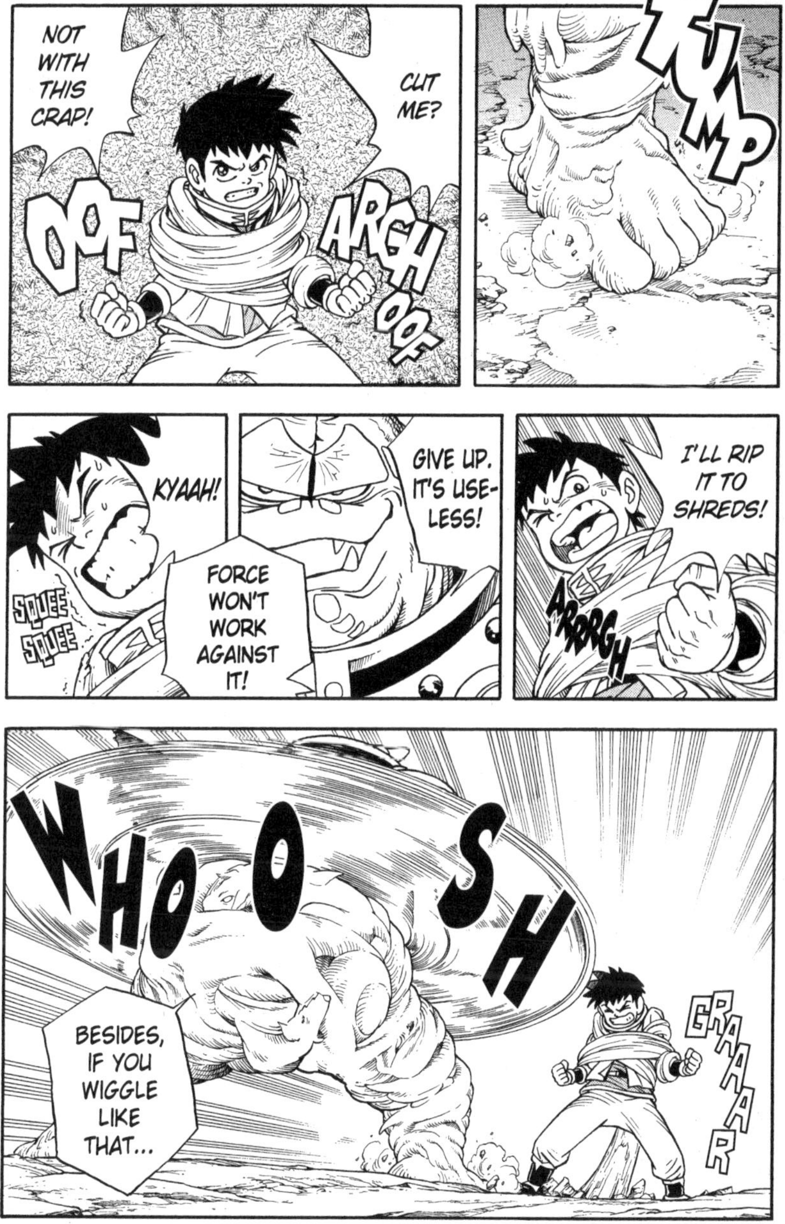
TUMP
CUT ME?
NOT WITH THIS CRAP!
ARGH
OOF
OOF
I'LL RIP IT TO SHREDS!
ARRRGH
GIVE UP. IT'S USE-LESS!
FORCE WON'T WORK AGAINST IT!
KYAAH!
SQUEE SQUEE
GRAAAAR
WHO-O-OSH
BESIDES, IF YOU WIGGLE LIKE THAT...

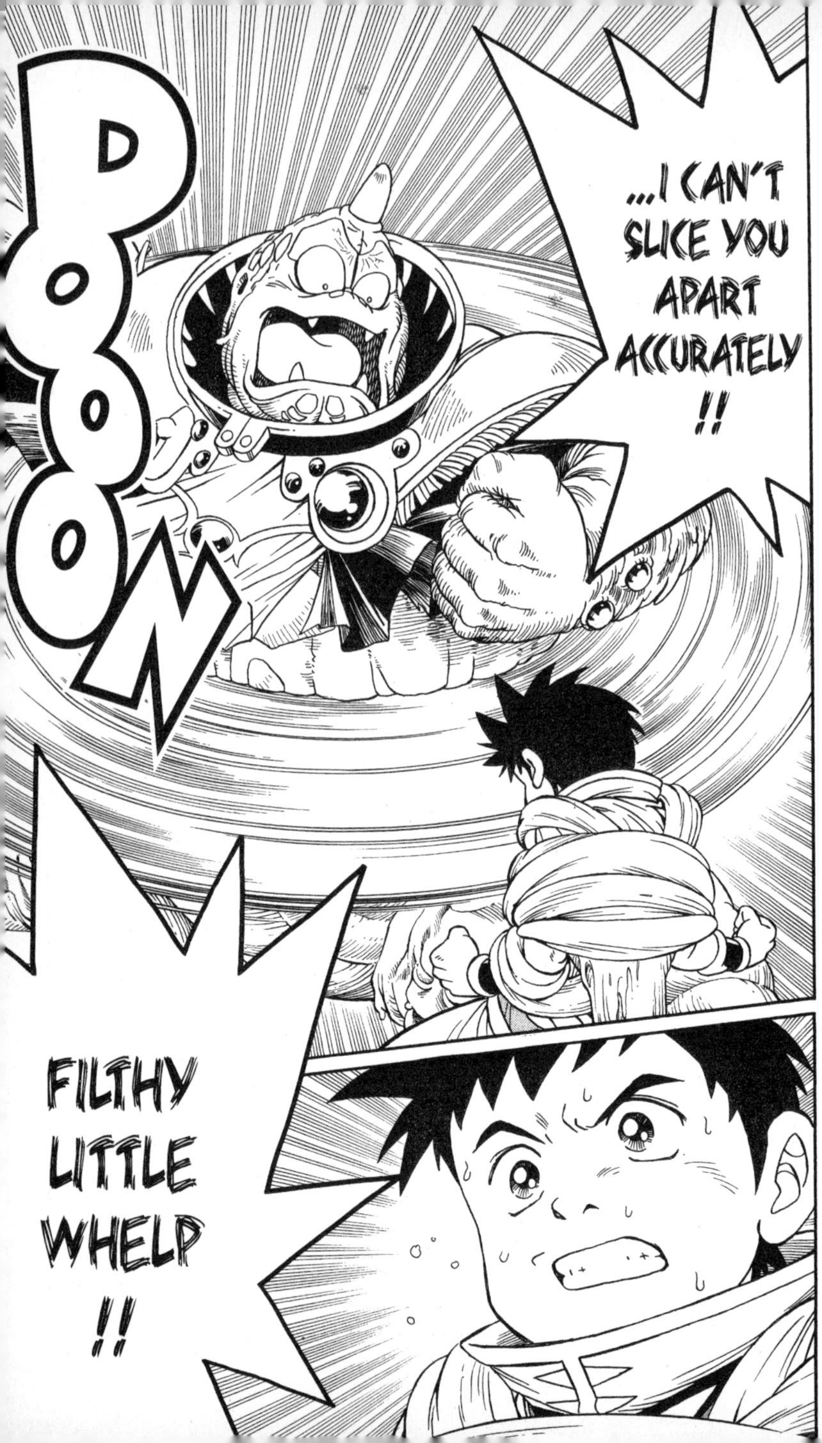
...I CAN'T SLICE YOU APART ACCURATELY !!
DOOOOM
FILTHY LITTLE WHELP !!

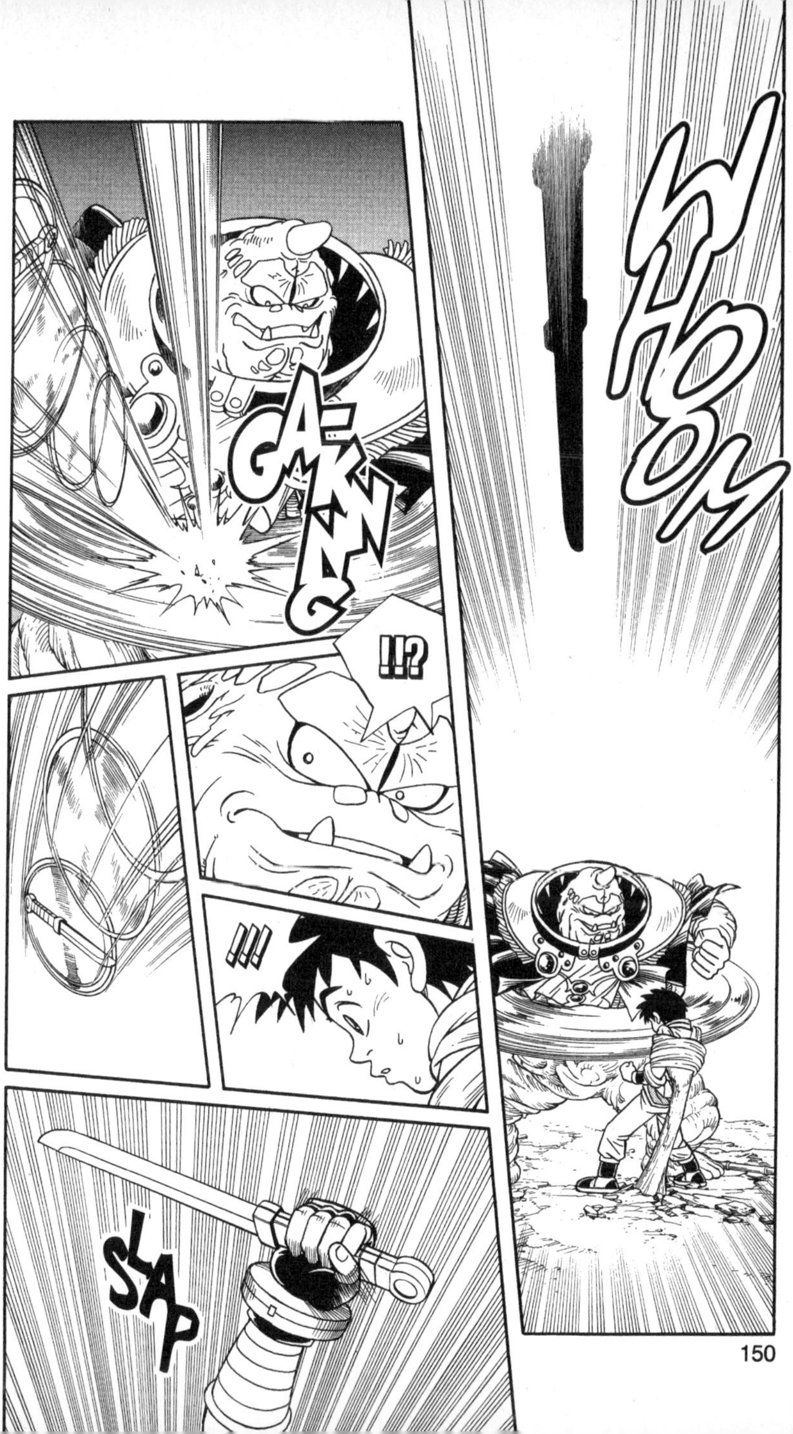
WHOOM
GA-KANNG
!!?
!!!
SLAP

READ THIS WAY

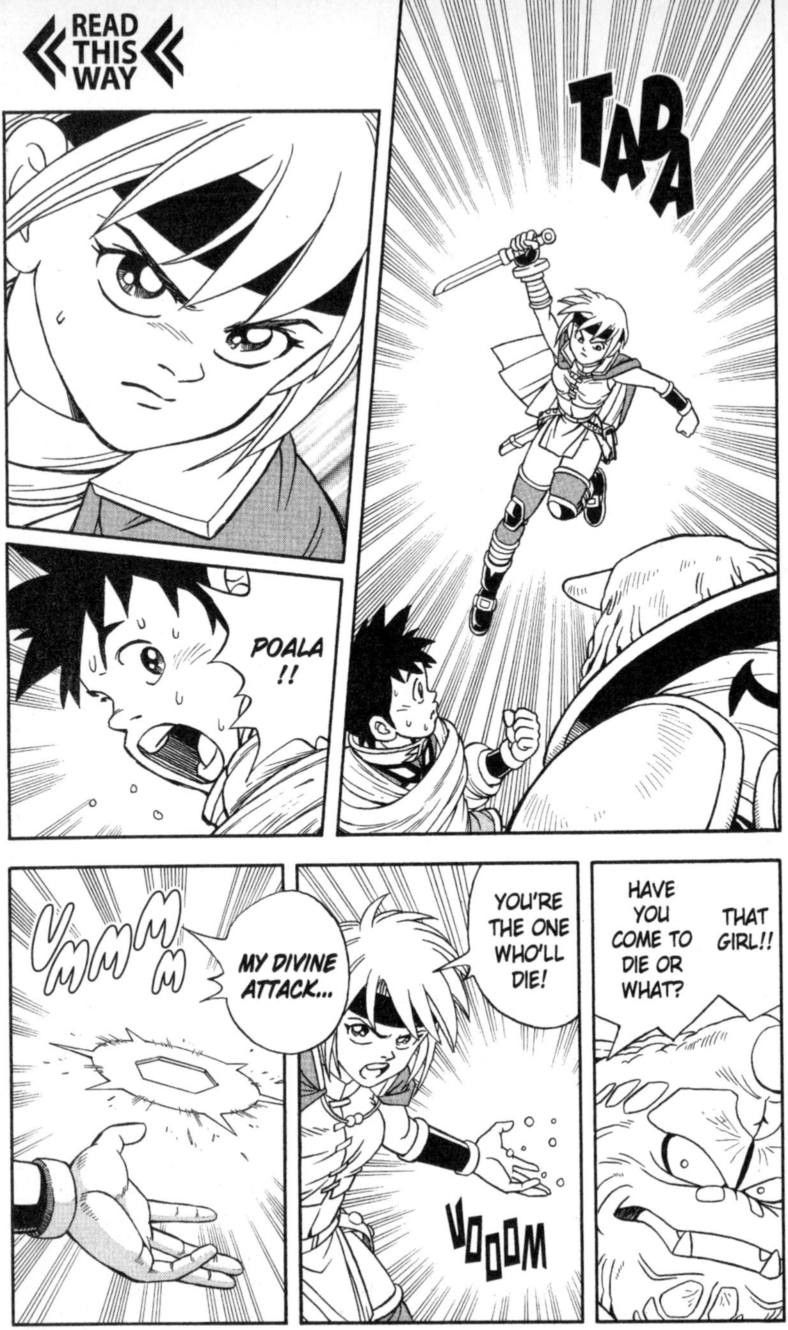
TADA
POALA !!
THAT GIRL!!
HAVE YOU COME TO DIE OR WHAT?
YOU'RE THE ONE WHO'LL DIE!
MY DIVINE ATTACK...
VOOOM
VMMMMM

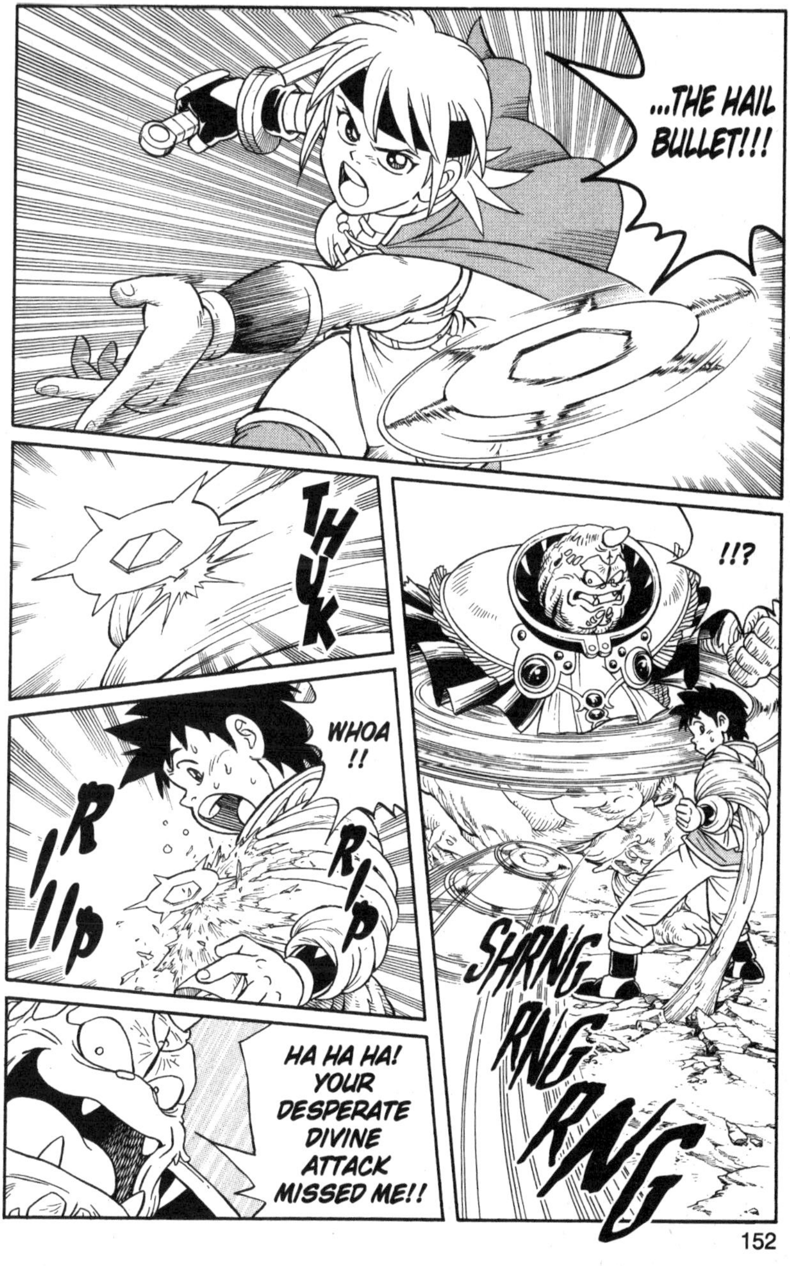
...THE HAIL BULLET!!!
!!?
SHRNG RNG RNG
THUK
WHOA!!
RIIIP
RIP
HA HA HA! YOUR DESPERATE DIVINE ATTACK MISSED ME!!

READ THIS WAY

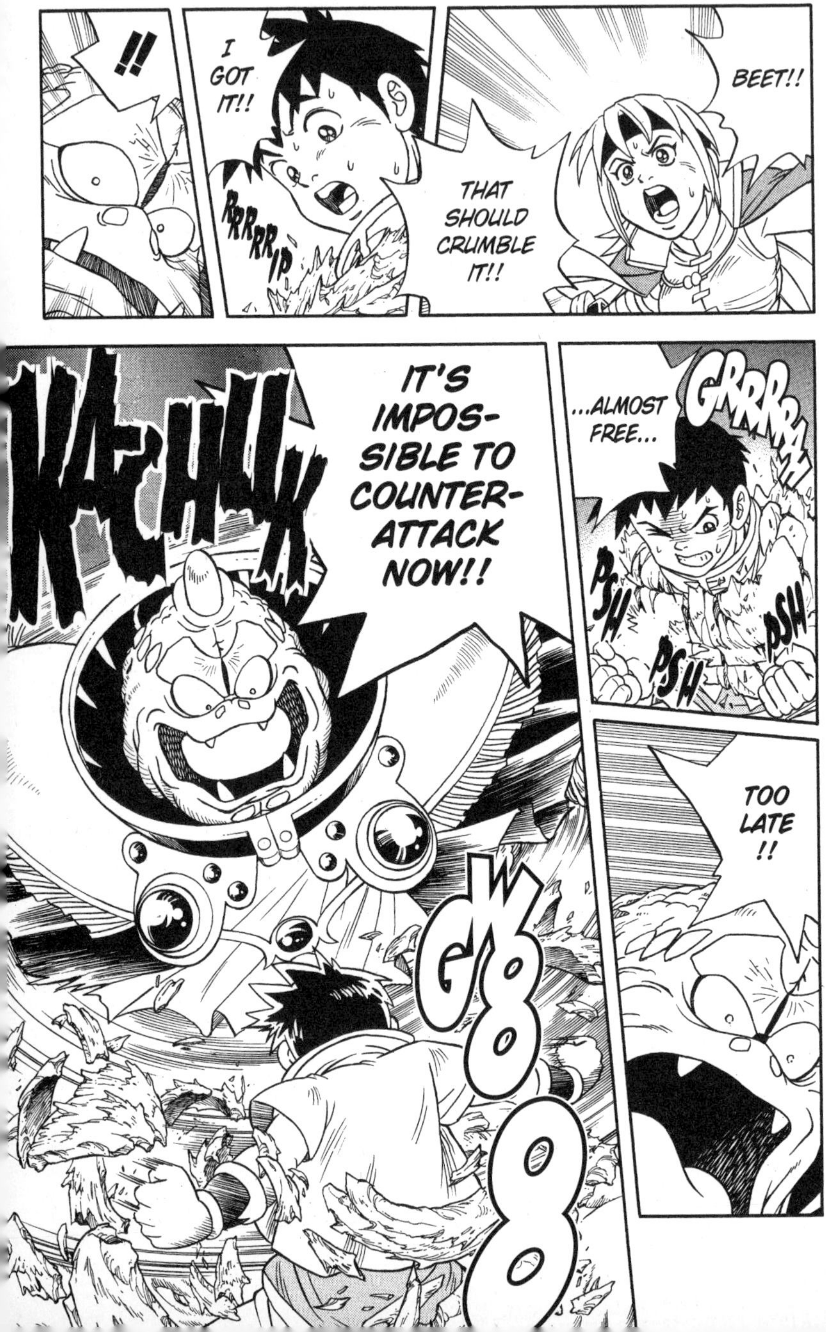
BEET!!
THAT SHOULD CRUMBLE IT!!
I GOT IT!!
!!
...ALMOST FREE...
PSH
PSH
PSH
TOO LATE!!
IT'S IMPOSSIBLE TO COUNTER-ATTACK NOW!!

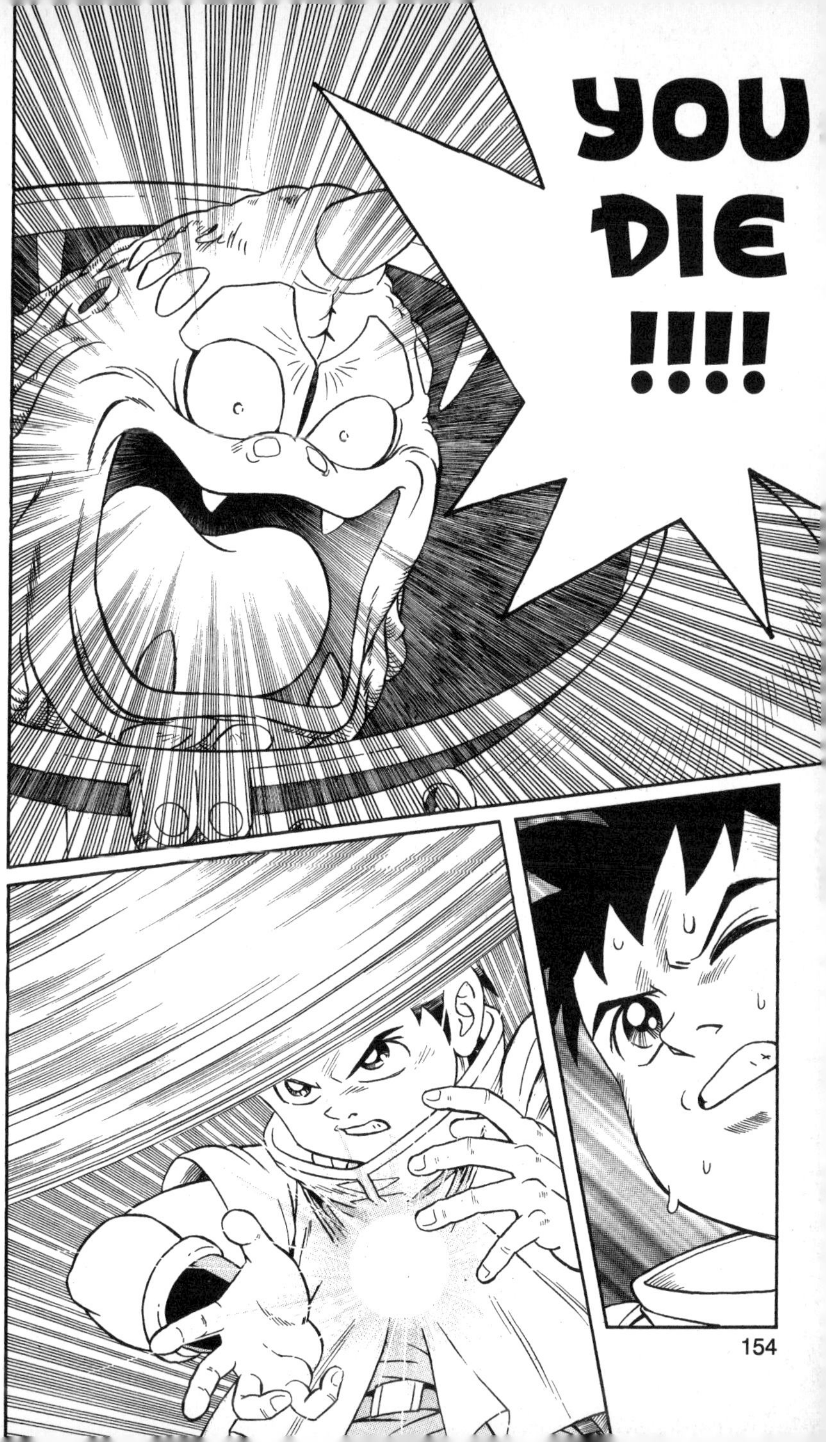
YOU DIE !!!!

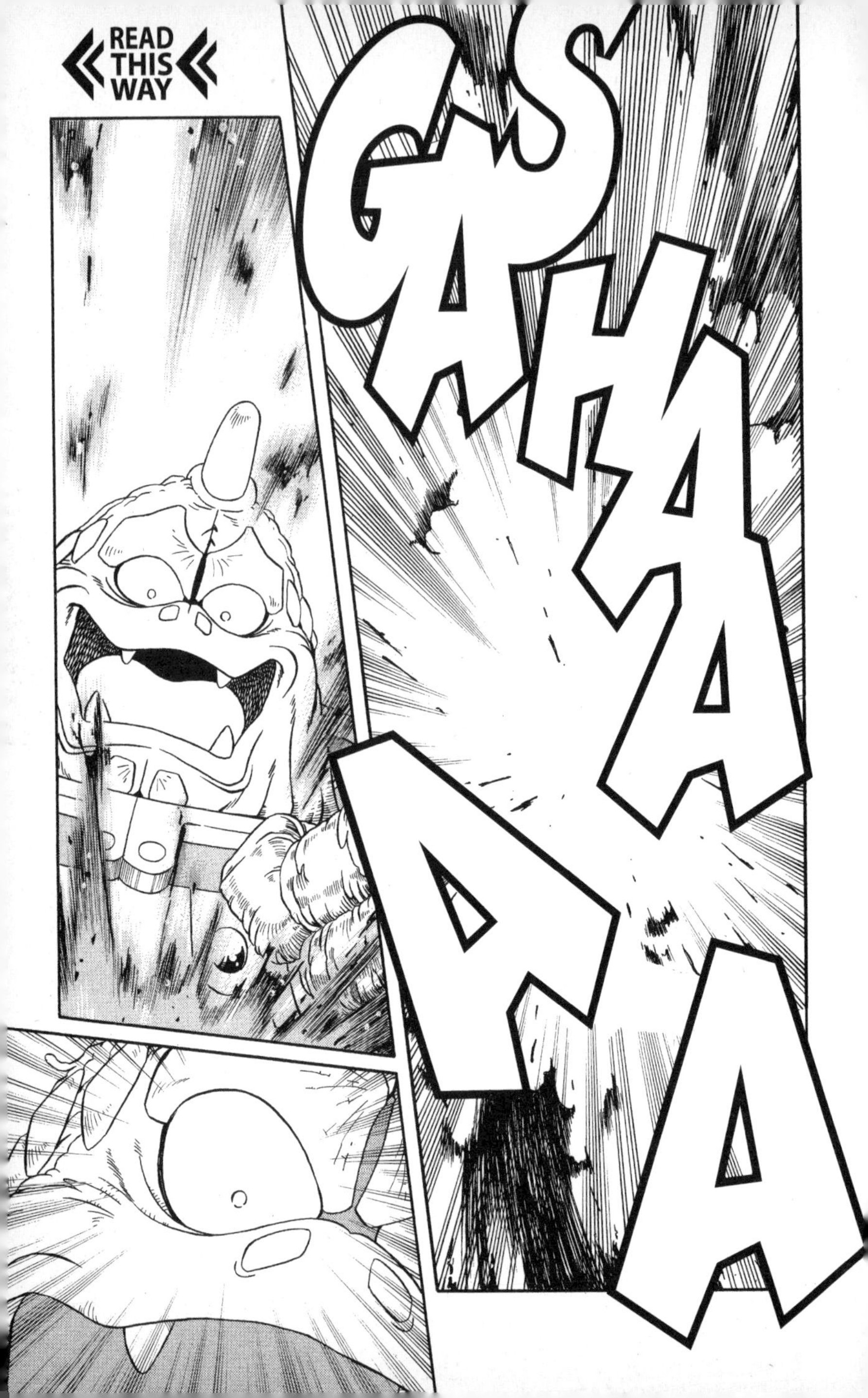
READ THIS WAY
GASHAAAA

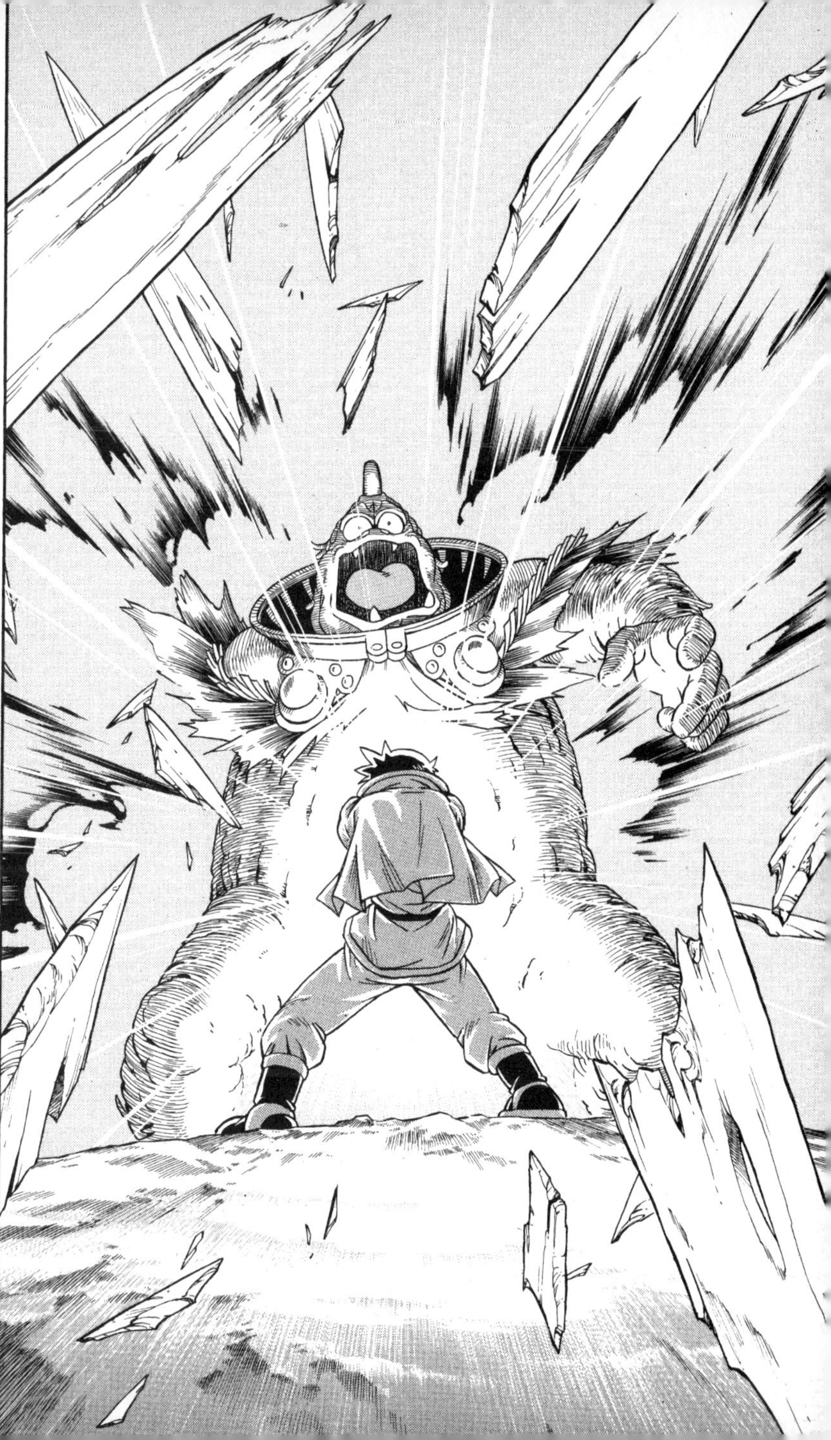

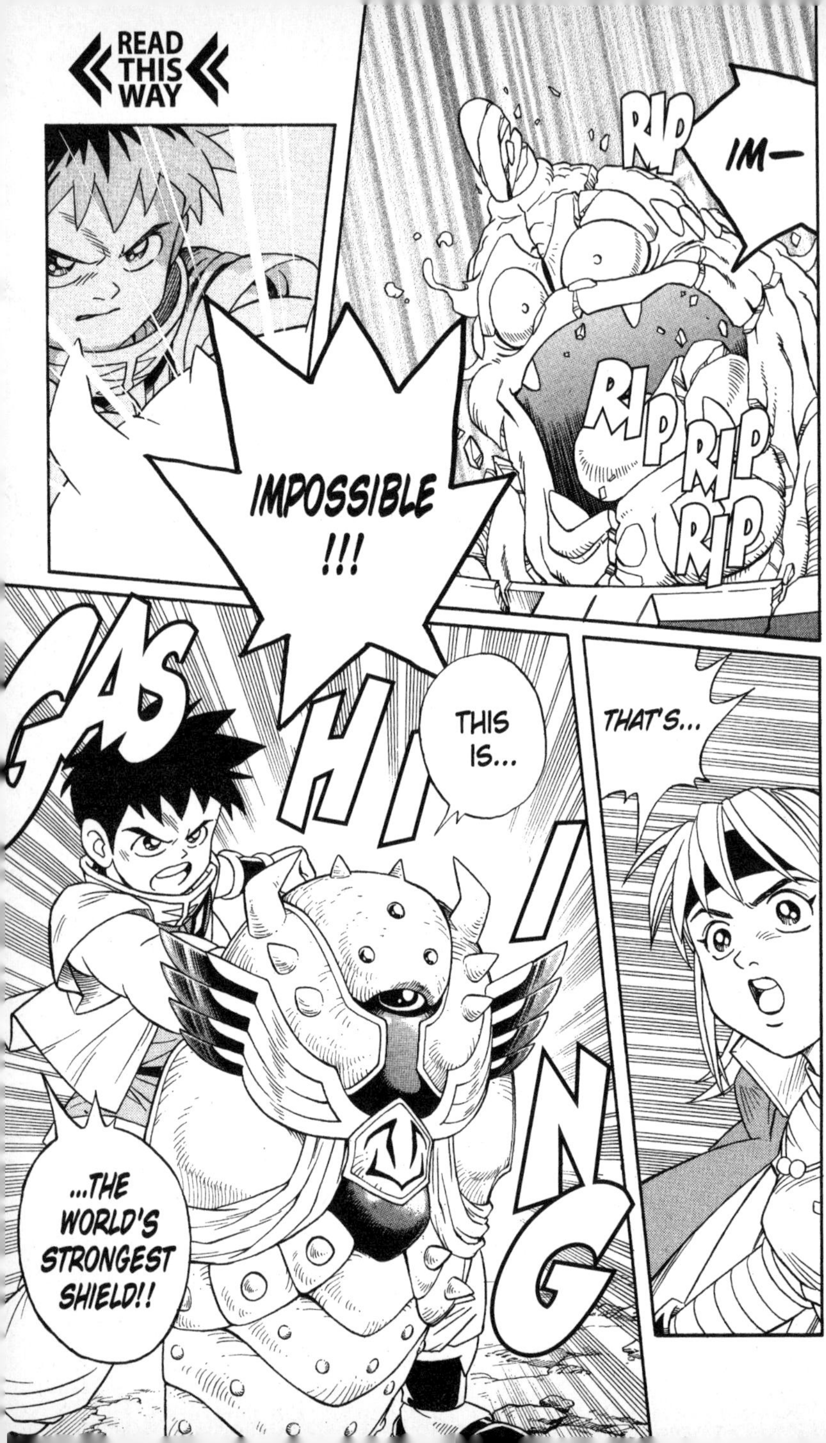

READ THIS WAY
IM—
RIP
RIP RIP RIP
IMPOSSIBLE !!!
THAT'S...
CASHIING
THIS IS...
...THE WORLD'S STRONGEST SHIELD!!

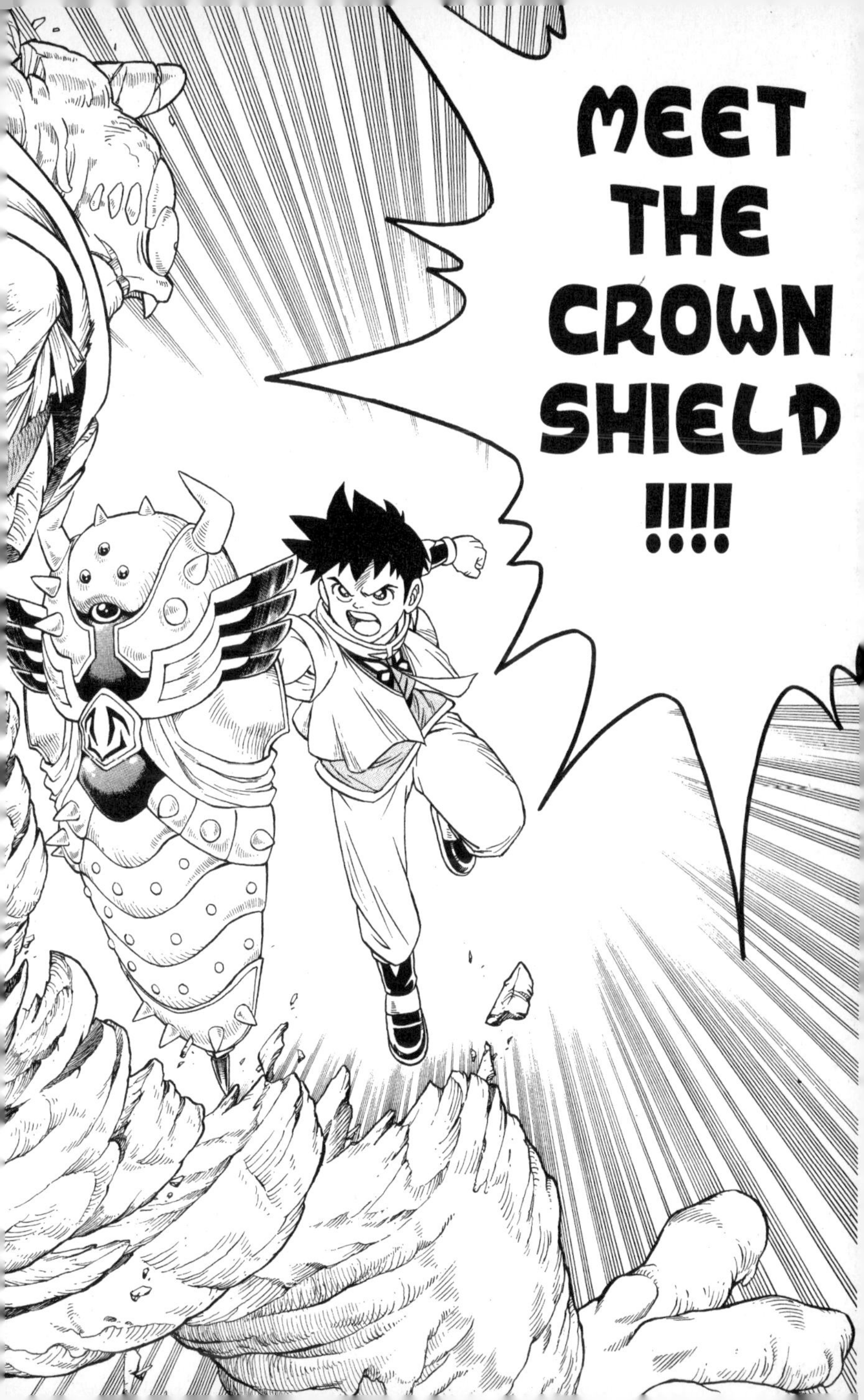
MEET THE CROWN SHIELD !!!!

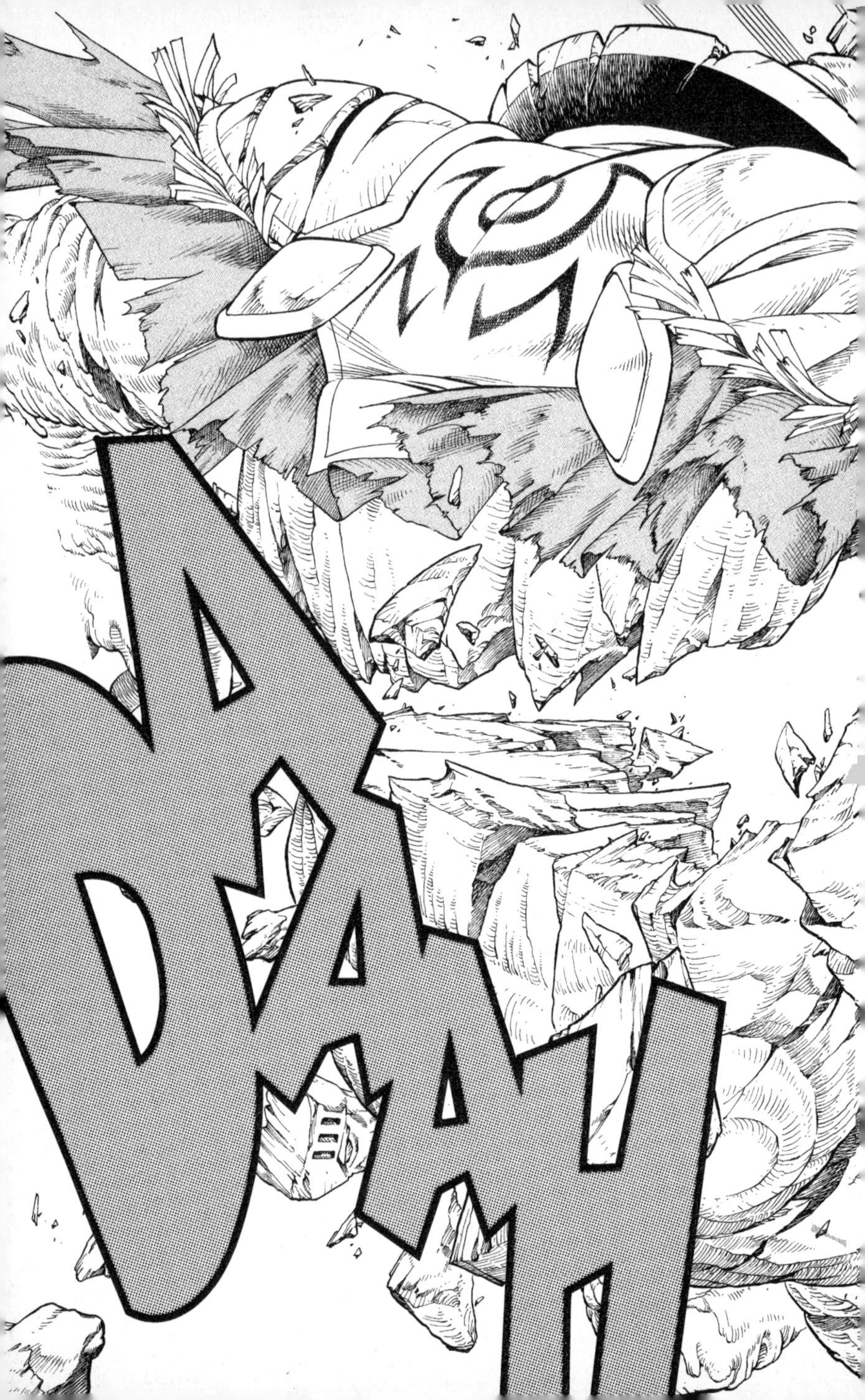

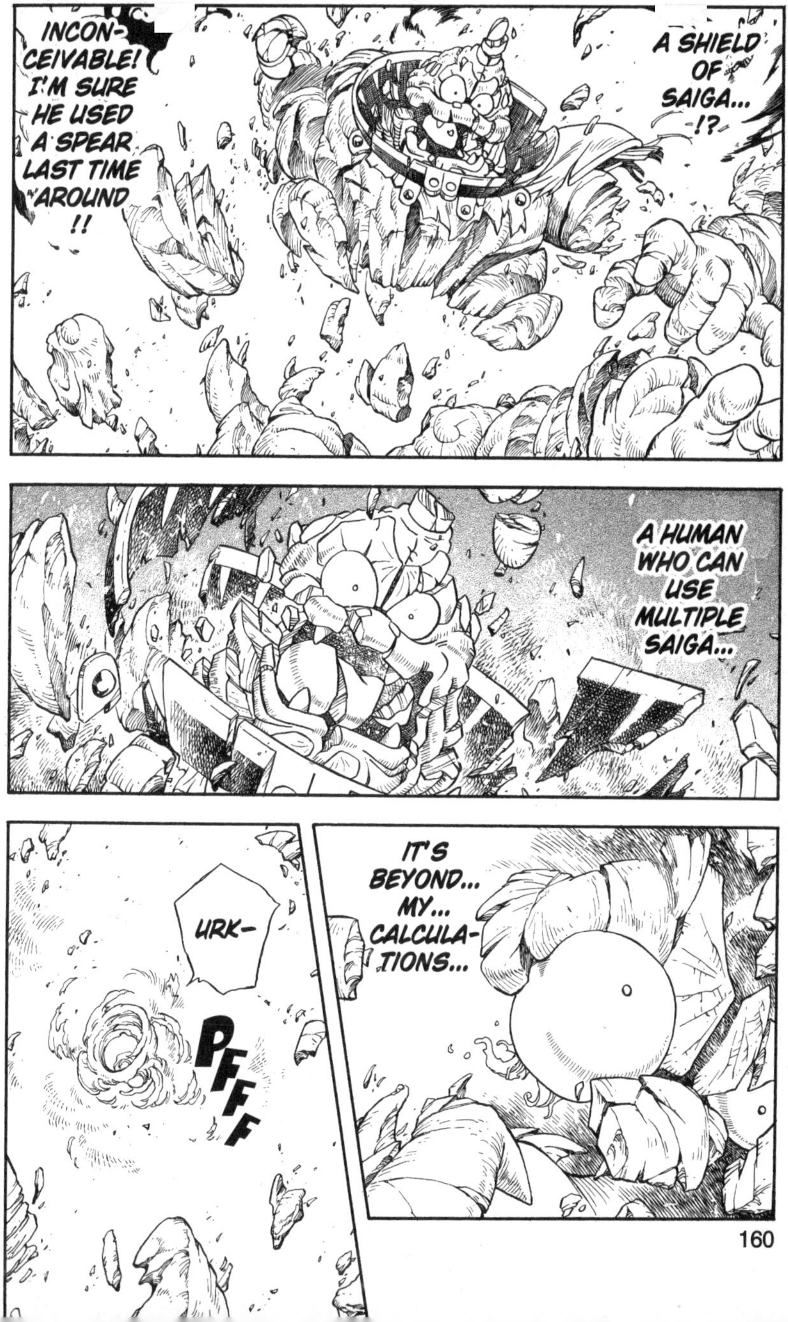
A SHIELD OF SAIGA...!?
INCONCEIVABLE! I'M SURE HE USED A SPEAR LAST TIME AROUND!!
A HUMAN WHO CAN USE MULTIPLE SAIGA...
IT'S BEYOND... MY... CALCULATIONS...
URK-
PFFF

READ THIS WAY

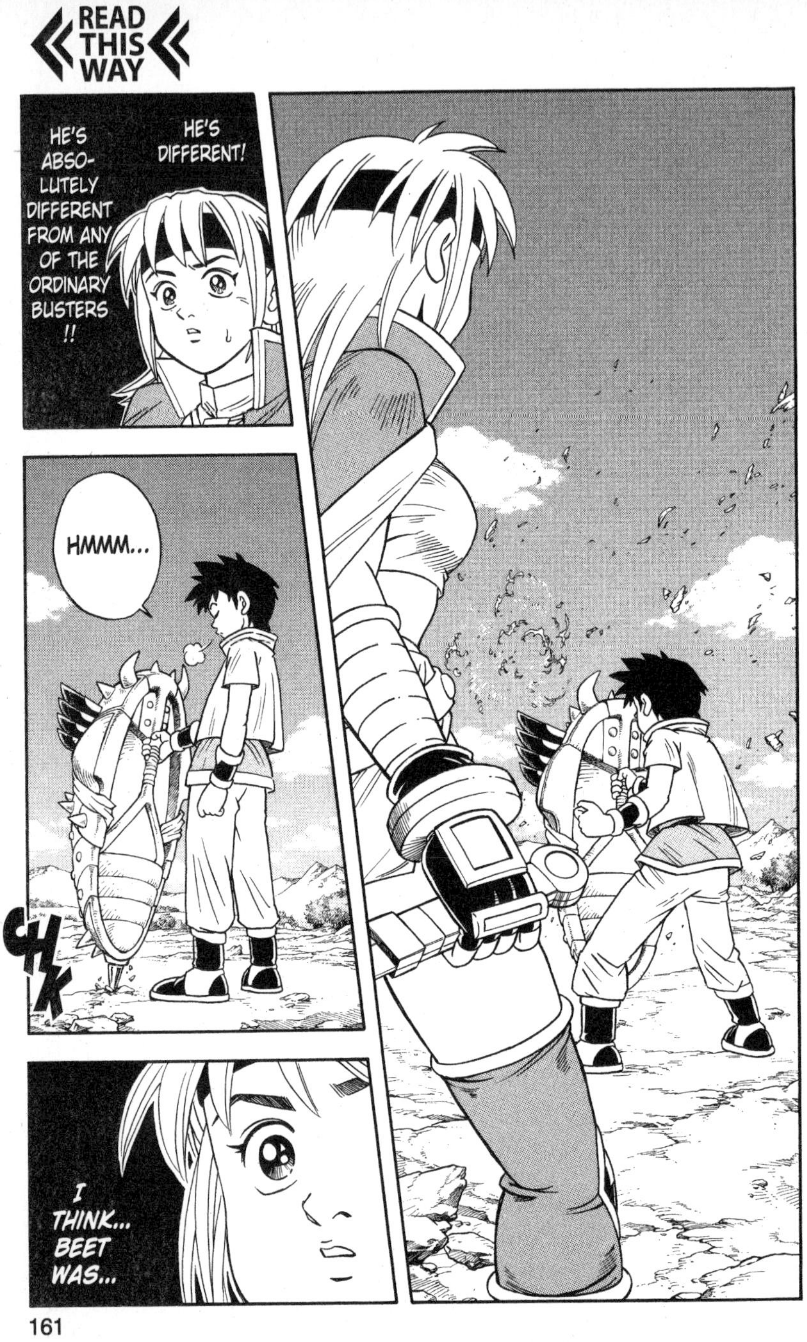
HE'S DIFFERENT!
HE'S ABSO-LUTELY DIFFERENT FROM ANY OF THE ORDINARY BUSTERS !!
HMMM...
CHK
I THINK... BEET WAS...

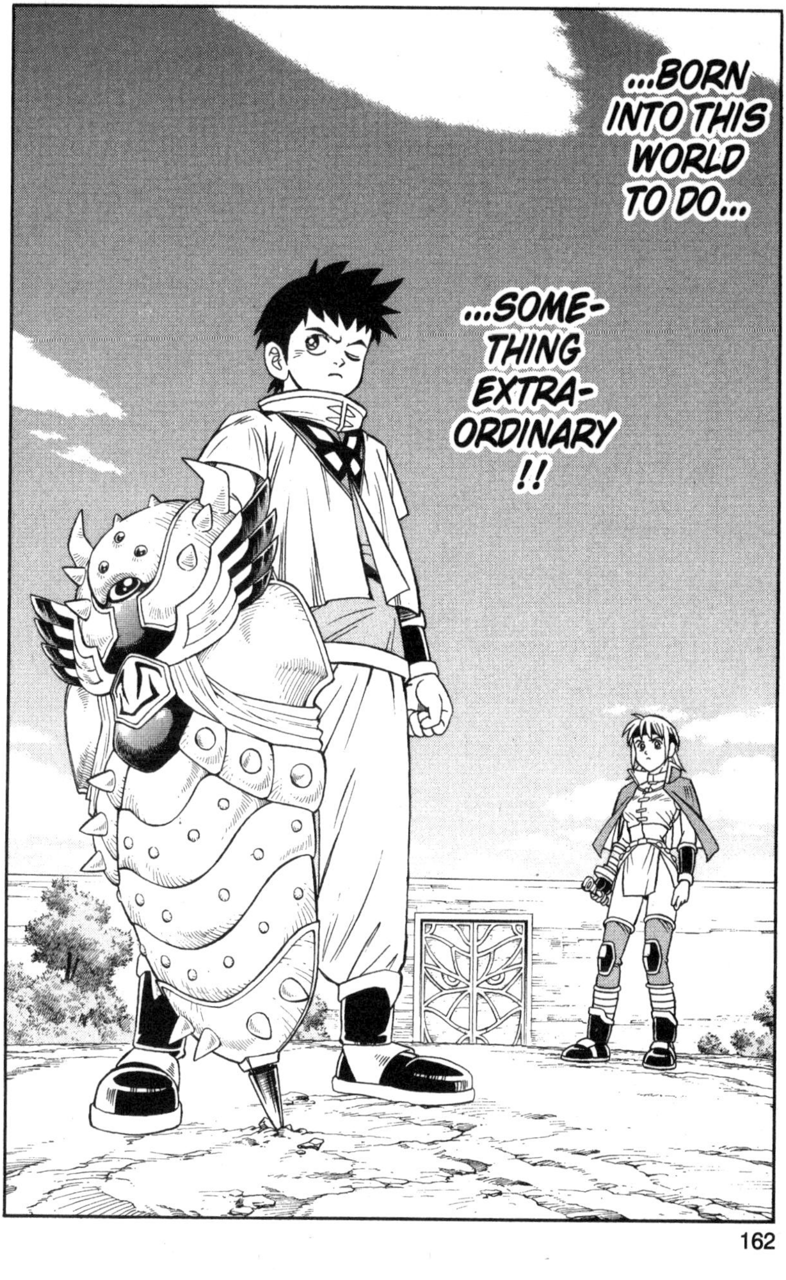
...BORN INTO THIS WORLD TO DO...
...SOME-THING EXTRA-ORDINARY !!

READ THIS WAY

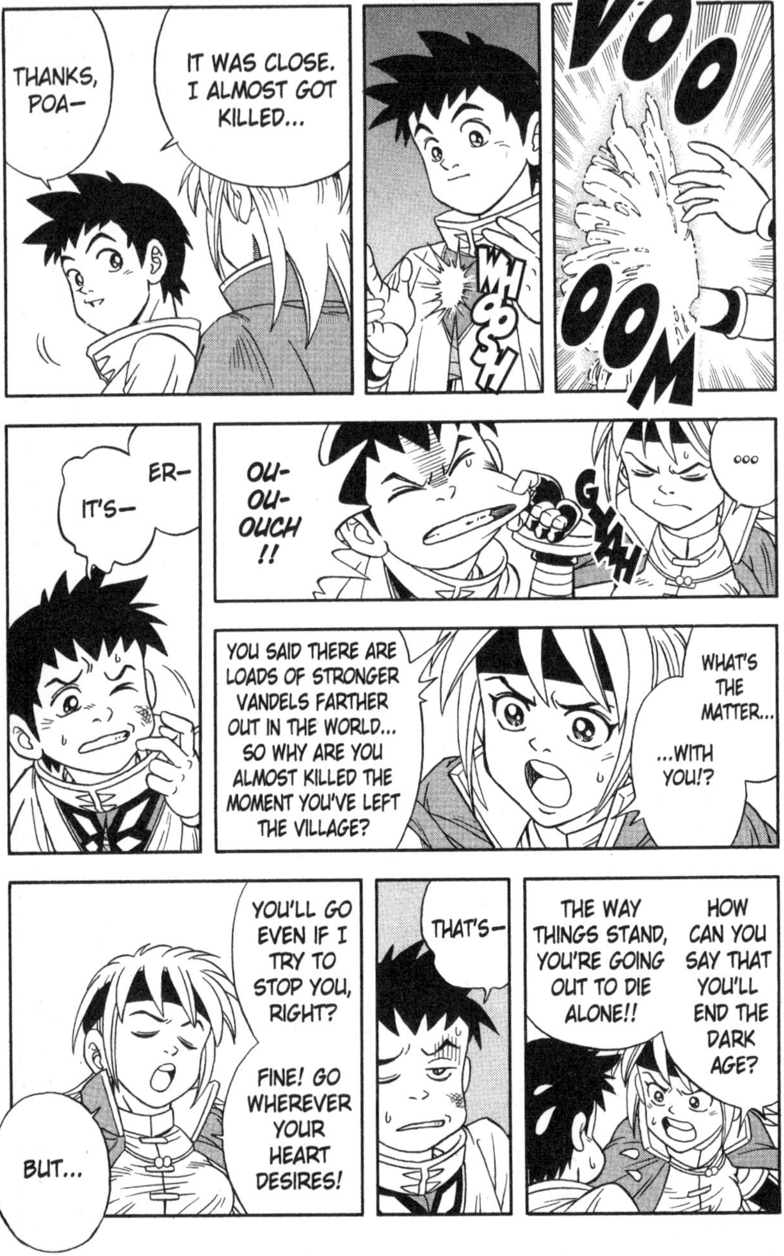
VOOOOOM
WHOOSH
IT WAS CLOSE. I ALMOST GOT KILLED...
THANKS, POA—
...
GWAAH
OU-OU-OUCH!!
WHAT'S THE MATTER...
...WITH YOU!?
YOU SAID THERE ARE LOADS OF STRONGER VANDELS FARTHER OUT IN THE WORLD... SO WHY ARE YOU ALMOST KILLED THE MOMENT YOU'VE LEFT THE VILLAGE?
ER—
IT'S—
HOW CAN YOU SAY THAT YOU'LL END THE DARK AGE?
THE WAY THINGS STAND, YOU'RE GOING OUT TO DIE ALONE!!
THAT'S—
YOU'LL GO EVEN IF I TRY TO STOP YOU, RIGHT?
FINE! GO WHEREVER YOUR HEART DESIRES!
BUT...

READ THIS WAY

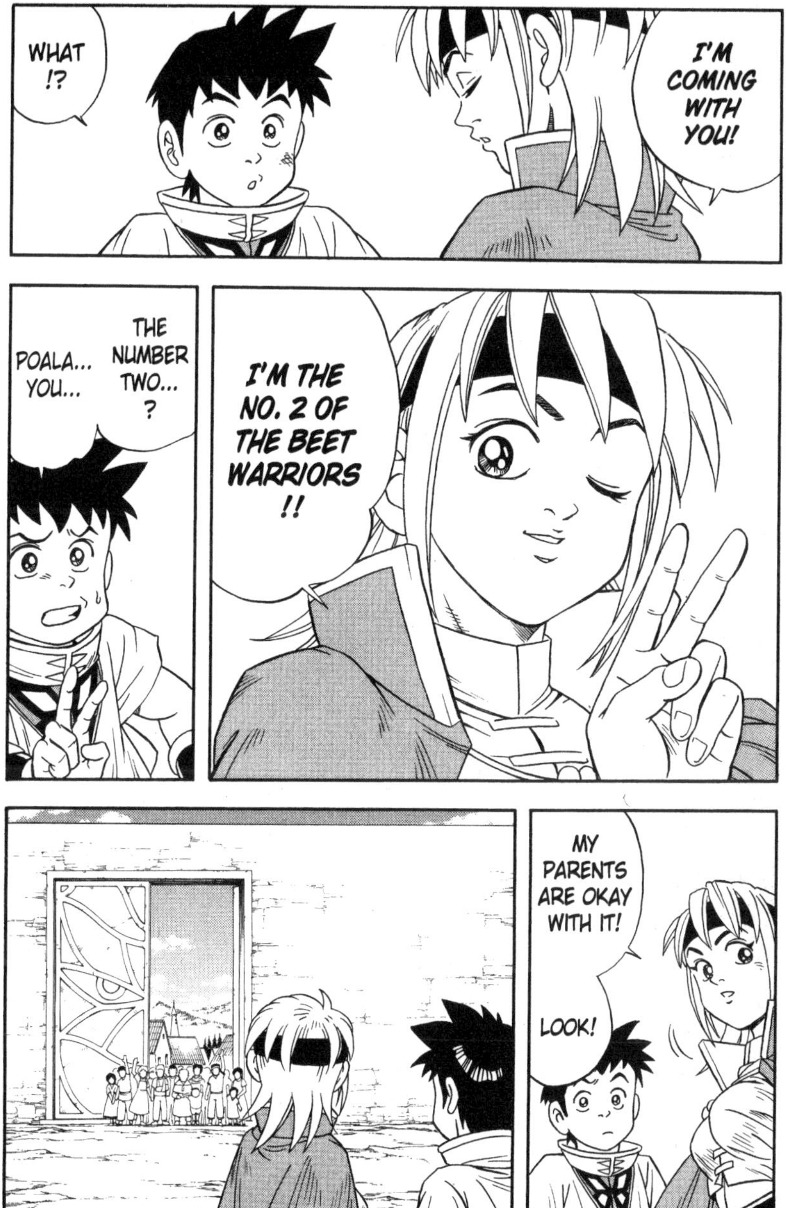
I'M COMING WITH YOU!
WHAT !?
I'M THE NO. 2 OF THE BEET WARRIORS !!
POALA... YOU... THE NUMBER TWO... ?
MY PARENTS ARE OKAY WITH IT!
LOOK!

READ THIS WAY

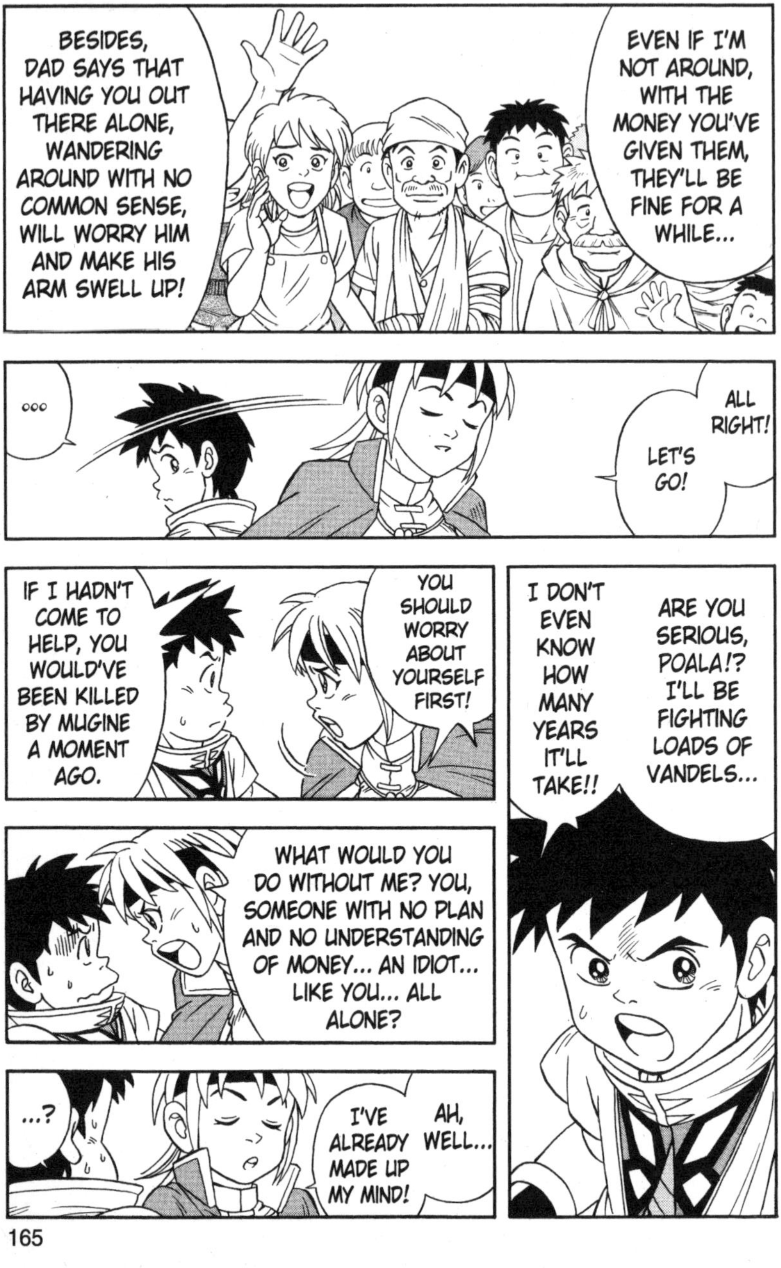
EVEN IF I'M NOT AROUND, WITH THE MONEY YOU'VE GIVEN THEM, THEY'LL BE FINE FOR A WHILE...
BESIDES, DAD SAYS THAT HAVING YOU OUT THERE ALONE, WANDERING AROUND WITH NO COMMON SENSE, WILL WORRY HIM AND MAKE HIS ARM SWELL UP!
ALL RIGHT!
LET'S GO!
...
ARE YOU SERIOUS, POALA!? I'LL BE FIGHTING LOADS OF VANDELS...
I DON'T EVEN KNOW HOW MANY YEARS IT'LL TAKE!!
YOU SHOULD WORRY ABOUT YOURSELF FIRST!
IF I HADN'T COME TO HELP, YOU WOULD'VE BEEN KILLED BY MUGINE A MOMENT AGO.
WHAT WOULD YOU DO WITHOUT ME? YOU, SOMEONE WITH NO PLAN AND NO UNDERSTANDING OF MONEY... AN IDIOT... LIKE YOU... ALL ALONE?
AH, WELL...
I'VE ALREADY MADE UP MY MIND!
...?

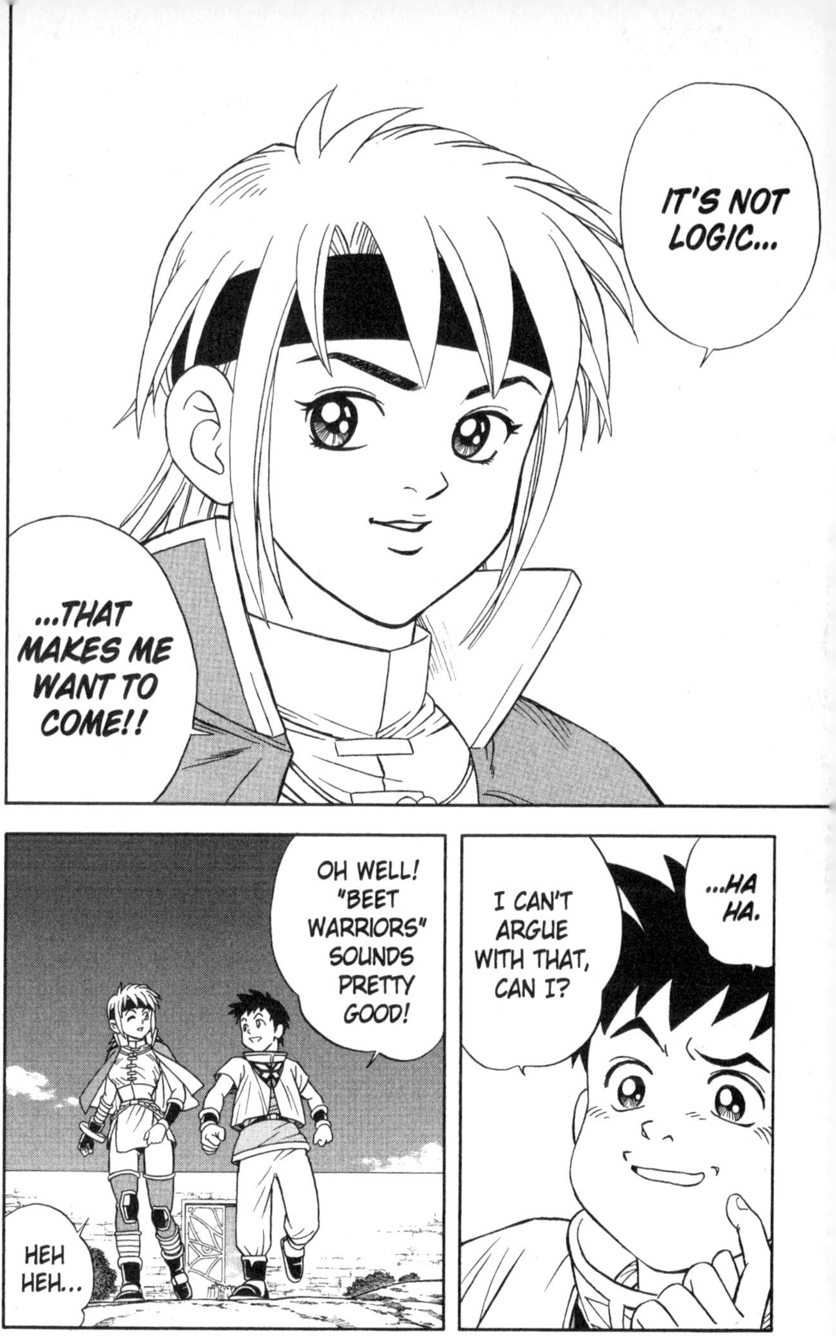
IT'S NOT LOGIC...
...THAT MAKES ME WANT TO COME!!
...HA HA.
I CAN'T ARGUE WITH THAT, CAN I?
OH WELL! "BEET WARRIORS" SOUNDS PRETTY GOOD!
HEH HEH...

READ THIS WAY

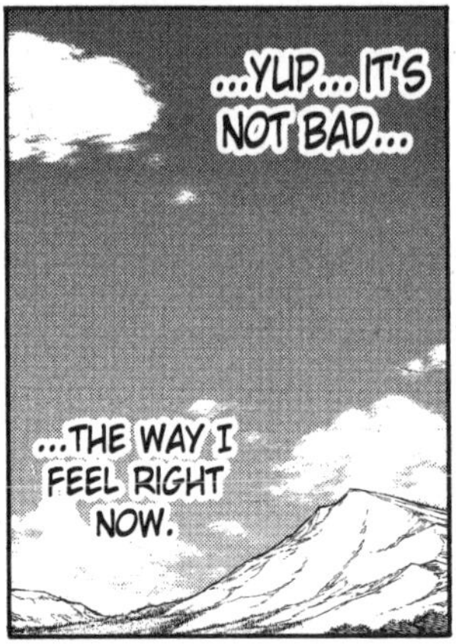
...YUP... IT'S NOT BAD...
...THE WAY I FEEL RIGHT NOW.

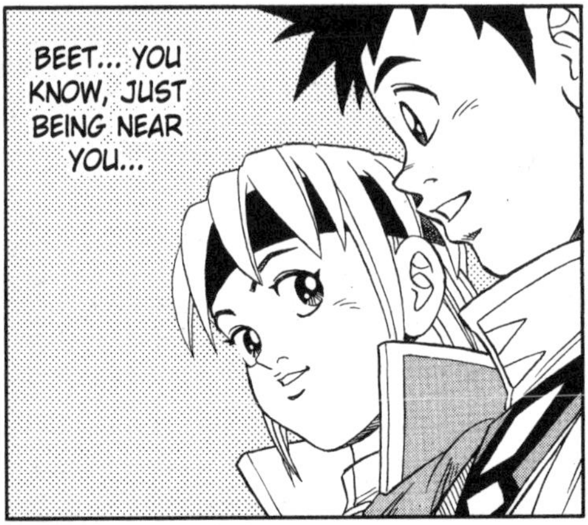
BEET... YOU KNOW, JUST BEING NEAR YOU...

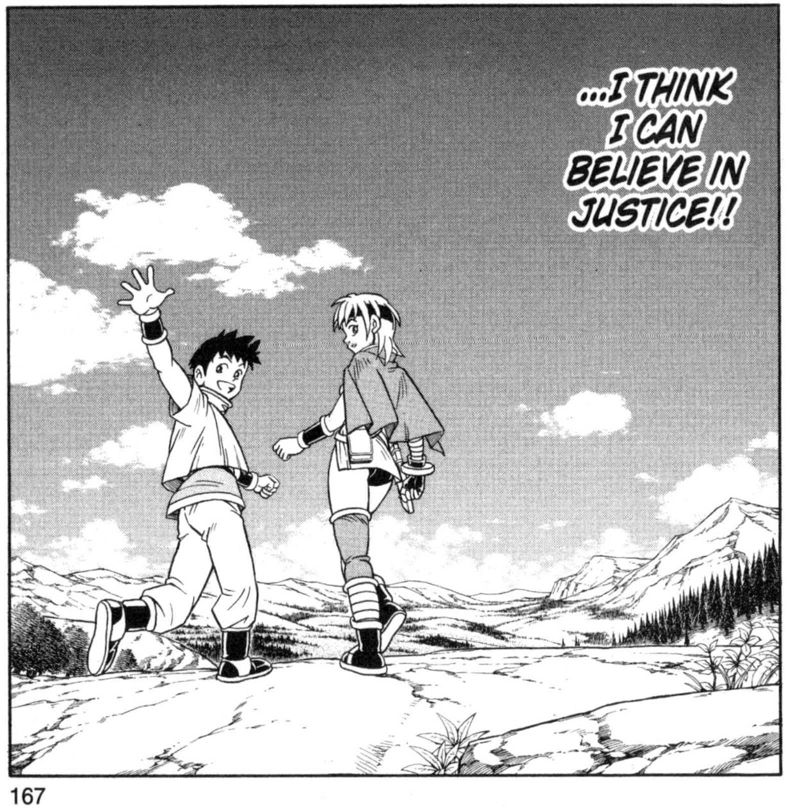
...I THINK I CAN BELIEVE IN JUSTICE!!

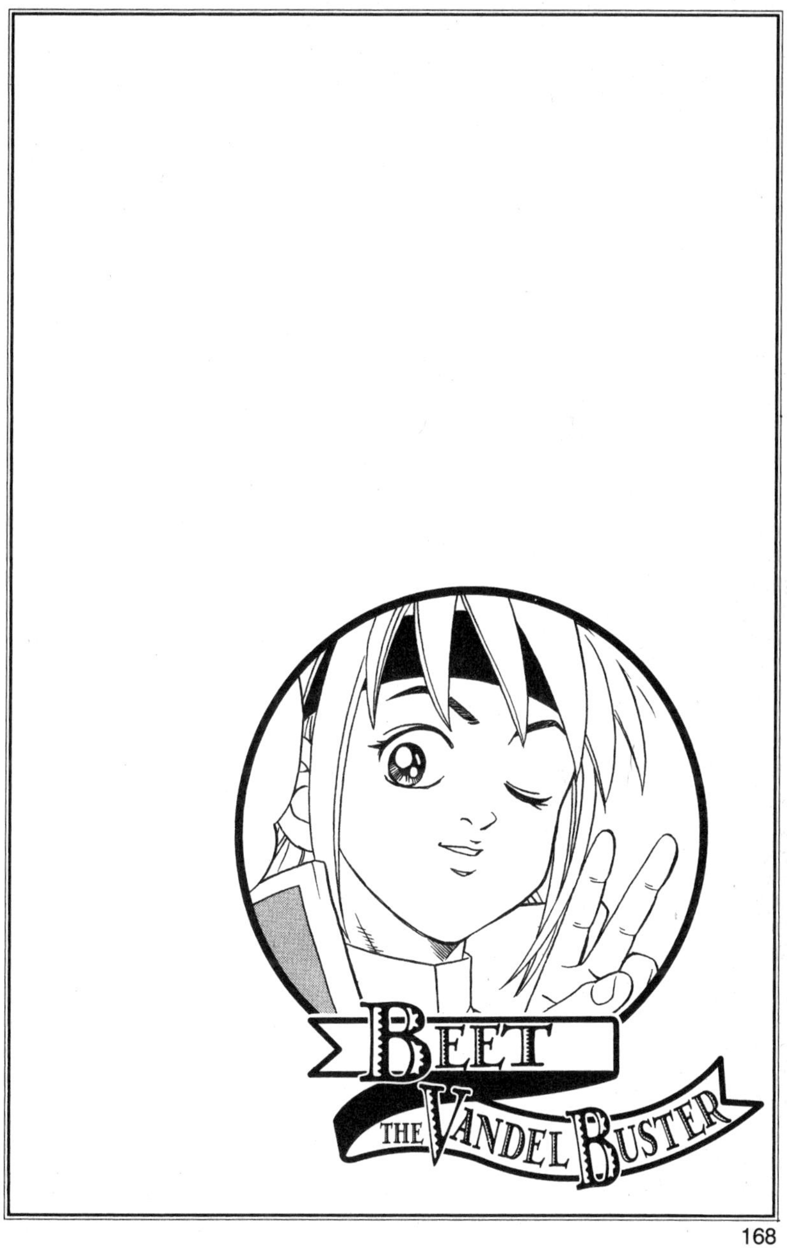
BEET
THE VANDEL BUSTER

BEET THE WORLD

THE WORLD OF
BEET the VANDEL BUSTER • PART 1

Let's look at the exotic and expansive world of "Beet." Here we'll analyze it in its entirety. Listed in this section are the main figures of the Dark Age...

VANDEL BUSTERS

THEY ARE THE DARK AND DIRTY PROFES-SIONALS WHO HUNT DOWN EVIL!

The Vandels are humanity's greatest threat. Vandels create monsters in the blink of an eye, devastating the earth and forcing humans to live in fear. People have come to call the endless, hellish era created by the Vandels the "Dark Age," and they regret living in such a terrible reality. In an attempt to break this vicious cycle, a new occupation has been born: the Vandel Busters, warriors dedicated to conquering the Vandels. At first they were simply bounty hunters, but now the system for Vandel Busters is formally established with supporting nations and organizations. Vandel Busters are usually called Busters for short. They each have unique battle skills, and they live off of the commissions they earn by killing Vandels and monsters.

▲Warrior groups all over the world are fighting against Vandels.

Anyone can become a Buster without having any specific qualifications. All one needs to do is sign a contract. However, only a few Busters become powerful enough to actually defeat Vandels. Large commissions are promised to those who kill Vandels, and many strong Busters dream of becoming rich overnight, but most of them end up dead. It is, indeed, a very risky occupation.

BASIC GEAR OF A BUSTER

THESE ARE THE MARKS OF A DEMON-HUNTING WARRIOR!

SAIGA

This is the ultimate weapon. Only the most capable Buster can learn to use it. It's the last weapon a Buster resorts to in battle. See the next page for more details.

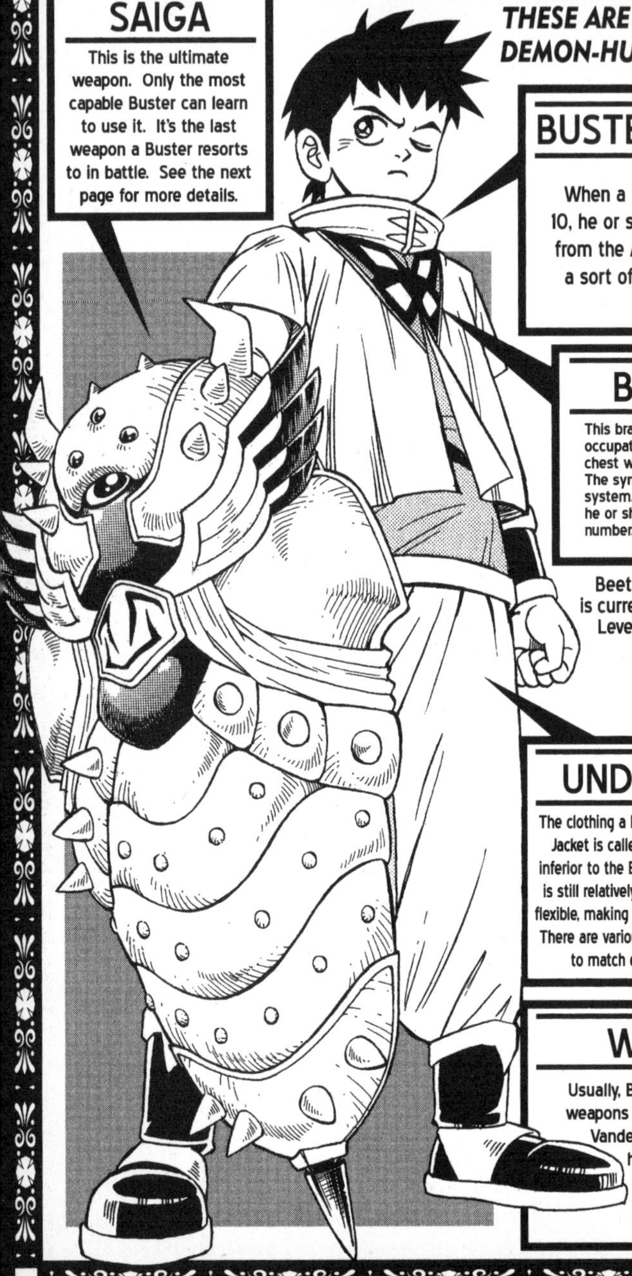

BUSTER'S JACKET

When a Buster reaches Level 10, he or she receives this jacket from the Appraiser's House. It's a sort of uniform for Busters.

BRANDING

This brand, the proof of a Buster's occupation, is stamped on his or her chest when the contract is made. The symbol uses an ancient number system. When a Buster's level rises, he or she is branded with a higher number.

Beet ▶ is currently Level 28.

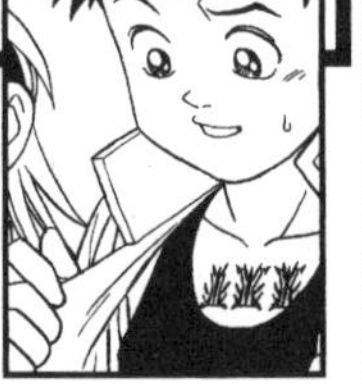

UNDER JACKET

The clothing a Buster wears under the Buster's Jacket is called the Under Jacket. Although inferior to the Buster's Jacket, the Under Jacket is still relatively strong protective gear, and it's flexible, making it perfect for all kinds of actions. There are various types of Under Jackets made to match each Buster's fighting style.

WEAPON

Usually, Busters choose whatever weapons they prefer to fight against Vandels and monsters. Beet uses his handmade spears, while Poala uses two daggers.

SAIGA

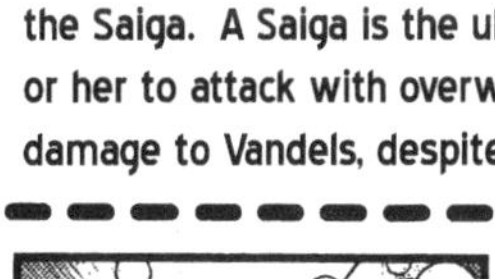

THIS IS THE STRONGEST PROOF OF A BUSTER. IT'S AN ULTIMATE WEAPON HIDDEN WITHIN HIS OR HER BODY.

ISN'T THAT RIGHT ...
...GUYS ?

The powerful magic Vandels use is called the Dark Power, and it is known to tap evil energy from the depths below ground. The counterpart, which humans use, is a superhuman force called "Divine Power." Divine Power taps the energy within the atmosphere. The power from the atmosphere is transformed into fire and ice, enabling the Divine Attack. When the Divine Power reaches its extremity, it allows the energy of the atmosphere to produce a physical substance. This is the power a Buster uses as his or her last resort: the Saiga. A Saiga is the ultimate weapon of a Buster, allowing him or her to attack with overwhelming Divine Power, inflicting fatal damage to Vandels, despite their powerful bodies.

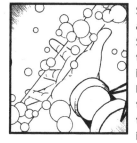

▲ An enormous amount of Divine Power is required to materialize a Saiga.

Saiga do not usually exist in the atmosphere. Instead, during a battle, a Saiga is brought out of a Buster's chest in the form of a glowing ball of light before it changes into its physical form. The Buster's body channels and materializes the elements in the atmosphere. Using the Divine Power, a Buster creates an ideal weapon that he or she has visualized in his or her mind. Beet received five Saiga from the Zenon Warriors, which still exist as glowing balls of energy inside Beet's body.

BEET THE WORLD

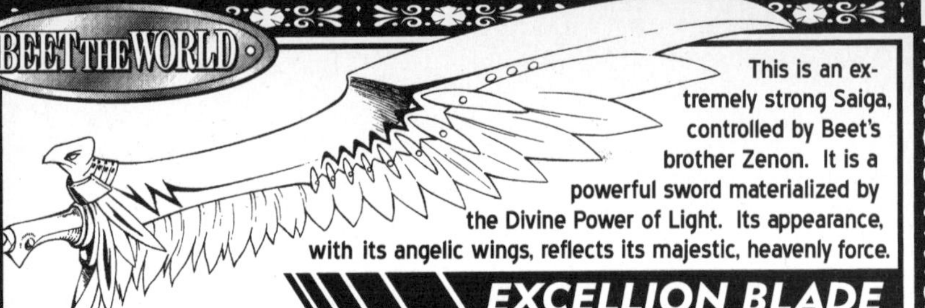

This is an extremely strong Saiga, controlled by Beet's brother Zenon. It is a powerful sword materialized by the Divine Power of Light. Its appearance, with its angelic wings, reflects its majestic, heavenly force.

EXCELLION BLADE

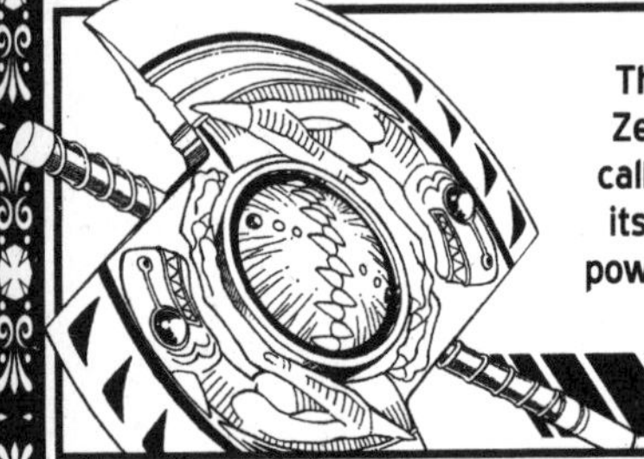

This Saiga is a gigantic axe used by one of the Zenon Warriors, the heavyweight masked giant called Bluezam. The Divine Power of Thunder is its basic element. With its extreme power, this powerful weapon can chop the enemy into pieces.

BOLTIC AXE

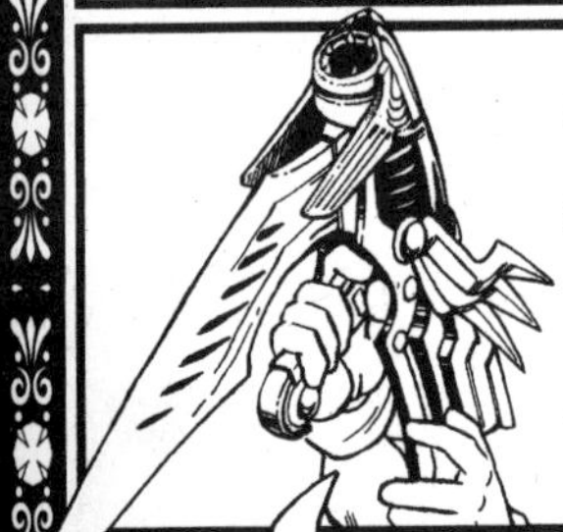

This is the Saiga of Alside, another member of the Zenon Warriors. He is known for his silent presence and his accurate shots. Materialized by the Divine Power of Wind, it has incredible speed. The damage it can inflict is immense, and it can bring forth an enormous plume of smoke wherever its bullet hits. The blade that stretches below the muzzle is sharp and can be used during close combat.

CYCLONE GUNNER

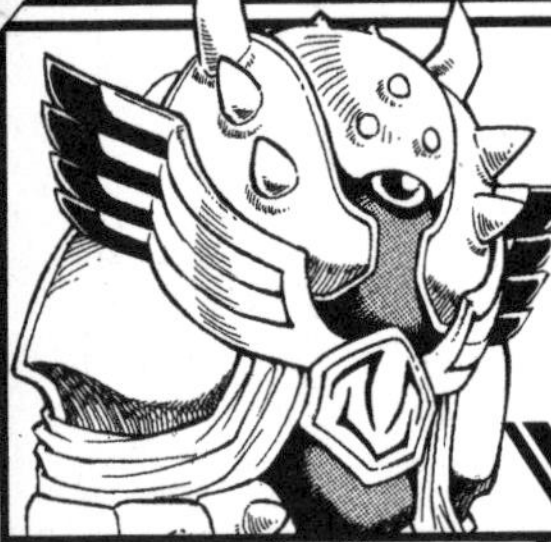

This is a strong shield produced by Cruss, the brain of the Zenon Warriors. Cruss is cool, calm and good-looking. The shield's external shell is protected by the Divine Power of Water. Its steadfast protective power has saved the Zenon Warriors from numerous attacks. Unless repelled with extreme skill, the Crown Shield can inflict enormous damage on an attacker.

CROWN SHIELD

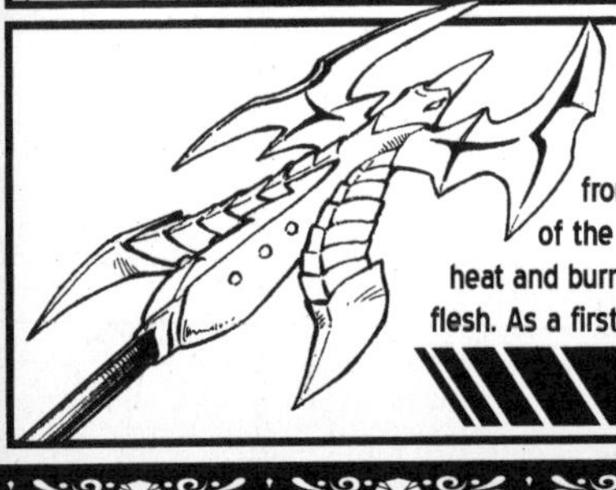

This is the Saiga of Laio. Laio, the lead attacker of the Zenon Warriors, was closest to Beet. Since Beet learned the Sohjutsu (Art of the Spear) from Laio, he uses this Saiga the most often. Born out of the Divine Power of Fire, this spear always radiates with heat and burns the bodies of its enemies as it slices through their flesh. As a first choice, it's the best weapon to use against Vandels.

BURNING LANCE

APPRAISER'S HOUSE

THIS IS THE BASE FOR THE VANDEL BUSTERS' ACTIVITY!

The Appraiser's House is the base of activities for the Busters. The Association of Busters has established Appraiser's Houses all over the world. The Association pays out commissions to subjugate Vandels and the overflowing number of monsters. The amount of commission the Association pays out is based on the strength of the opponent. At the house, the managing appraiser acknowledges the work done, pays out the commission, and approves an increase in level.

In addition, the Appraiser's House is an effective place to gather information. Busters can learn the price of various Vandels, as well as available jobs from nearby towns and villages. Most of the appraisers are old men or old women, but they're all experienced Busters and are expert Divine Attackers. Unsuspecting intruders can be easily beaten away.

RETINAL APPRAISAL

This is a special way of appraising Busters using Divine Power. Appraisers examine a Buster's eyes and verify the images of enemies' deaths imprinted on the Buster's retina. Once the deaths are ascertained, the Buster is entitled to the commission and promotion points. If the death of the enemy is in doubt, the Buster is denied the commission. This is the standard and only method of evaluating the work of Busters throughout the world, and a Buster can go from one Appraiser's House to the next without disturbing his or her record.

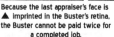

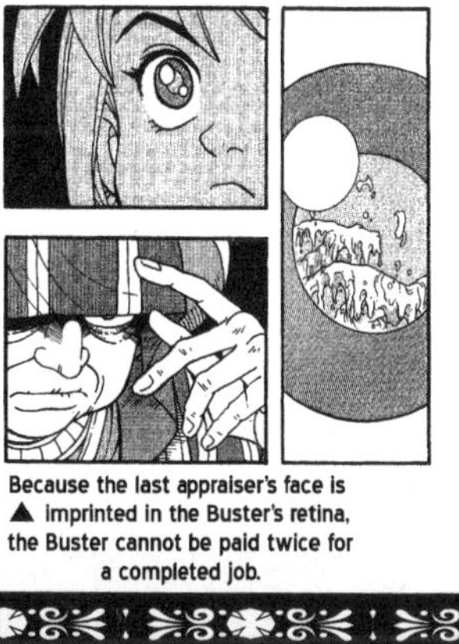

Because the last appraiser's face is ▲ imprinted in the Buster's retina, the Buster cannot be paid twice for a completed job.

LEVEL UP

In accordance with standardized scoring, Busters accumulate promotion points as they get rid of Vandels and monsters, and Busters' levels are upped accordingly by an appraiser. Busters' levels are clearly marked on their chests. The process is called Branding. Busters are pressed with hot iron, and ancient numbers are burnt onto their chests. The ancient numbers look somewhat similar to Roman numerals. Each line represents one point. With just a glance, a Buster's level is easily known by anyone.

▼ For Busters, the brand works as an I.D.

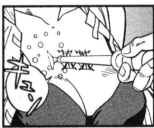

◀ Busters insist that the branding does not hurt much.

WANTED NOTICE

VANDEL
MUGAIN
MG 85000
MUGAIN
MG 85000

On the wall of the Appraiser's House, there are usually numerous Wanted Notices. The most important type is the notice relating to Vandels. Basic information, such as the place where the Vandel is based, the number of his stars, and the amount of commission, is written on the notice. Multiple of copies are readily available, and Busters can take as many copies as they want. The moment a Vandel is dead, a notice for that Vandel is eliminated from every Appraiser's House around the world.

MG

In this world, all money is in coin form. The basic denomination is the MG, or Maggie. The lowest value of a coin is 1 MG. There are numerous coins, from 1MG coins to 10,000MG coins, and, depending on the total amount of money, various combinations of coins can be used. An Appraiser's House typically contains huge sums of MG, but the appraiser of the hut is the only one who knows where the money is hidden.

VANDELS & MONSTERS

THEY ARE THE MAIN PLAYERS OF THE DARK AGE. THEY ARE THE FORCE OF DARKNESS THAT DEVASTATES THE EARTH.

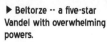

▶ Beltorze -- a five-star Vandel with overwhelming powers.
He is also known as the King of Tragedy.

▼ Mugine -- a Vandel with numerous abilities who lives in the Bog of the Dead. Although he's only a two-star Vandel, he's not easy to defeat.

The natural enemies of humans, Vandels are the strongest and the most terrible beings in the world. Their fighting power is tremendous, their vitality is unlimited, and it is not too much to state that they're physically the most perfect creatures that have ever lived. They are the reason behind the Dark Age, this long era of struggle that humans face. Some go about inflicting violence around the world, while others produce armies of monsters, causing disorder in human society. They're truly evil.

A common characteristic of the Vandels is the tremendous power they use, called Dark Power. When Dark Power is transformed into aggressive energy for an attack, it is called a Dark Attack. Another common characteristic is their immense physical power, which ranges from ten to one hundred times that of ordinary human beings.
But the strongest bond all Vandels share is the pleasure they feel in annihilating humans and destroying the world.
In accordance with their standard of distinction, jewels called "stars" are embedded in their left arms. The number of stars determines their status. Naturally, the more stars a Vandel has, the stronger he is. Therefore, stars can be used to figure out the strength of each Vandel, and humans are well aware of their meaning.

UPPER CLASS MONSTERS

Vandels create numerous monsters as their subordinates, and some of them are as strong as the Vandels themselves. Some understand language, work as partners, and can serve as the Vandels' personal guards. Busters must deal with these types of monsters carefully.

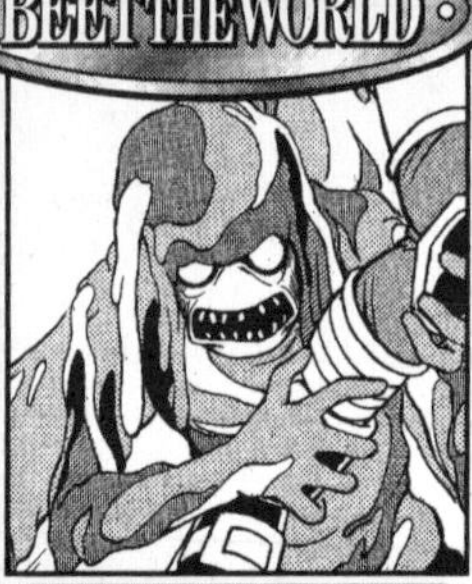

DRAWMASTER

Stronger version of a Drawman. It has a powerful talent for mimicry.

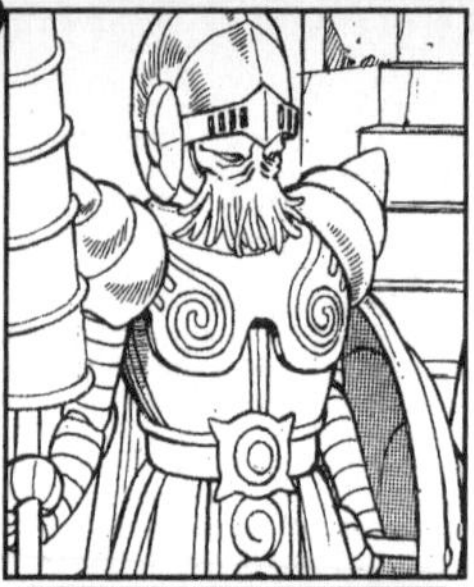

IRON KNIGHT SHELL

Covered in a tough shell, it belongs to the strongest class of shellfish monsters.

MIDDLE CLASS MONSTERS

These are what ordinary humans refer to as monsters. They have moderately high intelligence and are able to make decisions. They are well suited as opponents for trained Busters, but common people are no match for their strength. They are strong opponents and should not be engaged without a determined focus.

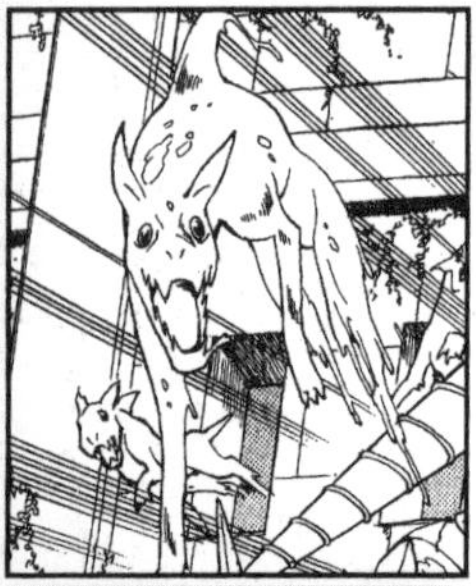

AQUA DOG

A monster whose body is made of water. It is a competent guard dog.

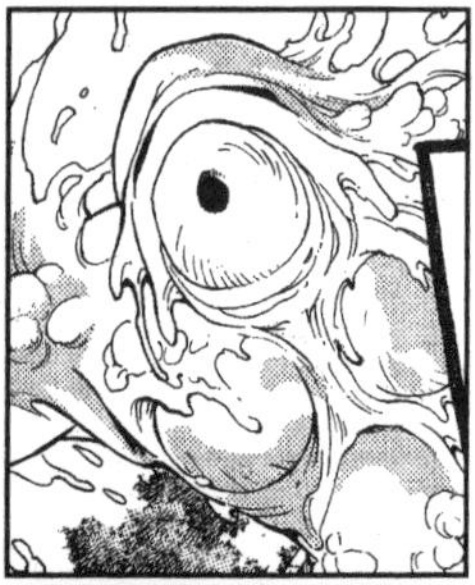

DRAWMAN

This shape-shifting monster infiltrates villages by impersonating a villager.

LOWER CLASS MONSTER

These are vicious creatures resembling animals or insects. They don't take direct orders from Vandels. Once released, they reproduce and attack uncontrollably, inflicting massive damage on the human world. They're not very strong, but they should not be overlooked.

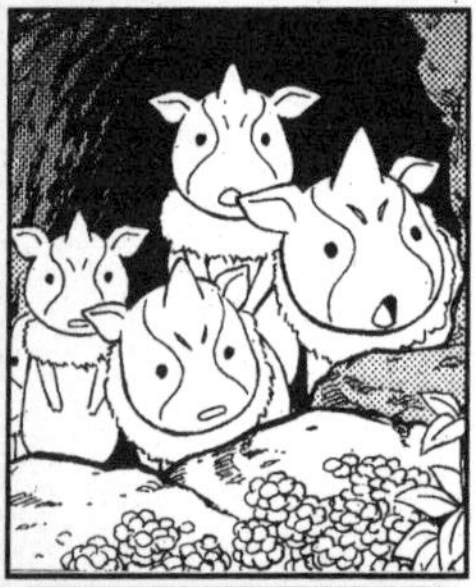

CANNECK

It likes to eat coins and is troublesome.

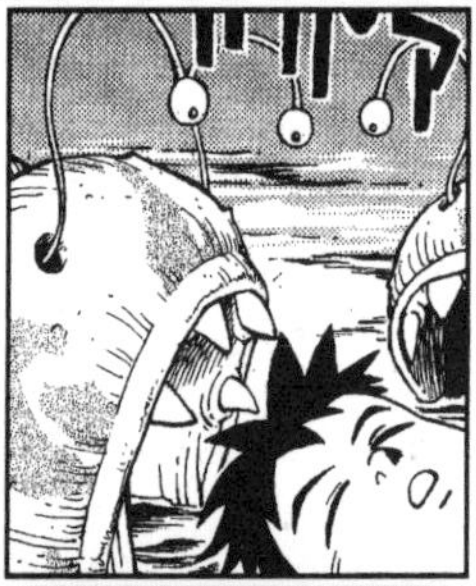

BITING CLAM

The first monster Beet defeated. It has a strong set of teeth.

Coming Next Volume

Beltorze is back and more powerful than ever—the strongest Vandel of all. And after shopping for some new monster minions at the Dark House of Sorcery you can bet that he's out to cause more trouble! Meanwhile, Beet and Poala have to duke it out with another powerful Vandel, Grineed. But he's just the beginning of their troubles...

Available in December 2004!

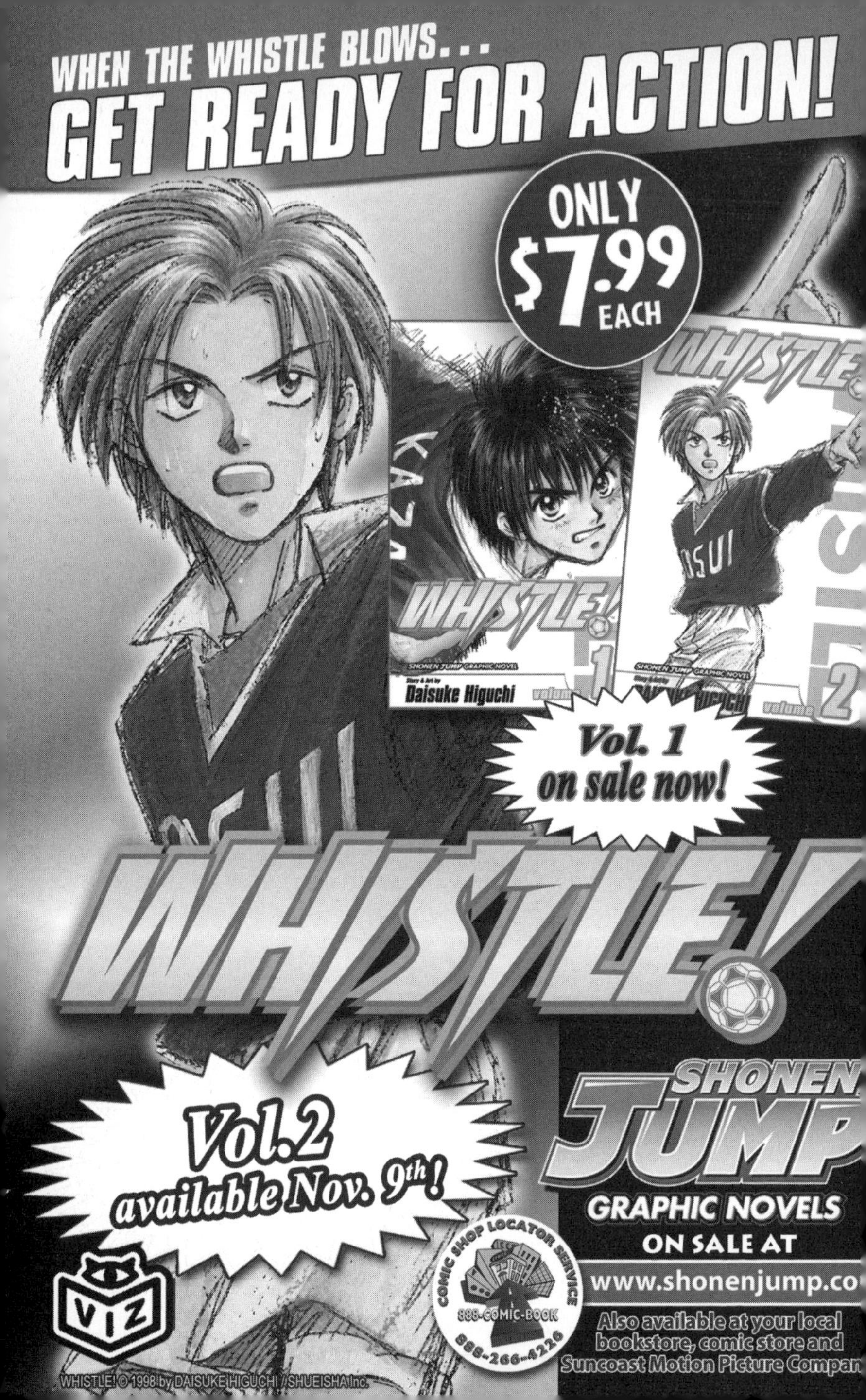

WHEN THE WHISTLE BLOWS...
GET READY FOR ACTION!
ONLY $7.99 EACH
WHISTLE!
SHONEN JUMP GRAPHIC NOVEL
Story & Art by Daisuke Higuchi
volume 1
volume 2
Vol. 1 on sale now!
WHISTLE!
Vol.2 available Nov. 9th!
SHONEN JUMP
GRAPHIC NOVELS ON SALE AT
www.shonenjump.com
Also available at your local bookstore, comic store and Suncoast Motion Picture Company
COMIC SHOP LOCATOR SERVICE
888-COMIC-BOOK
888-266-4226
VIZ
WHISTLE! © 1998 by DAISUKE HIGUCHI / SHUEISHA Inc.

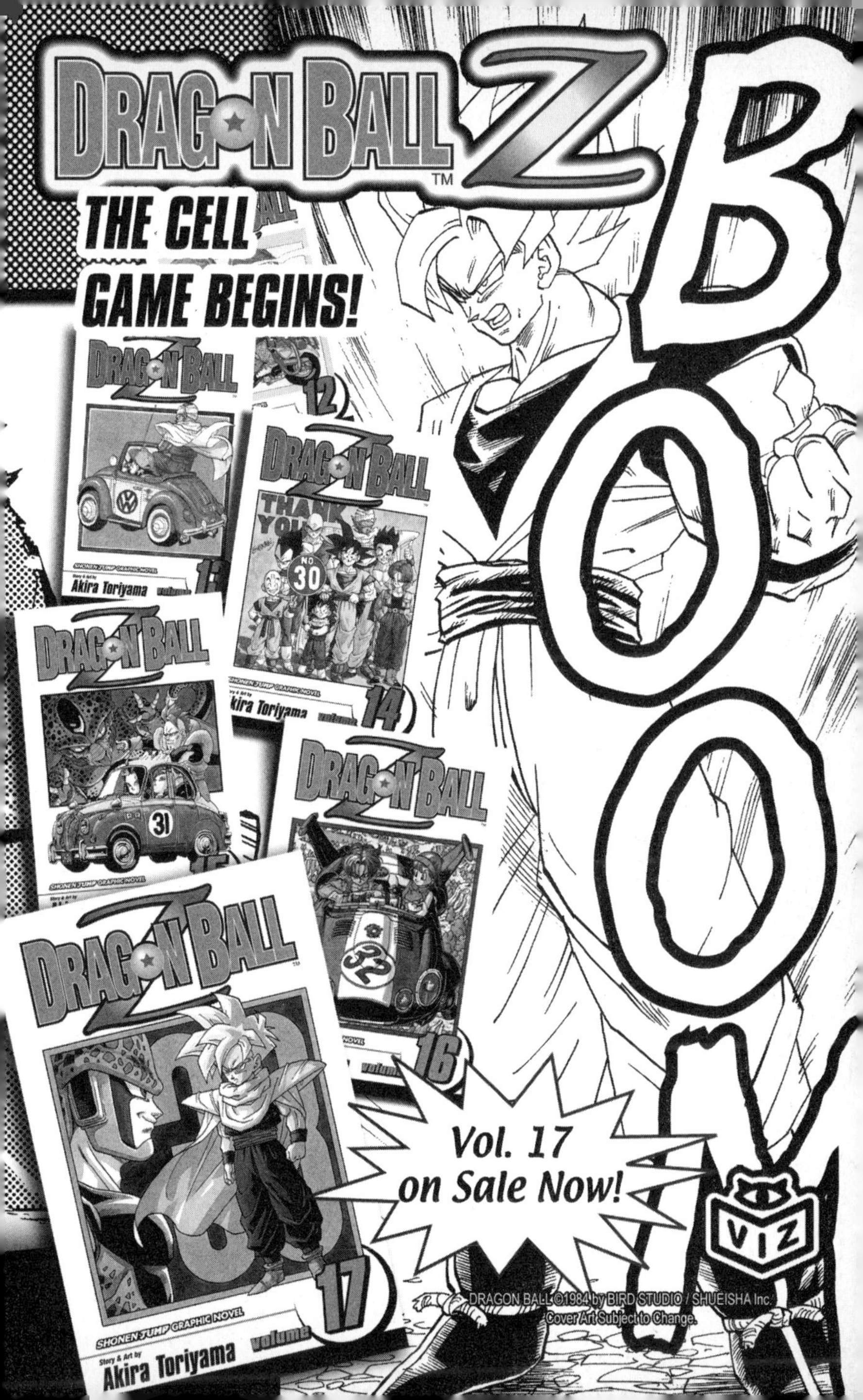
DRAGON BALL Z
THE CELL GAME BEGINS!
Vol. 17
on Sale Now!
VIZ
DRAGON BALL ©1984 by BIRD STUDIO / SHUEISHA Inc.
Cover Art Subject to Change.

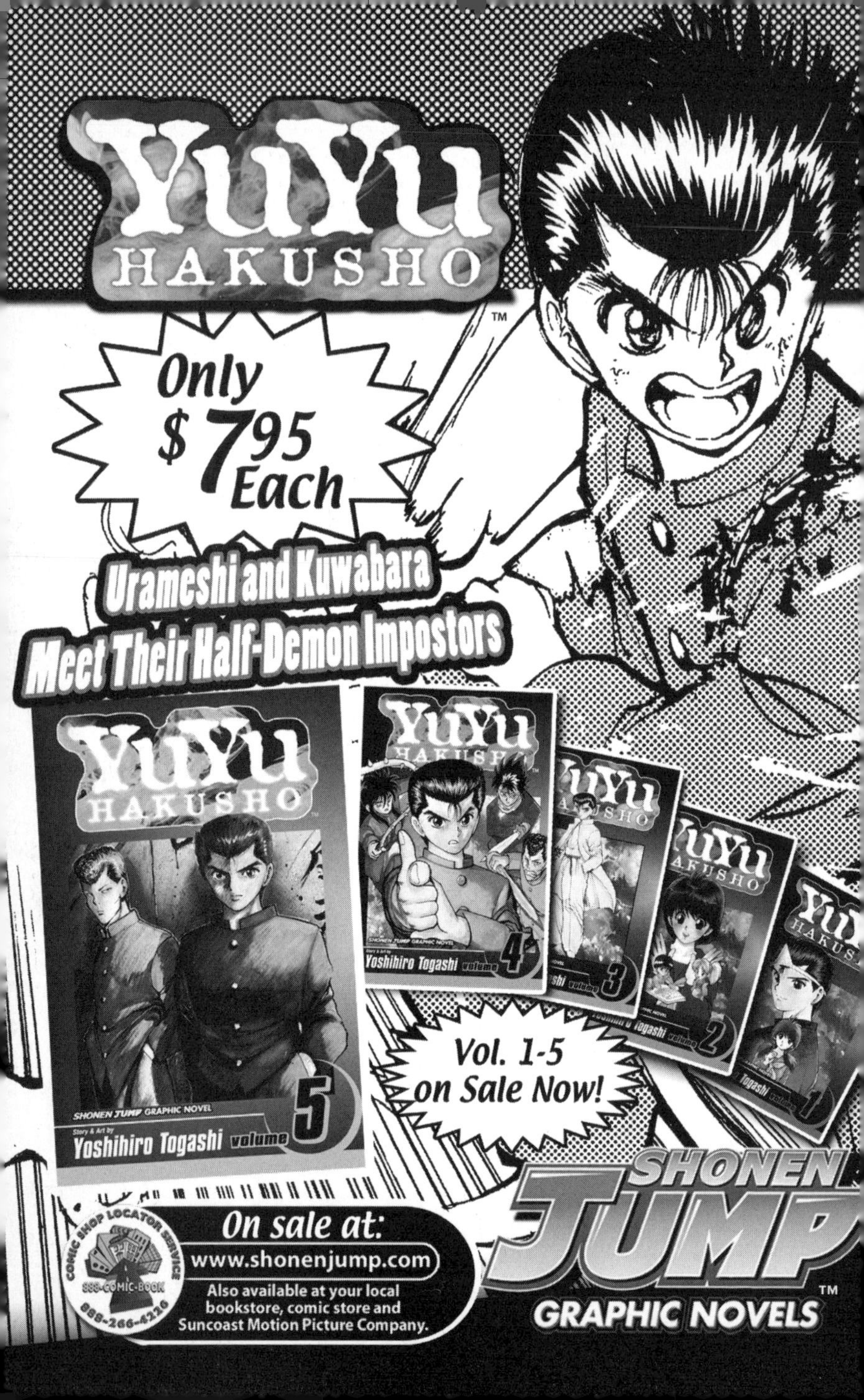
YuYu HAKUSHO™
Only $7.95 Each
Urameshi and Kuwabara Meet Their Half-Demon Impostors
YuYu HAKUSHO
SHONEN JUMP GRAPHIC NOVEL
Story & Art by
Yoshihiro Togashi volume 5
Yoshihiro Togashi volume 4
volume 3
volume 2
Togashi volume 1
Vol. 1-5 on Sale Now!
SHONEN JUMP GRAPHIC NOVELS™
On sale at:
www.shonenjump.com
Also available at your local bookstore, comic store and Suncoast Motion Picture Company.
COMIC SHOP LOCATOR SERVICE
888-COMIC-BOOK
888-266-4226

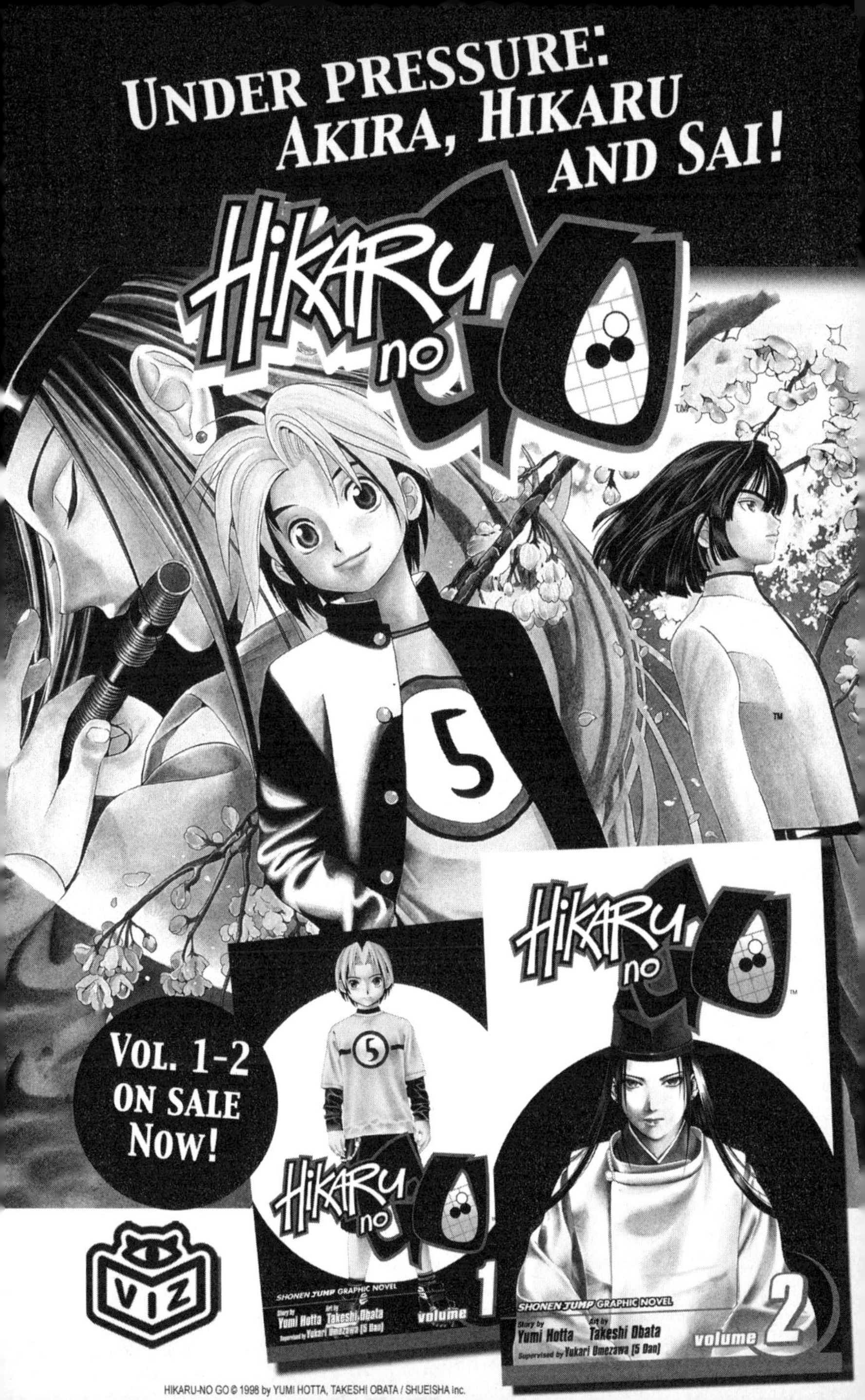
UNDER PRESSURE:
AKIRA, HIKARU
AND SAI!
HIKARU no GO
VOL. 1-2
ON SALE
NOW!
VIZ
SHONEN JUMP GRAPHIC NOVEL
Story by Yumi Hotta Art by Takeshi Obata
Supervised by Yukari Umezawa (5 Dan)
volume 1
volume 2

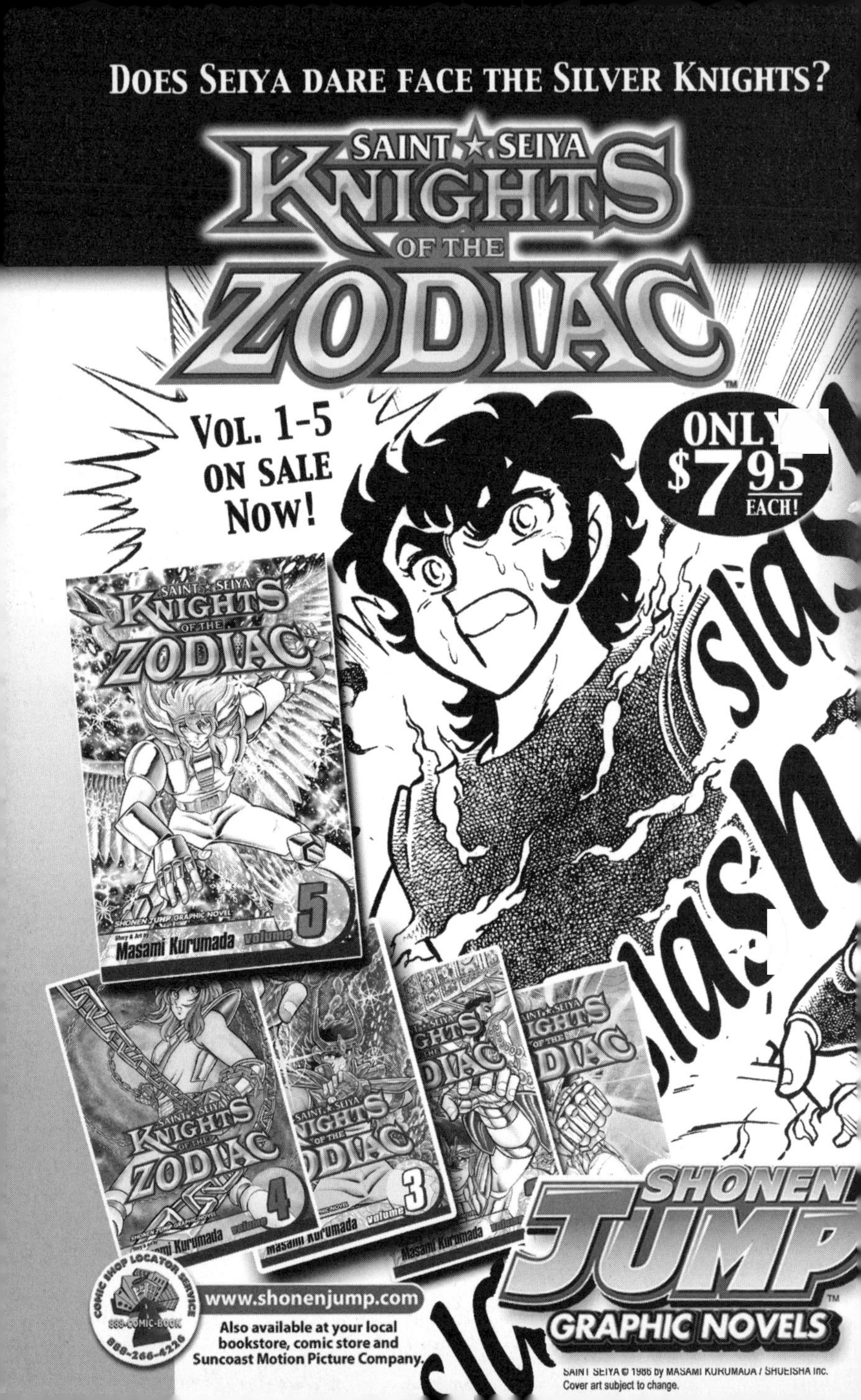
DOES SEIYA DARE FACE THE SILVER KNIGHTS?
SAINT ★ SEIYA
KNIGHTS OF THE ZODIAC
VOL. 1-5 ON SALE NOW!
ONLY $7.95 EACH!
COMIC SHOP LOCATOR SERVICE
888-COMIC-BOOK
888-266-4226
www.shonenjump.com
Also available at your local bookstore, comic store and Suncoast Motion Picture Company.
SHONEN JUMP GRAPHIC NOVELS
SAINT SEIYA © 1986 by MASAMI KURUMADA / SHUEISHA Inc.
Cover art subject to change.

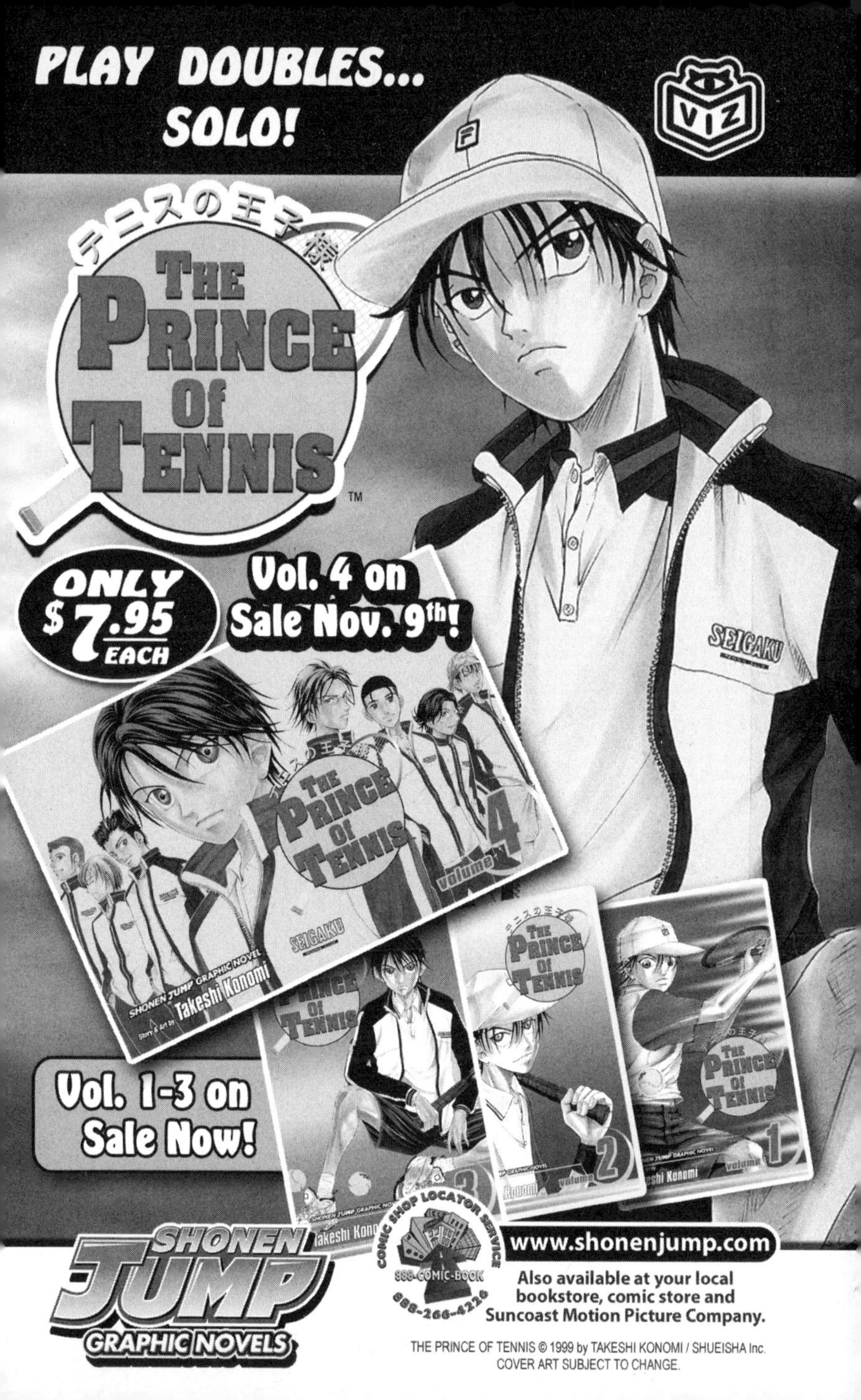
PLAY DOUBLES...
SOLO!
VIZ
テニスの王子様
THE PRINCE OF TENNIS™
ONLY $7.95 EACH
Vol. 4 on Sale Nov. 9th!
THE PRINCE OF TENNIS volume 4
SEIGAKU
SHONEN JUMP GRAPHIC NOVEL
Story & Art by Takeshi Konomi
Vol. 1-3 on Sale Now!
SHONEN JUMP GRAPHIC NOVELS
COMIC SHOP LOCATOR SERVICE
888-COMIC-BOOK
888-266-4226
www.shonenjump.com
Also available at your local bookstore, comic store and Suncoast Motion Picture Company.
THE PRINCE OF TENNIS © 1999 by TAKESHI KONOMI / SHUEISHA Inc.
COVER ART SUBJECT TO CHANGE.

SHONEN JUMP
THE WORLD'S MOST POPULAR MANGA

COMPLETE OUR SURVEY AND LET US KNOW WHAT YOU THINK!

☐ Please check here if you DO NOT wish to receive information or future offers from VIZ

Name: ______________________________

Address: ______________________________

City: ______________ **State:** ________ **Zip:** ____________

E-mail: ______________________________

☐ **Male** ☐ **Female** **Date of Birth** (mm/dd/yyyy): ___/___/_____ (**Under 13? Parental consent required**)

What race/ethnicity do you consider yourself? (please check one)

☐ Asian/Pacific Islander ☐ Black/African American ☐ Hispanic/Latino

☐ Native American/Alaskan Native ☐ White/Caucasian ☐ Other: ____________

What SHONEN JUMP Graphic Novel did you purchase? (indicate title purchased)

____

What other SHONEN JUMP Graphic Novels, if any, do you own? (indicate title(s) owned)

____

____

Reason for purchase: (check all that apply)

☐ Special offer ☐ Favorite title ☐ Gift

☐ Recommendation ☐ Read in SHONEN JUMP Magazine

☐ Other ______________________________

Where did you make your purchase? (please check one)

☐ Comic store ☐ Bookstore ☐ Mass/Grocery Store

☐ Newsstand ☐ Video/Video Game Store ☐ Other: ____________

☐ Online (site: ______________________________)

Do you read SHONEN JUMP Magazine?

☐ Yes ☐ No **(if no, skip the next two questions)**

Do you subscribe?

☐ Yes ☐ No

If you do not subscribe, how often do you purchase SHONEN JUMP Magazine?

☐ 1-3 issues a year

☐ 4-6 issues a year

☐ more than 7 issues a year

What genre of manga would you like to read as a SHONEN JUMP Graphic Novel?
(please check two)

☐ Adventure ☐ Comic Strip ☐ Science Fiction ☐ Fighting

☐ Horror ☐ Romance ☐ Fantasy ☐ Sports

Which do you prefer? (please check one)

☐ Reading right-to-left

☐ Reading left-to-right

Which do you prefer? (please check one)

☐ Sound effects in English

☐ Sound effects in Japanese with English captions

☐ Sound effects in Japanese only with a glossary at the back

THANK YOU! Please send the completed form to:

VIZ Survey
42 Catharine St.
Poughkeepsie, NY 12601

All information provided will be used for internal purposes only. We promise not to sell or otherwise divulge your information.